CQ GUIDE TO

CURRENT AMERICAN GOVERNMENT

Spring 2004

CQ PRESS

A Division of Congressional Quarterly Inc.

Washington, D.C.

Congressional Quarterly Inc.

Congressional Quarterly Inc., an editorial research service and publishing company, serves clients in the fields of news, education, business and government. It combines the specific coverage of Congress, government and politics contained in the *CQ Weekly* with the more general subject range of an affiliated service, the *CQ Researcher*.

Under the CQ Press imprint, Congressional Quarterly also publishes college political science textbooks and public affairs paperbacks on developing issues and events; information directories; and reference books on the federal government, national elections and politics. Titles include the *Guide to the Presidency*, the *Guide to Congress*, the *Guide to the U.S. Supreme Court*, the *Guide to U.S. Elections* and *Politics in America*. CQ's A–Z collection is a reference series that provides essential information about American government and the electoral process. The *CQ Almanac*, a compendium of legislation for one session of Congress, is published each year. *Congress and the Nation*, a record of government for a presidential term, is published every four years.

CQ publishes *CQ Today* (formerly the *Daily Monitor*), a report on the current and future activities of congressional committees. An online information system, CQ.com on Congress, provides immediate access to CQ's databases of legislative action, votes, schedules, profiles and analyses. Visit www.cq.com for more information.

CQ Press
1255 22nd St. N.W., Suite 400
Washington, DC 20037
202-729-1900; toll free, 1-866-4-CQ-PRESS (1-866-427-7737)

www.cqpress.com

ISBN 1-56802-807-5
ISSN 0196-612-X

Contents

Contents

Introduction

Guide to Current American Government is a collection of articles from the CQ Weekly. The Weekly has long been a trusted source for nonpartisan reporting and meticulous analyses of congressional actions, presidential activities, policy debates and other news and developments in Washington. The articles have been chosen to complement introductory American government texts with up-to-date examinations of current issues and controversies. The Guide has four sections: Foundations of American Government, Political Participation, Government Institutions and Politics and Public Policy.

The articles in the section Foundations of American Government examine issues and events that involve interpretation of the U.S. Constitution. This edition of the Guide provides extensive analyses of homeland security one year after the creation of the Cabinet-level Homeland Security Department and of the debate in Congress over how to ease the strain on the U.S. military.

Political Participation turns to electoral and party politics. The articles examine the challenges Democrats face as they prepare for the 2004 elections; the roles of House Majority Leader Tom DeLay and Senate Majority Leader Bill Frist; and the growing number of congressional Republicans who are beginning to question President George W. Bush about the aftermath of the war in Iraq and the problem of unemployment in the U.S. economy.

The section Government Institutions explores the inner workings of the major institutions of American government—Congress, the presidency and the judiciary—as they respond to recent events at home and abroad. In this edition of the Guide, the articles focus on President Bush's widening "credibility gap" regarding postwar Iraq and the federal budget deficit, the increasing influence of congressional caucuses and the struggle in the Senate over appellate court nominees.

The articles in the section Politics and Public Policy focus on major policy issues, such as trade, homeland security, Medicare and the environment.

Foundations of American Government

This section approaches issues that are at the heart of American democracy, including the balance of powers among the three branches of the federal government and the role of Congress. The articles focus on the Homeland Security Department's progress in repairing security problems and preventing future security breaches, and Congress and the Pentagon's debates over what can be done to ease the burden on an undermanned and overdeployed U.S. military.

The first article provides a topic-by-topic analysis of homeland security one year after the creation of the Cabinet-level Homeland Security Department—the most extensive government overhaul in five decades. From improving port security to funding first responders, to balancing passenger screening and civil rights, to untangling counterterrorism programs from 45 federal departments and agencies, securing the homeland has proved a huge challenge for the federal government. Special interests and rival bureaucracies continue to buffet the department, which made few tangible improvements to domestic protection.

A battle has begun on Capitol Hill over the need to add more troops to the army. The wars in Iraq and Afghanistan, coupled with increased threats to national security, have put a strain on the U.S. military. The second article discusses the Pentagon's struggles to manage its largest overseas deployment in two generations, while Congress grapples with ways to address falling morale among troops and strategizes about what can be done to ease the strain.

Is Homeland Security Keeping America Safe?

A look at the year since the White House embraced the Cabinet-level department

Like a drag racer going zero to 60 in a few short seconds, the creation of the Homeland Security Department seems like a blur.

Just over a year ago, the Bush administration stood pat in its refusal to create a homeland security agency, probably because it had been the idea of Democrats. Nine months later, the doors opened on a brand new Cabinet-level agency with 170,000 employees and a $40 billion budget.

How is it working out? So-so at best, in the estimates of most people who follow the issues seriously. To be sure, obstacles to fixing the problems that led to Sept. 11 are formidable, and probably outside the reach of Homeland Security Secretary Tom Ridge. No less than President Bush himself said last June: "This is going to be a tough battle, because we're going to be stepping on some people's toes. I understand that. You see, when you take power away from one person in Washington, it tends to make them nervous."

How prescient he was. From port security to protection of the nation's critical electronic and concrete infrastructure, from funding first responders to untangling the rat's nest of counterterrorism programs that in June 2002 could be found in the budgets of 45 departments and agencies of the federal government, the new Homeland Security Department has been buffeted by special interests and rival bureaucracies.

In what most would agree is a positive note, the creation of the department can at least be credited with resolving an old bureaucratic logjam: It at last broke up the widely criticized Immigration and Naturalization Service (INS), which, among other mistakes over the years, infamously approved visa applications for two al Qaeda hijackers six months to the day after they flew planes into the World Trade Center.

The Big Split

Now, along with the old Customs and Border Patrol services and the Transportation Security Agency, INS has been split up and reconstituted as most critics always wanted, with separate offices for visa applications and border security. Along with state-of-the-art visa tracking and passenger identification systems, Ridge may succeed where INS so blatantly failed: keeping terrorists out of the country.

It is an entirely different story with intelligence, the other major failure exposed by the Sept. 11 attacks that the Homeland Security Department was supposed to fix. So far, the fix has been a twofold headache. First, the department has been unable to gather the information streams of rival agencies from the CIA, FBI, Defense Intelligence Agency and others. Worse, the domestic counterterrorism projects and legislation associated with homeland security but not under the department's control have stirred so much fear and animosity that more

The battle to repair security problems and win over critics has just begun for Homeland Security Secretary Tom Ridge, some experts say.

than 100 local legislatures have passed resolutions vowing not to cooperate with the new law enforcement powers granted in the anti-terrorism legislation known as the USA Patriot Act.

Fair-minded people can argue about whether this is good or bad, but the fact remains that the responsibility for collecting, analyzing and coordinating intelligence on terrorists remains outside the Homeland Security Department, at the Justice Department, Defense Department, FBI and CIA.

Likewise, outside forces have defeated measures to bolster the security of critical infrastructure. The chemical industry, for example, crushed legislation that would have required it to beef up the protection of refineries and tank farms.

With firehouses closing in Manhattan, questions remain about whether safety has improved for Americans at home. What follows is a topic-by-topic examination of anti-terrorism protections one year after the creation of the Homeland Security Department.

Department of Homeland Security
Major Operational Divisions

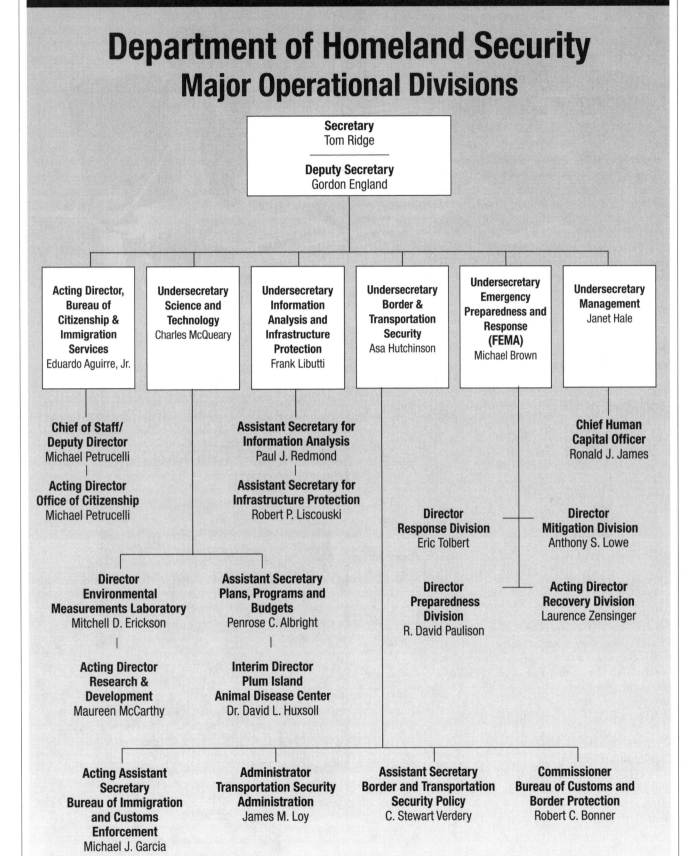

Secretary
Tom Ridge

Deputy Secretary
Gordon England

Acting Director, Bureau of Citizenship & Immigration Services
Eduardo Aguirre, Jr.

Undersecretary Science and Technology
Charles McQueary

Undersecretary Information Analysis and Infrastructure Protection
Frank Libutti

Undersecretary Border & Transportation Security
Asa Hutchinson

Undersecretary Emergency Preparedness and Response (FEMA)
Michael Brown

Undersecretary Management
Janet Hale

Chief of Staff/ Deputy Director
Michael Petrucelli

Acting Director Office of Citizenship
Michael Petrucelli

Assistant Secretary for Information Analysis
Paul J. Redmond

Assistant Secretary for Infrastructure Protection
Robert P. Liscouski

Chief Human Capital Officer
Ronald J. James

Director Response Division
Eric Tolbert

Director Mitigation Division
Anthony S. Lowe

Director Preparedness Division
R. David Paulison

Acting Director Recovery Division
Laurence Zensinger

Director Environmental Measurements Laboratory
Mitchell D. Erickson

Assistant Secretary Plans, Programs and Budgets
Penrose C. Albright

Acting Director Research & Development
Maureen McCarthy

Interim Director Plum Island Animal Disease Center
Dr. David L. Huxsoll

Acting Assistant Secretary Bureau of Immigration and Customs Enforcement
Michael J. Garcia

Administrator Transportation Security Administration
James M. Loy

Assistant Secretary Border and Transportation Security Policy
C. Stewart Verdery

Commissioner Bureau of Customs and Border Protection
Robert C. Bonner

QUESTION #1

Can the United States sufficiently secure its borders without hindering foreign commerce?

Before Sept. 11, coming to America was relatively simple.

Hop a plane in Paris after breakfast and arrive in New York City in time for dinner. Drive truckloads of goods back and forth between Windsor, Ontario, and Detroit several times a day. Customs was usually a breeze, with agents rarely giving European passports or Canadian driver's licenses a second look. The same went for cargo: If inspectors opened a container of Pakistani shirts arriving in a U.S. seaport, it was probably to check that importers were following rules set up to protect U.S. textile workers, not because they thought it might be hiding a dirty bomb.

In the year since President Bush announced that his administration would create a Department of Homeland Security, the government has struggled with initiatives designed to shine a bright light on every foreign student, business traveler, tourist and cargo load seeking entry into the United States.

Because it is impossible to check every person and item that comes across the border, success will be a matter of accurately — and speedily — determining which "low risk" individuals and shippers can receive faster processing by agreeing to extensive background checks.

The challenge is to find a way to efficiently screen out terrorist threats without choking off the routine flow of people and goods that is America's economic lifeline.

Administration officials and a bevy of contractors insist technology is the key. New systems are quickly being dispatched on every front: at — and between — highway border crossings, at airports and shipping ports of call. Some programs even aim to track cargo and individuals while they are here.

"[I]n the 21st century border, security can no longer be just a coastline or a line on the ground between two nations. It's also a line of information in a computer telling us who is in this country, for how long and for what reason," said Asa Hutchinson, the former Arkansas Republican congressman running the new department's border and transportation security directorate, in a May 19 address to the Center for Strategic and International Studies.

But each new system also brings its own challenges.

Checkpoint Gadgetry

Hutchinson was referring to the Visitor and Immigration Status Indication Technology, or U.S. VISIT, system, an ambitious and controversial project that will use biometric identifiers in travel documents to screen arriving visitors who are required to have visas against terrorist watch lists and track foreign visitors' entries and departures.

Although Hutchinson argues that an entry-exit control system could have tipped off officials when Sept. 11 hijackers Hani Hanjour and Mohamed Atta violated the terms of their visas, it is unclear whether Congress is prepared to give the department enough money to meet deadlines it has set for the program.

Homeland Security Secretary Tom Ridge has promised that U.S. VISIT will be functioning at every airport and seaport of entry by the end of this year, and at the nation's 50 busiest border crossings by the end of 2004, as required by a sweeping border security law enacted in 2001 (PL 107-173). Congress has appropriated $380 million for the project so far, but some estimates put its cost well into the billions.

Moreover, a request for a proposal to develop the technology behind the program, which Hutchinson has promised the department will issue by this fall, is already a year late. The former INS was supposed to solicit bids last summer.

Regardless, many lawmakers continue to worry about the long stretches of undefended border between ports of entry. The Mexican border, where the vast majority of drug and immigration arrests occur, is naturally more heavily manned than the U.S.-Canadian frontier. But each boundary has gaping holes, illustrated last month by the deaths of 19 illegal immigrants abandoned in a hot, airless trailer in south Texas.

"My worry is all the focus on crossings may push aside the fact that a terrorist could just slip across the border in an unguarded area," Maine Republican Sen. Susan Collins, chairman of the Senate Governmental Affairs Committee, said June 3.

One approach to tackling that problem, which has gained currency on Capitol Hill and in the Homeland Security De-

Examples of Biometric Identification

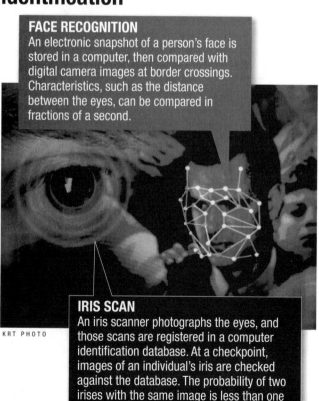

FACE RECOGNITION
An electronic snapshot of a person's face is stored in a computer, then compared with digital camera images at border crossings. Characteristics, such as the distance between the eyes, can be compared in fractions of a second.

KRT PHOTO

IRIS SCAN
An iris scanner photographs the eyes, and those scans are registered in a computer identification database. At a checkpoint, images of an individual's iris are checked against the database. The probability of two irises with the same image is less than one in 1 trillion.

partment, is the use of unmanned aerial vehicles, or UAVs, such as the ones the Pentagon used with great effect to track enemy forces in Kosovo, Afghanistan and Iraq.

Balancing Passenger Screening and Civil Rights

After deploying an army of federal airport screeners and training the first group of commercial pilots to carry guns in the cockpit, the Transportation Security Administration (TSA) is counting on a computer-based profiling system to spearhead its efforts. The Computer-Assisted Passenger Pre-screening System (CAPPS II), scheduled for deployment next year, would match passengers' names against the government's terrorist watch lists as well as credit bureau reports and other commercial databases, assigning each passenger a color-coded terrorist threat "score."

According to the TSA, the system will be better than an existing government "No Fly List," which is prone to errors and misinterpretation by airline clerks, resulting in erroneous detentions and an American Civil Liberties Union (ACLU) lawsuit.

But the ACLU and other groups — plus lawmakers in both parties, the European Union and even some U.S. officials — worry that CAPPS II's potential usefulness in stopping another hijacking may not outweigh its potential impact on privacy and civil liberties.

CAPPS II and U.S. VISIT are arguably Homeland Security's most complex undertakings to date. But while the department has streamlined border-security functions and broken up the dysfunctional INS, many other elements of border and transportation security policy have been just as problematic.

For instance, U.S. VISIT will incorporate the Student Exchange and Visitor Information System (SEVIS), an Internet-based foreign student tracking system meant to replace an older, unreliable paper-based INS database. Keeping tabs on foreign students has been a congressional priority because Hanjour, Atta and others among the 19 Sept. 11 terrorists posed as foreign students. But SEVIS, in place since February, has been plagued by technical glitches, staffing shortages and general confusion.

Now that the Department of Homeland Security sets the rules for State Department consular offices to follow when issuing visas, State plans to hold in-person interviews for nearly all overseas visa applicants, to the delight of security and immigration hawks. But the U.S. Chamber of Commerce warns that a lack of resources to help overseas consulates deal with tighter security measures already has created backlogs and delays that have hurt small U.S. businesses competing in international markets.

Also, since last fall, males 16 and older holding temporary visas from 25 countries on a list of terrorist havens have had to register and periodically check in with the federal government. Supporters say the "special registration" program has proven successful in netting at least 11 suspected terrorists.

More than 13,000 of the men who came forward to register have been found to be living illegally and could face deportation, according to the Bureau of Immigration and Customs Enforcement. The wave of cases suggests the degree to which the administration believes the immigration system can be used to weed out potential terrorists.

But immigration lawyers, Muslim groups, civil liberties

Technology is key to protecting U.S. borders while maintaining the benefits of commerce, White House officials say.

activists and some Democrats have complained that the initiative smacks of racial profiling. They say it has led mainly to the arrests of law-abiding men who overstayed their tourist visas while waiting years for the INS to act on their green card applications.

The TSA is now scrambling to complete criminal background checks on thousands of screeners whose pasts were not thoroughly checked before they were hired. It also is cutting thousands of screener positions to stay within budgetary limits imposed by congressional overseers who say the TSA has become a bloated bureaucracy.

In November 2004, all 429 of the nation's airports will be allowed to "opt out" of the federal system and instead use private screeners with TSA training. Airport managers and some lawmakers, including House Aviation Subcommittee Chairman John L. Mica, R-Fla., already are suggesting that the TSA should permit airports to opt out earlier.

The Weakest Link

TSA Administrator James M. Loy has promised that his agency will focus more heavily this year on securing other modes of transportation. But the TSA has come under fire this spring for seeking to divert port security grant money to pay for cost overruns in aviation security.

Indeed, although the Bureau of Customs and Border Protection has placed agents in major foreign seaports and now requires ocean carriers to send detailed manifests 24 hours before their cargo is loaded overseas, analysts continue to see shipping containers that come through U.S. seaports as a dangerously weak link in security.

Inspecting every container would grind international commerce to a halt, so the government has emphasized targeting those coming from lesser-known companies or from the least secure overseas ports.

But the Coast Guard, intended to be the lead agency on port security, is still waiting for funding to help it verify that foreign ship owners and port authorities are complying with last year's comprehensive port security law (PL 107-295). U.S. port authorities, meanwhile, say they are not receiving anywhere near enough federal funding to secure their own facilities. The law enacted last fall did not include a funding mechanism because the shipping industry lobbied fiercely for Congress to scrap a proposed user fee.

As Democrats have seized every opportunity to point out, the money woes facing the Coast Guard and local ports are just one example of a hard truth about the homeland security era: Everyone agrees on the need for more security, but there is wide dispute over how to pay for it.

QUESTION #2

Are state and local 'first responders' getting the federal funding they say they need?

State and local governments disagree on how funding for 'first responder' emergency personnel should be dispersed.

"We have a saying inside our department," Homeland Security Secretary Tom Ridge said recently. "The homeland will be secure when the hometowns are secure."

It's a nice turn of a phrase, but homilies do not pay the bills, and if anything has drowned out Ridge's avuncular assurances over the past year, it is the incessant cries of state and local authorities for more money to make their hometowns secure.

"I think it will come up again and again, and in spades, if there is another attack," said New Haven, Conn., Mayor John DeStefano Jr., who is also president of the National League of Cities.

If rescue units ever again race to smoking ruins comparable to the World Trade Center, indeed there probably will not be much debating over first responder spending. But until then, Washington and local governments will continue to wrangle over not just how much the federal government will provide, but who should distribute the funding and how to rejigger grant "formulas."

When President Bush on June 6, 2002, announced his support for a Department of Homeland Security, the political landscape in Washington shook like an earthquake. But the foundation for many of the state and local issues that have preoccupied homeland officials, members of Congress, governors and mayors since then arrived a few months before — on Feb. 4, 2002, when Bush unveiled his fiscal 2003 budget request.

At the time, Congress had appropriated $1 billion for first responders for fiscal 2002. Now, Bush was proposing that $3.5 billion in counterterrorism grants be made available to state and local programs for training and equipping firefighters, police officers and other emergency crews — all of which would be lumped together as "first responders." He also wanted the grants managed solely by the Federal Emergency Management Agency (FEMA).

Consolidating these programs under FEMA was an idea the administration floated the year before, but this first post-Sept. 11 budget proposal gave the White House the opportunity to really push it onto the agenda.

On its face, the idea of consolidating the programs in FEMA was logical. But the president's shift would have required the Justice Department, whose Office for Domestic Preparedness (ODP) handled a lot of this territory, and the members of Congress who authorize and appropriate its funding, to cede some control. It also would have called for local police officials to deal with an agency that had no law enforcement responsibilities or experience, another thing they were not eager to embrace.

But what really irritated state and local officials was the idea that almost all of the $3.5 billion in counterterrorism funding was not new money. In the same budget, the president proposed consolidating or eviscerating popular Clinton-era law enforcement grant programs, such as the Community Oriented Police Services (COPS) program.

To officials outside the Beltway it sounded like the administration was killing those programs to raise counterterrorist funds without really boosting the budget. The U.S. Conference of Mayors said such shifting and consolidation amounted to a nearly $800 million budget cut for programs.

"We must not rob Peter to pay Paul," New Orleans Mayor Marc Morial, then-president of the conference, said in March 2002. "We cannot afford to cut funding that helps prevent street crime in order to finance needed efforts to prevent terrorism."

The White House argued that COPS was a temporary program meant to help hire more police officers. And it insisted there was no proof that any of the other programs were actually contributing to the falling crime rate.

Rivals for Dollars

Adding to the roil was the reality that states and cities might well be united as a group in their pursuit of federal dollars, but they were rivals on the question of who should get them and how.

Local governments argued that funds should go directly to them because state bureaucracies would not only add more delay to the process, they would take sizable cuts off the top.

The states, which had an ally in Ridge, countered that sending money to them first would ensure that it was spent according to statewide plans that would help maximize dollars and avoid equipment duplication or incompatibilities, such as with radios.

The stage was set for a battle. Because Congress could not disentangle itself from election-year standoffs over spending and left for the year with 11 of its 13 annual appropriations bills on the shelf, the rhetoric only grew hotter.

Adding to the intensity was the fact that states and

cities, which are almost all required to balance their budgets, have huge deficits hanging over them.

In February, Congress did not come close to quenching the thirst for more federal dollars when it finally appropriated $3.5 billion for first responders. That money was not all new, either. Appropriators chose to include programs such as COPS in their tally for the $3.5 billion, much to the consternation of state and local officials.

In April, members used the wartime supplemental bill (PL 108-11) to try to pacify some of those complaints by providing $4.3 billion for first responder, emergency planning and critical infrastructure protection programs.

As for who would get what when, Congress — with the administration's support — sided with the states but offered an olive branch to local officials: Money would go first to state capitals, but they would be required to "pass through" 80 percent of it to local governments.

As far as who would hand out the money, the law enforcement community and its congressional allies won out over the administration, which wanted the new department's Emergency Preparedness directorate to handle the grant programs once the law (PL 107-296) creating the Homeland Security Department was passed in November. Instead, the authority was given to ODP, which sits in Homeland's law enforcement wing, the Border and Transportation Security directorate.

But even this issue remains somewhat unresolved.

Ridge has announced his support for legislation (S 796) sponsored by Maine Republican and Senate Governmental Affairs Chairwoman Susan Collins that would move ODP up the organizational chart into the Office for State and Local Government Coordination, which reports directly to the secretary.

Now, dispersing money but wearing its green eyeshade, the department is turning a magnifying glass on the criteria, or "formula," it will use to award funding.

The formula passed by Congress in fall 2001 requires that about 35 percent to 40 percent of first responder funds be split equally among all states. ODP has distributed the rest based mostly on population.

But Ridge and many in Congress would like to tweak the formula so that while a state minimum would remain in place, the department could direct the rest by using criteria such as the likelihood that an area would be attacked and whether it had vulnerable sites such as nuclear or chemical plants nearby.

Collins has made revisiting the formula a top priority for her committee, while Congress set aside $100 million in the omnibus and $700 million in the supplemental spending bills for high-threat cities, such as New York and Washington.

Sending more money to those cities is again an idea few would dispute, but Ridge already has had to deal with questions from lawmakers about why cities in their states did not make the cut.

Still, the issue of redoing formulas and deciding which box on a chart will mail the checks may soon be relegated to a sideshow when Congress starts working on next year's spending bills and vectoring grants to cash-strapped hometowns.

"You're going to go where the game is being played," DeStefano said of this year's lobbying action. "And the game is going to be played in the appropriations bills."

Homeland Security Money Finding Its Way to the States

Since the department opened in 2002, it has sent more than $2.2 billion to states and territories in grants from two agencies. The Office of Domestic Preparedness sends money—largely to police departments — for equipment, planning and training exercises. Emergency Management Performance grants go toward the same kind of programs for firefighters.

State grants:

(in millions of dollars)

State	ODP grant	EMP grant	Total
Alabama	$39.8	$5.2	$45.0
Alaska	21.0	2.8	23.8
Arizona	44.5	5.4	49.8
Arkansas	31.1	4.0	35.1
California	189.1	23.7	212.8
Colorado	39.8	4.9	44.7
Connecticut	34.8	4.6	39.4
Delaware	21.8	2.8	24.6
Florida	99.3	11.7	111.0
Georgia	59.6	7.3	66.8
Hawaii	23.9	3.2	27.2
Idaho	24.4	3.1	27.5
Illinois	79.5	9.4	88.9
Indiana	48.0	5.9	53.9
Iowa	32.2	4.1	36.3
Kansas	31.2	3.9	35.1
Kentucky	37.9	4.6	42.5
Louisiana	39.8	5.1	44.9
Maine	24.2	3.2	27.4
Maryland	44.5	5.4	49.9
Massachusetts	49.3	6.3	55.6
Michigan	67.0	8.5	75.5
Minnesota	42.4	5.2	47.6
Mississippi	31.9	4.0	36.0
Missouri	45.6	5.7	51.3
Montana	22.3	2.8	25.2
Nebraska	26.3	3.4	29.7
Nevada	28.4	3.5	31.9
New Hampshire	24.1	3.2	27.2
New Jersey	59.8	7.7	67.5
New Mexico	26.8	3.5	30.3
New York	111.6	13.8	125.4
North Carolina	58.5	7.3	65.8
North Dakota	21.0	2.7	23.7
Ohio	73.8	9.4	83.2
Oklahoma	35.0	4.4	39.3
Oregon	35.1	4.4	39.4
Pennsylvania	78.3	9.8	88.1
Rhode Island	23.1	3.1	26.2
South Carolina	37.9	4.9	42.9
South Dakota	21.6	2.6	24.2
Tennessee	46.2	5.7	51.9
Texas	124.0	14.8	138.8
Utah	29.2	3.7	32.9
Vermont	20.9	2.6	23.5
Virginia	53.5	6.7	60.2
Washington	47.5	5.8	53.2
West Virginia	26.7	3.2	29.9
Wisconsin	44.5	5.5	50.0
Wyoming	20.3	2.7	23.0

QUESTION #3

How willing is private industry to identify its vulnerabilities and protect critical infrastructure?

If there is one word that sums up the Bush administration's approach to securing privately owned infrastructure since the Sept. 11 terrorist attacks, it is volunteerism.

The White House has quashed proposed regulations for the chemical industry, opposed legislation to increase security at nuclear plants, and steered clear of imposing new requirements to secure the nation's computer networks. In place of these top-down approaches, the administration has largely relied on the private sector, which owns an estimated 87 percent of the nation's factories, rail lines, power plants and computer networks, to come up with its own strategies to defend against terrorist attacks.

In June 2002, for example, the American Chemistry Council, the trade and lobbying association for the nation's largest chemical manufacturing companies, told its members to study the physical security of their plants and to fix any problems they found. The security enhancements were to be verified by independent third parties, such as firefighters, police officers, insurance auditors or federal or state government officials.

In March, the council announced that its 165 member companies had completed vulnerability studies for their 120 highest priority facilities.

The program is part of the chemistry council's Responsible Care program, described by the organization as "a voluntary program to achieve improvements in environmental, health and safety performance beyond levels required by the U.S. government."

But critics complained the program relied on the good will of the industry, and noted the plan has no requirement that facilities near large population centers stop using chemicals such as chlorine, which could form deadly gas clouds if released accidentally or by terrorist saboteurs. And, critics said, the industry group represents only a small percentage of the nation's chemical infrastructure. Thousands of water and sewer treatment plants, which use chlorine as a purifier, were not covered by the program.

Sen. Jon Corzine, D-N.J., meanwhile, launched his own campaign in late 2001 to impose tough new anti-terrorism security requirements on the U.S. chemical industry.

Legislation that Corzine introduced in the 107th Congress would have required chemical plants to carry out vulnerability assessments, limit the types and quantities of chemicals they keep on hand and, when possible, phase out the use of chlorine and other potentially dangerous chemicals. The bill granted the EPA a lead role in enforcing the new security restrictions.

Corzine's bill also had teeth. Plant operators who failed to comply with the new regulation faced up to a year in prison and fines of $25,000 a day. Repeat offenders faced fines of up to $50,000 a day and prison terms of up to two years.

The bill was approved unanimously by the Senate Environment and Public Works Committee in July 2002.

But after the committee vote, the chemical industry launched an aggressive lobbying campaign against the legislation. It argued that forcing the phase-out of some chemicals would result in costly process changes and strongly opposed the EPA's role, saying the agency had no experience as a security regulator.

Seven committee Republicans eventually opposed the Corzine bill on the floor. It never came up for a vote.

Security for Americans

Meanwhile, the EPA was writing new security rules of its own, using its regulatory authority under the Clean Air Act. But the rules never appeared. Several sources — all of whom favored an expanded EPA role — said last fall that the regulatory approach was scuttled inside the White House.

Corzine reintroduced his legislation early in the 108th Congress, with some changes designed to make it more palatable to the industry — notably granting the new Department of Homeland Security the lead oversight role.

By then, however, the White House was drafting its own bill, which Sen. James M. Inhofe, R-Okla., introduced shortly after Congress returned from its spring break.

The Inhofe bill (S 1043) looks a lot like the American Chemistry Council's industry program. It requires chemical plants to assess their vulnerability to terrorism and to develop plans to fill any holes. And, like Corzine's bill, it includes fines for failure to comply — $50,000 a day for each violation and administrative penalties of up to $250,000.

But as was true of the council-sponsored industry program, Inhofe's legislation sets no minimum security criteria. It includes no requirements for the protection of aboveground chemical storage tanks and says nothing about phasing out the use of chlorine and other dangerous chemicals.

"Unfortunately, the bill does very little to secure Americans who work and live around these facilities," Corzine said in response to the bill's introduction. "The bill may provide an illusion of security, but it's little more than a fig leaf that would leave chemical plants highly vulnerable to terrorism."

Sen. Harry Reid, D-Nev., has met similar hurdles in his efforts to push through stiff new security requirements for the nuclear industry. Legislation Reid sponsored in the 107th Congress would have federalized the private security forces that now guard the nation's nuclear power plants. Reid's bill also would have changed the so-called design basis threat, the number of intruders that guards are required to repel, to include more numerous and more heavily armed attackers.

But the nuclear industry, like the chemical industry, launched an effective campaign to derail Reid's legislation. The Nuclear Energy Institute, the industry's trade association, paid for full-page ads in Washington-area newspapers with large Capitol Hill circulations. The ads featured photographs of well-armed, menacing guards and descriptions of the guards' law enforcement and military backgrounds.

The ads worked. Although Reid's bill passed the Environment and Public Works Committee unanimously in the 107th Congress, it was never brought to the floor for a vote.

Reid, joined by Sens. Hillary Rodham Clinton, D-N.Y., James M. Jeffords, I-Vt., Joseph I. Lieberman, D-Conn., John Edwards, D-N.C., and Tom Harkin, D-Iowa, reintroduced the bill in January. But Inhofe, now the chairman of the Environment and Public Works Committee, had his own legislation ready to roll.

Inhofe's bill would require the Nuclear Regulatory Commission (NRC), to assess the security of nuclear facilities under its authority, as well as the hiring and training standards for plant guards. The legislation also would require more stringent background checks for all individuals who have access to nuclear facilities.

But it would not require the industry itself to bolster security around nuclear facilities.

NRC's Revised Regulations

After the Sept. 11 attacks, the NRC, which oversees the commercial nuclear industry, endured withering criticism from a variety of public interest groups for doing little more than "recommending" that the nuclear industry increase the security around its plants.

The Washington, D.C.-based Project on Government Oversight (POGO) was particularly vocal, accusing NRC of ignoring whistleblower reports of overworked and lightly armed guards who would be hard-pressed to turn back one or two intruders, never mind an armed team of terrorists intent on stealing nuclear materials or causing a reactor meltdown.

This spring, NRC revised some of its existing regulations, changing the design basis threat to include more armed intruders and increasing the regularity of the force-on-force exercises used to test guards' abilities.

But critics said the new requirements are insufficient.

"The NRC seems to have this backwards. NRC appears to be tailoring its requirements to meet the existing capabilities of the plants' private security forces," said Peter Stockton, a senior investigator with POGO. "Instead, NRC should be determining the realistic threat, then sizing the forces to meet that threat."

Sean Moulton, a policy analyst at OMB Watch, a Washington public interest group, said the administration is relying too heavily on the private sector's willingness to share information about vulnerabilities and to fix its own security problems.

"The administration says this information is critical. If it's so critical, why not require that it be submitted?" Moulton asks. "They're trusting the companies to tell them what's wrong and then trusting them to do something about it."

Apparently stung by the criticism, the Department of Homeland Security proposed a new strategy in April for dealing with the security of privately owned infrastructure. A rule it published April 15 in the Federal Register encourages the private sector to share information about security vulnerabilities, threats or attacks with the government by establishing a system to keep that information out of the public realm.

"The Department recognizes that its receipt of information pertaining to the security of critical infrastructure, much of which is not customarily within the public domain, is best encouraged through the assurance that such information will be utilized for securing the United States and will not be disseminated to the general public," the department said in the proposed rule.

But critics say issuing a blanket disclosure exemption for voluntarily submitted information could keep a lot more than security reports from the public. Companies with poor environmental or worker safety records could keep that information secret by "voluntarily" submitting it to the Homeland Security department.

"The lack of accountability is staggering," Moulton said. "I'm not even sure Congress will be able to get the full story."

Robert P. Liscouski, the Homeland Security Department's

Private companies have been assigned the task of defending nuclear plants and other important infrastructure.

point man for infrastructure protection, conceded that balancing the need to encourage industry to volunteer information with the public's right to know about safety and security issues is a tricky job. "We don't have the answer yet," he said.

Liscouski, a former security executive at the Coca-Cola Co. in Atlanta, sat down with reporters at the department's northwest Washington, D.C., headquarters on June 6 to discuss the department's new cybersecurity division, which will serve as a threat information clearinghouse for public and private computer systems.

The division will monitor threats, help private-sector companies prepare for attacks, coordinate the response to attacks, and provide assistance in recovering from attacks. But Liscouski said the department would not require the owners of the nation's cyber-infrastructure to do anything to bolster network security.

"We don't want to be a regulatory agency," he said. "We don't want to force the private sector to do this."

The best approach, he said, is to give companies as much information as possible and count on the market to force them to do the right thing. Not only will market forces reward companies who protect the physical, personnel and procedural security of their networks, Liscouski argued, they will encourage companies to find ways to assuage consumers' fears about the security of personal data, including credit card numbers and transactions such as bank transfers and online purchases.

Asked whether the department will set standards against which companies would have to perform, Liscouski said no. What it can do, he said, is build awareness within the private sector to existing threats. "We can set expectations for behavior," he said. "The federal government won't solve this problem on its own because everyone owns it."

QUESTION #4

Have intelligence-gathering efforts been unified among agencies?

Ten years to the day after Ramzi Yousef moved into a gritty one-bedroom apartment in Jersey City, N.J., and began building the bomb that would gut the underground parking garage of the World Trade Center in 1993, Eleanor Hill sat before the House and Senate Select Intelligence Committees on the Sept. 11 Intelligence Failures.

"Information about the hijackers and about al Qaeda can be found in disparate databases spread among a range of intelligence and civilian agencies," Hill said during a hearing on Oct. 1, 2002, rendering her verdict as chief counsel leading the investigation.

It had been a months-long struggle, but Hill and her staff had dug through the underground mine of classified details about al Qaeda in the government's databases and files.

The FBI and the CIA knew al Qaeda was planning new attacks, her investigation had found; they knew Osama bin Laden and his lieutenants had seriously considered using commercial aircraft as weapons.

By now, Hill also knew about the Phoenix Memorandum, wherein an FBI agent urged a nationwide investigation of flight schools enrolling students from the Middle East. Already she had put under a microscope the frustrated attempts of FBI agents in Minneapolis to unzip the secrets of Zacariah Moussaoui and his laptop.

In her files, too, was proof that before the 9/11 attacks the CIA had fingered two of the al Qaeda hijackers for immigration authorities, but put no special emphasis on the danger they posed.

Unorganized Power Centers

Equally important, Hill had taken the time to drill down into the crust of claims by the CIA and the FBI that they had waged a "seamless" war against al Qaeda for years, operating in concert from two richly endowed counterterrorism centers.

Proceeding with a rigorous focus on the particulars, Hill found that deep divides still yawned between the three power centers of the U. S. intelligence community — the CIA, the FBI and the National Security Agency.

"Furthermore," Hill said in her testimony, "law enforcement, immigration, visa and intelligence information related to the 19 hijackers was not organized in any manner to allow for any one agency to detect terrorism-related trends and patterns in their activities."

To try to explain the bureaucratic group-think that let these "systemic" obstacles stay in place through a full 10 years of escalating terrorist attacks by Middle Eastern groups, Hill summarized the consensus views of the many witnesses she and her staff had interrogated.

All hands blamed "a range of political, cultural, jurisdictional, legal and bureaucratic issues that are ever-present hurdles to information sharing," Hill said, a conclusion that squared with the findings of earlier national commissions and government panels.

Six months after the Bush administration pulled a U-turn and declared its advocacy of a Cabinet-level Homeland Security Department (DHS), the joint House and Senate Committee issued its final report. Thus, on Dec. 1, 2002, members of Congress had every reason to believe they had knocked down the "walls" that were blamed for leaving the nation vulnerable to attack.

At considerable risk to civil liberties, the House and Senate had passed by large margins the anti-terrorism bill known as the USA Patriot Act (PL 107-56), a comprehensive bill that forcefully erased from federal law the jurisdictional and legal provisions that executive-branch witnesses said obstructed the sharing of intelligence among government analysts.

To bring down the bureaucratic, organizational and cultural walls that were said to keep the government's best intelligence analysts from examining the entire mosaic of terrorist-related intelligence, Congress used a bulldozer. The Homeland Security Act (PL 107-296) authorized the largest reorganization of government in 50 years.

Aside from shifting agencies that dealt with border security into a more logical alignment, the defining feature of the new department was a Directorate of Information Analysis and Infrastructure Protection.

The plain language of the law authorized a new center for the U.S. intelligence community that would do one thing well: analyze all terrorism-related intelligence gathered by law enforcement and intelligence agencies for warning signs of new threats.

In taking this dramatic step, the Congress followed the lead of the president's own National Strategy of Homeland Security. In that July 2002 document, President Bush declared that the new DHS information analysis directorate would be "responsible for analyzing terrorist threats to the homeland."

Just do it, said the legislation.

On Nov. 25, Bush had signed the bill and endorsed its chief objective. "First," he said in his signing statement, "this new department will analyze intelligence information on terror threats collected by the CIA, the FBI, the National Security Agency and others."

Thus, when the ranking Republicans and Democrats on the House Senate Joint Inquiry issued their final report Dec. 1, they did not belabor the need for a solution that the nation's civilian leadership had already adopted.

Keep the faith was their message.

"Congress and the [administration] should ensure the full development within the Department of Homeland Security of an effective all-source terrorism information fusion center that will dramatically improve the focus and quality of counterterrorism analysis. . . ." their report said.

So far so good.

Then, in much less time than it took the al Qaeda hijackers to carry out their complex plot, the locomotive force of this overhaul collided with an immovable object: The mountainous bulk of the bureaucracies most heavily implicated in the 9/11 intelligence failure.

In his Jan. 28 State of the Union speech, President Bush declared, "I am directing the leaders of the FBI, the CIA, the Homeland Security Department and the Department of Defense to develop a Terrorist Threat Integration Center to merge and analyze all threat information in a single location."

Missing: Its location. But it would be outside the new Homeland Security Department, at the CIA. Ridge's intelligence staff could come out and play, along with the FBI and other agencies, but that was it. By executive fiat, the deed was done.

Politically, Bush's sudden change of heart had the feel of an asymmetric attack on the prerogatives of Congress. But if the announcement came as a surprise, the creation of a new unit to correlate terrorist information was not without a compelling logic.

Focused on al Qaeda

In his Oct. 17, 2002, testimony for the joint House and Senate inquiry, CIA Director George J. Tenet conceded no error, acknowledged no miscalculation. Beyond removing "the wall" of legal restrictions on intelligence sharing and increasing his budget, he saw no need for fundamental change. In his view, any suggestion that the CIA was not joined at the hip with the FBI in pursuit of al Qaeda was not just a fiction, it was very nearly a blood libel.

"One of the most critical alliances in the war against terrorism is that between CIA and FBI," Tenet testified.

As early as 1996, they had set up a "Bin Laden Issue Station" staffed with CIA, NSA and FBI officers who did nothing but pursue al Qaeda, Tenet said. CIA-FBI teams conducted numerous joint operations against the terrorists, stopping plots, making arrests and saving thousands of lives.

The agency's analysis of intelligence on al Qaeda, Tenet contended, consistently hit the bull's-eye.

In 12 separate intelligence reports, he said, the CIA had warned civilian agencies that al Qaeda might use aircraft as weapons. In the months preceding the 9/11 attacks, CIA assets "lit up" with alerts that multiple attacks were in the offing.

"By long-established doctrine, we disseminated these raw reports immediately and widely to policymakers and action agencies such as the military, State Department, the FAA, FBI, Department of Transportation, the INS and others," Tenet said. "This reporting, by itself, stood as a dramatic warning of imminent attack."

The FBI witnesses elaborated on Tenet's theme. Yes, the legal "walls" had been a problem, they contended, but any alleged bureaucratic obstacles were old news, problems long since solved.

In fact, said former FBI Director Louis J. Freeh, if any institution was to blame for the horror of the 9/11 attacks, it was Congress itself, for failing to heed his many pleas for bigger budgets and a better computer system.

Current FBI Director Robert S. Mueller III praised Freeh's "thoughtful" comments, then hailed his own prompt "reorganization" of the FBI. He was, he explained, creating a new Counterterrorism Division, setting up an Office of Intelligence and seeking funding to hire more intelligence analysts.

In other words, at no time during the debate over the Homeland Security Act last year did the two agencies with the greatest culpability in the 9/11 intelligence failure admit that a failure had occurred, or accept that the tragedy justified creation of an "all source" analysis in the new Homeland Security Department.

During the Homeland Security Act debate in 2002, FBI Director Robert S. Mueller III and CIA Director George J. Tenet said their agencies were unified.

All of which helps explain the festivities that took place during the May 1 opening day ceremony for the new Terrorist Threat Integration Center (TTIC) in a room at CIA Headquarters.

Each armed with his own pair of scissors, Mueller, Tenet and Assistant Homeland Security Secretary Gordon England stood side by side with other officials and cut a white ribbon hung between two chairs.

"TTIC is absolutely crucial to the Department of Homeland Security," England said in a news release. "We could not do our job without a center like this."

And that was that.

A National Intelligence Plan

As for the CIA, Associate Director Winston P. Wiley has told Congress that TTIC will "provide integrated analysis of potential terrorist threats to all U.S. interests, physical and cyber," and then distribute threat warnings through DHS and the FBI to "state, local, and private-sector officials who have homeland security-related responsibilities."

Meanwhile, the Justice Department is moving fast along two parallel tracks to deepen its own ability to gather and analyze terrorist-related intelligence. One of them is its joint project with the International Association of Chiefs of Police to develop a "National Intelligence Plan," whose goal is to knit together hundreds of state and local law enforcement agencies into a domestic intelligence-gathering force that funnels terrorist-related information to new Anti-terrorism Task Forces lodged in local U.S. Attorneys offices.

Simultaneously, the FBI is surging ahead with its own plans to expand its network of FBI-police Joint Terrorism Task Forces, and bulking up a new cadre of intelligence analysts with foreign language skills.

Voices of dissent are stirring, though.

"This is a positive first step," Homeland Security Chairman Christopher Cox, R-Calif., and ranking member Rep. Jim Turner, D-Texas, said in joint statement on TTIC's opening day, but the CIA-led facility was "no substitute for the DHS center Congress had in mind."

They added: "By law, the Department is required to conduct its own analysis of raw intelligence received from federal, state and local government agencies."

Undermanned and Overdeployed? Congress Debates Expanded Army

Too many demands, drooping morale could leave troop levels dangerously low

U.S. military force levels have remained relatively static over the last half-dozen years, but the same thing cannot be said of overseas deployments.

Before the Sept. 11 terrorist attacks, if U.S. troops were sent overseas they usually headed to one of a few longstanding bases in such countries as Germany and South Korea. Since Sept. 11, that has all changed, as large numbers of soldiers, sailors and Marines have shipped off for extended tours in Afghanistan, Iraq and — in smaller numbers — such far-flung places as the Philippines and the former Soviet Republic of Georgia.

As the Pentagon struggles to manage its largest overseas deployment in two generations, and as falling morale threatens re-enlistment and recruitment, Congress is beginning to ask what, if anything, it can do to ease the strain.

There is strong support among some House members — led by Armed Services Chairman Duncan Hunter, R-Calif. — to add troops. And there is equally strong reluctance among senators to take that course before the Pentagon can assess its needs. It is a

CQ Weekly August 2, 2003

fight that may play out next year, but one that is already taking shape.

The debate over troop levels came into focus July 29 when Army Chief of Staff-nominee Gen. Peter J. Schoomaker testified at his confirmation hearing that "intuitively" he believes the Army needs more people. In the next breath, Schoomaker also asked the Senate Armed Services Committee to give him time to conduct a study of what is needed.

"This is a major issue," Sen. Carl Levin of Michigan, ranking Democrat on the panel, said at the hearing. "How much stress can we put on our active duty forces . . . and reserve forces?"

After the hearing, senators seemed more than happy to give Schoomaker and Secretary of Defense Donald H. Rumsfeld time to complete their manpower studies. "I personally don't think we've built a foundation for increasing troop strength yet," said Jeff Sessions, R-Ala. "It's good for Congress to study. That is our responsibility."

But Hunter and other House members already are agitating for more troops, arguing that burnout rates among active duty personnel are about to crest and that by the time studies are completed troop levels will have fallen to dangerously low levels. The time to act, they say, is now.

"You can only deploy them so often," said Ike Skelton of Missouri, ranking Democrat on the House Armed Services Committee.

Looking to 2005

Hunter has said he plans to include a provision next year in the fiscal 2005 defense authorization bill that would require the Army to add two new divisions of troops — possibly as many as 38,000 more soldiers. That comes as defense authorizers try to work out a minor disagreement over troop strength in the fiscal 2004 defense authorization bill (HR 1588).

House members have advocated an increase of 4,643 Army and Air Force personnel above the administration's request. The increase is not echoed in either the Senate version of the bill or either chamber's version of the fiscal 2004 defense appropriations bill (HR 2586). (*2003 CQ Weekly, p. 1842*)

Armed Services Total Force Subcommittee Chairman John M. McHugh, R-N.Y., makes no apology for the proposed increase, despite administration complaints that the proposal is

A U.S. soldier talks to a family at a Baghdad roadblock. Troops have grown frustrated over their role in Iraq and the uncertainty about how long they will be there.

"unnecessary," given ongoing Pentagon reviews of troops levels.

"There is sufficient evidence, given our commitments around the globe, that we need to be taking at least some moderate steps," he said.

Waiting for the Pentagon

But senators are not so sure, arguing that the kinds of nuts-and-bolts decisions that determine troop levels are best left to the Pentagon, at least initially. While Schoomaker reviews his new command, many are also anticipating reports from Rumsfeld that would offer ways to streamline military operations, emphasizing technology over manpower-heavy traditional systems. Until they get those reports, they say it would be irresponsible to jump into a debate.

"I want to wait to get a response back," said Sen. Ben Nelson of Nebraska, ranking Democrat on the Armed Services Personnel Subcommittee, after Schoomaker's confirmation hearing. "This isn't just a study. This is the general, the chief of staff of the Army, saying he'd study it."

What most legislators agree on is that something must be done to restructure the armed forces to make sure troops are not overwhelmed by the demands of a post-Sept. 11 world.

There is widespread anecdotal evidence that members of the National Guard and reserves are growing increasingly unhappy with their frequent and lengthy deployments since the terrorist attacks — first to provide extra security after the attacks and then to bolster the military operations in Afghanistan and Iraq. Legislators are worried that the discontent could drive away recruits and persuade other troops not to re-enlist.

Even active duty soldiers, who should be ready for sustained activity, have begun to complain. Grumbling has started among troops who have been in Iraq longer than they had anticipated and who see no hope of going home any time soon. Several Pentagon officials were surprised in mid-July when troops interviewed on ABC's "Good Morning America" show openly castigated Rumsfeld's management of the troops and said they would demand his resignation if they could meet with him.

Such displays of discontent worry legislators, who want to make sure that the Pentagon maintains the ability to attract highly qualified recruits and to retain the personnel it already has.

To the consternation of legislators,

there is no simple answer.

"The right approach is some rigorous analysis," said Michele Flournoy, who was a Pentagon official during the Clinton administration. "I personally would like Congress to do something a little more creative than just throw money at the problem."

Flournoy, now a military analyst with the Center for Strategic and International Studies, probably will not be disappointed. Capitol Hill is rife with ideas for keeping troops in the armed services.

Some would prefer to shift more menial tasks — domestic truck driving, for instance — from soldiers to civilians, leaving troops free for military actions. Others would overhaul the military's promotion system, making it easier for soldiers to stay in the service. Yet others advocate a blend of active duty personnel and reservists to share the workload more equitably.

For now, any fights seem destined to wait until the fiscal 2005 authorization and appropriations process starts. If Pentagon officials can have the results of their studies available for Congress by then, they likely will be able to sway the debate.

But many members will not be willing to wait if the Pentagon takes too long. "In some ways, I think it's an overly deliberative way to look at the process," said McHugh.

The first concern is that the problem cannot be readily solved simply by throwing money at it — the cost would be very high.

Schoomaker said the service may indeed need more troops. But he also told the Senate Armed Services Committee it would be expensive.

Each soldier costs about $60,000 per year. Adding troops in significant numbers would be "a price the Army can't absorb," he told the panel.

Every 1 percent increase in manpower — or about 14,000 troops — would cost about $3 billion, said Michael O'Hanlon, a defense analyst with the Brookings Institution. That would mean Hunter's proposal for two new divisions — along with the support they would require, a total of 80,000 people — might quickly add up to about $20 billion a year.

Hunter has long argued that Congress underfunds the military by tens of billions of dollars each year. But it is not clear that legislators would be willing to add so much money in a lump sum without looking for some offsets.

Flournoy said there is little doubt the Bush administration would find the extra $20 billion for those divisions if necessary. She notes that the Pentagon easily could trim some of its more traditional weapons programs — which it has threatened to shelve for years — if it wants to free up some money.

"There's still plenty of excess in the [Pentagon] budget," she said. "They have avoided making hard choices because they haven't wanted to."

But just because the money is there does not mean the Pentagon should simply open its checkbook, she adds. The real questions to be answered are those of force mix and management.

"It's important not to talk about end strength in a vacuum," she said. "It may be that we need more forces. Two more divisions might not be the right answer."

Nelson said that before Congress decides to spend more money, lawmakers need to decide if they can make ends meet within the existing budget by reorganizing troop arrangements.

"It might mean the same amount of money spent a different way," he said.

Alternatives to More Spending

Several members have proposals that they contend would go a long way toward easing military burdens.

Rep. William M. "Mac" Thornberry, R-Texas, said one of the easiest fixes he would recommend comes in the way soldiers are promoted. He notes that many officers are expected to make regular promotions if they are to stay in the military. But some military careers, notably operators of unmanned aerial vehicles, have limited advancement potential. Once a pilot hits the top of the promotions ladder and stalls there, Pentagon officials eventually discharge that person for lack of progress, forcing out a trained worker.

"It's up or out," said Thornberry. "We're forcing them to retire. That doesn't make a lot of sense."

The problem is only highlighted, he added, by the fact that many of these soldiers would gladly stay in the service, while the Pentagon is hungry to keep qualified workers on hand.

In the short term, others suggest international solutions. Levin said the Pentagon could ease some of its load if the administration would reach out to other countries to find ways to internationalize overseas missions.

Sessions is also looking abroad, but in a different way. He suggests that disman-

Where Is the Army Today?

House Armed Services Committee Chairman Duncan Hunter, R-Calif., says the Army needs more personnel, after its size has shrunk by almost half over two decades and the demand for overseas deployments are rising. The problem may be how to pay for up to two new divisions — possibly as many as 38,000 troops, costing up to $20 billion per year.

Where the Largest Army Units Are Stationed

The major units of the Army are headquartered across the globe. An Army Corps consists or two or more divisions. Divisions range in size from 10,000 for light infantry to about 18,000 for heavy armor.
(Army corps and their divisions are designated by color below)

Army troop strength over the past two decades

(in thousands)

- 779,643
- 710,821
- 610,450
- 486,542

1983 fiscal year — 1987 — 1992 — 1997 — 2002

I Corps
(Headquarters, Fort Lewis)
Wash.

101st Airborne division
(Air assault)
Fort Campbell

10th Mountain division (light)
Fort Drum
N.Y.

Ky.

N.C.

Ga.

Texas

Hawaii

25th Infantry light division

III Corps
(Headquarters, Fort Hood)
1st Cavalry division
4th Infantry division

XVIII Airborne Corps
(Headquarters, Fort Bragg)
82nd Airborne division

3rd Infantry division (mechanized)
Fort Stewart/Hunter Army Airfield

Germany

V Corps
(Headquarters, Heidelberg)
1st Infantry division
1st Armored division

South Korea

2nd Infantry division

Army overseas deployment	
Iraq 150,000	South Korea 38,000
Kuwait 34,000	The Balkans 5,000
Afghanistan 10,000	

SOURCE: U.S. Army

CQ GRAPHIC / YOLIE DAWSON

tling several U.S. military bases in Germany and South Korea would free up troops stationed there for deployment, easing the current manpower strains.

"If we redirect our forward presence, we may not have to add a significant number" of troops to the Army, he said.

Rep. Mark Steven Kirk, R-Ill., is one of the few members of Congress who also trains regularly as a reservist. His time in the reserves has made him aware that many fellow reservists are grumbling about their jobs and considering ways to get out of the military.

Part of the problem, he said, is that certain duties — such as medical and intelligence work — have been set aside solely for reserve units, meaning they do not work for long stretches of time, but are then called up for lengthy periods of time during a war.

"You are going to have to reprioritize," Kirk said.

McHugh argues that it is exactly those priorities he is trying to work through, which is why he needs to con-

sider all of these ideas in an effort to improve conditions for troops.

Corrosion of Low Morale

The main issue, he said, is making sure the Pentagon can retain the specially trained troops in whom the government already has invested its resources. Although recruitment and retention have remained strong since the Sept. 11 attacks, McHugh said he is worried that troops are going to grow tired of the long regular deployments and soon reconsider a career with the military. Although that has not yet happened, he said it is only a matter of time.

"Given life in the forces at this time, there's a real risk of recruiting and retention falling off the ball," he said.

Reservists and Guardsmen are most vulnerable to these problems. Many of these troops signed up to be so-called weekend warriors, prepared to train at regular intervals and be on standby in case of emergencies, but not for the prolonged war-time deployments where

they now find themselves.

Opinions are mixed about the complaints of this group. Many lawmakers note that the reservists signed up for a job with the understanding that they could be called up for regular duty.

"It's not unusual for people to be overseas for a year," said Vic Snyder of Arkansas, ranking Democrat on the House Armed Services Total Forces Subcommittee.

But, he added, he can see how their discontent can become corrosive.

"It's the frequency [of deployments]," he said. "Their expectation is that they would be called out in the event of a real emergency. Peacekeeping operations were not what they had in mind."

Sen. Robert C. Byrd, D-W.Va., proposed a fix to the problem during debate on the fiscal 2004 defense appropriations bill. His amendment, which was tabled 64-31, would have limited the amount of time any reservist would spend overseas in a one-year period. (2003 CQ Weekly, p. 1842)

"I'd rather not see us get that specific," McHugh said. "You can't just mandate it into law and not solve the other part of the problem."

That other part is significant, indeed. If McHugh's concerns are well-placed — and several of his colleagues say they are — it is only a matter of time before the Pentagon finds itself struggling to maintain its current roster of troops.

Army Bears the Brunt

The service most affected by the great increase in deployments is the Army. In addition to almost 150,000 soldiers in Iraq, the Army maintains almost 10,000 in Afghanistan, about 34,000 in Kuwait, almost 38,000 in South Korea and about 5,000 in the Balkans. These deployments reflect the largest number of U.S. forces serving overseas on active duty since the Vietnam War.

To cope with the strains troops face, the Army announced a new rotation plan for troops to Iraq on July 23. Most Army troops rotate out of a theater of operations after six months. The exception is South Korea, where U.S. troops spend one year without their families.

Gen. John Keane, the Army's acting chief of staff, announced July 23 that most troops would stay in Iraq for one-year rotations — after reports of sharply critical comments from troops in Iraq.

This approach may work in the short term for the Army, said Andrew Krepinevich, head of the Center for Strategic and Budgetary Assessment, a nonpartisan think tank that performs studies for the military and defense companies. But "they are firing their silver bullet," he added, leaving few alternatives should the fighting drag on for years.

Skelton said he can easily see a day when soldiers will leave the military en masse because of the current workload.

"We're wearing these people out," he said, noting that he has long called for about 40,000 extra troops.

A high rate of deployment can only last so long, especially in a military staffed predominantly with family men. Skelton and others note that during World War II, soldiers were not hesitant to spend two or three years fighting in Europe because most were single. Also, troops then signed up "for the duration."

That equation has changed. Married soldiers are not eager to spend so much time away from their families. Their families are not happy with the situation either and are lobbying the military to bring back troops as soon as possible. As re-enlistment

Defense Secretary Rumsfeld, left, talking with Sens. Lieberman, Warner, Byrd and Levin last September about Iraq, is studying ways to more effectively deploy existing troops.

dates pop up and soldiers begin to balance the needs of their social lives with their professional lives, Skelton worries many troops will decide to leave the military if current situations continue.

Facing that exodus makes members all the more interested in seeing the Pentagon reports, but unwilling to wait overly long to see the results.

Looking to Rumsfeld

Kirk said he puts a lot of hope in the anticipated Rumsfeld report, which he thinks will include provisions to lighten the load of the reserves.

"Unless you follow what Rumsfeld's talking about, you are going to drive the reserves into the ground," he said.

That plan should be coming to the Hill soon, he said. Senators say Schoomaker's plan could be on a similar timetable, meaning both will be seriously studied during consideration of the fiscal 2005 defense bills.

Meanwhile, the Army is also considering a longer term solution to the problems associated with lengthy deployments, called "unit manning."

Generally, unit manning would mean that once a soldier is assigned to a unit, such as the Army's Third Infantry Division, he or she would remain with that unit for much longer than a soldier does now. Currently, a soldier can be transferred from job to job several times during a tour.

Military planners say this change

would reduce a soldier's chances of being transferred to another division and then deployed overseas soon after returning from a deployment with his previous unit. It would also mean soldiers and their families would live longer in one place.

"You create more of a community within the battalion or the brigade," Krepinevich said. The Army has considered such an approach many times before but never moved ahead because of the enormous cultural and budgetary changes it would entail.

"We will have all next year to figure out which . . . vision is the right one," said Kirk, noting that competing studies from the administration mean there is probably little need for more congressional studies.

O'Hanlon suggests a mixed approach. "Congress should always weigh in on this kind of stuff. It is often wrong, but the Pentagon is often wrong, too, and if you believe in our system of government, the interaction is more likely to produce good policy than either branch left to itself," he said.

But for legislators worried that deployments may soon wear out troops and leave recruiters with smaller turnouts, there is little time to wait, and they hope to jump on proposals in the next round of defense legislation.

"I think we need to let [troops] know that help is on the way," said Sen. James M. Inhofe, R-Okla. ◆

Political Participation

Several challenges confront the Democrats as they organize to mount a strong offensive for the 2004 elections. As the first two articles in this section spotlight, congressional Democrats are looking ahead and strategizing about how to retake control of the House and the Senate.

Only two seats separate the Democrats from control of the Senate, but achieving that net gain will not be easy. At issue are key vulnerable seats in southeastern states that are increasingly GOP-friendly. Democrats have few takeover opportunities; most Republican incumbents appear likely to be reelected.

The election outlook is much the same for the House. Democrats have to gain twelve seats to take the majority from the Republicans; that will be difficult to achieve for several reasons. Recent redistricting successes have improved the Republicans' chances in the contest for House control. Democrats will also have to muster the financial resources and recruit strong candidates in enough districts to overcome the GOP advantage, which results from population growth in areas that favor the Republican Party and, as in most of the Senate races, the presence of strong incumbents.

The third article examines the role of House Majority Leader Tom DeLay. As the floor manager for House Republicans, a group that is far more conservative than the party in general, DeLay is a leader of the conservative wing of a party whose ultimate success—the re-election of President Bush in 2004—depends on pleasing the more moderate Republican electorate. Thus DeLay must straddle the line between advancing his own staunch conservative principles and helping President Bush appeal to a wider constituency.

DeLay's counterpart in the Senate, Bill Frist, was elevated suddenly to Senate majority leader in January 2003. The fourth article discusses how Frist has worked diligently to prove himself to doubting conservatives. So far, he has maintained the good will and trust of both his Democratic and Republican colleagues, as well as that of the White House. But the real test may arise when the Medicare bill hits the floor and Frist must direct the agenda. Medicare is a topic on which he is universally regarded as an expert, but the shape of the Medicare bill will be closely watched by his critics and will be used as a barometer of how well he is handling the job.

The final two articles examine how a growing number of Republicans—acutely aware of the 2004 elections—are joining Democratic critics in pressing President Bush about the financial and emotional toll of the war in Iraq and its aftermath, and the high U.S. unemployment rate. Four months after an unexpectedly swift victory in Iraq, daily guerilla warfare has impeded the reconstruction effort, and public concern is rising over the postwar death rate and the administration's inability to show how and when U.S. troops will get out. Republicans—once solidly allied with their president—are now echoing the Democrats in urging President Bush to accept international help and to justify the expense. With about 2.7 million jobs lost in the past two years, Republicans in Congress are increasingly worried about the recovering economy's inability to produce employment opportunities and are working overtime to show voters that they are acting to meet the needs of their states and districts.

Politics to the Power of Two

Senate Democrats weigh important and must-win races to gain the majority

Two seats: That is all that separates the Democrats from winning control of the Senate in the 2004 elections.

They might even grab control of the chamber with a net gain of one should a candidate from their party unseat President Bush and give a Democratic vice president the tie-breaking vote as president of the Senate.

But 15 months out from Election Day, Republicans do not appear vulnerable enough for the Democrats to eke out even that small a gain. In fact, given the obstacles that confront them, the Democrats may be just as likely to lose seats next year as to win them. That means the Republicans might widen their current Senate majority of 51 — the narrowest possible — in the 109th Congress.

"Democrats have got a big problem," said Keith Gaddie, a political scientist at the University of Oklahoma. "In a lot of states where senators are retiring, the cupboard is kind of bare for them for candidates," he said.

A shortage of talent "makes it very tough for the Democrats to take back the Senate, even if they win the presidency," Gaddie said.

Nineteen seats currently held by Democratic senators will be up for election, compared with 15 held by Republicans. But that disparity in itself does not mean the Democrats will suffer a longer exile in the minority. Republicans had more seats at risk in 2002, yet they managed the two-seat gain they needed to claim their current majority.

The bigger hurdle for the Democrats is the location of next year's Senate battleground. Four of their seats are in a block of conservative-leaning states that make up the nation's southeastern corner. In each race, the Democrats will probably have to fend off vigorous Republican takeover bids without the benefit of an incumbent on the ballot.

Democrat Ernest F. Hollings announced Aug. 4 that he would not seek another term for the South Carolina

Democratic efforts to pick up two Senate seats are complicated by the decisions of two incumbents, North Carolina's Edwards, left, and Florida's Graham, to run for president.

seat he has held since 1966. Georgia Democrat Zell Miller announced his retirement plans earlier this year. North Carolina's John Edwards and Florida's Bob Graham are pursuing the 2004 presidential nomination and may forgo re-election bids.

In addition, some Democrats who are running — including Minority Leader Tom Daschle of South Dakota and Minority Whip Harry Reid of Nevada — may face serious GOP opposition.

At the same time, the Democrats may have few bona fide takeover opportunities. Republican Sen. Peter G. Fitzgerald's decision to retire has opened up a seat in Illinois, a state that has been trending Democratic. Popular former Alaska Gov. Tony Knowles' challenge to Republican Lisa Murkowski gives the Democrats a shot in Alaska, usually a GOP stronghold.

Democratic strategists say they can also make a run at seats held by Republican incumbents Arlen Specter of Pennsylvania, Christopher S. Bond of Missouri and Ben Nighthorse Campbell of Colorado.

But the other Republican incumbents look either solidly favored or safe

for re-election at this point.

The 2004 presidential campaign also will be a factor in the outcome. With Bush heading the ballot for the Republicans, Democrats must defend seats in 10 states that he carried in his 2000 victory. Republicans are defending just three seats in states that Democratic presidential nominee Al Gore won three years ago.

"When you look at the terrain where the competitive races are going to be fought, we have a lot to be encouraged about," said Dan Allen, communications director for the National Republican Senatorial Committee (NRSC).

Illinois, Alaska Are Key

But Democratic strategists contend that their candidates' strengths will enable them to win on Bush-friendly turf.

"When you take a look at the Senate races and the individuals who are running and the characteristics that they bring and the record of their achievements, the concept of Bush being able to provide a sustainable bounce for Republican candidates is just not one that we buy into," said Michael Siegel, communications director for the Democratic Senatorial

Campaign Committee (DSCC).

Given the Democrats' paucity of opportunities, Illinois and Alaska loom as their "must win" states in 2004.

Recent victories in Illinois have given the Democrats control of every statewide office, except for the Senate seat Fitzgerald is giving up after one term. Democrats also have carried Illinois in each of the past three presidential contests.

The Democrats caught a big break when the Republican Party's top 2004 Senate prospect, former Gov. Jim Edgar, decided not to run.

Still, a Democratic primary field crowded with seven candidates — and no definite front-runner — clouds the outlook for a Democratic takeover. Among the top candidates are state Comptroller Dan Hynes, wealthy businessman Blair Hull and state Sen. Barack Obama.

Candidates seeking the Republican nomination include Jack Ryan, a former investment banker at Goldman Sachs; Jim Oberweis, a dairy company owner who lost a Senate primary in 2002; and Andrew McKenna, a paper products company executive.

Alaska is a less obvious target for Democrats. Since it became a state, Republicans have won 10 of 11 presidential contests there, and Bush ran up a 31 percentage-point victory margin.

But Democrats see an advantage in running against Murkowski, whose appointment to the Senate in December stirred controversy. She was appointed by her father, former Sen. Frank H. Murkowski (1981-2002), who had vacated the seat after he was elected governor to succeed the term-limited Knowles, who has set his sights on the Senate.

In Knowles, the Democrats recruited by far their best possible challenger to Murkowski. He was regarded as a conservative Democrat during his two terms as governor, and his zeal for developing Alaska's natural resources — a popular position among state voters — matches that of his opponent and her father.

Other Democratic Hopes

Pennsylvania is a third Democratic target. Not that Republican Specter, seeking a fifth term, is a sitting duck: He won easily in 1998, and his aggressive fundraising left more than $8.6 million in his campaign account as of June 30.

But Specter's image as a Republican centrist, which has sustained him in the politically competitive state, has attracted a vigorous primary challenge from conservative three-term Republican Rep. Patrick J. Toomey. Democratic strategists are hoping either for a primary win by Toomey, who they would brand as too far to the right, or for a bruising battle from which Specter emerges victorious but weakened for the general election.

Waiting for the outcome is the presumptive Democratic nominee, three-term Rep. Joseph M. Hoeffel.

Democrats filled a void in their candidate slate in late July when Missouri state Treasurer Nancy Farmer announced that she would challenge Bond.

Winding up his third Senate term, Bond is bolstered politically by a key legislative position: He chairs the Appropriations Subcommittee on Veterans, Housing, NASA and EPA. But Bond does not have a history of putting Senate races away easily. He won re-election with 52 percent of the vote in 1992 and 53 percent in 1998.

In Colorado, Democrats would love to make a serious bid to oust two-term incumbent Campbell, who was elected in 1992 as a Democrat but switched parties after the Republicans took over the Senate in 1994.

Campbell's fundraising so far has been somewhat tepid, but the Democrats' ability to contest the seat will not be measurable until they produce a candidate. Rep. Mark Udall would give them a top-tier challenger, but neither he nor any other well-known Democrat has yet committed.

Still on the Democrats' wish list, but much further down, is the race in Kentucky. First-term Republican Jim Bunning, winner of a very close 1998 contest, was expected to face a challenge from two-term Democratic Gov. Paul E. Patton. But Patton's long-planned Senate candidacy was torpedoed last year by a personal scandal.

Offsetting any optimism Democrats have for pickups is the urgent problem they face in the South.

The large-scale migration of Southern conservatives since the 1960s from their traditional home in the Democratic Party to the GOP has made the region the foundation of the Republicans' national successes.

As recently as 1987, Democrats held 18 of 26 Senate seats in the 13 states Congressional Quarterly defines as Southern. The Republicans now hold 17 of those seats and have a ripe opportunity to increase their share.

"The South plays a big part," the NRSC's Allen said. "It's an area that historically has done well for Republicans in presidential years, plus having President Bush at the top of the ticket . . . helps us and helps our candidates."

Holding South Carolina

The most difficult seat for Democrats to hold may be in South Carolina. Under the longtime leadership of Sen. Strom Thurmond (1954-2003), who died June 26 at 100, South Carolina made one of the earliest and strongest shifts to Republican loyalties.

Hollings survived tough re-election campaigns in 1992 and 1998, and four Republicans — three-term Rep. Jim DeMint, former state Attorney General Charlie Condon, businessman Thomas Ravenel and Myrtle Beach Mayor Mark McBride — jumped into the 2004 race even before the incumbent announced he would retire.

Democrats contend, however, that their likely candidate, Inez Tenenbaum, can defend the seat. Tenenbaum is the state superintendent of education and has been a big statewide vote-getter for that down-ballot office.

In Georgia, the retirement of Democrat Zell Miller gives the GOP an opportunity to build upon the electoral successes from 2002, when Republicans unseated one-term Democratic Sen. Max Cleland and Gov. Roy Barnes.

The crowded 2004 Republican primary field includes Reps. Johnny Isakson and Mac Collins. Democrats are still searching for a strong candidate.

"Georgia is a seat right now that has a large question mark on it," the DSCC's Siegel said. "But it has a pretty brutal Republican primary going on."

Also problematic for Democrats are the seats held by Edwards and Graham. Democrats would have the edge with the two incumbents on the ballot, but Republicans begin the likely open-seat campaigns as even-money bets.

In North Carolina, Erskine Bowles — a former White House chief of staff in the Clinton administration who lost the 2002 Senate race to Republican Elizabeth Dole — is prepared to try for his party's nod if Edwards does not seek re-election. The Republicans already have a highly competitive candidate in five-term Rep. Richard M. Burr.

CQ's 2004 Senate Race Rankings

The chart lists the 2004 Senate contests based on Congressional Quarterly's assessment of their level of competitiveness at this early point in the campaign. The rankings of some races will change over the course of the election season. Each state's listing shows the name of the incumbent, any possibility (where relevant) that the incumbent will not seek reelection, the year the incumbent first won the office, and the incumbent's vote percentage in the most recent election.

CLOSE SENATE RACES
In the West

Leans Democratic (3)
ARKANSAS — Blanche Lincoln (D), 1998, 55%
The centrist Lincoln has solid approval ratings. Republican hopes hinge on a candidacy by Gov. Mike Huckabee or ex-Rep. Asa Hutchinson, a top official in the Homeland Security Department. If neither runs, Lincoln's stock soars.

NEVADA — Harry Reid (D), 1986, 48%
Reid nipped Republican John Ensign — now his Senate colleague — in 1998's closest Senate race. GOP Rep. Jim Gibbons would provide a serious challenge, but hasn't committed.

SOUTH DAKOTA — Tom Daschle (D), 1986, 62%
Daschle is one of the most popular Democrats ever in this usually Republican state, and his position as the top Senate Democrat enables him to deliver. But Republicans are casting him as a liberal adversary to President Bush. A tough race ensues if Daschle faces ex-Rep. John Thune, who lost a close challenge to Democratic Sen. Tim Johnson in 2002; Daschle becomes the strong favorite if Thune demurs.

Leans Republican (1)
COLORADO — Ben Nighthorse Campbell (R), 1992, 63%
Campbell, an ex-Democrat, easily dismissed a weak 1998 opponent. He has had to quell 2004 retirement rumors and his fundraising so far is modest, but the Democrats need a blue-chip contender in Republican-leaning Colorado. Rep. Mark Udall is mulling.

No Clear Favorite (1)
ALASKA — Lisa Murkowski (R), 2002, appointed
Alaska's long history as a Republican stronghold benefits Murkowski. But her challenger is one of the Democrats' strongest 2004 recruits, ex-Gov. Tony Knowles. A conservative Democrat, Knowles reached the state's two-term limit as governor and left office with strong approval ratings. Knowles matches Murkowski in his support for natural resource development, neutralizing an issue that usually works to the Republicans' advantage in Alaska. A big issue: whether voters are rankled over Murkowski's appointment by her father, Frank H. Murkowski, to the Senate seat he vacated after winning the governorship in 2002.

Races Where Democrats Have a Clear Advantage

Democrat Favored (4)
CALIFORNIA — Barbara Boxer (D), 1992, 53%
Turmoil over the vote on recalling Democratic Gov. Gray Davis lends some unpredictability to California politics. But the state has trended Democratic, and Republicans have no Senate candidate with a statewide base.

NORTH DAKOTA — Byron L. Dorgan (D), 1992, 63%
Dorgan is popular, and GOP hopes deflated when ex-Gov. Edward T. Schafer declined to challenge. But North Dakota is too strongly Republican to declare Dorgan a shoo-in.

WASHINGTON — Patty Murray (D), 1992, 58%
GOP likely will rally around candidacy of Rep. George Nethercutt. But he is a conservative in a Democratic-leaning state; Murray easily beat conservative Rep. Linda Smith in 1998.

WISCONSIN — Russell D. Feingold (D), 1992, 51%
Feingold won a 1998 cliffhanger over GOP Rep. Mark W. Neumann. But the incumbent is bolstered by his co-authorship of the new campaign finance law. The GOP sought a bid by ex-Gov. Tommy G. Thompson, but he is staying as on Bush's Health and Human Services secretary.

Safe Democratic (8)
These Democratic incumbents appear to be maintaining their popularity, and the Republicans thus far have yet to present candidates who appear capable of an upset:

VERMONT — Patrick J. Leahy, 1974, 72%

CONNECTICUT — Christopher J. Dodd, 1980, 65%

HAWAII — Daniel K. Inouye, 1962, 79%

INDIANA — Evan Bayh, 1998, 64%

LOUISIANA — John B. Breaux, 1986, 64%

MARYLAND — Barbara A. Mikulski, 1986, 71%

NEW YORK — Charles E. Schumer, 1998, 55%

OREGON — Ron Wyden, 1996, 61%

CLOSE SENATE RACES
In the East

Leans Republican (2)

SOUTH CAROLINA — Ernest F. Hollings (D) (retiring), 1966, 53%
Hollings' retirement reinforces this seat as a top Republican takeover target. A strong state GOP trend has spurred a crowd of Republicans — including Rep. Jim DeMint, ex-state Attorney General Charlie Condon and businessman Thomas Ravenel — into the race. Democrats may turn to state Education Commissioner Inez Tenenbaum.

PENNSYLVANIA — Arlen Specter (R), 1980, 61%
Specter has more than $8 million in his campaign account; being a senior member on the Appropriations Committee doesn't hurt. But the GOP centrist faces a hard-charging primary challenge by conservative Rep. Patrick J. Toomey. Democrats hope for a bruiser that helps their likely choice, Rep. Joseph M. Hoeffel.

No Clear Favorite (4)

FLORIDA — Bob Graham (D)
(running for president), 1986, 63%
Both major parties have crowded fields with no front-runners yet, in anticipation that Graham will not seek re-election; confirmed candidates include Democratic Reps. Allen Boyd and Peter Deutsch, and Republican Rep. Mark Foley. Popular Gra-

ham would be the favorite if he runs, but would face a serious challenger in this GOP-trending state.

GEORGIA — Zell Miller (D)
(retiring), 2000, 58%
An open seat in this conservative-leaning state has spurred a crowded Republican field that includes Reps. Johnny Isakson and Mac Collins. Democrats hope a primary battle damages the GOP nominee, but so far lack a candidate of their own. Rep. Jim Marshall is thinking about it.

NORTH CAROLINA — John Edwards (D)
(running for president), 1998, 51%
Republicans, who have a top-tier contender in Rep. Richard M. Burr, contend Edwards would be vulnerable if he ran for re-election — which he probably won't. Possible Democratic candidates include financier Erskine Bowles, the former chief of staff to President Bill Clinton, who was the Democrats' Senate nominee in 2002 but ran into the juggernaut of Republican Elizabeth Dole.

ILLINOIS — Peter G. Fitzgerald (R)
(retiring), 1998, 50%
This is a must-win for the Democrats. Fitzgerald, a conservative in a Democratic-leaning state, was labeled the most vulnerable GOP incumbent before he

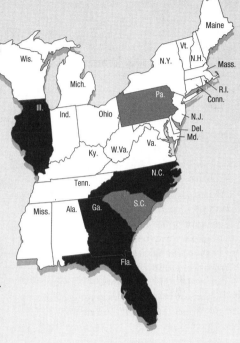

decided not to run. Democrats have been on a roll in Illinois, and hold almost all statewide offices. A packed Democratic field with no clear front-runner lends uncertainty. But Republicans failed to entice their best prospect, ex-Gov. Jim Edgar.

Races Where Republicans Have a Clear Advantage

Republican Favored (3)

KENTUCKY — Jim Bunning (R), 1998, 50%
Bunning won narrowly in 1998 and has had a relatively low profile in his freshman term. But Democrats have not found a top-flight contender since scandal-plagued Gov. Paul E. Patton dropped his expected challenge. Kentucky has an "off-year" election for governor that is the focus of political attention this year, and the Democratic field may not come into focus until after that is completed in November.

MISSOURI — Christopher S. Bond (R),
1986, 53%
Bond has never been a landslide winner, and Democrats think they can challenge. But the incumbent is bolstered by his seat on the Appropriations Committee. State Treasurer Nancy Farmer jumped in for the Democrats

after some better-known prospects eschewed.

OHIO — George V. Voinovich (R),
1998, 57%
Voinovich has been popular throughout a long career as Cleveland mayor, governor and senator. But Ohio can be a "swing" state, and Democrats hope to generate a backlash against Republican economic policies. State Sen. Eric D. Fingerhut, a former House member, is the choice of the Democratic establishment. "Trash TV" host Jerry Springer's trial balloon candidacy provided an air of adventure until he ruled out a bid.

Safe Republican (8)

These Republican incumbents appear to be maintaining their popularity, and the Democrats thus far have yet to present candidates

who appear capable of an upset:

ALABAMA — Richard C. Shelby,
1986, 63%

ARIZONA — John McCain, 1986, 69%

IDAHO — Michael D. Crapo, 1998, 70%

IOWA — Charles E. Grassley, 1980, 68%

KANSAS — Sam Brownback, 1996, 65%

NEW HAMPSHIRE — Judd Gregg,
1992, 68%

OKLAHOMA — Don Nickles, 1980, 66%

UTAH — Robert F. Bennett, 1992, 64%

Anticipation that Graham will stick to his presidential campaign has sparked Florida primary free-for-alls in both parties.

Reps. Peter Deutsch and Allen Boyd, Miami-Dade Mayor Alex Penelas and Betty Castor, the former president of the University of South Florida, are seeking the Democratic nomination. Rep. Mark Foley, former Rep. Bill McCollum (1981-2001) and state House Speaker Johnnie Byrd are in on the Republican side. Other candidates may join the contest.

Elsewhere, Republicans are stalking big game in targeting high-ranking Democratic incumbents. But their efforts hinge on recruiting top challengers.

In South Dakota, former Republican Rep. John Thune (1997-2003), who narrowly lost his 2002 challenge to Democratic Sen. Tim Johnson, is being urged to take on Daschle. In Nevada, Republican officials are lobbying Rep. Jim Gibbons to take on Reid, winner of the closest Senate race of 1998.

But neither Thune nor Gibbons has decided, while Daschle and Reid have run up big campaign cash reserves to discourage high-level opposition.

Arkansas Democrat Blanche Lincoln may face a tough 2004 race. But neither of her serious potential challengers — Gov. Mike Huckabee or former Rep. Asa Hutchinson (1997-2001), now the undersecretary for border and transportation security in the Department of Homeland Security — has shown enthusiasm for a bid.

Republican strategists are watching a challenge to Democrat Patty Murray in Washington, where Rep. George Nethercutt announced July 30 he would run for the seat, giving the Republicans a candidate with a solid political base. But he was not the party's first choice: The White House wanted Rep. Jennifer Dunn, but she declined.

The political environment in California, where Democrat Barbara Boxer is seeking re-election, has been destabilized by the campaign to recall Democratic Gov. Gray Davis. Boxer's liberal record will give Republicans material to use against her. But Democrats have dominated recent elections in the most populous state, and Republicans have no top-tier candidate as of yet.

Unlikely to face threatening opposition is first-term New York Democrat Charles E. Schumer, who has armored himself with the biggest campaign bankroll among 2004 Senate candidates: He had $16.5 million cash on hand as of June 30. ◆

Senate Incumbents Up in 2004

Most senators who may face tough races in 2004 have gotten early starts on their fundraising: Facing a serious primary and targeted by his Democratic opposition, Pennsylvania's Specter had nearly $9 million in the bank at last report. But others have used fundraising as inoculation: New York's Schumer and Alabama's Shelby, topping the cash list, have no well-known challengers.

(ranked by cash on hand as of June 30)

STATE	INCUMBENT	CASH ON HAND
New York	Charles E. Schumer (D)	$16,504,981
Alabama	Richard C. Shelby (R)	$10,630,579
Pennsylvania	Arlen Specter (R)	$8,664,835
Indiana	Evan Bayh (D)	$5,541,490
Iowa	Charles E. Grassley (R)	$4,266,067
Ohio	George V. Voinovich (R)	$3,404,452
California	Barbara Boxer (D)	$3,194,420
Nevada	Harry Reid (D)	$3,114,426
South Dakota	Tom Daschle (D)	$2,856,971
Missouri	Christopher S. Bond (R)	$2,822,869
Connecticut	Christopher J. Dodd (D)	$2,783,535
Oregon	Ron Wyden (D)	$2,373,868
Washington	Patty Murray (D)	$2,371,082
Kentucky	Jim Bunning (R)	$2,048,455
Wisconsin	Russell D. Feingold (D)	$1,904,756
Arkansas	Blanche Lincoln (D)	$1,866,949
Louisiana	John B. Breaux (D)	$1,387,791
North Carolina	John Edwards (D)*	$1,372,512
North Dakota	Byron L. Dorgan (D)	$1,308,171
Arizona	John McCain (R)	$1,091,925
New Hampshire	Judd Gregg (R)	$1,091,231
Maryland	Barbara A. Mikulski (D)	$1,091,130
Kansas	Sam Brownback (R)	$1,035,617
Vermont	Patrick J. Leahy (D)	$972,551
South Carolina	Ernest F. Hollings (D)**	$970,012
Alaska	Lisa Murkowski (R)	$814,430
Oklahoma	Don Nickles (R)	$743,695
Idaho	Michael D. Crapo (R)	$736,288
Colorado	Ben Nighthorse Campbell (R)	$724,757
Illinois	Peter G. Fitzgerald (R)**	$548,191
Utah	Robert F. Bennett (R)	$534,270
Hawaii	Daniel K. Inouye (D)	$465,863
Florida	Bob Graham (D)*	$242,711
Georgia	Zell Miller (D)**	$52,353

* Running for the Democratic presidential nomination, but has not definitively declined to run for Senate re-election

** Retiring

Daunting Task of Takeover

Democrats know they face long odds in their quest to recapture the House

There is little doubt that the 2004 congressional elections will be influenced by broad factors such as the strength of the economy, President Bush's re-election fortunes and the state of the war against terrorism.

But the next campaign for control of the House is not shaping up to be a "macro" contest, in which those national trends primarily determine the outcome. Instead, which party runs the House in the 109th Congress will probably be determined on the "micro" level — the aggregate of the elections in each of the 435 congressional districts. And that poses a monumental challenge for the Democrats, who will be seeking to retake control of the chamber after a decade in the minority.

Democrats need a wide playing field of politically competitive districts if they hope to gain the 12 seats required to take the majority from the Republicans, who now hold 229 seats, to 205 for the Democrats and 1 for an independent who sides with the Democrats. That is a tall order in an era when most incumbents are "safe" — and made safer by redistricting in 2001 and 2002 that narrowed the universe of competitive races. (*2003 CQ Weekly, p. 1364*)

The structural advantage Republicans enjoy in the 2004 House campaign can be gleaned from the following statistics: Although he won the presidency in the Electoral College, Bush took only

CQ Weekly Aug. 9, 2003

47.9 percent of the popular vote, which Democrat Al Gore won by 540,000 votes. Nonetheless, under the congressional maps that now are in place, Bush carried 237 of the 435 districts — or 54 percent of all the House seats that will be contested next year.

That is in part the result of continued population growth in the South and the West, areas largely favorable to Republicans; the reapportionment following the 2000 census shifted seats mainly to those regions. And the GOP's edge also is in part the result of partisan redistricting plans that Republicans succeeded in enacting prior to the 2002 elections in states where they controlled the process — including such population centers as Florida, Pennsylvania, Michigan and Ohio.

The GOP is seeking to press its advantage even further by pushing — against emphatic resistance from the Democrats — to redraw the House map in Bush's home state of Texas, where Democrats now hold a 17-15 advantage in the delegation under a map invoked by a court panel. A special session of the state Legislature is deadlocked on the issue, but Republicans have vowed not to give up. (*2003 CQ Weekly, p. 1728*)

Democratic leaders acknowledge that they will need some sort of national political "wind" to form at their backs if they are to be propelled to the majority in 15 months. Since 1982, when the party picked up a net of 26

seats, its biggest gains have been nine seats in both 1990 and 1996 — short of their 2004 target of 12.

Democratic strategists insist that their prospects have improved in recent months. They say they have candidates who are very interested in running; that Bush's popularity has declined, reducing the likelihood that he will have "coattails" for his fellow Republicans; and that voters are raising questions about the Republicans' stewardship of the economy.

"There's a breeze behind us now, and I think that is helping us," said Robert T. Matsui of California, chairman of the Democratic Congressional Campaign Committee (DCCC).

But a big question is whether Democrats can muster the resources and recruit strong candidates in enough districts to overcome the GOP advantage.

"There are only a limited number of takeover targets," said John J. Pitney Jr., a political scientist at Claremont McKenna College. "The great majority of Republican seats are safe."

GOP's to Win or Lose

But Republicans cannot afford overconfidence. They will be pressed to make the case to voters for continued GOP control of the federal government.

The Republicans controlled both halves of Congress as well as the White House during the first five months of 2001, but the Senate flipped to the Democrats that June after Vermont's

"There's a breeze behind us now, and I think that's helping us."
— Rep. Robert T. Matsui of California,
chairman of the Democratic Congressional Campaign Committee

"2004 is very much going to be a referendum on us."
— Rep. Thomas M. Davis III of Virginia, former chairman
of the National Republican Congressional Committee

James M. Jeffords quit the GOP.

So the 108th Congress is the first sustained period in which the Republicans have controlled the Senate, the House and the presidency at the same time since the 83rd Congress of 1953 and 1954. And unlike in 2002 — when they were able to run against the Democratic-run Senate as an obstacle to progress — the Republicans must stand on their own record this time.

"2004 is very much going to be a referendum on us," said Thomas M. Davis III of Virginia, the previous chairman of the National Republican Congressional Committee (NRCC). "You'll find that when one party controls the presidency, the House and the Senate, these are referendums on the incumbents."

Davis said that he is counseling House Republicans to ignore Democratic strategy and concentrate instead on priorities such as conducting the war against terrorism, boosting the economy and enacting a prescription drug plan. "Whatever the Democrats do is irrelevant," Davis said. "It's really what we do, what we're able to pass and how we're able to frame things."

Republicans and independent analysts agree that Democrats stand to benefit if the economy worsens, given that the GOP is the party in charge.

"The economy remains a national problem and a Democratic opportunity," Pitney said. "A bad economy is always an opportunity for the 'out' party, especially the Democrats."

But the Democratic Party's own financial hardship — a shortage of campaign cash — may undercut it efforts to convince voters that it would be the better steward of the economy. In the first six months of this year, the NRCC reported raising more than three times as much as the DCCC — $45.5 million to $14.5 million.

Playing Under New Rules

The Democrats had been more competitive in fundraising when the parties were allowed to collect and spend unregulated "soft money," but those were exactly the kind of donations that were banned by the campaign finance law (PL 107-155) that took effect for this election cycle. (*2002 Almanac, p. 14-7*)

Thomas M. Reynolds of New York, who succeeded Davis as NRCC chairman, expressed skepticism that Democrats would be capable of producing more competitive challengers in 2004

than they did in 2002, when they benefited from soft money.

Democrats argue that they will have adequate resources to get their message out. And they say the key fundraising statistic is cash on hand. Because the DCCC had spent far less, it had nearly as much of a reserve ($6.4 million) as the NRCC ($6.6 million) at the end of June, when the organizations made their most recent filings to the Federal Election Commission. However, the DCCC also was carrying $2.7 million in debt, while the NRCC was debt-free.

Without soft money to rely upon, the House campaign organization is turning to incumbents who are politically safe and who can part with some of their huge campaign treasuries in the form of smaller "hard money" contributions.

Well-financed incumbents have also steered money to the campaign committees of more vulnerable members. The GOP has held two Retain Our Majority Program (ROMP) events that boosted the campaign treasuries of 20 lawmakers from competitive districts. The DCCC has identified 18 Democrats who are most in need of campaign cash.

It is unclear how many "open seats" — which tend to be more competitive than districts defended by incumbents — will emerge in 2004. At this early stage, there have been few announced departures, and most of them are in solidly partisan districts. (*2003 CQ Weekly, p. 2009*)

One exception to that rule is Pennsylvania's 15th District, which three-term Republican Patrick J. Toomey is leaving open to challenge the renomination of GOP Sen. Arlen Specter. The district, which includes the Lehigh Valley cities of Allentown and Bethlehem, could be a bellwether of the 2004 campaign. Republicans, having already recruited a strong candidate in state Sen. Charles Dent, might have an early edge. But the district's voters preferred Gore in 2000; it was represented from 1993 to 1999 by Democratic moderate Paul McHale and could swing back to that party in tough economic times.

Shaky Seats Targeted

Recognizing the difficulty in dislodging veteran incumbents, Democratic strategists are focusing heavily on members of the Republican freshman class who represent politically competitive districts.

The most vulnerable among them may be Max Burns of Georgia's 12th

District. He won by 10 percentage points in 2002, even though the district along the state's eastern edge had been drawn by the Democratic-controlled General Assembly to elect a Democrat. Voters there favored Gore by 10 points, and Democrats describe Burns' win as an aberration; their nominee, businessman Charles Walker Jr., was hobbled by revelations of past arrests. So far, two Democrats are seeking the nomination to challenge Burns: Athens-Clarke County Commissioner John Barrow and state Sen. Doug Haines. Barrow has jumped out to an early lead in fundraising, posting $272,000 in overall receipts.

Georgia Democrats also are aiming to take on another upset Republican winner from last year: Phil Gingrey of the northwestern 11th District. He raised $846,000 in the first half of this year, more than any other House freshman.

Democratic strategists are eyeing Arizona's 1st District, a vast, rural expanse in the northeastern part of the state that has a large percentage of veterans and American Indians. Republican Rick Renzi won by 4 points in 2002 over Democrat George Cordova, a politically inexperienced businessman.

Cordova is seeking a rematch. But also trying for comebacks are three of his top 2002 primary opponents: Steve Udall, a former county attorney and a cousin of Colorado Democratic Rep. Mark Udall and New Mexico Democratic Rep. Tom Udall; attorney Diane Prescott; and Fred DuVal, a former Clinton administration official, who finished fourth. Paul Babbitt, a county supervisor and brother of former Gov. Bruce Babbitt, also is looking at the race.

As the winner of the closest House election in 2002, Republican Bob Beauprez would be expected to face fierce Democratic opposition in Colorado's 7th District, in the Denver suburbs. But the Republican-controlled Legislature altered the state's congressional map to give Beauprez more GOP voters. That map faces a legal challenge from Democrats, though. If the new lines are overturned, Beauprez could face a vigorous challenge in 2004.

The Democrats are not only targeting newcomers. High on their hit list is Republican John Hostettler, who has won five close races in southern Indiana's 8th District. Hostettler, who largely shuns the fundraising circuit, raised just $1,100 in the second quarter of this year. Democrat Jon Jennings, a former assistant coach for the Boston

Celtics, is making a bid.

Party strategists also are eyeing districts in which Democratic statewide candidates traditionally have done well. These include eastern Alabama's 3rd, held by freshman Michael D. Rogers; eastern Connecticut's 2nd, represented by two-term Republican Rob Simmons; and Kentucky's Louisville-based 3rd, where Anne M. Northup has won a quartet of nail-biter victories.

In other potentially competitive districts, Democratic strategists say they expect to field more competitive challengers to Republicans than they did in 2002. These include northwestern Missouri's 6th, held for two terms by Sam Graves; central New Jersey's 7th, held for two terms by Mike Ferguson; and Pennsylvania's 18th in the Pittsburgh area, represented by freshman Tim Murphy.

Democratic-Held Seats

Already in the majority, Republican strategists will emphasize protection of the seats they hold. But they have no intention of playing only defense. The GOP is targeting conservative and moderate Democrats who represent districts that voted strongly for Bush in the 2000 presidential election.

In several districts, Republican challengers who narrowly lost last year are back for a second try.

In northern Kentucky's 4th District, businessman Geoff Davis has been laying the groundwork for a rematch with Ken Lucas, one of the most conservative House Democrats. Former state Rep. John Swallow is bidding for another shot at Democrat Jim Matheson, who won a second term in Utah's sprawling 2nd District by less than 1 percentage point in 2002. Pilot Adam Taff is gunning for another go-round with Democrat Dennis Moore, who has held Kansas' suburban 3rd District since 1999. But Davis, Swallow and Taff are likely to face primary opposition.

Republican officials are not waiting for the theatrical battle over redistricting to run its course in Texas. They are weighing serious challenges to two veteran Democrats in mainly rural districts that are expected to overwhelmingly favor Bush's re-election: Charles W. Stenholm of the 17th District and Chet Edwards of the 11th. GOP strategists are also looking at the 4th District, east of Dallas, held by Democrat Ralph M. Hall, who at 80 is the House's oldest member and may not seek a 13th term. ◆

Close Winners Bankrolling Early

Lawmakers liable to serious challenges tend to make aggressive and early fundraising drives, and this year is no exception. The following list summarizes the most recent fundraising figures for House members who won by some of the narrowest margins in 2002 and expect to face competitive races in 2004. The receipts are for the second quarter of this year, ending June 30, and the cash on hand is as of that date.

INCUMBENT	RECEIPTS	CASH ON HAND	'02 VICTORY*
Democrats			
Rodney Alexander, La. (5)	$257,525	$253,348	0.6
Jim Matheson, Utah (2)	247,190	346,380	0.7
Jim Marshall, Ga. (3)	122,251	191,568	1.0
Timothy H. Bishop, N.Y. (1)	230,357	203,301	1.6
Tim Holden, Pa. (17)	232,227	258,775	2.8
Dennis Moore, Kan. (3)	216,475	351,974	3.3
Ken Lucas, Ky. (4)	262,943	332,925	3.6
Charles W. Stenholm, Texas (17)	208,765	191,427	4.0
Michael H. Michaud, Maine (2)	192,144	146,241	4.0
Rick Larsen, Wash. (2)	215,301	338,934	4.3
Chet Edwards, Texas (11)	268,576	306,947	4.4
Earl Pomeroy, N.D. (AL)	292,755	300,056	4.8
Baron P. Hill, Ind. (9)	268,431	290,803	5.0
Lincoln Davis, Tenn. (4)	165,305	150,607	5.6
Leonard L. Boswell, Iowa (3)	158,483	255,348	8.4
Julia Carson, Ind. (7)	58,503	145,520	9.0
Darlene Hooley, Ore. (5)	244,046	610,054	9.6
Republicans			
Bob Beauprez, Colo. (7)	$179,735	$407,670	0.1
Ginny Brown-Waite, Fla. (5)	154,528	323,241	1.7
Mike D. Rogers, Ala. (3)	347,606	490,065	2.1
Jim Gerlach, Pa. (6)	318,782	399,142	2.7
Anne M. Northup, Ky. (3)	212,059	402,751	3.2
Phil Gingrey, Ga. (11)	316,357	573,695	3.3
Rick Renzi, Ariz. (1)	146,390	244,315	3.6
Henry Bonilla, Texas (23)	415,355	656,674	4.3
Chris Chocola, Ind. (2)	129,027	311,164	4.7
John Hostettler, Ind. (8)	1,100	5,018	5.3
Jim Leach, Iowa (2)	153,335	137,933	6.5
Bill Janklow, S.D. (AL)	7,669	25,640	7.8
Rob Simmons, Conn. (2)	316,227	372,284	8.2
Robin Hayes, N.C. (8)	317,141	336,683	9.0
Max Burns, Ga. (12)	211,500	309,169	10.4
Heather A. Wilson, N.M. (1)	332,845	391,628	10.7

* Percentage point margin over closest competitor
SOURCE: Federal Election Commission

Alexander   **Matheson**   **Beauprez**   **Brown-Waite**

DeLay's Conservatism Solidifies GOP Base for Bush

House majority leader is president's not-so-secret weapon

It was not a particularly warm moment in the White House, when President Bush and House Majority Leader Tom DeLay squared off in mid-June at a breakfast with the top five House and Senate leaders.

DeLay, according to congressional and administration officials, complained to the president about White House press secretary Ari Fleischer, who had publicly urged the House to pass the Senate's version of a child tax credit bill for low-income workers — not the House version, which contained further tax breaks favored by conservatives. Bush could have collegially distanced himself from Fleischer's comment. Instead, the president firmly told DeLay that Fleischer "speaks for me."

Days later, DeLay insisted the exchange had not happened. "They're lying," he said sharply, before adding that if Bush "said something like that, it didn't register."

On one level, the story plays to the Beltway notion, often overstated, that the two most powerful Texans in the nation's capital do not get along. But this brief spat shows more than a mere personality clash: It highlights the central conflict of loyalty that marks DeLay's tenure as the second-highest ranking Republican in the House.

In his six months as majority leader, DeLay has shown he can be more than just a strident right-winger, a role that only reinforced the nickname of "The Hammer" that he had as majority whip for the previous eight years. Indeed, he has positioned himself as the congressional leader that no high-level negotiation will be without.

Yet he straddles the line between advancing the staunch conservative principles in which he believes — for the wing of the party he most potently represents — and serving a Republican president who must satisfy a far broader constituency.

As the floor manager for House Republicans, a group that is far more conservative than the party in general, DeLay is an effective prosecutor for the ideology espoused by the party's core, more than his predecessor, fellow Texan Dick Armey (1985-2003). Armey, for example, was never part of the presidential breakfasts where DeLay raised the child tax credit matter.

Therein lies DeLay's conflict: He is a leader of the conservative wing of a party whose ultimate success — Bush winning re-election in 2004 — is predicated on pleasing the broader, more moderate, Republican electorate.

So, while he still urges conservatives not to compromise on some issues, DeLay now also persuades them to back Bush programs they may be chary of, such as a recent $15 billion package to fight the international spread of HIV and AIDS (PL 108-25). And while he still keeps most moderates out of the power loop, he also lets them vent when they think he has moved too far to the right and is threatening to undermine Bush's "compassionate conservative" message.

"It's interesting that there are some weeks in which we are urged to support the president and then there are weeks in which we are urged to support Tom DeLay," said Rep. Michael N. Castle of Delaware, leader of the GOP moderates.

DeLay's dual role as Bush loyalist and standard-bearer for the far right seems to suit the White House just fine. The administration frequently strategizes with DeLay, using him as a master tactician to win House approval of its priorities.

Thus Delay provides the right flank for Bush's version of triangulation, the political strategy mastered during the 1990s by President Bill Clinton and envied by Republicans in which Clinton adroitly positioned himself to the right of most Democrats and to the left of most Republicans to broker political deals around centrist policies.

DeLay helps Bush by pulling the Senate, and even his closest ally, House Speaker J. Dennis Hastert of Illinois, to the right, while quieting party moderates and intimidating Democrats so the president's final position ends up right of center, where Bush wanted to be all along.

The child tax credit bill is a case in point. After being upbraided by the president for challenging the White House decision not to back the House's version, DeLay quickly retreated from a public row over the matter. Yet in the end, DeLay prevailed: The administration later dropped its support for the Senate bill, and now it does not endorse either version. The child tax credit legislation, which DeLay does not want unless it includes the extra tax breaks, has stalled indefinitely.

"The president considers him an important part of his team," Fleischer said in a June 27 interview. "Tom DeLay is a valiant warrior. If Tom DeLay didn't exist, the Republican Party and the House of Representatives would need to invent him."

'A Method in the Madness'

Six months into his job as majority leader, after eight years as perhaps the most effective House majority whip in modern history, DeLay is a leading policy maker on Capitol Hill. He has moved beyond the whip's traditional tactician role — cajoling lawmakers and fine-tuning legislation to grow the vote for the party's program — to now shaping the program and the strategy by finding the House Republicans' consensus on issues.

With an always combative edge, he has moved debates to the right on major issues, including the Israeli-Palestinian conflict, tax cuts and prescription drug coverage in Medicare, where his loyalty to conservatives will once again be pitted against Bush's political need to get a bill before next year's election.

DeLay does not limit his reach for power to the workings of the House. He has stirred a fierce partisan fight in the Texas Legislature — where Bush bragged of practicing bipar-

While DeLay does not relish meeting with reporters, he uses weekly news briefings to trumpet the conservative line and to occasionally throw a barb at the White House. He keeps the Republican base satisfied and helps move policies right of center, where Bush wants to be.

tisanship while governor — by forcing a redrawing of congressional district lines to expand the GOP's majority in the House. (*Redistricting, p. 28*)

More than one Republican referred to "a method in the madness" of DeLay's strategic thinking, and those who agree with him admire his skills. Allies call him brilliant, tough, very effective, intense, possessive of power and always searching for more.

"He's very self-confident. He's always thinking about tactics. He thinks strategically, but he's a tactician," said Jennifer Dunn, R-Wash., a fellow conservative.

Those who do not see eye to eye with him — not just Democrats, but at times Republican moderates as well — envy his effectiveness.

"I obviously disagree with Tom on a variety of issues," Castle said. "On the other hand, I admire him. He has a very firm view of what he wants to get done and he has a strong grasp of the mechanism to get it done. It's a mixture of disagreement and envy."

Blunt and Effective

DeLay revels in his image as a major irritant for his political opponents. In recent interviews, he has called himself "a cocky Texan" and "just a bug man," a reference to his former occupation as an exterminator. But his big-footed comments have made fellow Republicans flinch on occasion.

There was the time during the 2000 presidential campaign when DeLay proposed postponing payment of a tax credit for low-income workers. Candidate Bush warned Congress not to "balance their budget on the backs of the poor." DeLay fired back that Bush "needs a little education on how Congress works."

House Science Committee Chairman Sherwood Boehlert recalled a floor speech DeLay gave when he was still whip that tore apart the EPA .

The tough talk might play well in DeLay's East Texas district, Boehlert protested at the time, but not in his "green" district in upstate New York.

DeLay responded with "a little bit stronger language," the moderate Boehlert said with a chuckle. "His attitude is, 'You've got your point of view, and I've got mine. And I'm not offended by that.'"

Most recently, when DeLay proclaimed that the child tax credit bill "ain't gonna happen" without a broader tax cut package, Democrats used his comments to portray Republicans as uncaring about working families.

Even Republicans felt he spoke too harshly. "For DeLay to speak out that way, in terms of the American people, really sounds like he's not sensitive to their concerns," said GOP Sen. George V. Voinovich. "I have to represent all of Ohio. I represent the suburbs and the urban areas and the poor and the rich. I am with the president on this. It's the compassionate thing to do."

Nonetheless, DeLay's words influenced policy. At a time when House Republicans could easily have caved into Democratic demands to move a narrow bill to expand the tax credit, House leaders chose to stand and fight. They passed a bill (HR 1308) that included $82 billion in tax cuts, more than eight times the Senate's total. (*Taxes, p. 81*)

DeLay perfected his reputation as a keen political strategist, vote-counter, enforcer of party loyalty and chief fundraiser among lobbyists while serving as majority whip, a job he won when Republicans took control of the House in 1995.

And he solidified his base of support within the GOP

conference — from conservatives and moderates — by meeting members' needs, ranging from feeding them barbecue on late work nights to raising millions of dollars in campaign cash. (*1999 CQ Weekly, p. 1322*)

In exchange, members learned to accurately report their intended votes and not defy the leadership when loyalty counted the most. If they did, punishment, or threats of it, followed.

In a high-profile delivery of leadership payback, moderate Christopher Shays of Connecticut was denied the chairmanship of the Government Reform Committee because he used procedural rules against the leadership to force a vote on his campaign finance overhaul (PL 107-155).

This year, conservative Christopher H. Smith of New Jersey was warned he could lose the helm of the House Veterans' Affairs panel if he pursued budget-busting legislation to move veterans' health spending from discretionary to mandatory accounts to guarantee funding. Smith has since worked on a compromise bill and is trying to avoid conflict.

When asked how DeLay has performed as majority leader, Smith said simply, "Fine." He quickly added: "I have my eye on the ball."

DeLay has worked to smooth some of his rougher edges. He capped his teeth, softened his hairstyle and agreed to hold a weekly news conference, even though he dislikes being interviewed. Asked by a reporter if he wants to be Speaker of the House, he replied curtly, "I don't know."

But he says the public image of him is off base. "Everybody, especially my detractors, has tried to write me as this mean-spirited, awful person," DeLay said in an interview. "I don't see myself as mean-spirited at all. I am passionate, I am passionate about what I believe in, I am aggressive about getting that done."

By his account, the way he does business has not changed, only his job title. "I still make controversial statements."

Driving Foreign Policy

DeLay says his dealings with the White House, the Senate and moderates are guided by what a majority of House Republicans want. If he deviates from that, "they will kick me off in a nanosecond," he said.

But in some foreign policy areas — Israel, Iraq and Taiwan, for example —

the majority leader has stepped forward to drive the debate, out of conviction that the United States should be in the business of "exporting democracy."

A Southern Baptist, DeLay often is driven by religious views, which hold that Jewish control over the West Bank is a fulfillment of biblical prophecy. DeLay and other conservatives say Israel should not be forced to make concessions in peace talks until Palestinian violence ends.

Within days after Bush's announcement June 4 that Israeli and Palestinian leaders had agreed to support his "road map" for peace, the region was rocked by a new cycle of violence. As Bush watched the fragile agreement begin to crumble June 10, he criticized Israeli retaliatory attacks against Palestinians, including an attempted assassination of Abdel Aziz Rantisi, the leader of the militant Islamic group Hamas. (*2003 CQ Weekly, p. 1469*)

DeLay protested privately to the administration and then spoke out in defense of Israel's right to strike back.

"America must stand by Israel as it fights its own war on terror," DeLay said, without specifically referring to Bush's comments. By the end of that week, Bush urged the world to "deal harshly with Hamas."

Similarly, DeLay prodded the administration on the issue of war with Iraq last August, at a time when Bush was still shaping his strategy.

For days, DeLay had watched leading Republicans, including Brent Scowcroft, national security adviser to Bush's father, question and criticize the ongoing war deliberations.

No one in the administration was effectively responding to the critics, DeLay thought. So he delivered a speech in Texas, in which he chastised those who second-guessed the wisdom of invading Iraq.

"Every generation must summon the courage to disregard the timid counsel of those who would mortgage our security to the false promises of wishful thinking and appeasement," DeLay said Aug. 21. (*2002 CQ Weekly, p. 2251*)

Five days later, Vice President Dick Cheney made the administration's first full argument for an invasion of Iraq.

"I think there have been times when DeLay was ahead of the administration's position. Eventually they were in the same place," a top GOP aide said.

They are not yet in sync on the issue

of Taiwan, however. As Bush courted new Chinese President Hu Jintao in early June, DeLay called for a free-trade agreement with Taiwan — which flies in the face of the administration's "one China" policy — and lashed out at the People's Republic of China, which he said was run by "decrepit tyrants: old apparatchiks." (*2003 CQ Weekly, p. 1429*)

An aide to DeLay said he is not yet pushing legislation, just a debate.

While much speculation has surrounded what one GOP lawmaker calls the "healthy tension" between DeLay and the president, the congressional leader is known to work closely with Cheney and with national security adviser Condoleezza Rice.

Drafts of his foreign policy speeches, such as the 2002 address on war with Iraq, are sent to the White House, not for approval, but to ensure he is not compromising sensitive diplomatic talks.

Managing the Conservatives

DeLay's strategy with the White House is founded on his relationship with conservatives. But his political skills and dual loyalties are about to be tested, as the administration and Congress try to settle major differences between the House and Senate versions (HR 1, S 1) of Medicare legislation.

As the House opened debate on the bill June 26, DeLay knew the vote would be one of the toughest to win in recent years. But in a way, DeLay had helped increase the risk of a loss. He had quietly urged conservatives to voice their objections to the leadership-backed bill and press for inclusion of conservative principles, such as controlling costs and bringing private competition into Medicare.

The conservatives spoke out, and so did other Republicans. DeLay suddenly had to shift from encouraging a discussion of conservative principles to helping save Bush from an embarrassing defeat at the hands of his own party.

During a meeting June 25, DeLay reminded Republicans that the House version contained funding to create incentives for private competition with Medicare. View the House bill not as an expansion of Medicare, but as a far better choice than the version Sen. Edward M. Kennedy of Massachusetts would support, DeLay advised — a play to conservatives' dislike of the liberal Democrat.

Still, the vote was a nail-biter, held

open for an extra 36 minutes as Hastert, DeLay and others scrambled to turn a four-vote deficit into a winning margin of one thin vote. In all, 19 Republicans voted against the bill, a "must-pass" legislative priority of Bush. (*2003 CQ Weekly, p. 1611*)

Now, conservatives are counting on DeLay and other House leaders to force a House-Senate compromise containing the private market mechanisms they were promised before the House vote; provisions that key Senate Democrats fiercely oppose.

"I cannot think of a single time that he has forced conservatives to swallow medicine they don't want to swallow," said Stephen Moore, president of the Club For Growth, a group closely allied with DeLay and other conservative lawmakers. Nor can Moore imagine DeLay voting for a bill that does not control the cost and expansion of Medicare.

But would DeLay go against any bill Bush wants passed? "I don't know," Moore said haltingly. "Tom is a good soldier for the party and for Bush."

Appeasing Moderates

Because he usually has the floor votes to push a conservative agenda, DeLay has his eyes on the Senate more than on finding compromise in the House. For this reason, Republican moderates in the House often find themselves cut out of the process: First they're pressured to vote for bills drafted by a team of primarily conservative committee chairmen. Then those right-leaning bills get negotiated against the more centrist Senate versions. The result often gets the backing of the White House.

This dynamic has played out in numerous debates, including the president's education programs, whether to make airport security screeners federal or private sector employees, tax cuts and other major bills.

"I have said to Tom, 'Let's figure out what the Senate is going to do and do that. Why do we have to fall on our sword all of the time?'" said Ray LaHood of Illinois, a leading moderate who last year waged a short-lived bid to succeed DeLay as whip. "Apparently they don't want to do that. They want to play to the base."

DeLay also offended moderates when they learned he gave $50,000 to the Club For Growth for their 2002 general election fund, even though the group has picked conservatives over

Bush holds DeLay's grandson, Brett Ferro, at a White House picnic June 18. The two Texans are not personally close, but they both want to win and understand each other completely.

moderates in GOP primary contests. The group is considering targeting Boehlert in the 2004 election cycle.

"Giving money to any group like that gives them credibility," Castle said. "To give any support that's going to do that in my judgment is poor politics and I don't agree with that."

Indeed, Boehlert questioned DeLay about the Club for Growth donation. But when the party's steering committee was picking committee chairmen for the current session, DeLay supported Boehlert's bid to take over the Science panel, making him the only moderate lawmaker and one of two from the Northeast to serve in that capacity.

Committee chairmen are key to DeLay's success.

Unlike his old handpicked whip team, for whom fealty to DeLay was paramount, the chairmen can be more independent. So when considering how to serve as majority leader, DeLay decided to hold weekly meetings with the chairmen to discuss the flow of legislation and work out problems, something his predecessor never did.

Members said it reflects DeLay's constant focus on how to keep the team together to expand the Republican hold on Congress, and his understanding that a moderate Republican is better than a Democrat in any seat.

In return for those efforts, Boehlert cuts DeLay some slack. "I don't really think in my heart of hearts that he is nearly as extreme as some of his state-

ments would suggest," Boehlert said. "He's got to occasionally throw some raw meat to certain segments of our conference and they eat it up."

DeLay has shown moderates he is willing to back off when they make a strong case. For example, when the House debated a bill (HR 760) that would ban a procedure known by its opponents as "partial birth" abortion, the leadership allowed Pennsylvania moderate Republican James C. Greenwood to offer an amendment that would have been less strict. It was rejected.

"Tom knows what he wants. He's very good at adjusting to the situation to get us as close to what we want as he can," said Vernon J. Ehlers, a moderate Republican from Michigan.

If not, Hastert is there to apply the brakes, effectively becoming the limit to how far to the right DeLay can go.

The Good Cop

Like Bush, Hastert is more conservative than his rhetoric sometimes suggests, though he is not regarded as the keeper of the conservative flame. Also like Bush, Hastert plays the "good cop" role against "bad cop" DeLay.

"We don't always see everything exactly alike," Hastert said, but added he would not change a thing about DeLay. "He has the courage to stand up and say what he thinks. It gets him in trouble sometimes. But he certainly has been a good part of this team."

Hastert and DeLay describe themselves as the perfect political match, working in tandem through a partnership formalized when Hastert was DeLay's chief deputy whip. When former Speaker Newt Gingrich (1979-99) resigned, DeLay helped move Hastert to the Speaker's chair in 1999. (*1998 Almanac, p. 7-4*)

"We complement each other," DeLay said. "I am passionate and he's more cool-headed and that's good to work off of each other." He also makes a critical bow to the Speaker: "He can be the voice of last resort."

DeLay's colleagues noted that the leadership has had to practice more patience as Republicans have matured in their role as the ruling party. With every major bill, DeLay and other GOP leaders sense a greater need to take more time answering members' questions, Republican lawmakers said.

"We have all developed more patience, more ability to listen. We have developed that as members have become increasingly confident with the responsibility of being in the majority," said Roy Blunt of Missouri, who succeeded DeLay as whip. (*2003 CQ Weekly, p. 1731*)

Senate Rules

DeLay has less patience with the Senate, which is governed by rules that force conservative leaders to cut deals with party moderates and Democrats in order to avoid filibusters.

"We call the Democrats our opponents and the Senate our enemy," Dunn said.

The frustration of GOP conservatives took hold early in the 107th Congress, when their high expectations for legislative victories with Bush in the White House were crushed by a Democratic takeover of the Senate.

As Republicans prepared to retake control after the 2002 election, disorder reigned when Majority Leader-elect Trent Lott of Mississippi was forced to step down after making a racially insensitive remark. (*2003 CQ Weekly, p. 16*)

Suddenly, Senate Republicans were being led by Bill Frist of Tennessee, a conservative with no previous congressional leadership experience.

At the start of the 108th, House and Senate GOP leaders committed to improved communications and a coordinated legislative strategy. But that pledge blew up in April during negotiations on the fiscal 2004 budget resolution (H Con Res 95). (*2003 CQ Weekly, p. 931*)

In a handshake deal with Hastert and other House leaders April 10, Frist agreed the budget would pave the way for $550 billion in tax cuts. But hours later, Frist promised two GOP moderates — Voinovich and Olympia J. Snowe of Maine — that tax cuts would not exceed $350 billion. House leaders did not find out about it until it was announced on the Senate floor the next day, and they were furious.

In their dual cop roles, Hastert left it to DeLay to lead their protests at a hastily called news conference, so the Speaker would still be available to straighten things out with Frist.

"This has long-term implications," DeLay warned. "This goes right to the heart of our ability to work together."

Interjecting himself in the management of the Senate, DeLay advised Frist to declare an agreement with the House and schedule a vote, maximizing pressure on moderates. "The pressure of the moment always works," he said.

It is a tactic DeLay has used repeatedly in the House where the rules favor the party in control. Sometimes, as with the recent Medicare vote, House leaders enter a roll call without enough votes, but with the confidence that arms can be twisted.

In the end, the tax cut enacted in May (PL 108-27) totaled just $350 billion, less than half of what Bush, DeLay and other conservatives sought. But House leaders persuaded Bush to back their language on corporate dividends tax cuts, which was closer to the president's mark than the Senate version. (*2003 CQ Weekly, p. 1245*)

Weekly Meetings With Bush

A contrite Frist said he and Hastert now meet at least every other day. But House leaders remain on guard. "Trust but verify," said House Budget Chairman Jim Nussle, R-Iowa.

It was around the time of the budget and tax cut debates that DeLay became a regular at the weekly leadership breakfasts with Bush, with the firm approval of Hastert and the White House. With a new, untested Senate leader in place, a strong conservative voice was needed at the table, administration and congressional sources said.

House leaders also point out that Hastert is a constitutional officer — the position of Speaker is technically nonpartisan — and that DeLay, as the floor leader, is equal to Democratic House Leader Nancy Pelosi of California, and therefore, should be present.

"He asserted himself in a way Dick [Armey] had not been willing to do," Blunt said.

That assertiveness frustrates DeLay's foes. DeLay "plays so far to the right, that he makes the regular right-wing position of the White House look reasonable and rational," said an aide to a top Democrat.

Over the years, DeLay's dealings with lobbyists and campaign donors have been questioned. Environmentalists have assailed him for trying to dismantle environmental laws. Democrats have called him an extremist.

"This is a man who says that there's not one regulation at EPA worth saving. This is a man who voted for a very discriminatory measure, an anti-immigrant measure," said Pelosi, referring to a failed amendment to the Homeland Security appropriations bill (HR 2555) that would have blocked federal aid to states or localities that restrict the sharing of information with the Bureau of Immigration and Customs. "Not even half of his conference supported it, but he did." (*2003 CQ Weekly, p. 1618*)

Still, Democrats have yet to succeed in turning DeLay's words and actions into voter anger against Republicans.

"He's a big, big target. But the president is a bigger shadow," said Democratic pollster Stanley Greenberg. "It's hard with the president there to battle it out at the level of DeLay."

The majority leader also is shielded by Hastert's non-confrontational, low-key style, which contrasts sharply with that of Gingrich, whose unpopularity rubbed off on all Republicans.

"Quite frankly, you'd be lucky to get 20 percent of the country who knows who the Speaker of the House is," said GOP pollster Ed Goeas. "Certainly there are some DeLay haters out there, but his numbers are nowhere near the kind of polarization and awareness that you saw with Newt Gingrich."

Democrats say their challenge is to go into districts of moderate Republicans and highlight the conservative votes ordered by House leaders.

For their part, moderates work to maintain a delicate balance between the politics of their districts and the political needs of the White House and DeLay.

On all sides, there are those who may not like his combative style or his conservative rhetoric. But no one denies his success.

"Maybe he has to say the most conservative things," said Jack Quinn, a GOP moderate from New York. "But so far so good. We're picking up seats." ◆

Management by Objective: How Frist Deals in 51-49 Senate

Many conservatives reserve judgment as biggest challenges await the GOP leader

Frist, middle, presides at a July 30 energy bill strategy session with GOP Whip Mitch McConnell of Kentucky, left, Energy Chairman Pete V. Domenici, R-N.M., right, Larry E. Craig, R-Idaho, and Energy Secretary Spencer Abraham, as Bush liaison Ziad Ojakli and others look on.

For such a deliberate place as the Senate, Bill Frist was an impulse buy. Republicans reached for the relatively inexperienced Tennessean last December at a moment of deepening political crisis, only after it became clear that Mississippi's Trent Lott could not continue as party leader.

Smart and telegenic, an expert on health care and a close ally of President Bush, the surgeon-turned-senator seemed the perfect man to be not only majority leader but also spokesman for a party hoping to appear more inclusive and compassionate.

But from the start, there were doubters in his own ranks as well as optimistic opponents. Conservatives worried that Frist was too moderate and would be too willing to compromise with Democrats. For their part, the Democrats hoped that Frist would emphasize accommodation in the closely divided Senate — or might prove out of his depth in running the place, and therefore outmaneuverable.

In the eight months since, Frist has seldom been outflanked by Democrats or accused of giving away too much. And his choice of staff and his statements in public and private have reassured and at times surprised conservative skeptics. Now, they say, they believe he will be not only attentive and sympathetic to their views but also a forceful advocate of their positions on judicial nominees, taxes and social policy.

"He's won me over," said Paul M. Weyrich, chairman of the Free Congress Foundation, an influential conservative think

tank. "I've come to be a fan of Frist. He's been very forthcoming," said Weyrich, who distrusted Frist initially.

Still, leading conservatives are withholding final judgment on Frist's performance until he has completed one full year as majority leader. As Congress returns from its summer break the week of Sept. 1, senators face a stack of must-do spending bills, post-blackout pressure to cut a deal on an energy policy bill and a deepening standoff over Bush's picks for the federal bench. Most politically pressing of all is the search for a deal to add a prescription drug benefit to Medicare, a topic about which Frist is universally regarded as an expert.

Many on and off Capitol Hill, conservatives and others, are looking to the coming weeks — and the debate on Medicare in particular — as the new majority leader's defining challenge. House and Senate negotiators are under significant pressure from Bush and others to produce a compromise Medicare bill (HR 1) by the end of the year. And it is Frist, by virtue of his position and credibility on the issue, who bears the greatest share of the responsibility for forging a deal and making it stick. (2003 CQ Weekly, p. 2064)

How he balances the competing interests and viewpoints will reveal a great deal about Frist as a leader and could determine the trajectory of his political career.

Putting a bill on Bush's desk that satisfies interests across the political spectrum would solidify Frist's position both inside and outside the Senate and add to his longstanding reputation as an overachiever. Stalemate or, perhaps worse, a backlash among seniors to whatever deal Congress strikes could wound him deeply. A deal that alienates the party's conservative base also could undermine him. It is generally assumed that he wants to succeed Bush as president in 2008, but Frist could see that aspiration dashed if he fails to strike the right balance.

So far, he has maintained the good will and trust of his colleagues — both Democrats and Republicans — as well as that of the White House and his wider party, even as he has shored up support among conservatives. He generally gets good marks for fairness and for keeping the president's agenda moving in a Senate where the GOP holds just a one-seat majority — no small accomplishment. His willingness to delegate authority to committee chairmen and his habit of staying in touch with colleagues through a ceaseless exchange of e-mail has won him praise from many lawmakers.

But like other majority leaders before him, Frist will be called upon this fall to choose between ideological purity and gridlock on the one hand and compromise and progress on the other on a wide variety of issues.

"I think the jury is still out on Frist," said Stephen Moore, president of the tax cut advocacy group Club for Growth and a prominent conservative voice in Washington. "For me to make an assessment before the fall, when we have Medicare and appropriations bills and judicial nominations, it's just premature to say whether he is succeeding or not."

Unique Responsibility

As a physician, Frist is presumed to have special insight into modernizing the system that provides health care for 40 million seniors. He has focused on the issue for years, investing untold hours working on the 1999 National Bipartisan Commission on the Future of Medicare and writing and promoting drug coverage legislation in the 107th Congress with centrist Democrat John B. Breaux of Louisiana.

As a result, Frist has almost unmatched prominence and credibility on the complex issues involved in a Medicare overhaul. That was part of the calculus when Republicans picked him as majority leader. He seemed the man to help Bush and the GOP claim the politically potent issue as their own before the 2004 elections, undermining the Democrats' traditional edge with voters on health care.

At the same time, Frist's expertise, poise and evenhanded temperament make him well-suited to sell a bill to a broad audience, said Joseph Antos, an expert on health care at the conservative American Enterprise Institute (AEI).

Acknowledging what he calls his special responsibility in the debate, Frist took the unusual step for a majority leader of assigning himself to the House-Senate negotiating committee that will try to fashion the final bill. His counterpart in the House, Speaker J. Dennis Hastert, R-Ill., did not.

"I could have stayed off the committee and sat back with Speaker Hastert to help make some of the fundamental decisions," Frist said. "But I wanted to be involved in the process, to fully understand, to listen to the debate on both sides and to be in the best position to help make some of the major decisions that inevitably are going to have to be made."

Nothing is getting through Congress without some support from Democrats and moderate Republicans, and Frist has a better track record of working with both than do the highest-ranking GOP House members on the conference committee: Majority Leader Tom DeLay of Texas and Ways and Means Chairman Bill Thomas of California, both polarizing figures.

"It's Bill Frist who will determine which direction that conference takes," Antos said. "Bill Frist is the dealmaker and the guy with the intellectual throw weight on this."

Shortly after the Senate adjourned Aug. 1 for its monthlong summer recess, Frist set the bar high. Showing a flash of the surgeon's self-confidence, he challenged his fellow conferees to finish work by the end of September.

"I think you can take the best principles out of both bills," Frist said. "Through negotiations, you can accomplish a solid, sound public policy that will accomplish the goals of health care security. So I don't think it's as complicated as people from the outside think."

No Cakewalk

But Congress is debating the single biggest expansion of Medicare since its creation in 1965, and the chance of failure is high. "I am not optimistic," said one lobbyist for physicians and a longtime Senate watcher. "You put a gun to my head right now and I'd say it's 30 for and 70 against."

Besides the complexities of the issue and his own inexperience as leader, Frist will have to overcome deep ideological divisions between the political parties and institutional jealousies between the House and Senate.

The latter was exacerbated by the biggest mistake Frist made in public during his rookie year as majority leader. In April, he announced a deal with two GOP senators to hold Bush's tax cut package to $350 billion after seemingly promising to work with House GOP leaders for a $550 billion tax cut. That misstep nearly

CQ photographs by Scott J. Ferrell

Secretary of Defense Donald H. Rumsfeld and Frist enjoy a light moment before a July 30 meeting. Rumsfeld is craning his neck to look at the artwork on the wall behind him.

brought the legislation down; only the intervention of Vice President Dick Cheney saved the day. (*2003 CQ Weekly, pp. 931, 866, 1306*)

Although Frist has apologized, and House members say they have forgiven and moved on, Republicans concede that traces of distrust still linger. These could complicate Frist's work on Medicare, perhaps weakening his leverage with the House.

No one wants a repeat of what was an embarrassing episode for all Republicans on the size of the tax cut — which was born of an impasse between conservative House Republicans and their generally more compromising Senate counterparts. Frist will have to be careful to avoid a similar standoff on Medicare.

The Senate voted 76-21 for its Medicare bill, but the majority coalition is far from solid. The House bill passed 216-215, and the support there remains tenuous. In conference, Democrats are demanding universal coverage and a strong federal role, while conservatives are taking a hard line on including "premium support," or private-sector competition with Medicare. A deal that moves too far to the right will cause Democratic votes in the Senate to fall away. One that moves even a bit to the left will prompt House conservatives to balk.

While they came around to the idea that $350 billion in tax cuts this year was the best Frist could have done, conservatives appear less willing now to take the pragmatic view on Medicare. Some would rather see Frist thwart a bill than embrace one that lacks significant private-market competition or creates a massive and expensive new government entitlement.

A segment of Frist's own caucus in the Senate is pressuring him to return from conference with a bill that looks like the House version — with premium support as its centerpiece — and dare Democrats to filibuster it.

"What we're looking for in the majority leader's position is a Republican Tom Daschle," Moore said, referring to the Senate Democratic leader from South Dakota. "Someone who will steer the public debate in the direction we want it to go, someone who will stand up for conservative principles the way Tom Daschle stands up for liberal principles."

Letting Chairmen Work

When Frist ascended suddenly to the leadership, the biggest question in many minds was whether a hot-shot doctor, unaccustomed to having his authority questioned, would have the patience to be majority leader. The Senate is an institution where big personalities and even bigger egos are the rule, and the majority leader's job is ill-defined, with little formal power. (*2003 CQ Weekly, p. 16; 2002 Almanac, p. 1-10*)

Unlike the House, where majority rules and the leadership can govern with an iron fist, no Senate leader can afford to squeeze too hard. All senators wield considerable power and can shut down the chamber if they choose.

But so far, the take on Frist is that he has been, if anything, too accommodating, too hands-off. Where Lott, Daschle and other previous leaders dominated news conferences and the television cameras, Frist routinely steps back and lets others do the talking.

Committee chairmen, it is generally agreed, are driving the process in the Senate to a greater degree under Frist than past majority leaders.

The chairmen themselves say that although Frist respects the committee process, there is never any doubt that he ultimately is the leader.

"He listens to the chairmen, but at the end, he says, 'We're going to do thus and such,'" said Arizona Republican John McCain, chairman of Commerce, Science and Transportation. "I don't hear the chairmen saying, 'We're going to do thus and such.'"

But Wendy Schiller, a political scientist at Brown University who has studied the internal workings of the Senate, said the relatively junior Frist comes to the leadership at a marked disadvantage. First elected in 1994 as a political novice and then thrown into the role of leader with little preparation, he lacks the relationships and chits with his colleagues to stare down balky chairmen, Schiller said.

"Frist hasn't shown that he has the capacity or the willingness to lean on chairmen, so his style de facto has had to be conciliatory," she said. "Most of the people he would lean on have been in the Senate a lot longer than he has. They have a great deal of independence and are electorally secure."

A prime example is Finance Committee Chairman Charles E. Grassley, Schiller said. It was the Iowa Republican who struck the agreement, later blessed by Frist, to keep the president's tax package at $350 billion last spring. And it was Grassley who wrote the Senate's Medicare bill with his committee's ranking Democrat, Max Baucus of Montana.

Headstrong committee chairmen — Grassley in particular — were a headache for leaders before Frist. Grassley is a force even the Bush White House has had difficulty controlling. (*2003 CQ Weekly, p. 542*)

But one senior Democratic aide complains that Frist is letting committee chairmen and senior members pursue their own agendas to such a degree that the Senate increasingly will be tied in knots. A pileup on the floor the week of July 28 — with some Republicans itching for a confrontation over judges while others were trying to get the energy bill done — was one example, the aide said. (*2003 CQ Weekly, pp. 1967; 82*)

"It's ultimately the responsibility of

Frist, who often stands back so that colleagues can have the spotlight, is nonetheless thronged by reporters as he makes his way through the Capitol corridors July 31.

the leader to lead," the aide said. "It helps move things along, it helps keep decorum between the parties because the leader has the big picture."

A longtime Republican Senate aide who is now a lobbyist acknowledged that Frist "has chosen not to make a significant number of issues leadership issues." But the former aide said: "Daschle made everything a leadership issue, and it played havoc with the workings of the Senate."

Ross Baker, a political scientist at Rutgers University, said stepping back and letting others take the limelight gets Frist "tremendous credit from his colleagues."

No Hard Lines

Frist has a group meeting with his chairmen every Monday, a session they say helps keep the legislative process transparent and the party's larger goals in view. Many days, after a regular meeting with staff around 8 a.m., he presides over small working groups in his office, with staff and senators key to the issue at hand, to discuss the day's floor strategy and political challenges.

He listens more than he talks, participants say. And he appears to come to debates with an open mind, sincerely seeking opinions and ideas.

He also is drawing input from a broader range of members than past leaders did, according to Appropriations Chairman Ted Stevens, R-Alaska, and others. "Other leaders have tried to work with one or two chairmen. He is talking to many," Stevens said.

Frist said it was former Majority Leader Howard H. Baker Jr. (1967-85), a fellow Tennessee Republican, who suggested that he meet regularly with the chairmen as a group. "In that room, when you look around, you look at the chairmen, the experience is broad and collectively is powerful," Frist said. "Do I depend on them for counsel? Absolutely I do."

On Medicare, conservatives were deeply disappointed that Frist did not intervene in the work of the Finance Committee as it wrote the bill. Angered by the final deal because it lacked a premium support component, they questioned Frist's grip on the reins and his commitment to an idea that had in previous years been the centerpiece of the Medicare legislation he sponsored with Breaux.

Senate Energy Chairman Pete V. Domenici, R-N.M., makes an emphatic point to Frist as they discuss July 31 how to push a massive energy bill through the chamber before adjourning for August.

As conservatives see it, Grassley acquiesced, and Frist just sat back and watched it happen. They complained that their liberal archenemy, Sen. Edward M. Kennedy, D-Mass., got the better of the GOP. (*2003 CQ Weekly, pp. 1611, 1455; 103*)

"I assumed — we all assumed — that Bill Frist was going to be the key to getting 60 votes in the Senate," said Antos of the AEI. "And actually, Ted Kennedy was the key to getting 60 votes. It wasn't Frist at all."

But while Grassley and Baucus led the drafting of the Senate's Medicare bill, those involved in the discussions say Frist was engaged and decisive, particularly in the endgame, as leadership and the bill's proponents worked to secure the final votes for passage.

At that stage, Frist presided over meetings with key players in his office, with Baucus, Grassley, Kennedy and others bustling between there and the Senate floor as the bill moved toward passage. "He was hell-bent for leather," said the Senate's No. 3 Republican, GOP Conference Chairman Rick Santorum of Pennsylvania.

What Frist said he did not do was draw hard lines and play dictator. No one holds all the answers on Medicare, he said; the issue is too complex.

"As majority leader, I sought the very best ideas, to get the very best out of individuals who care about the issue and have studied the issue," he said. "I did not approach it with biases.

"The alternative would be to take my old Breaux-Frist bill and cram it down everybody's throat and say, 'This is the way it's going to be,' " Frist said. "If I were certain that I had all the answers, that's probably what I would do. But that's not the approach I'm taking."

Frist and others point out that under him, the Senate finally has done something it has never achieved: It passed a Medicare drug bill, moving it to conference and closer than ever to becoming law.

Even Republicans who voted against the bill — or voted for it with reluctance — credit Frist with keeping the process moving. "He has put us in a position where a bill that is very important to the country and to Republicans is on a path to pass," said Santorum, one of 10 GOP senators who opposed the bill.

A Delicate Touch

Frist's personal style is a marked departure from that of his predecessors.

In communicating with colleagues and running the business of the Senate, he favors e-mail and working groups over the firm arm around a shoulder or the quiet ultimatum to a colleague. He sleeps little, and he e-mails colleagues on their wireless Blackberry pagers at all hours, keeping them twiddling with the little devices in hallways, in committee rooms, on the way to their cars, even at home.

Late the morning of July 30, Frist gets a rare few minutes alone to work at his desk and catch up on phone calls. President Bush's news conference from the White House Rose Garden plays live on television in the background.

His identity and style are ultimately rooted elsewhere. Few people in America ever knew what Lott or Daschle did before their elections to Congress (both were congressional aides). Frist, by contrast, came onto the public consciousness last year as the surgeon-senator, someone not at all a creature of Capitol Hill. There is a reminder of that for visitors to his leadership suite in the Capitol office. The shingle he has hung on the front door there reads, "Republican Leader William H. Frist, M.D."

He frequently uses stories from his career as a surgeon to illustrate points about the position he occupies now, and he clearly relishes recounting the details of a surgery or transplant.

On the Senate floor or in news conferences, he is affable but reserved, precise in his movements and speech, almost professorial — a demeanor some read as aloof or detached. A far cry from the expansive Lott or the fiery Daschle, Frist speaks in long and sometimes disjointed arcs, rarely sound bites.

Many senators love their pagers and say they are pleased that Frist uses them to stay in touch. "There's more communication than I have ever had with a leader," Stevens says.

But his heavy reliance on e-mail has left some colleagues a little cold.

"There have been concerns that he's not an old-fashioned politician," said Antos, who met with disgruntled Republican lawmakers during the Senate's Medicare debate. "The reputation is that he's into efficient communication and not grabbing your arm, slapping you on the back and then leading you into a vote. If you're not a back-slapper, you are at a disadvantage when you are surrounded by politicians."

Frist and his allies say he has the low-key, inclusive, open-handed style necessary to ease the Medicare bill through the Senate — and to keep other key items on the GOP agenda from screeching to a halt.

And it is true that Frist and his team are circumscribed as well as empowered by the fact that their party controls the House, Senate and White House.

"We're part of a larger team in moving the agenda," said Frist spokesman Bob Stevenson, a Senate aid for 23 years. "When you're in the minority or in control of one house, you can afford to be more demonstrative and abrupt. Here our agenda is to move things forward, and I think that thus far, we've been successful in accomplishing that."

Frist is no Lyndon B. Johnson of Texas, the famously strong-armed majority leader from 1955 to 1961. But in the modern Senate, Johnson's tactics no longer work, Stevenson and others say. Television in particular has made top-down leadership unworkable, they say. Individual senators, including freshmen, can reach a national audience more easily now, even grow to become celebrities of a sort. And they have become more autonomous. As a result, the Senate has become more difficult to tame, except by consensus and inclusion.

Frist speaks of himself as a "leader-manager," responsible for marshaling and directing Senate resources, setting the course and then putting the right people to work on the right problems.

"My responsibility, I think, is to search for the strengths and maximize those, minimize the weaknesses, in a direction that is consistent with a clearly defined mission, working with an agenda that the president sets out for our party," he said. "That tends to take some of the sort of Lyndon Johnson command-and-control out of one person and shares it through a broader group of people."

Keeping the Trains Running

Frist and his supporters also point out that the Senate has done most of what the majority leader promised it would do by this point in the year, including completing the overdue fiscal 2003 appropriations process, pushing the tax cut and economic stimulus package (PL 108-27) into law and working with Bush on a law (PL 108-25) authorizing $15 billion over the next five years to fight the global spread of HIV/AIDS.

Democrats say that by and large, Frist has kept the process fair and open. The debates on Medicare, medical malpractice caps and a bill to ban a procedure opponents call "partial birth" abortion (S 3) were full and unfettered, noted

Richard J. Durbin of Illinois, who as assistant Democratic floor leader is his party's chief message-maker in the Senate.

"He has not dropped the hammer, with the exception of judicial nominations, which is a high-profile issue," Durbin said.

Frist "offers us an opportunity for a debate and a vote, something that is not offered to the minority in the House," he said.

In the House, Republican leaders say Frist has done his best to fix the damage caused by the blowup earlier this year over the tax cut package.

"Bill was as up-front and apologetic as you could ever hope for," said Republican Whip Roy Blunt of Missouri. "He got substantial credit for admitting that it was a learning experience for him."

White House aides say Frist continues to have the trust of the president. The two have been close since early in Bush's 2000 campaign.

"It's been a very successful eight months, and he has shown himself to be a very strong leader," one White House official said of Frist. "He says the Senate is going to stay in until it gets the job done, and he keeps the Senate in until it gets the job done."

Bush himself has been a realist, willing to compromise to claim victory when necessary. The White House's negotiating line on Medicare so far matches Frist's. The administration prefers the House bill — and particularly wants to get some level of private-sector competition — but Bush has drawn no hard lines.

Just as his agenda is Bush's agenda, so too does Frist share the president's fundamental dilemma. By taking the lead on Medicare and other traditionally Democratic issues, they hope to expand the GOP's base of support. But at the same time, they risk upsetting their established conservative base.

Frist's voting record is conservative and runs almost straight down the party line. Still, since becoming leader, he has reached out to the right, working to enact the partial-birth abortion ban and a bill (S 1019) that would make harming a fetus during the commission of a federal crime a separate offense. (*2003 CQ Weekly, pp. 1827, 1825*)

Also, Frist hired as a senior policy adviser a man conservatives deeply trust: Bill Wichterman, who helped organize and lead the House Values Action Team, a GOP leadership effort to build coalitions with conservative groups off Capitol Hill.

Just before the Fourth of July, Frist appeared before a regular lunchtime gathering of influential conservatives at the Free Congress Foundation, and his audience liked what they heard.

"He left with a very pleased crowd," said Morton Blackwell, a prominent conservative who attended. Frist gave the impression that day that he would aggressively represent attendees' views on Medicare and other issues.

"I don't expect miracles," Weyrich said. "What we want to see is an effort, and we also want to see our positions defended. Too often, Lott would just walk away from our position and not defend it. Or if he did say something good, he backed away from it two days later."

A Chance to Govern

Attendees of the lunch pressed Frist to force up-or-down votes on Bush's judicial nominees — a cause célèbre with activists on both ends of the political spectrum. Some conservatives are urging Frist to try to weaken Senate filibuster rules to overcome Democratic tactics against Bush's judges. But that would so inflame partisan tensions in the Senate that it would bring near-certain paralysis. (*2003 CQ Weekly, p. 1079*)

As Weyrich tells it, Frist was pressed on the point several times before he finally said, "Remember, before I came here, I used to cut people's hearts out."

Said Blackwell, "With my own ears, I've heard him discuss this thing, and I think he's prepared."

Frist himself says, "In my guts, I'm more of a risk-taker. You don't do a heart transplant, heart surgery, if you're not a risk-taker."

But as Daschle, Lott and others before Frist have learned, dramatic displays and unyielding positions are often luxuries the Senate's majority leader cannot afford — particularly when the party's agenda is at stake.

Force an end to the Democratic filibusters of three appellate court nominees and the president's agenda comes to a halt in the Senate. Frist continues to say such a move is an option, but he has been noncommittal.

On Medicare, Frist says, "Ideologically, there are certain fundamentals that I believe are important. I believe in competition, private-sector involvement, individual responsibility. So those principles I want injected and maximized, more so than in the Senate bill."

Asked if he might consider pushing the legislation to the right and daring Democrats to filibuster, Frist redirects: He is convinced they can find an agreement, he says.

Stevenson called the issue a "Rubik's cube" — solving it will take a complicated series of twists and turns, any of which may disrupt the whole. Frist and his staff ask for time to prove they can bring all the pieces together. It has been five decades since Republicans controlled Congress and the White House.

"For years, Republicans have told the American public, 'Just give us a chance and we'll show you we can govern,'" Stevenson said. "They've done that. We have an opportunity now that we haven't had in a long, long time, and he wants to demonstrate to people that he can make this institution work." ◆

Frist listens to Dave Schiappa, secretary for the majority, at a July 30 meeting. The GOP leader faces growing pressure to find a way to end filibusters of Bush's judicial nominees.

GOP Starting to Waver On Support for Iraq

Unanticipated expenses — in both dollars and lives — undermines support

Even before President Bush took the nation to war with Iraq in March, a small group of moderate Republican lawmakers joined with Democrats to caution the administration that the actual fighting would not be the only challenge ahead. More difficult, they warned, would be the task of rebuilding the country and transforming it into a democracy.

Now, four months after an unexpectedly swift victory, followed by daily — and deadly — guerrilla warfare that has impeded the reconstruction effort, such skepticism is widening to the Republican rank and file, where a growing number of lawmakers are now raising their own questions about the administration's Iraq policy.

For example, Sen. Pete V. Domenici, R-N.M, a strong supporter of Bush and never an outspoken voice on foreign policy issues, is now quite vocal.

Meeting with Bremer in Iraq, Rumsfeld says other countries will have a say in Iraq's reconstruction commensurate with the size of the forces they send to help police the nation.

"I am expecting new ideas to evolve from the White House on how this is going to be handled — not only from the standpoint of the management of the crisis but also how the administration can put together a multi-year program that can be described to the American people on a regular basis, rather than the Americans learning most of their information each time a bad event occurs," said Domenici, chairman of the Senate Energy Committee.

Domenici says he is now discussing his concerns directly with the White House and the Pentagon — a step he has never taken before.

Sen. John McCain, R-Ariz., who was in Baghdad when the United Nations headquarters there were bombed, warned: "If we don't turn things around in the next few months, we're facing a very serious long-term problem."

Senate Intelligence Committee Chairman Pat Roberts, R-Kan., described an even more dire scenario: The U.S. invasion, predicated in part on the allegation that Iraq was in cahoots with the al Qaeda terrorist organization, may have made that a reality. "If Iraq was not a sanctuary for al Qaeda before, it certainly is now," Roberts said.

For the administration, the timing of such Republican concerns could not be worse. Returning from the August recess, a period that saw guerrillas destroy the U.N. headquarters and a Shi'ite shrine in Najaf and push the postwar U.S. death toll past the number of troops killed in the actual war,

Congress now faces important decisions on spending to fund military and reconstruction operations there. The timing is difficult for lawmakers, too. These decisions come as their constituents are complaining about the anemic economy and the mushrooming deficit and as polls suggest that Iraq poses political dangers for the president and his party.

Republican skepticism is now moving them closer to Democrats in three general areas: They are both now publicly chiding the administration for what they say was a lack of postwar planning and vagueness on the occupation's cost and duration. They have pressed Bush to make the case for the effort to the American people, echoing Democrats that without public support for his policy, Americans might lose confidence in the Iraq reconstruction effort. And like the Democrats, Republicans have urged Bush to share the burdens of money and manpower by internationalizing Iraq's occupation and reconstruction despite their reservations about sharing control of the country.

This Republican criticism has added a thumb to the scales of the Iraq debate, allowing Congress to assert its role in foreign policy and help prod the administration to respond. The president was scheduled to speak to the nation about the war Sept. 7 in his first such address since he announced May 1 that major combat operations had ended.

Tough Timing

The pressure is growing at a time when the administration most needs its allies on Capitol Hill. Congressional

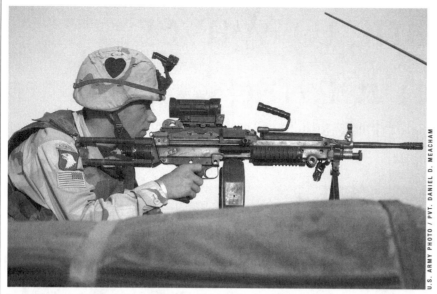

U.S. ARMY PHOTO / PVT. DANIEL D. MEACHAM

Republicans have joined Democrats in criticizing the Bush administration for insufficient postwar planning that has left American troops struggling to stabilize Iraq.

aides expect that the White House will request as much as $80 billion to pay for the growing costs of the Iraq occupation and reconstruction effort during fiscal 2004. The request, which could be presented to Congress as soon as this week, follows Congress' approval of a nearly $80 billion emergency Iraq supplemental (PL 108-11) last April. Several lawmakers said it confirmed what they have been saying for months: that the administration grossly underestimated the money required to restore order, rebuild the country's infrastructure, and provide Iraqis with basic services such as electricity, water and telephones. *(2003 CQ Weekly, p. 2136)*

The administration also disclosed Sept. 3 the details of a draft U.N. resolution that it will present to the Security Council in a bid to win international funding and troops for Iraq. The U.S. draft would create a multinational U.N. peacekeeping force that would operate under U.S. military command, urge Iraqis to come up with a plan for a government and a constitution, and give the United Nations limited political power while maintaining a dominant U.S. role.

Taken together, the administration's moves appear aimed at tamping down criticism of Bush's stewardship of the Iraq situation before it blossoms into a major political headache — particularly as the 2004 campaign season gets under way in earnest and Democrats begin to sense that the deepening Iraq morass could weaken Bush. In Congress, lawmakers say there is little question that Bush will get the money he seeks. But Democrats seem determined to make sure the process is not painless.

House Minority Leader Nancy Pelosi of California says the lack of planning for postwar Iraq has led to huge and unnecessary bills — costs for which she believes Bush should be held accountable. "The Bush administration's endless spending there could have been avoided if only they had had a plan — a reliable plan — for safety and security in Iraq," she said. "They did not."

The impetus for many formerly circumspect Republicans going public with a variety of concerns seems to be surprise at the ongoing unrest in Iraq — not only the bombings but the relentless attacks on U.S. soldiers whose 149 deaths as of Sept. 5, in hostile and accidental situations, exceed the 138

killed through May 1, when Bush declared the end of major combat operations.

When postwar deaths exceeded wartime deaths, "that set off some warning lights," said Jack Pitney, a professor of government at Claremont McKenna College in Southern California. "Whenever you have rough air out there, politicians put on their parachutes. They're not jumping out yet, but they're checking their chutes."

Said former Senate Majority Leader Trent Lott, R-Miss.: "I think most of us didn't think it would be as bad as it has been. I don't know why we didn't realize that, when you look at the violent history of Iraq over the past many years, 30 years, what they've done to each other and their neighbors. . . . But obviously we are not happy with the way it is."

Sen. George Allen, R-Va., suggested that the relative ease of the initial victory set people up for later disappointment. "The military-vs.-military action went so well, with such precision," said Allen, who supports Bush's handling of the effort. "So you expect, gosh, that went so much better than anybody could have envisioned, hoped for, prayed for, and now it'll all be easy. Well, it's not going to be easy."

Constituent Concerns

Many Republican lawmakers also said that during the August recess they heard constituents complain that planning for postwar operations in Iraq was insufficient. But at the same time, they are quick to add that they still found solid support for Bush and the war in Iraq.

"I find my constituents very supportive of the United States in Iraq and of the president," said Richard G. Lugar, R-Ind., chairman of the Senate Foreign Relations Committee. But, he added, "there is a feeling that planning was inadequate and more cogent planning is required."

Lugar says his constituents have focused not on money for Iraq but on the overall federal budget deficit, which is nearing $500 billion. And he warns the administration that if it keeps coming to Congress for emergency spending requests outside the normal budget process, it could undermine public confidence in the Iraq reconstruction effort.

Bush needs to build that confidence by "having a comprehensive, multi-year plan that shows staying power, shows responsibility," Lugar said.

Rep. Curt Weldon, R-Pa., a senior member of the Armed Services Committee, said, "The constituents that I talked with are still supportive of the president's battle against terrorism." He notes, however, that he has heard a lot of concern from families of reservists and National Guardsmen who have been called to active duty.

"With this new military, we rely heavily on the Guard and reservists," Weldon said. "Their families never expected to have them away for this period of time. They're concerned about the continued killings, the need for security in Iraq, whether we had our planning in order for postwar Iraq. That's something we could have done better."

In fact, Bush may be seeking more international help through the United Nations precisely because he does not want to call up more reservists, said Michèle A. Flournoy, a former Defense Department official under President Bill Clinton. Calling up more reservists is "not a politically attractive option when you're running for re-election," said Flournoy, now senior adviser at the Center for Strategic and International Studies in Washington.

A recent poll supports the legislators' soundings back home. A CNN/USA Today/Gallup poll conducted Aug. 25-26 and released Aug. 28 found 63 percent saying it was worthwhile to go to war with Iraq, and 57 percent approving of Bush's handling of Iraq. But 54 percent said the administration does not have a clear plan for handling the postwar situation. The poll involved a sample of 1,009 adults and had a margin of error of 3 percentage points.

Democratic strategists see political potential in such sentiments. Party strategists James Carville, Stanley Greenberg and Robert Shrum reported Sept. 4 that their poll of 1,004 likely voters indicated that Bush has become more vulnerable in next year's election because of Iraq and the doubts it has raised about his honesty. The poll, conducted Aug. 24-28, reported that Bush would defeat an unnamed Democrat by 46 percent to 42 percent, the closest margin so far this year.

Yet another potential liability for Bush is a report expected soon from his chief weapons inspector, David Kay, on Iraq's alleged weapons of mass destruction, which the president cited as the main reason to attack. Accounts citing sources familiar with the report say Kay is not expected to produce hard evidence of Iraq's proscribed weapons, but he will build a more circumstantial case that Saddam Hussein dismantled and dispersed his weapons programs to elude inspectors. Such conclusions could revive criticism of the administration's pre-war intelligence, which is being investigated by the House and Senate Intelligence panels. (*Intelligence*, p. 2168)

With many in Congress, even before the bloody month of August, urging the administration to beef up the 140,000 U.S. troop contingent in Iraq, Bush's move toward a U.N. military force has drawn quick praise from Democrats on Capitol Hill, though it is tinged with an "I told you so" flavor.

"I'm very pleased that the administration has made the decision to go to the United Nations," Senate Minority Leader Tom Daschle, D-S.D., said Sept. 3. "It's been a long time in coming. There has been, as you know, a lot of infighting within the White House with regard to whether to do this, and I'm very pleased that at long last, we are. Many of us have called for this for a long period of time."

Sen. Carl Levin of Michigan, ranking Democrat on the Armed Services Committee, called it "welcome news that the administration is finally waking up to the need to seek greater international support for, and participation in, our stabilization and reconstruction efforts in Iraq."

With Bush originally opposed to significant U.N. involvement in Iraq, analysts note, the U.S. draft resolution represents a major concession by the president. But they add that it is one that can help Bush politically at home.

"There's a sense that there are other people to share the burden, that we're not going to be Uncle Sucker again," Pitney said.

Tough Negotiations Ahead

But Bush's draft resolution has not been received so warmly by key members of the U.N. Security Council and other allies. German Chancellor Gerhard Schroeder and French President Jacques Chirac criticized the U.S. proposal Sept. 4, saying it neither gives responsibility to Iraqis nor offers the United Nations a large enough role in Iraq's reconstruction.

"We are quite far removed from what we believe is the priority objective, which is the transfer of political responsibility to an Iraqi government as quickly as possible," Chirac said.

With France, a permanent Security Council member, now demanding changes to the American draft resolution, U.S. officials are bracing for tough negotiations to produce a draft that can win the council's approval. In the meantime, lawmakers are weighing in with their own views and advice for the administration.

Levin says there is no need to compromise on U.S. leadership of the proposed U.N. peacekeeping force, given the similar precedents that were established in the 1991 Gulf War.

"There will, however, be a need for compromise with respect to the control of civilian reconstruction and political development of Iraq," Levin warned, calling for decision-sharing in those areas. "If we are willing to do so, Germany and Russia will probably go along, and France would then have little choice, I believe, but to go along as well."

Defense Secretary Donald H. Rumsfeld said Sept. 3 that decision-sharing would be part of the deal. "There's no question that to the extent that countries step up with troops and money and support, they're clearly at the table, and they have the opportunity to work with us and to work with the Iraqi Governing Authority."

But that power-sharing raises the dander of some GOP lawmakers.

Lott, in particular, expressed concern about the potential role of France, which led Security Council opposition to the war and ultimately forced the United States to drop its bid for a resolution for the war to avoid a defeat.

While allowing for "a lot of give and take" on control over governance, humanitarian aid and infrastructure, Lott said, "I would want to be very careful about relinquishing military command and also giving the French a chance to get their hands on the oil.

"Money is a consideration, and oil is a consideration in terms of what some people want. The French, specifically," he added.

The draft resolution also invites the U.S.-backed Iraqi Governing Council to create a blueprint and a schedule for turning Iraq into a democracy.

Lugar says the push to accelerate the Iraqi Governing Council's work could "bring about a sense of sovereignty that makes it possible for a lot of other nations and agencies to deal constructively with Iraq, in terms of both money and personnel."

As these logistical challenges come into greater focus, the question about Iraq is less was the war justified than can the occupation be managed.

"The main issue is that we were destined to win the war, and we won it more quickly than anyone expected, but the administration had a misguided view of what would come after the war," said Judith Kipper, a Middle East analyst at the Council on Foreign Relations. "It was an ideological view, rather than a practical view of the realities of Iraq." She added: "Since the Second World War, no one dances in the streets when they see foreign troops invading their country." ◆

'Jobs, Jobs, Jobs' Mantra Returns to Haunt GOP

Conflicted employment picture could re-emerge as top issue in 2004 election

As the Senate reconvened from its August recess, Majority Leader Bill Frist laid out a truncated but difficult agenda: appropriations, Iraq funding, prescription drug coverage and energy. That same day, Rick Santorum, a Pennsylvanian who heads up the Senate Republican Conference, circulated a memo to his colleagues urging them not to overlook what recent GOP polling showed to be voters' No. 1 concern: jobs.

"The top issue continues to be the economy/jobs. Let me repeat that. The top issue continues to be the economy/jobs," he wrote.

Republicans in Congress and in the White House are increasingly worried about the recovering economy's inability to produce employment opportunities. About 2.7 million jobs have been lost since President Bush took office — almost all of them in manufacturing — and he may become the first White House occupant since Herbert Hoover to see more positions vanish on his watch than are created.

With the election year approaching, administration officials and Republican lawmakers recognize the potency of a jobless rate that is just below a nine-year high. The fear is that the economy's jobless recovery will result in political layoffs next fall.

"Our jobs message is more important than ever, and I cannot stress enough how we need to keep talking about jobs and acting to strengthen the economy," Santorum wrote. "We should prioritize key legislation that has economic benefit, and present it as our fall Jobs and Growth Initiative."

The result is that GOP lawmakers have stepped up efforts to show voters that they are acting to meet the needs of their states and districts: advocating additional tax breaks for manufacturers and arguing for a more careful approach to trade that does not risk shifting more jobs overseas.

The president heralded his new focus on manufacturing jobs during a Labor Day speech in Ohio, where 160,000 factory positions have disappeared in the past three years. Bush assured union members that "better days" lie ahead, as the economy rebounds from a series of heavy blows with the aid of multiple tax cuts he championed.

To show workers in key industrial states that he plans to follow through, Bush proposed creating an assistant secretary position in the Commerce Department to focus attention on manufacturing, the new rallying point for job creation. In Kansas City on Sept. 4, Bush announced a six-point package of new and recycled proposals to spur growth.

As the president offered reassurances, Treasury Secretary John W. Snow scolded China for keeping the value of its currency artificially low. Some business leaders and economists blame currency valuations for making U.S.-made

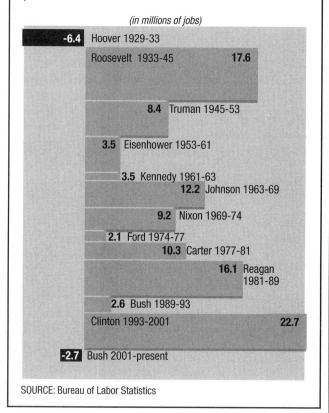

Job Losses Rare In Presidential Terms

No president since Herbert Hoover, who served during the Depression, has seen a net job loss during his time in office. At the current pace, President Bush could share that distinction. Net jobs created or lost during the tenure of presidents since 1929:

(in millions of jobs)

-6.4	Hoover 1929-33
	Roosevelt 1933-45 — 17.6
	8.4 Truman 1945-53
	3.5 Eisenhower 1953-61
	3.5 Kennedy 1961-63
	12.2 Johnson 1963-69
	9.2 Nixon 1969-74
	2.1 Ford 1974-77
	10.3 Carter 1977-81
	16.1 Reagan 1981-89
	2.6 Bush 1989-93
	Clinton 1993-2001 — 22.7
-2.7	Bush 2001-present

SOURCE: Bureau of Labor Statistics

goods more expensive than imports from China and other countries.

But the administration was playing catch-up. The day after Bush unveiled his manufacturing czar, the government announced that the economy lost 93,000 more jobs in August. While the White House has maintained for months that the tax cuts it supported would eventually create jobs, lawmakers in both parties responded much earlier to their constituents' anxiety over persistent unemployment and continuing job losses in manufacturing.

Democrats would delight in reprising the campaign theme that worked so well against Bush's father, who was the incumbent president 12 years ago when the economy's weak performance was issue No. 1. Democrats have been telling voters that the administration is ignoring the fact that jobs are vanishing and unemployment remains high despite Bush's tax cuts.

"After losing more than 3 million jobs since he took office, President Bush will need to do much more than just add one at the Commerce Department," said House Minority Leader Nancy Pelosi, D-Calif.

Rep. Tim Ryan, an Ohio Democrat representing Youngstown and part of Akron, said his constituents think Bush has been "asleep at the wheel" in his role as guardian of the economy. "If I heard it once, I heard a thousand times that he is beginning to look like his father," Ryan said. "People are beginning to wonder when the answer to everything is a tax cut."

Not Enough Good News

The widening awareness of job losses comes as the economy, including manufacturing, shows new signs of life in the aftermath of a recession that ran from March to November 2001. Some lawmakers and economists say the current 6.1 percent unemployment rate is modest compared with joblessness following previous recessions.

Bush, who took office just two months before the economy fell into its slump, argues that even with a push from tax cuts, growth needs time to bounce back from the effects of war on terrorism, the war with Iraq and a series of corporate scandals.

But the job creation that the administration said its tax cuts would trigger has yet to materialize. The president's Council of Economic Advisers predicted in February — before enactment of an additional $350 billion in tax cuts in May (PL 108-27) — that 510,000 jobs would be gained in 2003 and 891,000 in 2004. Instead, the economy lost 437,000 positions through the first eight months of this year.

Factory employment has declined in each of the past 37 months. Textile- and steel-state lawmakers warn that those industries are in danger of disappearing from the domestic economy. Textile mills employ about 250,000 fewer workers than they did a decade ago, and about 160,000 of those jobs have been eliminated in the past three years.

The wave of layoffs has not been confined to the nation's traditional industry giants. Computer and electronics manu-

> But the job creation that the administration said its tax cuts would trigger has yet to materialize.

facturers have eliminated 475,000 jobs in the past three years, leaving Silicon Valley and other communities reeling.

Economists explain manufacturing job losses as a natural product of an evolving economy. As Federal Reserve Board Chairman Alan Greenspan told the Senate Banking Com-

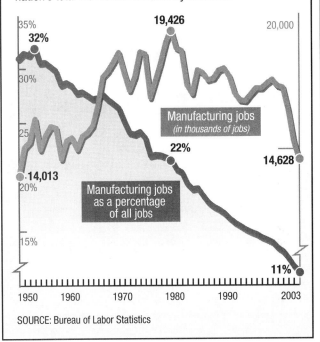

Factory Employment Slides

The number of manufacturing workers in the United States has had its ups and downs since 1950, peaking in 1979. But factory manpower has taken a nosedive since 1998 as a result of a recession, steady improvement in productivity and a growing trade deficit. Manufacturing's share of the nation's total workforce has steadily declined.

19,426

32%

20,000

Manufacturing jobs
(in thousands of jobs)

22%

14,628

14,013

Manufacturing jobs as a percentage of all jobs

11%

1950   1960   1970   1980   1990   2003

SOURCE: Bureau of Labor Statistics

mittee on July 16, a smaller percentage of Americans than ever before are "making stuff." Even before the current slide began, the number of factory workers was about the same as the figure in the early 1970s, although the nation's population had grown by 70 million people.

"[Management guru] Peter Drucker told us 30 years ago the days of the high-wage, blue-collar worker were gone forever," said former Rep. Bill Frenzel, R-Minn. (1971-91), now a guest scholar at the Brookings Institution. He noted that Americans once worried about the exodus from farm employment to factories the way they now fret over the shift to service industries.

But evolution is not the only explanation that rings true to those lawmakers whose constituents are waiting in the unemployment line.

House Small Business Committee Chairman Donald Manzullo, R-Ill., said manufacturing jobs moving overseas are not being replaced by comparable numbers of the high-tech, high-wage jobs Americans were told to expect as the economy evolved in an era of free trade. In fact, he added, white-collar jobs also are leaving the country.

"I think Democrats are starting to see this as a more significant issue, even those in the free-trade camp," said Rep. Robert T. Matsui of California, chairman of the Democratic Congressional Campaign Committee.

Democratic presidential candidates have turned up the heat on the incumbent. Sen. Joseph I. Lieberman of Connecticut blasted Bush for not moving aggressively against China's alleged trade practices. Massachusetts Sen. John

Kerry charged that Bush's policies are "destroying America's economic security." And Rep. Richard A. Gephardt of Missouri said he has been fighting what he sees as harmful trade policies longer and harder than his rivals.

Tired of seeing Democrats monopolize the jobs issue, Republicans welcomed the president to the cause of saving manufacturing jobs.

> **"** *The president, who has always believed manufacturing was an important sector, now realizes it is the important sector.* **"**
>
> — Donald Manzullo, R-Ill.
> House Small Business
> Committee Chairman

"I am happy that more and more members are thinking through our economic strategies," said Rep. Phil English, a Republican who represents a manufacturing district centered in Erie, Pa. "The administration is clearly gearing up on the issue but needs to show results — quickly."

Rep. Chris Chocola, R-Ind., said unemployment was his constituents' leading concern during the August congressional recess, outweighing questions about U.S. policy in Iraq, although the jobless rate in his district is below the national average. GOP Rep. Vernon J. Ehlers of Michigan reported that "it was just China, jobs, China, jobs, in meeting after meeting."

"What the president has realized is that the prophesies that said employment is cyclical were not correct," Manzullo said. "The president, who has always believed manufacturing was an important sector, now realizes it is *the* important sector."

Ryan and Manzullo head the newly formed House Manufacturing Caucus. Members of both parties from Southern states that have lost textile jobs and the Northern states of the Rust Belt are among the charter members.

Congress Seeks Solutions

As job losses mount, Bush's pursuit of tax cuts and trade agreements and his administration's willingness to live with record budget deficits are likely to come under increasing attack on Capitol Hill. New tax breaks for manufacturers might gain momentum. But free-trade agreements could drop lower on the administration's agenda.

Policymakers are concerned that there are few tools left in the box to stimulate job creation and economic growth. Interest rates have been cut to 50-year lows, nearly $2 trillion in tax relief is either already flowing into the economy or on its way, and government spending on war and homeland security has accelerated.

Jared Bernstein of the Economic Policy Institute, a liberal think tank, said that despite some positive indicators, the economy is not poised for a "virtuous cycle" that generally marks a rapid escape from recession — a big boost in con-

sumption, business investment, job growth, income gains and consumption, all adding up to a self-sustaining recovery. The tax cuts provided by Congress and the windfalls many homeowners have collected by refinancing their mortgages cannot provide the type of economic boost that would result from larger payrolls, Bernstein said.

A recent report prepared by economists at the Federal Reserve Bank of New York explained that structural changes in the economy may mean that many old jobs are gone for good and it will take more time to create new ones.

Nevertheless, members of Congress have offered a variety of remedies for the decline in factory employment.

In the spring, House Ways and Means Trade Subcommittee Chairman Philip M. Crane, R-Ill., teamed up with the full committee's ranking Democrat, Charles B. Rangel of New York, and Manzullo to sponsor a bill (HR 1769) that would give manufacturers a tax incentive to keep jobs in the United States. The impetus for the legislation was a World Trade Organization ruling that an existing corporate tax break for exporters is an unfair trade subsidy. But the bill, along with a competing measure (HR 2896) sponsored by Ways and Means Chairman Bill Thomas, R-Calif., are being touted as job-creation measures.

On Sept. 10, Michigan Democratic lawmakers proposed a 14-point plan to boost manufacturing that included federal assistance to help employers meet health and pension costs, steps to make international competition fairer, and more federal funding for the Manufacturing Extension Partnership and Advanced Technology Program.

Bush has embraced a plan by freshman Michigan Republican Rep. Thaddeus McCotter to create an assistant secretary of Commerce for manufacturing (HR 2172). The sponsor of the Senate version of that legislation (S 1326) was Ohio Republican George V. Voinovich.

Rep. Robert B. Aderholt, R-Ala., added language to the committee report on the fiscal 2004 spending bill for the Transportation and Treasury departments (HR 2989) that would tell the Treasury Department to report to Congress when countries manipulated their currencies to gain a competitive advantage in trade.

English offered legislation (HR 3058) that would impose tariffs on Chinese imports to counter the effects of China's devaluation of its yuan. Lieberman and Sen. Charles E. Schumer, D-N.Y., have offered similar measures (S 1592, S 1586).

Economists say factories have reduced their payrolls for a number of reasons. Demand for the high-end products Americans make is soft as the global economy remains weak. And U.S. manufacturers are constantly learning how to produce more with fewer workers on their assembly lines.

But the favorite scapegoat among lawmakers is the allegedly unfair competition that U.S. manufacturers face from overseas. Critics of U.S. trade policy say the persistent loss of manufacturing jobs validates their warnings that free-trade pacts and the Bush administration's lax enforcement of trade laws consign American workers to a "race to the bottom" with lower-paid workers in Asia and elsewhere.

"No one cares about trade policy in the boom times," said Barry P. Bosworth, a senior fellow at Brookings. "But whenever you get into the bad times, there is a drive to look at imbalance of trade because you are looking for someone to blame."

When legislation to implement free-trade agreements with Chile (PL 108-77) and Singapore (PL 108-78) was debated in the House and Senate in July, job losses were the centerpiece of an unsuccessful campaign by opponents to derail them. (*2003 CQ Weekly, p. 1985*)

Free-traders have long argued that globalism will reallocate jobs, leaving Americans with better-paying employment. Such reassurances helped overcome opposition to the removal of trade barriers during the 1990s, and helped President Bill Clinton win backing for the North American Free Trade Agreement (NAFTA). Robust U.S. economic growth in the second half of the last decade overwhelmed warnings of erosion of the nation's industrial base.

But Bosworth and others conceded that the economic ship supporting free trade has now sprung a leak.

House Ways and Means Trade Subcommittee ranking Democrat Sander M. Levin of Michigan and other lawmakers argue that the trade debate should focus on the administration's efforts to enforce the ground rules for expanded commerce.

In May, Republican Frank R. Wolf of Virginia used a hearing of the House Appropriations Commerce, Justice, State and the Judiciary Subcommittee, which he chairs, to challenge the administration's trade enforcement. The panel's fiscal 2004 spending bill (HR 2799) would provide the U.S. Trade Representative's office with $5 million more than requested and direct the Commerce Department to better monitor China's trade conduct.

Max Baucus of Montana, the top Democrat on the Senate Finance Committee, has introduced legislation (S 676) that would establish a commission of retired judges to review World Trade Organization (WTO) rulings to determine if the United States has been treated fairly.

Tough Choices on Trade

Second only to the world trade body on the lawmakers' list of villains is China.

Frank Vargo, a vice president for the National Association of Manufacturers (NAM), said the $100 billion U.S. trade deficit with China last year would have been much smaller had China not undervalued its currency, making its exports less expensive.

Snow won commitments from the Chinese to address the issue at some unspecified time. Manufacturing groups will press for more action.

"You've got to start somewhere," Vargo said of Snow's effort. "It isn't often that you see a secretary of the Treasury telling a foreign country to let their currency float."

Bosworth said manufacturers are entitled to be angry about China's currency deflation. But he cautioned against attributing too many U.S. job losses to competition from Chinese imports. China, he noted, had nothing to do with job losses in high-technology industries.

U.S. Chamber of Commerce lobbyist William J. Morley said currency manipulation is a problem, but noted that American companies that manufacture overseas benefit from the strength of the dollar.

Litigation costs and tax policies also make it difficult for U.S. companies to compete globally, Morley said.

Bush and backers of free trade maintain that their faith is unshaken by U.S. manufacturing job losses. "NAM has not done a good job explaining that free-trade agreements are not the culprit," Vargo said. "It is the solution."

State-by-State Job Losses

Figures compiled by the National Association of Manufacturers show that 48 states suffered net losses of manufacturing jobs between July 2000 and June 2003. Nationwide, more than 2.6 million factory jobs disappeared during that period. Nevada gained 100 jobs, and North Dakota's factory employment was unchanged.

States losing the most jobs:

New York 129,100
Pennsylvania 136,000
Mich. 162,300
California 280,600
Illinois 140,900
Ohio 160,400
Indiana 87,300
North Carolina 151,000
Texas 151,800
Georgia 80,800

SOURCES: NAM, Bureau of Labor Statistics

When Bush signed the Chile and Singapore implementing legislation on Sept. 3, he said free trade produces jobs for Americans. The president called on world trade officials headed to Cancun, Mexico, during the week of Sept. 8 to do their best to get back on track the world trade talks launched in Doha, Qatar, two years ago.

But winning congressional acceptance of new trade agreements may prove difficult, particularly if employment fails to rebound.

The proposed Central American Free Trade Agreement, which the administration hopes to conclude by the end of the year and send to Congress in 2004, may be slowed, lawmakers warned. Levin said Bush will have to work hard to assemble majority support for that agreement.

Concern over manufacturing job losses may make it politically difficult for Bush to remove tariffs he imposed in 2002 on some steel imports in response to charges of unfair trade.

The ranks of steelworkers had thinned to 225,000 by 2000, or about half of the industry's 1980 workforce. The losses have been slowed by the tariffs, but the WTO has ruled that they were an improper trade barrier and must be removed. The administration is deciding how to respond, and lawmakers from Ohio, Pennsylvania, Indiana and West Virginia are determined to keep them in place. Members from districts that are home to other manufacturers are eager to scuttle import barriers that have made a raw material used by their industries more expensive.

The steel tariffs fulfilled a Bush campaign promise, and steel-state lawmakers — including English, who heads the Congressional Steel Caucus — warn that backtracking would hurt Bush in their states next year.

Free-traders are dismayed that Bush imposed the tariffs, and insist that the United States cannot promote a free-trade agenda to the rest of the world while maintaining steel tariffs in defiance of a WTO ruling.

Administration Prepares a Policy

In addition to proposing a manufacturing czar at Commerce, the administration plans to unveil by the end of September a "white paper" on aid to manufacturers.

Undersecretary of Commerce for International Trade Grant D. Aldonas said Bush previewed some of the proposals in his Kansas City speech. They include protecting companies from some types of litigation, easing some federal regulations, helping companies reduce health care costs, and preventing them from being required to put larger amounts of money into their employee pension plans. The president's six-point plan also includes making sure energy sources are affordable and reliable, expanding trade opportunities and making permanent the tax cuts already enacted.

The administration is also looking at ways to help small and medium-sized manufacturers acquire advanced technology and train workers, Aldonas added. NAM officials recently told a government panel that the United States will suffer a shortage of workers with needed skills unless training and education improve.

Aldonas said the administration's initiatives are products of nearly a year of active work on manufacturing issues. He dismissed attempts by Democrats to paint the administration as disengaged.

But Thea Lee, the AFL-CIO's assistant director for international economics, called the proposal to create a new assistant Commerce secretary "lame," and chided the administration for being slow to react to the drumbeat of factory job cuts. "It is unlikely his job record will be any better a year from now," she said. "And that is a good thing."

The recovery continues to send mixed signals about its strength and significance for workers. According to the most recent data from the Labor Department, even as companies pare their payrolls, the economy is expanding and productivity is rising, surging at a 6.8 percent annual rate during the second quarter of 2003. That's twice as fast as worker efficiency increased at the end of the 1990s and suggests that businesses need less manpower to grow.

Economists say it is not unusual for joblessness to persist well into a recovery — a potential political problem for the ad-

> *The recovery continues to send mixed signals about its strength and significance for workers.*

ministration. "I've got a manufacturing district," English said. "We usually come out of a recession six months later than everyone else."

Amid the good news for the manufacturing sector in recent months is an increase in orders for durable goods in July, as well as increases in business investment in May, June and July.

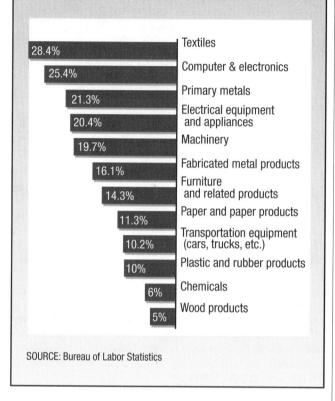

Hard-Hit Manufacturing Jobs

More than 1.8 million manufacturing jobs have been lost since the beginning of 2001. The computer and electronics industry lost 475,000 jobs, and machinery producers lost 286,000. The textile industry was particularly hard hit, losing 291,000 jobs — more than one of every four. Below are the industries losing the largest percentages of their workforces:

- Textiles — 28.4%
- Computer & electronics — 25.4%
- Primary metals — 21.3%
- Electrical equipment and appliances — 20.4%
- Machinery — 19.7%
- Fabricated metal products — 16.1%
- Furniture and related products — 14.3%
- Paper and paper products — 11.3%
- Transportation equipment (cars, trucks, etc.) — 10.2%
- Plastic and rubber products — 10%
- Chemicals — 6%
- Wood products — 5%

SOURCE: Bureau of Labor Statistics

Republicans insist Bush is not in serious trouble. The GOP did well in the 2002 congressional elections, they note, in a worse economic climate.

Ehlers said voters know there are limits to what Congress and the president can do to improve the economy. "The mere fact that recessions exist means we can't control them," he said. "We can only tinker around the edges."

With Hoover's legacy and his father's fate in mind, Bush appears eager to acknowledge that manufacturing job losses are a problem and demonstrate his administration's willingness to help U.S. companies and workers.

What voters will care about are the results of the administration's economic policies, Chocola said. And economists do not rule out an acceleration of economic growth to 5 percent toward the end of the year and into 2004.

As Santorum's warning suggested, the timing will be important to Bush and Republican congressional candidates. The economy had begun a recovery in 1992, but it came too late to help Bush's father win re-election.

"If they do not have anything by the end of the year, people will have made up their minds," Bosworth predicted.

For Hoover, better days never came. Instead, he lost the 1932 election to the strains of "Happy Days Are Here Again" that heralded the economic program of Franklin D. Roosevelt and a revived Democratic Party. ◆

Government Institutions

The articles in this section provide insight into the inner workings of the major institutions of American government, focusing in turn on the presidency, Congress and the judiciary.

The first article in the Congress section features Representative Bill Thomas, a California Republican who is chairman of the Ways and Means Committee. Thomas has become one of the most effective members of Congress and has restored his committee—which has the broadest policy jurisdiction in the House of Representatives—to its powerful reputation of years past.

The next two articles discuss questions that have been raised about the veracity and reliability of intelligence reports regarding the presence of weapons of mass destruction in Iraq. Some in Congress fear that without proof that Saddam Hussein was armed with such weapons, the United States, and Congress itself, will lose credibility. The inclusion in President Bush's State of the Union speech of a discredited allegation about attempts by Iraq to buy bomb-making uranium in Africa has awakened bipartisan interest in congressional hearings.

The last article in this section takes readers inside congressional caucuses. In the past, caucuses provided a way for lawmakers with common interests to plan legislative strategy. As these informal organizations have proliferated, they have become powerful lobbying forces that fundamentally change the way interest groups pursue their legislative agendas.

The four articles in the presidency section return to the issue of President Bush's widening "credibility gap." His once-solid footing in Congress—and in public opinion polls—is on softer ground. For most of 2003, Bush enjoyed a strong relationship with Congress. But by the fall, Republicans once solidly allied with their president had begun to raise concerns over his supplemental spending request for Iraq and Afghanistan, the continued U.S. occupation of Iraq and climbing postwar casualties, the stubbornly high U.S. unemployment rate and the ballooning budget deficit. If the strains in the Bush–Congress relationship continue into 2004, it could make it more difficult for Republicans to present a unified front as they campaign to keep a one-party government in place beyond the 2004 elections.

The first two articles in the judiciary section examine the Senate's contentious fight over appellate court nominations. Stung by Democratic filibusters blocking appeals court nominees, Senate Republicans may drop the "blue slip" policy that allows home-state senators to halt nominations by a single objection. Such a step would make the judicial appointment process even more contentious; that it is being considered illustrates the erosion of traditional Senate norms. Congressional members also debated the role of anti-Catholic sentiment in Democrats' resistance to some nominees.

The third article discusses the passage by the House of a bill banning "partial birth" abortion, a huge win for abortion foes. But even after the bill clears Congress and President Bush signs it into law—both considered inevitable—the fight will continue, as abortion rights advocates are ready to challenge the law in federal courts.

The last article examines the Supreme Court's ruling that Congress acted within its authority in writing a law that required libraries and schools to install filtering software on computers to block pornography. The ruling reaffirmed the constitutionality of Congress's making policy through the appropriations process.

A Rough but Steady Hand At Helm of Ways and Means

Chairman Thomas boosts his panel's stature with a feel for power and partisanship

Bill Thomas makes a point about his plan to add prescription drug coverage to Medicare at a rally June 26, the day before the House passed the bill. Behind Thomas are Rep. Billy Tauzin, R-La., chairman of the Energy and Commerce Committee, and Speaker Hastert.

The story of how the $350 billion tax cut of 2003 was finally drawn is the story of how Bill Thomas told the president of the United States just how things had to be. And that tells the story of Bill Thomas, who may be the most potent legislator in Congress.

Back in April, Thomas, a California Republican and chairman of the House Ways and Means Committee, wrote a bill to trim the tax rate on corporate dividends and capital gains to 15 percent. That was in contrast to the bill the Senate had forced on Finance Committee Chairman Charles E. Grassley, R-Iowa. Following President Bush's own proposal, the Senate bill focused strictly on complete elimination of the tax that investors pay on dividends, and ignored capital gains altogether.

So in mid-May, with each chamber having passed different versions of the bill and with little scent of compromise in the wind, the two men were summoned to the White House along with three GOP leaders: House Speaker J. Dennis Hastert of Illinois, House Majority Leader Tom DeLay of Texas and Senate Majority Leader Bill Frist of Tennessee.

It was there that Thomas, a former political science professor, explained to Bush that while the Senate bill stayed true to the president's vision, "the structure didn't make sense." The tax break would end too soon, and it would fail to require companies to pay income taxes before distributing dividends tax-free. That last oversight would do more than end double taxation of corporate profits — Bush's goal — it would allow them to be tax-free altogether.

Worse still, Thomas informed the president, Senate rules would forbid inserting a new provision in conference to fix the problem.

The meeting disbanded with participants expecting negotiations to resume the next day. But Thomas stayed behind and pressed the president to accept the House approach as the only way to get a bill enacted before Congress recessed for Memorial Day.

Senate rules would, in fact, permit the corporate tax problem to be fixed in conference. But by the time Senate aides got that message to the White House a few hours later, it was already too late. Thomas had won the day; he and Bush sealed a deal to bring the House version of the tax cut out of the conference. A week later it was law (PL 108-27). (*2003 CQ Weekly, p. 1245*)

The performance was vintage Thomas, proffering his view of Senate rules, whether correct or not, to win a point. Using preparation, bluff and bluster, he has gotten his way at every major turn since triumphing over the seniority system to grab the Ways and Means gavel in January 2001. In the process, Thomas has directed his wrath at his GOP colleagues almost as readily as at his Democratic adversaries.

With the committee's sweeping jurisdiction and Thomas' drive, he has steered three major tax cuts — totaling almost $2 trillion over 11 years — and an overhaul of trade policy into law.

Now, Thomas faces two more major challenges in this Congress: completing the biggest change in Medicare since the program was created 40 years ago, and revising the tax code for international business by Jan. 1 to prevent European countries from imposing $4 billion in sanctions on U.S. exports. He, no doubt, expects to get his way on both of them.

His enemies and friends alike speak of his arrogance and partisanship. But in his 2fi year tenure as chairman, Thomas has restored the clout and prestige of Ways and Means to where it was a decade ago, when then-Chairman Dan Rostenkowski, D-Ill. (1959-95), told an audience of reporters and editors: "I am the House."

When asked who holds the reins of power, Thomas says he understands his position, but he also knows he carries authority, too. "The Speaker is the most powerful," Thomas said in an interview June 26. "The chairman of the Rules Committee is very powerful, but he follows the lead of the Speaker. I'm chairman of Ways and Means."

If the Speaker wanted to take a different tack on a particular bill, Thomas said, "I might have a discussion about it."

Ways and Means' stature was diminished in 1994 when Rostenkowski was indicted on criminal charges and stepped aside after 13 years as chairman. He had been credited with helping manage a wholesale overhaul of tax law in 1986 (PL 99-514), a rewrite of trade law in 1988 (PL 100-418) and several tax increases in the early 1990s that helped put the federal budget on a path toward surplus. (*1986 CQ Almanac, p. 491, 1988 CQ Almanac, p. 209*)

The two men who led the committee in the interim, Sam Gibbons, D-Fla. (1963-97), and Bill Archer, R-Texas (1971-2001), could count few such accomplishments between them. (*Chairmen, p. 49*)

His Own Way

Thomas is different. He is not an ideological visionary like Archer, who hoped, but failed, to scrap the multitiered progressive income tax code in

favor of a national sales tax. Thomas may be less ambitious, but he is much more effective at getting bills enacted, which has given rise to the notion that he is nothing more than Bush's quarterback or delivery man. Yet he is clearly charting his own agenda to turn bills into laws.

Last year, Thomas was told to write a bill adding prescription drug coverage to Medicare so Republican House members could cast a politically popular vote on the issue before the 2002 elections.

He did so, but tediously created a measure that he thought might get through the House and help him in conference, even though the Senate had no intention of acting on the issue.

This year, Thomas produced a new bill, (HR 1) that passed 216-215 less than two weeks ago, with some heavy arm-twisting by the White House and GOP leadership. The Senate has acted this time on a different measure (S 1) , but Thomas' success in conference has yet to be measured. (*Medicare, p. 103*)

Even so, DeLay, with whom the less ideological Thomas has an uneasy relationship at times, credits him with taking steps both to revive the economy and reinvent Medicare.

"He is the center," DeLay said June 26, the eve of the vote on Medicare. "It's a stellar performance." (*Thomas' record, p. 48*)

Abrasive, Abusive, Partisan

Some critics say Thomas could be even more effective if he were not so adamant about how things ought to be done. His proposal for realigning U.S. tax law on foreign transactions to comply with international law and avoid a trade war with Europe has sparked a rare uprising among Republicans on his committee, where an alternative Democratic measure is more popular. (*2003 CQ Weekly, p. 1528*)

And his success on complex issues has been paired with difficulties on what appear to be simpler matters.

Over the spring, Thomas attached a controversial health care provision to a popular bill (HR 1528) that would overhaul IRS filing procedures and help millions of taxpayers, nearly killing it. Sponsor Rob Portman, R-Ohio, said adding the health care amendment was Thomas' decision. The bill finally passed the House on June 19 after it was pulled from the floor schedule twice, but now the Senate has shown little interest in acting

47

on it. (*2003 CQ Weekly, p. 1556*)

Another bill (HR 1664), to provide tax breaks to military personnel, was thought to be headed for quick passage during the Iraq war. But the measure, which passed the House three times in various forms this year, has withered, partly because Thomas initially made it a Christmas tree of tax breaks for obscure industries, from off-track bettors to makers of bows and arrows. (*2003 CQ Weekly, p. 870*)

Thomas' legendary partisanship is frequently on display.

Ten years ago, he accused Speaker Thomas S. Foley, D-Wash. (1965-95), on the House floor of asking Attorney General Janet Reno to seal files on a scandal at the House Post Office. Thomas later apologized and admitted he had no evidence.

In March 2003, he accused Democratic Sen. Dianne Feinstein of lacking "guts" on the medical malpractice issue. He wrongly attributed Feinstein's position, similar to his own, to the fact that she was facing re-election in their shared home state of California, while her term runs to 2006. He apologized hours later.

Last year, in the House tussle over the trade bill, he labeled questions from Florida Democrat Alcee L. Hastings "dumb and outlandish." A week earlier, he was challenged on the floor for using the phrase "Maloney baloney," in referring to Jim Maloney, D-Conn. (1997-2003).

But he has likewise been known to play hardball with fellow Republicans.

Grassley was aghast when Thomas stormed out of a negotiating session in late May as they tried to put the finishing touches on the tax bill.

"I hope to educate Mr. Thomas in the next month that he ought to show a little more respect to people of equal rank," Grassley said. "I've never walked out on him, and I think I deserve equal consideration. He's a very conflicting guy."

And Nancy L. Johnson, R-Conn., chairman of the Ways and Means Health Subcommittee, speaks from personal experience about Thomas' demeanor. "He doesn't pussyfoot around," Johnson said. "If you've got a dumb idea, he'll tell you that you've got a dumb idea."

Johnson felt the sting of Thomas' heavy-handedness when she took over the Health Subcommittee from him at the time he claimed the full committee chairmanship two and a half years ago.

Making Law Is Job No. 1 For California's Thomas

Since becoming chairman of the House Ways and Means Committee in January 2001, Thomas has compiled an enviable record of accomplishments that led The Wall Street Journal on May 22, in an editorial headlined "President Thomas," to say he was "about to impose his will on American tax policy." The following day, Congress cleared the third major tax cut bill in three years.

MAJOR LAWS

- Economic Growth and Tax Relief Reconciliation Act of 2001 (PL 107-16). Cut taxes by $1.35 trillion through 2011. Signed June 7, 2001.

- Job Creation and Worker Assistance Act of 2002 (PL 107-147). Provided short-term business investment tax breaks worth $42 billion to stimulate the economy. Signed March 9, 2002.

- Trade Act of 2002 (PL 107-210). Restored the president's power to negotiate trade pacts with foreign countries that Congress cannot alter and may only accept or reject. Signed Aug. 6, 2002.

- Jobs and Growth Tax Relief Reconciliation Act of 2003 (PL 108-27). Cut taxes by $350 billion through 2013. Signed May 28, 2003.

MINOR LAWS

- Fallen Hero Survivor Benefit Fairness Act of 2001 (PL 107-15). Made survivor benefits tax-free to families of public safety officers killed in the line of duty. Signed June 5, 2001.

- Railroad Retirement and Survivors' Improvement Act of 2001 (PL 107-90). Authorized $4 billion to improve benefits of railroad workers. Signed Dec. 21, 2001.

- Victims of Terrorism Relief Act (PL 107-134). Authorized $360 million in tax relief to those killed or injured in Sept. 11 attacks or 1995 Oklahoma City bombing. Signed Jan. 23, 2002.

- Clergy Housing Allowance Clarification Act of 2002 (PL 107-181). Cracked down on $33 million in excessive clergy deductions on homes and furniture. Signed May 20, 2002.

Thomas installed his top health care aide, John E. McManus, as the subcommittee's chief of staff, and he did not allow his Medicare bill to go through Johnson's subcommittee.

Knowledge Is Power

In the 24 years since Thomas arrived on Capitol Hill, he has not only accumulated power, he has shown he has the wiles to use it.

"Knowledge is what's powerful, not your position," Thomas said.

It helps that Thomas' position is at the top of Ways and Means, which has the broadest policy jurisdiction in the House. It oversees taxes, trade, health care, Social Security, retirement, unemployment and welfare. Because tax incentives are used to promote so many national policies, the committee's jurisdiction is even larger than it appears, playing a major role in energy, charitable giving and transportation.

Thomas works hard. Armed with file folders and analyses, he comes to meetings, no matter how insignificant, wanting to be better prepared than his adversaries — or his would-be allies, as happened in the meeting at the White House.

"At the end of the day, people — if they're open-minded — would think I have a better argument as to the course we should take," Thomas said, in explaining his legislative success. "But that's always done on the basis of presentation of information and analysis, not because I'm 'powerful.' "

Age is barely slowing Thomas down. At 61, he rises at 4:30 a.m. to read policy briefs. "I don't retain things well at night," he said.

Thomas' distinctive speech pattern, possibly one of the most mimicked on Capitol Hill, uses the enunciation of Strother Martin, the character actor who played the prison camp captain in "Cool Hand Luke." Thomas does not mispronounce words, but adds extra stress to the dominant syllable, accentuating his tendency toward pedantry. ("I don't care about the POL-i-tics, I care about the POL-i-cy," he is fond of saying.)

Yet Thomas' attention to detail can charm visitors and aides, as he recalls tiny aspects of their lives and families to flatter them and demonstrate that he cares. Once he interrupted a scrum of reporters' questions to tell an industry trade reporter that he had seen her on television the previous day and offered advice for improving her performance.

Thomas mostly pens legislation solo inside his Capitol hideaway along the same secluded corridor as the Capitol physician's office. He has a two-room suite: One room holds nothing more than a conference table, encircled by an outer ring of chairs against the walls. It serves both as Thomas' desk and as his negotiating venue.

Aides are always flitting about, commuting between the committee suite in the Longworth House Office Building and the Capitol hideaway. One tax aide, always on his mobile phone, is rarely far from Thomas' side.

But Great Results

In markups and in conference battles, Thomas pursues a brutal all-or-nothing course that leaves egos battered and bruised.

Ways and Means member Jim McCrery, R-La., calls Thomas one of the best negotiators he has ever seen. He portrays Thomas as a Republican version of Bill Clinton, with a mastery of minutiae and an ability to own a situation.

"I normally have an idea of what we should do and can back it up with a lot of evidence," Thomas said. He anticipates rebuttals from his colleagues and prepares counterarguments. In tense budget negotiations with the Senate this spring, Thomas was ready for any outcome, fully plotting how to produce a dozen different tax cut packages ranging from $350 billion to $726 billion.

It is hard to argue with results. Soon after taking over the chairmanship in 2001, Thomas helped deliver Bush's first tax cut, a 10-year plan that slashed revenue by $1.35 trillion principally by lowering individual income tax rates (PL 107-16). To fit almost all of Bush's proposed $1.6 trillion in cuts under a compromise ceiling, Thomas joined with Senate tax writers to limit cost by phasing in tax breaks. *(2001 CQ Almanac, p. 18-3)*

Thomas used a similar tactic even more boldly this year, condensing $1 trillion in tax cuts into $350 billion by setting early expiration dates. Most political analysts presume that Congress will never let the cuts expire and will vote to extend them, meaning the cost estimates were illusory.

The result of using these budget devices is that tax accountants have needed complicated matrix charts to figure out when new lower rates phased in and out. Still, Republicans were able to claim they had eliminated the estate tax, even if only for one year.

In 2002, Thomas pushed through Bush's second tax cut of $42 billion in business tax breaks (PL 107-147), intended to boost the sluggish economy. *(2002 CQ Weekly, p. 633)*

As soon as the stimulus measure was signed into law, Thomas moved on to dozens of stalled free-trade agreements. He engineered enactment of a bill (PL 107-210) to break the logjam by giving the president the authority to negotiate a final pact that Congress could not alter and had to either accept or reject.

Thomas virtually bypassed the official party whip organization, run at the time by DeLay, and assembled his own head-counting operation to figure out exactly how many votes he needed and what he would have to give away to House members from industrially depressed districts who were uneasy about supporting liberalized trade.

At 3:05 a.m. on July 27, 2002, Thomas walked over to Rep. Adam H. Putnam, a Republican citrus grower from Florida, and handed him a manila folder. Moments later, Putnam cast his "aye" vote for the conference report on the measure. Inside the folder was a letter Thomas had secured from U.S. Trade Representative Robert B. Zoellick, asking Putnam to assemble a task force of citrus industry leaders to advise him on the best way to open overseas markets to Florida's crops.

The bill squeaked through the House and into law with a three-vote margin, and Thomas later quipped to his aides that he had two votes too many — he had given away too much. *(2002 CQ Weekly, p. 2201)*

Poor Beginnings

Thomas was born on the eve of the Japanese attack on Pearl Harbor to a working-class family in the mining hills of Idaho. Soon after, his family

How Past Chairmen Made Their Mark

Archer

Bill Archer, R-Texas (1995-2001), turned down a run for the Senate to hold the gavel. Undercut by the newly empowered GOP leadership, Archer did fashion a $275 billion tax cut in 1997, the first major reduction since 1981.

Rostenkowski

Dan Rostenkowski, D-Ill. (1981-94), reclaimed the chairman's historical function of power broker. His career ended after he was caught in the House Post Office scandal. **Sam Gibbons,** D-Fla. (1963-97), was acting chairman for the rest of the 103rd Congress.

Ullman

Al Ullman D-Ore. (1975-81), had a permissive leadership style that flowed from the post-Watergate era. Ullman delegated authority to his six subcommittee chairmen and broke with tradition, opening many committee meetings to the public.

Mills

Wilbur D. Mills, D-Ark. (1958-75), was the longest serving chairman in the panel's history. His legendary record of accomplishment came in part from carefully selecting committee members, so his bills had widespread support in the House.

moved to the West Coast in search of work and lived in government housing projects. Jobs were so scarce that his father, a union plumber and pipe fitter, took an 18-month contract in Saudi Arabia after World War II.

With that money, the family bought a first car and a house in Orange County, where Thomas eventually attended Santa Ana Community College. He later received bachelor's and master's degrees from San Francisco State University — the first in his family to receive a college education.

"There's no wealth in my background," said Thomas, whose only employment before his election to the state legislature in 1974 was as a community college teacher. After four years in the California Assembly, he was elected in 1978 to a House seat that had been held since 1973 by Republican William Ketchum, who died that year following the June primary. While Thomas had to fight to win that first nomination, he has managed to win re-election easily since. (*Thomas at home, p. 50*)

He has found success calling himself a pragmatic conservative. "I understand the need and difficulty in making money," he said. "If you don't really have a starter batch, you can never really get the sourdough bread going. I'm very sensitive to enabling whatever an average person needs to accumulate their own wealth and pass it on."

The Tinkerer

An interest in the money woes of middle-income families may explain his favoring elimination of the estate tax and giving tax breaks for saving.

Thomas remains relatively less well off than his millionaire colleagues in Congress. Along with his congressional salary of $154,700 this year, he reports no income from investments on his financial disclosure reports.

He was close to his mother and his three sisters, who taught him to sew. His last project was denim slip covers for two recliners at his home. "Denim wears well, has a rustic look to it. It looked fine," Thomas said.

Not only can he sew, Thomas can repair a sewing machine. And he restores vintage sports cars, recently refurbishing a yellow 1971 MGB-GT that he sold to a former student "for an extremely low amount." He's looking for a new project, but said he has not yet found one he can afford.

Tinkering is something Thomas has in common with Speaker Hastert, who collects old fire engines. The two bonded over discussions of their mechanical hobbies, and that helped when Thomas sought to become Ways and Means chairman after Archer's retirement in 2001.

In typical fashion, Thomas engineered his promotion through a deft maneuver. Phillip M. Crane, a Republican from Hastert's Illinois delegation, was No. 2 to Archer and in line to take over. But his reputation over more than two decades in the House was of a low-profile member with episodic interest in legislating.

Thomas, who was next in seniority, did not appeal to GOP leaders directly, asking panel members instead to sign a letter to Hastert urging the GOP leadership to appoint Thomas. Two-thirds of the Ways and Means Republicans signed on.

"Either [the leadership] had to say the people we put on Ways and Means weren't as good as we thought they were because we're not going to honor how they think the committee ought to go, or they had to seriously take [the petition] into consideration," Thomas said.

Crane's consolation prize was to hold the chairmanship of the Trade Subcommittee, despite a term limiting rule that would have required him to give that up, too. But when it came time to re-enact the president's trade negotiating authority last year, Thomas pushed Crane aside and ran the show himself.

McIntyre vs. McCloskey

Thomas learned the ropes in Sacramento's partisan pits in the 1970s. His fierce partisanship was further honed after a bruising battle in early 1985 over a House election in Indiana between Republican Richard D. McIntyre and Democrat Frank McCloskey.

Indiana's GOP secretary of State had declared McIntyre the winner by 34 votes, but House Democrats refused to seat him, appointing a three-member task force to review the election.

The task force recounted the ballots and declared that McCloskey had won by four votes, a decision ratified by the full House on a party-line vote. (*1985 Almanac, p. 28*)

The four-month contest of wills between the two parties that year — when Democrats had a 253-182 majority in the chamber — was a defining

moment for Thomas and the GOP. Thomas, the lone task force Republican, called the result a "rape" and "arrogant use of raw power." He helped lead a GOP walkout from the chamber.

"In the context of a political battle, I am very political," Thomas said.

Thomas is more than happy to have Democratic support for his initiatives, but he sees no need to seek bipartisanship on his committee. Democrats are not included in the lunches Thomas holds each Wednesday in the Capitol for his 23 Republican committee colleagues. Democrats are barred from using the committee's hearing room for private meetings. Thomas did not even invite Democrats to the annual holiday party.

"We are not included. If at all, as window dressing," groused Pete Stark of California, the No. 2 Democrat on Ways and Means.

The panel's top Democrat, Charles B. Rangel of New York, says the two men do not have a relationship. Thomas did not invite Rangel, who represents Harlem, on a trade trip to Africa. And trade is one area where the committee operates on a bipartisan plane.

"My one consolation is that you are just as inconsiderate of your Republican colleagues," Rangel said to Thomas during a hearing earlier this year.

John Tanner, a "Blue Dog" conservative Democrat from Tennessee, is often the only person from his party who hops the fence. Thomas, though, does not make much of an effort to broker Tanner's support. Often it is Tanner who calls the chairman. "I see if there's something I can do to work it out so there will be some bipartisanship," Tanner said, adding that there was "honest give and take" on last year's trade bill.

Even so, Tanner laments the polarized atmosphere on the committee and in the House. And he blames the Republicans. "Only the majority can make it bipartisan," he said. "The minority can only take what the majority dishes out."

Thomas contends it is the Democrats who have become more partisan on his committee, and he produces his own vote study to prove it.

A number of Democrats used to vote with Republicans frequently, Thomas points out. "Those type of Democrats are not put on the committee any more," he said, complaining that Democratic leaders exact a "brutal" discipline against rank-and-file members who support Thomas.

'Thomas Machine' Extends Beyond 22nd

Bill Thomas and his central California congressional district make for an odd match.

His hometown of Bakersfield is a little more than 100 miles from Los Angeles, yet Thomas' 22nd District is a distant world of oil wells and grape vineyards. Steinbeck's violent Grapes of Wrath was set in the fertile San Joaquin Valley. Cesar Chavez got his start there advocating for immigrant workers.

Sometimes dubbed "Appalachia West," it is home to country music star Buck Owens. Like Appalachia, unemployment is high, about twice the national average. The region's largest employer is Edwards Air Force Base, and this cowboy country leans very conservative politically.

Thomas is something of a carpetbagger, having moved to the area from Orange County for a teaching job at Bakersfield Community College. Still, the voters have returned the moderate

Bakersfield
California 22nd District

Republican to the House with little or no opposition since 1979.

One secret to his success is that Thomas has installed political allies in local positions of power, and the "Thomas machine" has warded off attacks from the right. Former Thomas aide Kevin McCarthy is in line to be Republican leader in the

state Assembly in Sacramento.

Thomas' support also helped elect freshman Republican Rep. Devin Nunes from the adjacent 21st District. And while Thomas has one of the largest war chests in the House, he has not had to use much of it for his own campaigns, instead doling it out in key races across the country.

After the Bakersfield newspaper wrote in 2000 that Thomas was having an extramarital affair with a top health care lobbyist, the fallout was minimal. Thomas never acknowledged or denied the affair, but wrote to his constituents: "Any personal failures of commitment or responsibility to my wife, family, or friends are just that, personal."

And Thomas does deliver to his economically depressed district. Recently he worked with Democrat Cal Dooley to secure $15 million for Meadows Field airport in Kern County.

Stark proves Thomas' point. "It's nice when we can get unanimity on the Democratic side so they can't say it's bipartisan," he said.

Historically, Ways and Means had a reputation for rising above partisan rifts. Lawmakers saw themselves as tax experts and worked closely together under the stewardship of Wilbur D. Mills, D-Ark. (1939-77). But that has changed, especially in recent years.

Archer, who ran the committee from 1995 until 2001, acknowledges that he began his chairmanship "on a completely, totally partisan basis."

Now a tax lobbyist for PricewaterhouseCoopers, Archer said that while chairman he once approached Rangel and suggested they work together. "If I give you this provision, will you support me?" Archer recalled asking, and Rangel replying that he would have to check with Minority Leader Richard A. Gephardt and the White House. "Well, I'm not going to negotiate three times," Archer said.

But while the breakdown of collegiality may have accelerated under Archer, it began before then.

The committee under Rostenkowski had produced its major tax and

trade bills in 1985 through 1987 with bipartisan support, though not always with majorities from both parties.

Things changed as Republicans were emboldened by the rise of Newt Gingrich, R-Ga. (1979-99), and his call for Republicans to confront 40 years of Democratic dominance. "The last two years of my service, every vote we [had], we didn't get one Republican vote. We had to pass it with all Democratic votes," Rostenkowski said.

Rostenkowski, who now works as a political consultant, blamed Republicans. "I was always criticized by Archer for not having him in the room when I was designing legislation. But what I found out was, when I brought Archer in, he would go back to Gingrich and poison the well," he said.

Influenced by Gingrich

Thomas, who is no conservative ideologue, may have had his partisan motor revved by Gingrich at the same time. Gingrich and Thomas, both members of the Class of 1978, were roommates during their freshman term.

In 1992, Gingrich was concerned that Thomas — then-ranking Republi-

can on the House Administration Committee — was too cozy with the panel's Democrats and not beholden to GOP leaders. He tried to push Thomas out of the top job.

Thomas says he does not see the point of bipartisanship. And he retains a long-simmering desire for payback. "Remember, for 16 years I was in the minority, and they never, ever let me be a major participant," he said.

He recalls his role in the McIntyre-McCloskey fight as "the point person to illustrate how arrogant the majority had become."

The result was the GOP sweep to power in the House in 1994. "It took a while for [the Democratic majority] to rot from the inside out, which it eventually did," Thomas said.

And without a bit of irony or concern that the same fate might befall an arrogant Republican, he suggests that his opponents on the other side of the aisle might benefit from more time in the wilderness.

"If Democrats would accept the fact that we are in the majority, I'd be more than happy to work with them as a junior partner." ◆

Foreign Policy Credibility Gap Worries Many in Congress

Fruitless weapons searches in Iraq spark larger question of trust among nations

Two disparate images of the Middle East are coming into focus as the region preoccupies both ends of Pennsylvania Avenue.

For the White House, one of the images, the latest, is a hopeful picture, with Israeli and Palestinian leaders responding positively to President Bush as he tries to halt more than two years of communal violence and help them down the road toward peace. Administration officials say Bush's diplomatic effort could have been undertaken only after he established his bona fides in the region by toppling the regime of Iraqi President Saddam Hussein.

But as Bush moves to the next phase of his planned Middle East makeover, Congress is still struggling to make sense of the disturbing picture of the Iraq war's aftermath. A primary argument for going to war with Iraq had been to disarm Saddam, who administration officials said was developing or possessed weapons of mass destruction. But it has been two months since Baghdad fell, and so far no evidence of such weapons has been found.

That situation, coupled with security and civil administration problems in the postwar reconstruction effort, has some lawmakers worried that the credibility of the administration — and of Congress, which voted last October to approve the use of force — is in jeopardy. Although Bush's chief antagonists are Democrats, some Republicans have been treading, albeit more lightly, on similar ground.

There are new suspicions of another intelligence failure over the estimates of Iraq's biological and chemical weapons capability, along with fears of diplomatic repercussions, and the possibility of political fallout at home.

"It raises the credibility bar when assertions are made in the future about Iran or Korea or anywhere else in the sense that it'll allow those who are not our friends to say, 'They don't have the evidence. They're dead wrong,' " Joseph R. Biden Jr., ranking Democrat on the Senate Foreign Relations Committee, said June 3, referring to lack of evidence to corroborate Bush's charges that Iraq possessed weapons of mass destruction.

"Even friendly countries wary of getting involved in controversial circumstances might say, 'Show me. We don't believe you. We doubt your credibility. We doubt the accuracy of your intelligence.' So it makes it harder," Biden said.

Added Sen. Herb Kohl, D-Wis., a Defense Appropriations Subcommittee member who voted to authorize the use of force: "We were told unequivocally by those who were in the know that this regime had very dangerous weapons that had to be eliminated, and if necessary, we were going to go to war to do that." While Kohl stopped short of saying he would feel betrayed by the administration if no weapons were found, he said, "We just hope very much that the reason for having gone to war is validated. Any American feels that way."

Confused Emotions

Other lawmakers argue that it makes no difference if weapons are found. Even if Saddam destroyed the weapons as the United Nations demanded — something the administration now admits is possible as it confronts demands to explain why none have been found — some senior foreign policy experts say Saddam still deserved to be attacked for failing to reveal evidence of that effort.

"I would argue that Saddam Hussein, if he didn't have [the weapons anymore], certainly misled everybody," said Senate Foreign Relations Committee Chairman Richard G. Lugar, R-Ind. "By hiding it or obfuscating, he's been a casualty of his failure to inform us that nothing was there."

Quick Contents

As President Bush moves on to tackle the Israeli-Palestinian conflict, lawmakers are still struggling with the aftermath of the Iraq war.

For Congress, hopeful scenes of Bush's meeting with Sharon and Abbas to discuss Mideast peace do not obscure problems in Iraq and a possible intelligence failure.

WHITE HOUSE PHOTO VIA BLOOMBERG NEWS / PAUL MORSE

Absence of Weapons in Iraq Pulls Democrats Together

The debate in Congress over how to address the dearth of weapons of mass destruction in Iraq is starting to fracture along partisan lines.

Those lawmakers calling for a probe and open hearings into the matter are mostly Democrats, while Republicans tend to defend the White House and counsel for more time for weapons to be unearthed.

At the same time, a puzzle lies at the heart of this debate. Lawmakers from both parties on key committees such as Intelligence and Armed Services saw the same material from U.S. intelligence agencies about the presence of chemical or biological weapons in Iraq. Yet among those who voted for the war resolution (PL 107-243), including a number of Democrats, opinions are wildly mixed on whether the failure so far

to find weapons is a surprise, as well as whether this failure will damage American credibility abroad.

There is growing concern among those Democrats that U.S. intelligence on the Iraqi threat was flawed or manipulated. If Congress does not investigate this matter soon, they say, the United States will find it even more difficult to persuade allies to act against other proliferation threats.

One is Sen. Tom Harkin, D-Iowa, who says he voted for the resolution because he was assured Iraq had weapons of mass destruction.

Harkin says he was told by a high-ranking official: "We have [weapons sites] so pinpointed that before the action starts we're going to drop parachuters in, special forces, to secure those sites."

"What happened?" Harkin asks.

Sen. John D. Rockefeller IV, D-W.Va., vice chairman of the Intelligence committee, also is more surprised than his GOP counterparts, even though he also backed the war.

"I think most people expected that there was [weaponry]," says Rockefeller, who has hinted he may try to force the intelligence committee to conduct its own investigation.

In sharp contrast, Republicans who had access to the same material say more time is needed for weapons of mass destruction to be uncovered.

House Intelligence Chairman Porter J. Goss, R-Fla., says his panel will conduct only "routine oversight" into the analytical process of pre-war intelligence.

But for now, Goss says he sees "no reason for these cries for investigations and joint hearings."

Meanwhile, many lawmakers say they believe the weapons did exist and may still turn up.

As a result, a third picture is surfacing — one of fractiousness on Capitol Hill as lawmakers argue over what it means that no weapons have yet been found, or if it matters at all. The issue has even caused at least one lawmaker to take issue with himself.

In a July 1 interview with the Los Angeles Times, John. W. Warner, chairman of the Senate Armed Services Committee, suggested that senior administration officials, including Defense Secretary Donald H. Rumsfeld and CIA Director George J. Tenet, may have misled him before the war by promising specifically that U.S. forces would find the weapons quickly and display them on television for all the world to see. (*Briefings, p. 53*)

But in a statement the next day, Warner said, "I remain of the opinion there has been no deception by the administration."

Congress is dealing with the growing political problem of the unfound weapons in its customary fashion: in-

vestigations and hearings. Or at least talking about investigations and hearings. Warner, Senate Intelligence Committee Chairman Pat Roberts, R-Kan., and Rep. Porter J. Goss, R-Fla., chairman of the House Intelligence Committee, all have mentioned an interest in investigating the intelligence that assessed the threat posed by Saddam's weapons programs.

Roberts and Goss are poring over loads of documents the White House and the CIA sent to Capitol Hill last week. These are the intelligence documents the administration relied upon in making its claims about Iraq's weapons, which it said justified the decision to go to war.

Hearings, or 'Witch Hunt'?

While Warner was initially outspoken about the need for public hearings into the possibility of an intelligence failure, or at least miscalculation, he later softened, saying a thorough closed-door examination of the intelligence documents was needed first.

Nevertheless, lawmakers of both parties have expressed support for hearings

on intelligence and other Iraq matters.

"We've had hearings after every conflict that we've been involved in, whether it be Kosovo or Bosnia or Grenada or Panama, ever since the first Persian Gulf War, and it's appropriate that we have hearings following the Iraqi conflict," Sen. John McCain, R-Ariz., said after Vice President Dick Cheney joined Senate Republicans for lunch. "One of the issues, and I emphasize one, is the issue of weapons of mass destruction." He said lawmakers also would examine the deaths of U.S. forces that resulted from friendly fire.

But some House members are not eager for hearings. Ray LaHood, R-Ill., a House Intelligence Committee member, said, "I think it's a dumb idea" because "the intelligence community has been very forthcoming. I think it's a witch hunt." Said Republican Steve Buyer of Indiana: "This place lacks the virtue of patience."

Thus far, the only evidence of unconventional Iraqi weapons has been two trailer trucks, which Bush said were mobile biological weapons laboratories. No biological agents were found in ei-

Goss, a former CIA officer, also emphasizes that he is not surprised at the minimal results of the weapons hunt in Iraq.

"Saddam Hussein was a master of deception," Goss says. "We will find his [weapons]."

Rep. Rob Simmons, R-Conn., takes the same view as Goss. But he adds that Democratic criticism is fueled by unrealistic expectations.

"I never expected to find Fat Man or Little Boy," Simmons said, referring to the two U.S. atomic bombs dropped on Japan in World War II. "I expected to find evidence that validated the intelligence. And we have."

Simmons, also a former CIA officer, was mainly referring to the mobile labs recently found in Iraq. Although they did not contain any, the White House says they were probably used to produce biological weapons.

Much of the intelligence on Iraq provided to those lawmakers remains classified. But the CIA released some of that material in February to Secretary of State Colin L. Powell before he headed to the United Nations to make the administration's case that Saddam Hussein was concealing his weapons programs in defiance of UN Resolution 1441.

Among Powell's key claims: Iraq shifted material from nearly 30 chemical weapons sites before U.N. inspectors arrived; weapons were being developed in at least seven mobile labs; and al Qaeda cells were in the Kurdish autonomous zone in northern Iraq.

Jane Harman of California, ranking Democrat on Goss' committee, says much of the information she saw last fall came out in that testimony.

Harman, who also voted for the war resolution, said she thought Powell made "a very careful case."

So far, Sen. John W. Warner, R-Va., appears to be alone among key

Warner, right, and Foreign Relations Chairman Richard G. Lugar, R-Ind., want to wait on hearings.

Republicans in calling for a probe. But in an ironic turn, the mystery of Iraq's missing weapons of mass destruction has so far unified Democrats far more than the much debated, bitterly divisive Iraq war ever did.

ther vehicle; the administration says the trucks had been scrubbed.

Some lawmakers — focused on the positive side of Saddam's downfall — dismiss the possibility of an adverse public reaction to the failure to find more evidence of the weapons.

"I think all of those questions are over with, they're meaningless," Sen. Pete V. Domenici, R-N.M., said heatedly June 3. "The war was justified in the eyes of most Americans, justified in the eyes of most Americans who sent their young ones over there. They're for the most part thrilled that we got rid of Saddam Hussein. Whether we can prove in any more detail the weapons of mass destruction seems to me to be not a very big issue."

For now, polls appear to back him up. Approximately 56 percent of Americans believe the war with Iraq "was justified even if the United States does not find conclusive evidence that Iraq has weapons of mass destruction," while 23 percent believe it was justified only if the evidence is found, according to a CNN/USA Today/Gallup Poll conducted May 30 to June 1. The poll of 1,019 adults had a margin of error of plus or minus 3 percentage points.

House Majority Leader Tom DeLay, R-Texas, said, "You don't necessarily need to find the actual weapons. The detractors from our successes might want to congratulate Saddam Hussein on his ability to hide them or to destroy them." Critics are "just playing politics, and I think it's shameful."

Trusting Intelligence

At the same time, other members have expressed concern that this latest challenge to U.S. intelligence gathering, coming less than two years after the Sept. 11 terror attacks caught the intelligence community unprepared, could cause problems for them in making future policy decisions. What will happen, these lawmakers ponder, if they feel they can no longer trust the intelligence they receive?

The situation is "deeply troubling" to Dianne Feinstein, D-Calif., a Senate Intelligence Committee member who voted for attacking Iraq.

"We had been given before the war an enumeration of specific chemicals and biologicals that were unaccounted for and presumed to be present in Iraq, possibly to be dispersed on the battlefield," she said.

Sen. John D. Rockefeller IV, D-W.Va., vice chairman of the Intelligence Committee, said the ability of the administration and Congress to rely on American intelligence is critical given the Bush administration's willingness to wage pre-emptive wars.

"Under a doctrine of pre-emption, you really have to have absolutely first-rate intelligence," said Rockefeller, who is seeking an investigation even if Roberts does not want one.

"If you can't find weapons of mass destruction, you have to raise the question that either the intelligence was not good, or it was manipulated or misused. . . . All of those choices are dreadful."

Feinstein, like many lawmakers, said "it is still quite possible that weapons of mass destruction will in fact be found as inspections continue."

Lugar agrees, but he emphasizes that it will not be easy to find them, and he knows something about such searches.

With former Sen. Sam Nunn, D-

Ga. (1972-97), Lugar cosponsored the Nunn-Lugar Act of 1991 (PL 102-228), under which the United States has spent about $7 billion to find unsecured nuclear and other dangerous weapons in the former Soviet Union.

Lugar recalled a trip a few years ago to Pokrov, where two local Russians led him to a "Green Mama" shampoo plant that also had produced anthrax a few months earlier. Inside, the Russians handed over 14 vials of the biotoxin.

Many lawmakers return to the theme of lost credibility and their concern that a failure to find the much-touted weapons might undermine international support for the United States in a future foreign situation.

"It's not a matter of whether war was justified — Saddam Hussein was an evil despot — but that we now have credibility problems," said John P. Murtha of Pennsylvania, ranking Democrat on the House Defense Appropriations Subcommittee. "What do we do in the future? Will people doubt us internationally?"

That is a question that also could affect Bush's efforts to resolve the Israeli-Palestinian conflict. The positive images that have been generated so far — of Bush, Israeli Prime Minister Ariel Sharon and Palestinian Prime Minister Mahmoud Abbas conferring beneath a palm tree in Aqaba, Jordan — have little substance behind them, save for Israeli and Palestinian statements of their willingness to make peace. Bush's credibility on the Middle East peace process will be judged, in part, by how credible his performance is in Iraq.

Lugar dismisses such worries.

"It will be an interesting historical footnote as to how we went about this," Lugar said, referring to the country's march to war. "Right now, it's an interesting flap. . . . Eventually even that will be dissipated, and then we'll have to start arguing about something else, mainly how well are we doing in Iraq generally."

Occupation Blues

That is another cause for concern among lawmakers. Since Bush on May 1 declared the end of major combat operations in Iraq, 10 American soldiers have been killed in skirmishes with Iraqi guerrillas as of June 6. Meanwhile, U.S. occupation authorities continue to have trouble restoring basic services, such as water and electricity.

Lugar's committee hearing June 4 focused on the postwar reconstruction ef-

fort, generating some heat of its own as senators tried to pin down the administration on such matters as costs, how many troops would be needed and for how long — questions that have vexed members of both parties since before the war began in March. Bush did not send Congress his request for a $74.7 billion supplemental for the war until a week after it began. Congress ultimately approved $78.5 billion (PL 108-11).

But Seriously

Sen. Chuck Hagel, R-Neb., who has long criticized the Republican administration for providing insufficient information on Iraq, went toe-to-toe with Pentagon Comptroller Dov S. Zakheim on a variety of matters, some of them seemingly simple, without getting much for his efforts.

"Could you provide this committee with a number of American troops in Iraq?" Hagel asked.

"Well, I believe the actual number right now is a classified one," Zakheim responded.

"You're kidding me?" Hagel said.

"No, I'm not kidding you, sir, " Zakheim said.

Zakheim eventually produced the number — almost 147,000 as of June 3 — explaining that he had demurred because he had seen the information on a classified chart. "I wasn't trying to obfuscate at all," he said.

Yet Sen. Russell D. Feingold, D-Wis., also ran into trouble when he tried to get Zakheim to give him the estimated cost of Iraq reconstruction and how much might be picked up by other nations.

"My constituents want to know how much we're going to pay," Feingold said. "They want to know as much as possible, what the total will be, and what can be expected as a percentage by other countries. . . . What's a realistic goal that I can tell my constituents we're going to try to get other people to help us with?"

"I think a realistic goal is to get them to contribute as much as we possibly can get them to," Zakheim said.

"That is a complete non-answer," Feingold said.

It is unclear how long the American public will be willing to pay. Kohl predicts that taxpayers may make their feelings known in 2004. "Once the election season comes around, these things become magnified because they're in the public discourse," he said.

Meanwhile, lawmakers also are worried about the dramatic shift in Muslim

public opinion against the United States. On June 3, the same day that Bush met with the leaders of Egypt, Jordan, Saudi Arabia, Bahrain and the Palestinians in Sharm el-Sheikh, Egypt, a Pew Research Center poll found that "the bottom has fallen out of support for America in most of the Muslim world."

"Negative views of the United States among Muslims, which had been largely limited to countries in the Middle East, have spread to Muslim populations in Indonesia and Nigeria," the survey said. "Since last summer, favorable ratings for the United States have fallen from 61 percent to 15 percent in Indonesia and from 71 percent to 38 percent among Muslims in Nigeria."

The poll, conducted by Pew's Global Attitudes Project, also found that in most countries friendly to the United States, only modest percentages had confidence that Bush would "do the right thing regarding world affairs." In the survey, Russian President Vladimir V. Putin, German Prime Minister Gerhard Schroeder, French President Jacques Chirac and British Prime Minister Tony Blair all received higher ratings than Bush in most countries.

The survey interviewed 16,000 people from April 28 to May 15 in 20 countries and the Palestinian territories, and more than 38,000 people in 44 nations in 2002. It had a margin of error of plus or minus 4 percentage points.

Meanwhile, the heat from the weapons issue is spreading. On June 6, after a closed hearing of the Senate Armed Services Committee, Vice Adm. Lowell Jacoby, director of the Defense Intelligence Agency, acknowledged that his agency had no specific intelligence last September on Iraqi facilities producing weapons of mass destruction. "We could not specifically pin down individual facilities operating as part of the weapons of mass destruction program," Jacoby said a news conference with Warner and Stephen Cambone, the Pentagon's intelligence chief.

It was around the same time that senior administration officials began building their public case against Iraq. "There is no doubt that Saddam Hussein now has weapons of mass destruction," Cheney said in an August speech. "There is no doubt he is amassing them to use against our friends, against our allies and against us." ◆

Hill Demands More Answers On Iraq — Not a Fall Guy

Hearings multiply as partisan split over intelligence failures grows increasingly bitter

Judging from the somber faces of the lawmakers coming out of the closed hearing of the Senate Select Intelligence Committee on July 16, it had been an extremely difficult session. For four-and-a-half hours, committee members questioned CIA Director George J. Tenet on how uncorroborated allegations of Iraq's efforts to buy uranium from Niger found their way into the State of the Union speech President Bush gave last January.

At one break in the session, when reporters asked whether she was happy with what she was hearing in the room, Dianne Feinstein, D-Calif., responded pointedly: "Happy is not the right word."

For several days, the administration tried to make the controversy go away, and Tenet obliged in that effort by taking full responsibility for the president's suspect words. But the question leading up to the hearing was whether Congress would let it stop there.

The answer came when Intelligence committee Chairman Pat Roberts, R-Kan. — who had previously castigated the CIA for "extremely sloppy handling" of the uranium issue and "press leaks" aimed at discrediting Bush — emerged at the end of the day to commend Tenet for being "very candid" and "contrite." Asked whether he thought the CIA director should resign, Roberts said, "No, I don't think so," and added that he felt Tenet had "done a good job in the war on terrorism."

More significantly, Roberts, who typically is a staunch administration defender, suggested that responsibility for the uranium claim did not lie solely with Tenet. "Mistakes were made up and along the chain," Roberts said.

Roberts' announcement was the clearest signal to date that the controversy will not easily blow over. He promised that the panel will hold an open hearing in September — an option that he had expressed little interest in only a month ago, when the panel's review of pre-war intelligence began — as well as a closed hearing on July 31 with U.S. officials leading the search for illegal weapons programs in Iraq.

Roberts' readiness to conduct open hearings into the matter not only appears to depart from his earlier stance, but suggests that Congress is not going to accept Tenet as a fall guy for pre-war intelligence failures. If anything, it shows that the Intelligence committees are starting to flex their oversight muscles in a strong assertion of the congressional prerogative to remain in the loop.

Recriminations over the uranium reference spilled out onto the Senate floor July 17, as one Democrat after another began demanding a fuller accounting from the Bush administration. The drumbeat came the same day British Prime Minister Tony Blair spoke before Congress and passionately

Durbin and Harkin have been among the most outspoken Democratic critics of President Bush's use of uncorroborated Iraq intelligence.

defended the decision to go to war.

"It's time for the president to come clean," said Sen. Tom Harkin, D-Iowa. "Does he believe his own claim? Did Iraq even have an active nuclear weapons program when we invaded? If so, then why have we not found any evidence for it in the months since the war ended? And if not, then why did we invade in the first place?

"This is not just about one statement," Harkin continued. "It is about a war justified by claims that Iraq was actively pursuing nuclear weapons, by dire warnings about mushroom clouds."

One of the panel's Democrats, Richard J. Durbin of Illinois, went on national television and dropped a tantalizing detail from the closed session: A CIA official gave the committee the name of a White House official who demanded that the uranium claim be included in the State of the Union address.

He immediately received a sharp rebuke from White House spokesman Scott McClellan, who called the charge "nonsense" and disparaged Durbin for trying to justify his own vote against the Iraq war resolution (PL 107-243).

In a sign that the administration sees the issue as potentially dangerous politically, the normally circumspect White House followed up on McClellan's remarks July 18 by releasing declassified portions of last October's National Intelligence Estimate — a consensus assessment of all the intelligence agencies — that the White House said corroborated Bush's uranium claim.

The report warned that if Iraqi leader Saddam Hussein went "unchecked," he would have a nuclear weapon "during this decade." It also said he had tried to buy uranium from Niger, Somalia and "possibly Congo."

The White House also won wide support from most Republicans, who argued throughout the week that regardless of the accuracy of the uranium claim, other justification for the war was ample.

Senate Majority Whip Mitch McConnell, R-Ky., said Democrats, "in their zeal to score political points," have "sacrificed the national interest on the altar of partisan politics and are making accusations that are grossly offensive against the president and those of us who believed and continue to believe that our liberation of Iraq was the right thing to do."

At the end of the week, partisan divisions over the intelligence controversy remained more bitter than ever. But just as significant, the House and Senate Intelligence panels — the only full panels conducting reviews on Iraq intelligence — still managed to preserve some bipartisan cohesion even as they moved their investigations into the public eye.

Committee Questions

The focus on the nation's intelligence-gathering capabilities is expected to intensify during the week of July 21 with the release of the report of the congressional joint inquiry into Sept. 11. The report's release is months behind schedule. In May, Bob Graham of Florida, the Democratic chairman of the Senate Select Intelligence Committee until January, charged that the administration was telling the CIA vetting team looking at the report to stall because it feared that embarrassing details would be released.

On July 24, the House Intelligence Committee will hold an open hearing with testimony from former CIA directors, focusing on how the intelligence agencies create their products.

That will be followed by the Senate panel's July 31 hearing, which Roberts and the panel's vice chairman, John D. Rockefeller IV, D-W.Va., said would be followed by more committee action in the fall. Roberts also said Tenet might return for another hearing and promised that both a classified and declassified report would be forthcoming in the fall.

But a senior administration official set the stage for a possible confrontation between Congress and the executive branch when he said July 18 that the White House would not send any of its staff members to testify before the investigating intelligence committees. "That is something we do not do," the official said.

Meanwhile, another, more restricted investigation has begun in the Senate Armed Services Committee, led by its ranking Democrat, Carl Levin of Michigan. That probe lacks the full support of the panel's Republican chairman, John W. Warner of Virginia, so Levin's powers are limited. But because he is also a member of the Intelligence panel, Levin — one of the most energetic critics of the administration on the Iraq intelligence front — has been able to participate in the full-committee review led by Roberts.

While some Republicans and the White House have painted the issue as one driven by partisan interests, other Republicans say they have serious questions about the use and possible misuse of pre-war intelligence.

Going into the July 16 hearing, Senate Intelligence Committee members Chuck Hagel, R-Neb., and Olympia J. Snowe, R-Maine, began pressing the administration for more answers after Tenet's statement. "We need to know why [the uranium statement] was in the State of the Union. It's very important, especially as a prelude to war," Snowe said. "It raises a very real question of U.S. credibility."

Meanwhile, Democrats in both chambers have tried and tried again, unsuccessfully, to find a way to broaden the investigation and pry more information from the White House.

On July 16, for example, the Senate tabled an amendment, proposed by Jon Corzine, D-N.J., during floor debate

Blair's speech before a joint meeting of Congress raised spirits but did little to halt the bitter partisan debate over pre-war Iraq intelligence.

CQ PHOTO/ SCOTT J. FERRELL

on the defense appropriations bill (HR 2658) that would have established an independent commission to investigate pre-war intelligence on Iraq.

The next day, Durbin offered another amendment to the defense bill that would have held up $50 million from the intelligence budget until Bush submitted a report to Congress on how the White House used intelligence to justify the war. It was tabled, and thus killed, 62-34. (*Senate vote 287, 2003 CQ Weekly, p. 1849*)

Senate Appropriations Chairman Ted Stevens, R-Alaska, who sponsored the tabling motion, said, "[T]he extended debate on this floor about the intelligence activities because of [Bush's uranium claim] is starting to have an impact on the intelligence-collecting activities in this country."

Tenet has survived so far because of his strong popularity on the Hill, and because, lawmakers say, Tenet made clear during the hearing that the agency recommended against using the uranium reference in Bush's January address.

Durbin said a CIA official "certainly told us who the person was who was insistent on putting this language in, which the CIA knew to be incredible."

The New York Times reported on July 18 that senior intelligence officials said in the hearing that Alan Foley, a CIA expert on weapons of mass destruction, said Robert Joseph, the National Security Council's director for non-proliferation issues, asked him whether the president's address could include a reference to Iraq's seeking uranium from Niger. According to the Times, officials said Foley has testified that he told Joseph the agency was not certain about the evidence and recommended it be taken out of Bush's speech.

As Durbin described it: "[T]here was this negotiation between the White House and the CIA about just how far you could go and be close to the truth, and unfortunately those sixteen words were included in the most important speech the president delivers in any given year."

Congress Asserts Prerogative

While Democratic measures such as Durbin's amendment may have failed, the aftermath of Tenet's meeting with the Senate Intelligence Committee signaled several other subtle but important shifts in the dynamics in the debate over America's pre-war intelligence on Iraq.

First, Durbin's remarks and the post-

hearing comments from panel members suggested that the focus of the congressional probes currently under way will no longer be only on the performance of U.S. intelligence agencies, but also on how the White House used the classified material to make the case for war with Iraq.

Second, the congressional Intelligence committees are taking seriously their oversight role, even though both the House and Senate panels are chaired by Republicans who generally support the Iraq war, believe it was justified and continue to state that justification will soon be plain to all.

Both committees have become more comfortable taking on an investigative approach that includes direct interviews with top administration officials, open hearings, and plans for a public disclosure once the panels' work is finished.

The change is more pronounced in the Senate panel, however. For several weeks in June, the committee was stuck in a partisan dispute over how far to take the Iraq intelligence review. Democrats sought a joint probe with the Senate Armed Services Committee that included the full array of investigative tools, including open hearings, while Roberts resisted taking any steps beyond the normal oversight functions of the committee. He even called the investigation "pejorative."

The panel arrived at a bipartisan compromise June 20 that kept the probe restricted to the Intelligence panel — and behind closed doors. But it also allowed for the possibility of open hearings in case the CIA material under review opened more questions than it answered.

Goss-Harman Unity

A stronger sense of partisan unity has been guiding the House committee, which also began reviewing CIA documents on Iraq in June. When the panel's leaders, Porter J. Goss, R-Fla., and ranking Democrat Jane Harman of California, announced their probe June 12, their joint statement already included mention of open hearings and a public report. Harman even embraced the word "investigation."

Although Goss and Harman have taken somewhat different positions in the unfolding weapons controversy, their history of cooperation has kept partisan disagreement on the panel under wraps. Meanwhile, their review

continues to move forward.

Still, the contrasting approaches of Goss and Harman were on display when the two, along with their panel colleagues Robert E. "Bud" Cramer, D-Ala., and Jim Gibbons, R-Nev., held a news conference July 15 following a fact-finding trip to Iraq. At that appearance, Harman announced the open hearing now slated for July 24.

In her comments, Harman underscored the need for "accurate, unbiased, timely, and actionable intelligence" for future proliferation challenges such as North Korea, and she argued that this context was behind her panel's work.

Harman, a moderate Democrat who voted for the Iraq war resolution, also offered several "tentative" conclusions: The White House relied more than it should have on circumstantial evidence of Iraq's illegal weapons programs; the intelligence community failed to emphasize the ambiguous nature of many of its claims to Congress and the administration; and the White House "consistently omitted" those qualifiers on Iraq that were attached to intelligence reports.

Harman noted that one of the 20 volumes under review does contain information on the uranium story.

Goss, for his part, said he agreed with some of Harman's conclusions, but made clear he is much less concerned about the credibility issue — or the specific question about Bush's uranium statement — than he is about the underinvestment in U.S. human intelligence in the 1990s.

That underinvestment, charged Goss, prevented the intelligence agencies from acquiring accurate information about Iraq.

"Human beings make mistakes, but I think we're doing as well as we can," Goss said. "I just wish we had more to work with — more language experts, more spies, more human intelligence."

Goss expressed "complete confidence" in Tenet, but underscored the areas where he felt U.S. intelligence was inadequate ahead of the war.

"The intelligence community underestimated the amount of trashing, looting, denial and deception, and it overestimated the crowd response we'd get from the [Iraqi] street once our troops came in," he said. "They also underestimated the real fear that the Iraqi people have of Saddam Hussein and the Baathist party." ◆

Caucuses Bring New Muscle To Legislative Battlefield

Informal Hill alliances wield influence across party, regional, committee lines

When gunmakers campaign in the Senate this fall for a shield from liability lawsuits, they'll have more in their lobbying arsenal than the clout of the National Rifle Association and some relevant committee chairmen.

The industry will also have an ally that falls somewhere between a lobby and a legislative committee: the Congressional Sportsmen's Caucus, a group with an industry-financed budget and more than 300 lawmakers who call themselves members.

Originally designed as informal groups of lawmakers with common interests, caucuses have evolved into powerful lobbying forces that play a largely unsupervised role in the legislative process, fundamentally changing the way interest groups pursue their legislative agendas.

Caucuses are increasingly aligning themselves with powerful private interests, including business organizations, that use caucuses of lawmakers friendly to their cause to build momentum for legislation or to block other proposals by working outside the traditional venues of party organizations and legislative committees.

The House in 1995 imposed rules to curb the largest caucuses by cutting off their taxpayer funding, but instead congressional caucuses have proliferated. There are now nearly 300, according to a count by Congressional Quarterly, and they range from large organizations such as the Sportsmen's Caucus to groups that could meet in a House subway car.

For lawmakers, caucuses offer an opportunity to be involved with issues important to constituents, even if those matters are far outside the range of their committee assignments. Junior members who can only dream of committee chairmanships can create caucuses and install themselves as chairmen, gaining at least some leverage over issues handled by the most powerful legislative committees.

Finding particularly fertile ground in the House, today's congressional caucuses reach across party and delegation lines — and come in every imaginable flavor. Some, such as the Republican Study Committee, reflect factions within party ranks. *(2003 CQ Weekly, p. 2338)*

Caucus names can be so broad as to be seemingly without controversy (the Building a Better America Caucus; the Results Caucus), or amusingly narrow (the Horse Caucus). Caucuses sometimes represent regions or institutions (the Northeast-Midwest Congressional Coalition; the Air Force Caucus). They can speak for foreign countries (Albanian Is-

> **"** *Frankly, there are so many caucuses it's getting harder and harder to keep track of them.* **"**
>
> — Bob Ney, chairman of the House Administration Committee, whose job includes keeping track of caucuses

sues Caucus), embattled industries, agricultural products (Potato Caucus), diseases (Congressional Diabetes Caucus), road projects and even hobbies (Philatelic Caucus). Sometimes competing caucuses focus on the same issue. Many lawmakers proudly list their caucus memberships on their Web sites, alongside their committee assignments.

Lawmakers join caucuses to impress voters and potential campaign contributors, said Rep. Mark Foley, R-Fla., chairman of the Congressional Travel and Tourism Caucus. "It's a first step toward establishing an identity. It's a way of saying, 'I am an advocate who is fighting for you.' "

Some lawmakers have also found that caucus membership can be a credential for post-congressional employment. Former Rep. John Edward Porter, R-Ill. (1980-2001), for example, was a founder of the Human Rights Caucus. He is now a lobbyist and registered foreign agent for several countries, including El Salvador, the Bahamas and Canada.

The role of caucuses as an increasingly popular point of entry into the legislative process has prompted watchdog groups and a few lawmakers to call for new disclosure requirements and tighter rules for caucuses and their support groups.

"Frankly, these groups raise a question about who lawmakers represent — their constituents, or some lobbyists," said Rep. John L. Mica, R-Fla. "That's why I don't join any of them. I worry now that we are seeing more and more caucuses. It seems as though we will have a caucus for just about everything before long."

Rising From the Ashes

The Sportsmen's Caucus is as big as they come. The group has been around since 1989, created to unite lawmakers who want to protect the interests of 14 million Americans who enjoy hunting and fishing. Caucus activities are supported by the nonprofit Congressional Sportsmen's Foundation, which is operating this year on $860,000 in contributions from the NRA, firearm manufacturers and the makers and retailers of other hunting and fishing equipment. The foundation is among a half-dozen nonprofit arms of caucuses operating

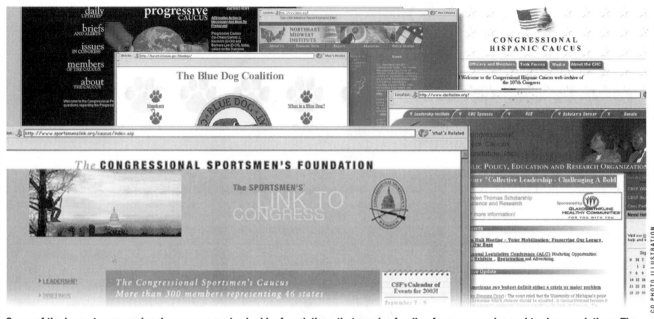

Some of the largest congressional caucuses are backed by foundations that receive funding from companies and trade associations. The nonprofit groups, including the Congressional Sportsmen's Foundation, lower left, often maintain Web sites that promote caucus activities.

from privately funded offices near the Capitol.

The clout of such groups today is remarkable, considering they were an endangered institution not even 10 years ago.

Led by then-Rep. Pat Roberts of Kansas, Republicans fresh from their triumph in the 1994 elections banned House members from using their expense allowances to pay dues to 28 legislative service organizations that had been certified by the House Administration Committee to receive funding in this way. GOP leaders complained that the former Democratic majority permitted public money to be used without sufficient oversight and to promote special interests. About $4 million had been spent on caucuses in 1994.

Large caucuses, including the Congressional Black Caucus and Democratic Study Group (DSG), were forced to scale back their activities and were ousted from their quarters in House office buildings. Congressional Quarterly Inc. in 1995 purchased DSG Publications, an arm of the DSG that published detailed information on legislation scheduled for debate on the House floor, and turned it into a nonpartisan publication named House Action Reports.

While the largest groups were forced to make painful transitions, the rules change had little impact on most of the more than 100 caucuses that were operating without dedicated staff or offices. (*1995 Almanac, p. 1-24*)

Caucuses have multiplied year after year. Congressional Quarterly has found at least 286 caucuses operating in the House, the Senate or in both chambers. A 1999 report by the Congressional Research Service identified 185 caucuses.

Trade groups representing high-technology companies, wireless telephone service providers, wineries, entertainment conglomerates, machine toolmakers, casino operators and racetracks all have contributed to the caucus explosion.

The current roster includes about 60 caucuses aligned with business and trade groups, 25 organized by lawmakers concerned about issues involving particular foreign countries, seven representing party factions and dozens concerned with public policy issues. More than 90 percent of congressional caucuses are found in the House.

Lobbyists are often the engine driving congressional cau-

cuses, sponsoring social events to recruit members, developing legislative strategies, running Internet sites and raising money for foundations that support caucuses. The lobbyists also help caucus members raise campaign funds.

Some lobbyists said they have increased their involvement with caucuses because of the difficulty of moving legislation through a narrowly divided Congress. Others said limited access to Capitol Hill offices since the Sept. 11 terrorist attacks is a factor.

Rules limiting lawmakers' committee assignments — and the overall decline in power of committees in recent years — also encourage the growth of caucuses, according to Christopher J. Deering, a political science professor at George Washington University.

Two Can Serve

House Republicans can serve on two committees, although members of the Appropriations, Ways and Means, Rules, and Energy and Commerce panels are limited to that single seat. Senators can serve on three panels, but on only one "Super A" committee such as Appropriations, Finance, Armed Services or Foreign Relations.

"Caucuses are growing because members are trying to expand their representational portfolios beyond these limits," Deering said.

Another factor in the proliferation of caucuses, according to Rep. George P. Radanovich, R-Calif., was the 1999 relaxation of another 1995 House rule that made it difficult for lawmakers to accept meals and entertainment from lobbyists.

Radanovich said the 1999 change prompted him and Sportsmen's Caucus co-chairman Mike Thompson, D-Calif., to revive the Congressional Wine Caucus. Recruitment was easy, thanks to a series of receptions featuring food and beverages provided by the industry.

House Speaker J. Dennis Hastert, R-Ill., has supported several caucuses, including the sportsmen's group. During the August recess, Hastert was a star attraction along with skeet shooting and fly fishing at the Sportsmen's Foundation's "Great Outdoors Weekend" in the Jackson, Wyo., area. Lobbyists and other supporters paid $3,000 apiece to attend the retreat sponsored by Browning Arms Co., the American Sportsfishing Association, the National Marine Manufacturers Association and others.

"Caucuses are small 'd' democracy," Hastert said. "There are a lot of people that want to be represented. That's a good thing."

Major caucuses survived the House Republican funding cut with the help of business lobbyists and a GOP leadership decision that has allowed some groups to have taxpayer-financed staff and office space.

About a half-dozen caucuses, or "congressional member organizations," are using aides paid from House members' personal payroll allowances. The aides typically receive portions of their salaries from multiple lawmakers. House office space assigned to an individual lawmaker, a committee or a House leader can be occupied by caucuses and their aides.

"It's an outrage if they are using public funds to support caucuses," said House Minority Whip Steny H. Hoyer, D-Md. "They took away rooms that caucuses occupied under the Democrats."

Setting the Agenda

Hastert rejected Hoyer's complaint, saying Republicans have honored the spirit of their 1995 decision to ban public funding for caucuses.

"There were reforms that we enacted," Hastert said. "I don't know if there are irregularities now. . . . But the principal thing is we try to create ideas, so that we can create legislation."

Each caucus has its own legislative ideas, and collectively caucuses help shape the congressional agenda. Caucuses played particularly significant roles in this year's tax cut debate.

Grover Norquist, president of Americans for Tax Reform, said his pro-business, anti-tax group has provided support for five congressional caucuses that have helped set GOP tax cut priorities.

"We knew that another tax bill would be coming," Norquist said. "And we thought these caucuses would provide a gauge for the level of support for different proposals that would be on the table."

The Zero Capital Gains Tax Caucus, headed by House Rules Committee Chairman David Dreier, R-Calif., quietly promoted a proposal to slash the taxation of capital gains at a time

early this year when the Bush administration preferred a tax cut for dividends. The dividend proposal drew lukewarm support from the business community because it was aimed at individuals, not corporations.

A proposal to cut taxes on both dividend and capital gains income offered in March by House Ways and Means Chairman Bill Thomas, R-Calif., was embraced by the capital gains caucus and eventually became the model for the centerpiece of the $350 billion tax cut package (PL 108-27) enacted in May. *(2003 CQ Weekly, p. 1245)*

Americans for Tax Reform provides Internet sites and advice for the anti-tax caucuses, hoping to maintain pressure on Republican leaders for additional tax cuts.

Another of Norquist's groups, the End the Death Tax Caucus, led by Rep. Jennifer Dunn, R-Wash., is pushing for permanent repeal of the estate tax. The Full Business Expensing Caucus is working to accelerate business investment write-offs, while the Abolish the Alternative Minimum Tax Caucus wants to eliminate a tax paid by some middle-class and upper-income families.

Rep. Rob Portman, R-Ohio, heads the Universal IRA Caucus, which wants to make savings tax free by eliminating restrictions on Individual Retirement Accounts (IRAs).

"What it comes down to is votes," Norquist said. "In the closely divided Congress, a lot of tax bills will be decided on close votes. Our caucuses will be persistent. And I think they will prevail if they take a stand and show they have broad support."

Other tax-related caucuses are following Norquist's lead, pushing for tax measures opposed by powerful committee chairmen or the White House.

The Congressional Manufacturing Caucus, led by Small Business Committee Chairman Donald Manzullo, R-Ill., is pushing a business tax cut package (HR 1769) designed to help domestic manufacturers that is competing with a bill (HR 2896) backed by Thomas, which would provide breaks for domestic and multinational companies.

Some caucuses promote additional spending. A flock of business-related caucuses — including the Interstate 49 Caucus headed by House Energy and Commerce Committee Chairman Billy Tauzin, R-La. — are working to promote federal funding of additional

highway projects, including extension of a Louisiana interstate north to Kansas City.

Keith Ashdown, vice president of the conservative fiscal watchdog group Taxpayers for Common Sense, said caucuses are formidable forces for both tax cuts and spending increases.

"They are extremely motivated," Ashdown said. "And it's hard to motivate people to go against them. There is usually not much of a political upside to opposing them."

Some caucuses or the groups backing them have set up nonprofit foundations or institutes in Washington to support their efforts in Congress. A half-dozen caucuses have support groups resembling a hybrid of a think tank and a lobbying team. *(Groups, p. 64)*

The supporting organizations help to recruit new members, provide research, promote bills and sponsor fundraising events such as those staged during the week of Sept. 22 by the Sportsmen's Foundation, the Congressional Hispanic Institute and the Congressional Black Caucus Foundation.

GOP Rep. Curt Weldon of Pennsylvania, a former fire chief, is the founder of a caucus representing firefighters, fire departments and companies that make firefighting equipment. Those organizations support the Congressional Fire Services Institute.

Weldon and Rep. Norm Dicks, D-Wash., recently launched the Homeland Security Caucus. A plan to raise funds for another institute is under consideration. "We want to provide a voice for lawmakers and companies with an interest in homeland security," Weldon said.

Signs of Concern

As caucuses grow in numbers and clout, not everyone has welcomed their growing presence. Lawmakers including Mica and Lloyd Doggett, D-Texas, contend that caucuses are too close to business interests and threaten to undermine public deliberation, and the traditional role of committees.

Mica and Doggett want to see the House rule against public funding of caucuses more tightly enforced, and they would require caucuses to disclose the support they receive from lobbyists.

Common Cause and other watchdog groups want caucuses to disclose sources of income, their use of shared employees and congressional office space, ties to any business groups, membership lists, legislative goals and any offers of employment as lobbyists or consultants received by caucus members.

In May, Rep. Charles W. "Chip" Pickering Jr., R-Miss., a leader of the two-year-old Congressional Wireless Telecommunications Caucus, revealed that he was offered a $1 million-a-year position as chief lobbyist for the Cellular Telecommunications Industry Association. Members of that trade group were the main beneficiaries of legislation promoted by Pickering, including a 2002 law (PL 107-195) that delayed the sale of electromagnetic spectrum dedicated to television broadcasters in order to allow possible future bids by wireless providers and other companies. (*2002 Almanac, p. 17-4*)

Pickering turned down the job offer after being urged by party leaders to remain in the House.

Common Cause called for a ban on lobbying by former members of Congress during their first year out of office. The group also wants the House to require members to disclose whenever they seek or are interviewed for lobbying jobs, and to prohibit members from voting on legislation that would benefit their potential future lobbying clients or employers.

"Business caucuses are raising new issues," said Celia Wexler, Common Cause's research director. "First of all, the leaders of business caucuses should not be seeking jobs from trade groups. If they do, they should disclose any interviews and recuse themselves from related legislation."

Regulatory Vacuum

The Senate has no official regulation or monitoring of caucus activities. House caucuses are required to file at the start of each Congress a statement of purpose, the name of at least one of their members and a list of House employees assigned to caucus business.

But in practice, the rule is not enforced, and there is little oversight.

House Administration Chairman Bob Ney, R-Ohio, said his staff can barely keep up with the registration forms pouring in as new caucuses are formed, let alone monitor the groups' activities.

Some well-known caucuses, including Radanovich's Wine Caucus and the influential Textile Caucus, are not registered. A check of House members' Web sites found more than 60 other groups that have not filed. Leaders of several of the groups said they were unaware of the requirement.

Ney, who is listed as the leading

member of the Caribbean Caucus, the Congressional Youth Civic Caucus and the US-Afghan Caucus, was surprised to learn that many groups have not complied with the registration requirement.

"Frankly, there are so many caucuses it's getting harder and harder to keep track of them," he said.

The ban on the use of public funds by caucuses is enforced, Ney said. "They are not allowed to use public funds. That's why we oversee them," he said. "If we ever found out that caucuses were using public funds . . . we would close them."

GOP leaders permit caucuses to use staff members employed by House members and to use space donated by lawmakers and committees as long as the caucuses do not receive or expend public funds.

Mica said the lack of enforcement of the registration requirement and the caucuses' use of shared employees and donated office space indicates that some caucuses are effectively receiving public funds. "I fear we are going back to where we were," he said.

Tighter regulation of congressional caucuses could become part of a broader effort by an unlikely alliance of liberal public interest groups and fiscal conservative groups to require lobbyists and lobbying coalitions to disclose more information about their activities.

Doggett wants to expand the 1995 lobbying disclosure law (PL 104-65) to require lobbying coalitions to report their sources of funding and donated services. Similar requirements should be imposed on congressional caucuses and their nonprofit affiliates, he said.

One Thing Leads to Another

Susan Webb Hammond, a professor of government at American University who has studied modern congressional caucuses, says the current caucuses evolved from groups created by party factions and organizations representing the interests of ethnic groups, women and regional constituencies. The first official caucus, the House's Democratic Study Group, was formed in 1959.

Hammond traces the first business-related caucuses back to groupings of lawmakers that focused on major industries in their districts. Midwestern and Eastern lawmakers formed the Steel Caucus, and Southern lawmakers launched the Textile Caucus in the 1970s and 1980s.

To win House votes in 2001for a law

(PL 107-210) renewing President Bush's fast-track trade negotiating authority, the White House and Republican leaders acceded to demands by the Steel Caucus for steel import tariffs. The Textile Caucus won an agreement that GOP leaders would back a requirement that apparel imported under trade agreements with Caribbean and Andean nations be produced from U.S.-made fabric. (*2002 Almanac, p. 18-3*)

Newer business caucuses have been set up to provide a way for single industries to be heard apart from major business organizations, including the U.S. Chamber of Commerce, the National Federation of Independent Businesses and the National Association of Manufacturers. Caucus sponsors may work within the large business alliances, while at the same time promoting narrower agendas.

Technology and entertainment companies, for example, backed formation of the Congressional Internet Caucus in 1996 to fight restrictions on the Internet, including the ban on indecency, that were viewed as barriers to development of online businesses.

That caucus grew rapidly, and its support group, the Internet Education Foundation, now has a Washington office and an annual budget of $591,000 funded largely by the high-tech industry. The Internet caucus and its supporting foundation do not take positions on bills, but caucus members have created new groups that focus on legislation.

"Our caucus was really the first of its kind, focusing on high-tech issues," said former Rep. Rick White, R-Wash. (1995-99), a founder of the Congressional Internet Caucus. "Members learned about issues in our caucus and then formed other caucuses to help promote bills."

The new high-tech caucuses include groups promoting testing and evaluation equipment, medical technology, biotechnology, and copyright protection for movies and recorded music.

Other industries are working with caucuses to move specific legislation.

"[A] caucus allows for one-stop shopping, if you will, to discuss with members the many facets of an issue," said Jeffrey D. DeBoer, president and chief operating officer of the Real Estate Roundtable, which represents large commercial property owners. "And when we need votes, we don't have to start from scratch. We have a ready base of support."

The Congressional Real Estate Caucus that DeBoer helped launch in 1998 with Reps. Phil English, R-Pa., and Richard E. Neal, D-Mass., helped win a 50 percent tax deduction for the cost of some equipment installed in buildings before 2005 as part of this year's tax cut package (PL 108-27).

Competing for Dollars

The proliferation of caucuses has spurred competition among related groups for corporate and interest group backing. In late 2001, such a feud erupted between some Republicans and a fledgling group, the New Economy Republicans Inc., headed by Rep. Jerry Weller of Illinois.

Both parties had promoted caucuses aimed at addressing the needs of Silicon Valley and gathering high-tech campaign contributions. Critics complained that Weller's group was preempting other GOP fundraising efforts to promote Weller's ultimately unsuccessful 2003 race against Thomas M. Reynolds of New York to become the chairman of the National Republican Congressional Committee (NRCC).

During the week of Sept. 15, Hastert moved to end the intraparty competition for the role of Silicon Valley champion by proposing revival of the House Republican High Technology Working Group. That caucus was formed in the 1990s to compete with the moderate New Democrat Coalition. Hastert prodded Weller, Dreier and GOP Reps. Lamar Smith of Texas, and Thomas M. Davis III and Robert W. Goodlatte, both of Virginia, to work together.

"A lot of people want to be a leader in dealing with the high-tech industry. Now, we're all working together," Weller said.

More common is partisan competition to appeal to business and issue-oriented groups. Republicans recently formed a Congressional Hispanic Conference to compete with the Democratic-backed Congressional Hispanic Caucus. Both parties have entertainment caucuses, as well as high-tech groups.

Gun Liability

In a packed hotel conference room near the Capitol on Sept. 24, Rep. Thompson helped Sen. Blanche Lincoln, D-Ark., sell raffle tickets for a camouflage-colored Browning shotgun Thompson was brandishing above his head.

Congressional Caucuses, A to Z

Lawmakers working closely with interest groups have formed nearly 300 congressional caucuses to promote legislative causes. Here is a sampling of the variety of issues that have inspired formation of caucuses.

Army Corps Reform Caucus
Reps. Earl Blumenauer, D-Ore., Wayne T. Gilchrest, R-Md.
Backed by environmental groups and the National Waterways Conference, seeks more rigorous review of proposed U.S. Army Corps of Engineers water projects.

Building a Better America Caucus
Rep. Gary G. Miller, R-Calif.
Champions the priorities of the construction industry. Business backers include the National Ready Mixed Concrete Association, National Stone, Sand & Gravel Association and Associated General Contractors.

Congressional Boating Caucus
Sens. Trent Lott, R-Miss., John B. Breaux, D-La.; Reps. E. Clay Shaw Jr., R-Fla., Gene Taylor, D-Miss.
Represents the recreational marine industry. Business backers include the National Marine Manufacturers Association.

Congressional Fitness Caucus
Reps. Zach Wamp, R-Tenn., Mark Udall, D-Colo.
Promotes exercise and good nutrition to improve fitness of American population. Business backers include the International Health, Racquet and Sportsclub Association, restaurants and makers of food, beverages and consumer products.

Horse Caucus
Reps. John E. Sweeney, R-N.Y., Ken Lucas, D-Ky.
Seeks tax breaks and other benefits for horse breeders and operators of racetracks. Backers include the National Thoroughbred Racing Association.

Congressional Vision Caucus
Reps. Gene Green, D-Texas, Pat Tiberi, R-Ohio
Backs funding for eye disease research and public health education. Supported by the American Academy of Ophthalmology.

Space Power Caucus
Reps. Jane Harman, D-Calif., Dave Weldon, R-Fla.
Supports space programs and research. Backed by aerospace and defense firms.

2015 Caucus
Reps. E. Clay Shaw Jr., R-Fla., Collin C. Peterson, D-Minn.
About 10 lawmakers who have survived cancer promote research to find a cure by 2015.

Western Caucus
Rep. Chris Cannon, R-Utah
Conservative Western Republicans support property rights and conservation, oppose restrictions on use of public land.

Wind Hazard Reduction Caucus
Reps. Walter B. Jones, R-N.C., Dennis Moore, D-Kan.
Promotes research and new standards to reduce damage from tornadoes. Backed by makers of manufactured housing and building materials, engineering firms and insurers.

Zero Capital Gains Caucus
Rep. David Dreier, R-Calif.
Promotes reduced taxation of capital gains income. Supported by Americans for Tax Reform.

The gun was one of several sold, along with an African safari and other hunting adventures, during the Sportsmen's Foundation's annual fundraising banquet and auction. Door prizes were awarded based on numbers touched by a duck in a cage. A wall behind the lawmakers was decorated with the corporate insignia of dozens of companies, including producers of firearms and ammunition.

A year ago, the proposed gun liability ban stalled in the House after a series of sniper attacks in the Washington, D.C., area increased public concern about the availability of firearms.

Leaders of the Sportsmen's Caucus revived the bill (HR 1036) this year, and are one large step away from delivering it to Bush. The House passed the proposed lawsuit restriction on a 285-140 vote April 9, and caucus members have lined up 55 Senate supporters. Sixty votes would be needed to break a filibuster.

The legislation would block some civil lawsuits against manufacturers, distributors, dealers and importers of firearms and ammunition. Trade groups would also be protected. Lawsuits would be permitted against manufac-

Fundraising by Caucus Support Groups

Some of the largest congressional caucuses are affiliated with nonprofit groups that conduct fundraising, cover expenses and coordinate lobbying campaigns and legislative strategies. Here are annual fundraising totals reported by those groups.

Congressional Black Caucus
$7.0 million

Northeast-Midwest Institute
$3.3 million*

Congressional Hispanic Caucus
$2.3 million

Congressional Sportsmen's Caucus
$860,000

Internet Education Foundation
$591,000*

Congressional Fire Services Institute
$236,000*

Congressional Wine Foundation
$25,000*

SOURCE: Internal Revenue Service filings. (Figures are for 2002. Those marked with an asterisk are 2001 figures.)

turers or sellers who marketed weapons illegally, or when injuries or damage resulted from defective products.

Opponents call the bill a favor to the gun industry, and complain that the measure would deny victims of gun violence access to the courts.

Supporters have won Majority Leader Bill Frist's agreement to bring the House-passed bill directly to the Senate floor without committee action.

Four leaders of the Sportsmen's Caucus — Lincoln and Sens. Michael B. Enzi, R-Wyo., Michael D. Crapo, R-Idaho, and Max Baucus, D-Mont. — are working to enlist the support of Senate moderates with an argument that the bill is needed to preserve conservation programs that benefit hunters. They say lawsuits against gun makers and retailers threaten the revenue the government receives for conservation programs from excise taxes on guns and ammunition.

"We are in a strong position now. The Sportsmen's Caucus has made an important contribution to educating lawmakers about the issue," said Larry E. Craig, R-Idaho, chief sponsor of the Senate version of the bill (S 659) and a member of the NRA board of directors.

The Sportsmen's Caucus has generally focused on less-controversial conservation issues.

"We wanted a bipartisan environment, one in which lawmakers from both parties would feel comfortable," said Ray Arnett, a former NRA lobbyist who helped launch the caucus. "We didn't want it to work directly on gun issues, primarily. But we wanted it to support, or at least never oppose, the NRA."

While the caucus is attempting to win support for the liability legislation by appealing to moderate lawmakers concerned about conservation programs, the NRA has made clear that opponents of the bill could pay a price the next time they face voters.

Merle Black, a political science professor at Emory University, said Geor-

gia Republican Saxby Chambliss benefited last year from his active role on gun and conservation issues when he upset Democratic incumbent Sen. Max Cleland (1997-2003).

Chambliss launched a "Sportsmen for Saxby" group and stressed his record of opposing "attacks on our hunting heritage" as a leader of the caucus. He criticized Cleland for backing gun control legislation after the 1999 shootings at Colorado's Columbine High School. The Senate passed gun restrictions that died in the House. (*1999 Almanac, p. 18-3*)

The Congressional Sportsmen's Foundation has been pushing to form affiliated groups in state legislatures.

"Before, hunters may not have had much of a voice because they were in their duck blinds and may not have been paying attention to what was going in Washington," said Melinda Gable, executive director of the caucus foundation. "We make sure they know what's happening and have their voices heard." ◆

New Tensions Test the Limits Of Bush's Sway in Congress

White House finds more Republicans willing to buck its agenda as troubles mount

For most of this year, President Bush has enjoyed the strongest relationship with Congress of any president in decades. He has benefited from a widespread network of allies in both the House and Senate, and rank-and-file Republicans have not forgotten who campaigned so hard to help them win back the Senate.

But this fall, Bush's safety net of support in the Republican-run Congress is being tested like never before.

All over Capitol Hill, jaws are hanging open over Bush's $87 billion request for a year's worth of military operations and reconstruction in Iraq and Afghanistan. The Treasury is expecting a deficit approaching $500 billion for the fiscal year that started Oct. 1, and a recent New York Times-CBS News Poll showed that a majority of the public says Congress should say no to the whole thing. That will not happen, but it is increasingly likely Congress will try to limit the damage by turning at least some of the $20.3 billion for rebuilding Iraq into a loan rather than a grant.

There is also the growing unease in GOP ranks over joblessness, the reach of the 2001 anti-terrorism law (PL 107-56) into Americans' privacy, and the deepening deficits that many believe will get even worse if Congress enacts an expensive Medicare prescription drug benefit. Furthermore, Bush's job approval ratings, once a source of phenomenal political strength for not only him but also congressional Republicans, have fallen to a new low. In fact, they have dipped below the approval ratings he was getting before the Sept. 11 terrorist attacks. *(Polling, p. 66)*

The conditions are producing the greatest tensions in the Bush-Congress relationship since Republicans won majorities in both chambers in the midterm election 11 months ago. Their differences are still relatively small, and they fall far short of all-out internal warfare. But the White House is finding that Republicans are willing to vote against its proposals, if only on second-tier issues — such as overtime rules and media consolidation — and in ways that do not threaten the central themes of Bush's presidency.

The frequency of these Republican push-backs against the president has been increasing, and shows signs of picking up even more as the first session of the 108th Congress moves into its final weeks. If the trend continues next year, it could make it more difficult for Republicans to present a unified front as they campaign to keep one-party government in place beyond November 2004.

Still, there are limits to how far Republicans will go in de-

“They're going to get some pretty tough questions because the people at home are asking us tough questions.”

— Sen. Chuck Hagel, R-Neb., on the tension
between Congress and the White House

fying Bush on the issues that define his presidency. On the economy, the war on terrorism and the war in Iraq, Republicans restrict themselves to tinkering at the margins.

In part, that is because Republicans say they agree with Bush on the broad themes — that tax cuts are the right way to stimulate the economy, that new criminal justice powers were needed to fight terrorism at home, and that giving up on rebuilding Iraq would allow that nation to slip into chaos and lead to greater problems down the road.

No Longer Invincible

"There are ways to push back. Members will find the right thing to do," said Jim Kolbe, R-Ariz., chairman of the House Appropriations Foreign Operations Subcommittee. In the end, Congress will approve Bush's spending request for Iraq, he predicted, "because people don't want to be seen as saying we didn't follow through. Regardless of whether you felt we should or should not be there, we have to follow through."

Hill Republicans also will probably limit their rebellions because an all-out defeat of Bush's basic principles on the economy or foreign policy could damage them as well in the process. Knowing that such an effort would not only undermine him but also might drag them down, they make sure any rebellion is more of a tap on the shoulder than a full-force shove. "If Bush does badly, they're likely to pay, too," said Barbara Sinclair, a professor of American politics at UCLA.

"They really don't have any alternatives right now," said Merle Black, a professor of political science at Emory University. Having invested themselves so deeply in Bush's agenda, he said, "they've just got to tough it out and hope the situation improves."

At the moment, public attitudes toward Iraq are not improving, for either the White House or congressional Republicans. Faced with incredulous questions from their constituents — why would the United States give money to a country that has the second-largest oil reserves in the world? — Republicans are warming to the idea of lending the reconstruction funds to Iraq and expecting the country to pay it back with its oil revenues.

When they return from a recess the week of Oct. 13, senators expect a showdown vote on an amendment to the fiscal 2004 supplemental spending package (S 1689) that would turn $10 billion of the reconstruction funds Bush has requested into long-term loans. The proposal is by two Republicans: Kay Bailey Hutchison of Texas, the vice chairwoman of the GOP Conference, and Susan Collins of Maine. (*2003 CQ Weekly, p. 2451*)

"In a rare instance, they're politically tone deaf to the way this is being perceived," freshman GOP Rep. Tom Feeney of Florida said of the White House. He co-wrote an article for National Review Online with Stephen Moore, president of the conservative Club for Growth, advocating the loan approach.

Making the reconstruction funds a loan would be a relatively mild rebellion compared with other proposals that will not succeed, such as separating the reconstruction money from the rest of the package and killing it entirely, as Senate Democrats tried to do. But it would be a rejection of the administration's insistence that Iraq has enough debt already and cannot take on any more.

Moreover, some of the specific details in the request have made Hill Republicans cringe. Democrats had a field day with such items as $3.6 million for 600 radios and satellite telephones — at a cost of $6,000 each — and $2.6 million for 80 pickup trucks, at a cost of $33,000 each. A statement released by Senate Minority Leader Tom Daschle, D-S.D., noted dryly that "prices in the United States for a new truck begin at $14,000."

Even Republican leaders who normally would line up quickly behind Bush are finding themselves short of material to work with.

"The level of detail presented by the White House is something that's going to cause us more trouble than help," said Ohio's Deborah Pryce, chairwoman of the House Republican Conference. She said the White House had more work to do to make "the complete and proper case" that the reconstruction money should be a grant, not a loan.

Second-Tier Setbacks

The loan-vs.-grant debate is the most visible congressional challenge to the White House at the moment, but it follows a series of recent rebukes on other issues, at the hands of Republicans as well as Democrats.

Last month, the Senate voted, with the support of six Republicans, to block the administration's proposed changes in overtime regulations, which Democrats contend could make as many as 8 million workers ineligible for the extra pay.

The provision of the Labor, Health and Human Services, and Education spending bill (HR 2660) could complicate negotiations on the final bill. On Oct. 2, the House approved a non-binding motion endorsing the Senate language, with 21 Republicans defying a veto threat from Bush. Such "motions to instruct" are only symbolic, but they often provide a low-risk way for lawmakers to express their true feelings on an issue. (*2003 CQ Weekly, p. 2440*)

There have been other setbacks to the administration. With the support of 12 Republicans, the Senate voted in September to overturn a Federal Communications Commis-

President Showing Vulnerability

Recent polls appear to show President Bush's standing with the American people slipping.

President's overall job approval has reached a new low

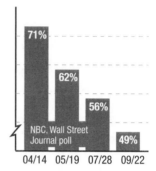

71% (04/14), 62% (05/19), 56% (07/28), 49% (09/22)
NBC, Wall Street Journal poll

Fewer than half of Americans approve of his handling of the Iraq situation.

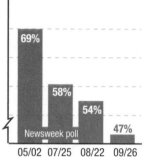

69% (05/02), 58% (07/25), 54% (08/22), 47% (09/26)
Newsweek poll

Half of the country fears the nation is generally moving in the wrong direction.

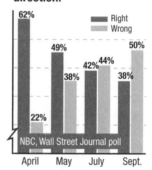

Right / Wrong
April: 62% / 22%
May: 49% / 38%
July: 42% / 44%
Sept.: 38% / 50%
NBC, Wall Street Journal poll

Republicans and Democrats in Congress are seeing their approval ratings slip as well.

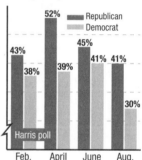

Republican / Democrat
Feb.: 43% / 38%
April: 52% / 39%
June: 45% / 41%
Aug.: 41% / 30%
Harris poll

Bush's rating for handling of the nation's economy has reached its all-time low.

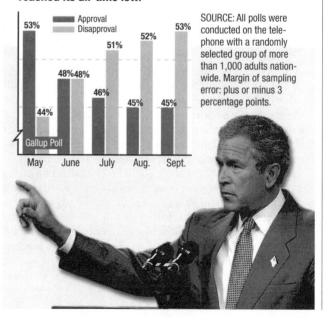

Approval / Disapproval
May: 53% / 44%
June: 48% / 48%
July: 46% / 51%
Aug.: 45% / 52%
Sept.: 45% / 53%
Gallup Poll

SOURCE: All polls were conducted on the telephone with a randomly selected group of more than 1,000 adults nationwide. Margin of sampling error: plus or minus 3 percentage points.

Recent Congressional Rejections of Bush Policy

Since July, President Bush has faced a series of setbacks from Congress, with Republicans joining Democrats to reject a half-dozen of the administration's policies. While most do not rise to the level of issues that will define the Bush presidency, taken together they have raised the level of tension between Bush and Congress. And they signal a shift in a relationship that since the 2002 election has been dominated by a powerful president at the height of his popularity.

PATRIOT ACT:
On July 22, in an amendment to the Commerce-Justice-State appropriations bill (HR 2799), the House voted 309-118 to kill funding for a provision of the 2001 anti-terrorism law (PL 107-56) that lets police conduct searches and seize evidence without advanced notice. *(2003 CQ Weekly, p. 1905)*

OVERTIME:
On Sept. 10, the Senate adopted 55-45 an amendment to the social services appropriations bill (HR 2660) to block changes in federal overtime rules. On Oct. 2, the House voted 221-203 to instruct conferees to accept the Senate position. *(2003 CQ Weekly, p. 2440)*

MEDIA CONSOLIDATION:
On Sept. 16, on a 55-40 vote, the Senate adopted a resolution (S J Res 17) to overturn a Federal Communications Commission rule that would let large media firms own more television stations and newspapers. *(2003 CQ Weekly, p. 2303)*

PRIVATIZATION:
In an amendment to the Transportation-Treasury appropriations bill (HR 2989), the House voted 220-198 Sept. 9 to stop the administration from privatizing thousands of federal jobs. *(2003 CQ Weekly, p. 2224)*

AVIATION:
Under pressure from Democrats and some Republicans, House GOP leaders are expected to send a bill to reauthorize the Federal Aviation Administration (HR 2115) back to conference committee to rewrite or drop its privatization language. *(2003 CQ Weekly, p. 2357)*

CUBA TRAVEL:
Also on the Transportation-Treasury bill Sept. 9, the House voted 227-188 to lift the ban on most travel to Cuba. *(2003 CQ Weekly, p. 2224)*

sion rule that would let large media conglomerates get larger. And the House, normally the chamber the White House can count on for support, has voted to stop the administration from privatizing thousands of federal jobs and to lift the ban on most travel to Cuba. *(Background, pp. 2303, 2224)*

Some Democratic strategists say those votes could create momentum for Congress to mount broader challenges on bigger issues. "One of the most important parts of the Bush image is effectiveness. He talks tax cuts, he gets tax cuts," said Democratic pollster Anna Greenberg. The recent defeats, she said, undermine that image.

"I really feel a different dynamic on Capitol Hill," said Democratic strategist Michael Lux. On issues such as Iraq, the economy and Medicare, Lux said, "they went home over the August recess, and I think they got the hell scared out of them."

But independent public opinion analysts say issues such as media regulation, overtime and privatization of federal jobs are not the kind that burn themselves into the public memory. "These were important issues, but they're not so large that they will resonate across the country," said Andrew Kohut, director of the Pew Research Center for the People and the Press.

Now, Republicans are taking heat on the big issues that do resonate. Constituents are critical of the rising costs

and mounting U.S. death toll in Iraq and are questioning whether the administration's economic and anti-terrorism policies are working. *(2003 CQ Weekly, p. 2198)*

"It's a very different situation than we've seen in the last two years," said Sen. Chuck Hagel, R-Neb., a member of the Foreign Relations Committee who has criticized Bush for not giving other nations a big enough role in rebuilding Iraq. The public sees "a drain on the Treasury. We're taking casualties. . . . We've never been in the Middle East as deeply as this. All of this adds up to a very unsteady public that wants some answers."

Damage Control

The White House has been concerned enough about Republican anxiety that Vice President Dick Cheney and other administration officials have been on Capitol Hill to press Bush's case for the funds.

They know any nervousness that spills into public view generates headlines and creates political problems for Bush. "I think everyone is concerned about the cost," said Sam Brownback, R-Kan., a member of the Senate Appropriations Committee. "People are starting to ask more questions now: Why $87 billion? Is it needed? Is it structured in the right way?"

To answer those questions, Cheney has met with the Senate and House Re-

publican conferences, and the administration has made top officials such as Defense Secretary Donald H. Rumsfeld, Ambassador L. Paul Bremer III, the top civilian official in Iraq, and General John P. Abizaid, commander of the United States Central Command, widely available to explain the request at length in committee hearings.

In addition, the White House has been circulating information to Hill Republicans who want to support the request but have no idea how to defend it to their constituents.

That strategy acknowledged the reality behind many of the criticisms during several recent hearings on Iraq. For Republicans such as Pete V. Domenici of New Mexico, a member of the Senate Appropriations Committee, the pointed questions were less about opposing the funding than about needing a good set of talking points to make the case to skeptics back home.

"I think there is a substantial majority of Americans who think we should have gone to war, who still think it was the right decision, but who are fragile because they don't understand the plan," Domenici told Bremer at an Appropriations hearing Sept. 22. He suggested Bremer hold news conferences on a regular basis to explain the plan for rebuilding Iraq and report on its progress.

"They're going to get some pretty tough questions, because the people at home are asking us tough questions," Hagel said.

Former lawmakers say the GOP is keenly aware that it can take dissent only so far, especially in the House.

"I think you'll see great reluctance among rank-and-file Republicans to pile on in this situation," said John Edward Porter, R-Ill. (1980-2001), a former House appropriator and now a partner at Hogan & Hartson LLP.

Instead, Porter suggested, Republicans may simply let Democrats pose the tough questions — including those they secretly would like to ask themselves — so the issues get aired without GOP fingerprints. "There will be enough questions raised . . . that it will give great pause to the administration if it decides to ask for another supplemental," Porter said.

Talking Points

To help congressional Republicans convince the public — and perhaps themselves — that the funding is justified, one set of White House talking points noted that $87 billion is less than 4 percent of next year's federal budget. While Iraq's total reconstruction needs are projected at $50 billion to $75 billion, the administration says it expects the United States to have to pay only $20 billion and that other nations and Iraq itself ultimately will cover the rest.

In addition, the White House says the Iraq costs have been higher than expected because it was difficult before the war to get an accurate picture of the deterioration of Iraq's electrical, water and sewage systems.

A second set of White House talking points offered explanations for some of the troublesome line items in the reconstruction funding request, such as $50,000 a bed for two new Iraqi prisons and $9 million to improve postal service. The administration said the cost for the prison beds is less than the U.S. average and Iraq is running out of prison space for criminals and terrorists, and that most of the postal money is actually to repair looted post offices.

Even that information may not be much help to the administration's cause. "I would have thought the one thing the Iraqis were good at was providing plenty of prison space," Rep. David R. Obey of Wisconsin, the ranking Democrat on Appropriations, remarked to Bremer during a Sept. 24 hearing of the Foreign Operations Appropriations Subcommittee.

Until now, the closest Bush came to a serious push-back from the Republi-

can Congress came in the spring, on his economic policy. Under pressure from Democrats and moderate Senate Republicans, Congress slashed the second major tax cut of his presidency from the $674 billion he requested to the $350 billion he signed (PL 108-27). Even there, however, Congress never seriously questioned whether there would be a tax cut at all. And conservative leaders have made it clear they hardly consider a $350 billion tax cut a defeat. (*2003 CQ Weekly, p. 1309*)

Now, despite real unease among Republicans over the stagnant jobs picture, the core of Bush's economic program is not under attack from within his own party. And the deteriorating deficit picture is still justified by many as acceptable in a time of war.

Aware that polls show jobs are the voters' top concern, Senate Majority Leader Bill Frist of Tennessee and other GOP leaders unveiled a "jobs and growth" agenda Oct. 2. But rather than outlining new initiatives, it was mainly a repackaging of legislation already moving through Congress — such as the energy bill (HR 6), limits on class action lawsuits (S 274) and a reauthorization of the Small Business Administration (S 1375) — that emphasizes their economic impact.

In general, Republicans agree that tax cuts have been the right way to stimulate the economy, so any new initiatives will continue in that vein. The Senate Finance Committee approved a tax package (S 1637) on Oct. 1 that

would give targeted tax relief to manufacturers. (*2003 CQ Weekly, p. 2428*)

The next day, the Senate rejected the latest Democratic attempt to pare Bush's tax cuts. An amendment by Democrat Joseph R. Biden Jr. of Delaware that would have raised taxes on the wealthiest Americans as a way to pay for the $87 billion Iraq supplemental was killed on a tabling motion, 57-42.

In the debate, Republicans advocated staying the course on Bush's economic policy. "The thing we need to do is to keep the growth occurring in this country, and you do that by low interest rates and low taxes," Brownback said.

Cornerstone of Terrorism War

Congress also is displaying the limits of its challenges to Bush on one of the cornerstones of the president's war against terrorism: the 2001 law known as the Patriot Act.

While polls have not shown strong public opposition to the law, there are other signs of anxiety. More than 175 cities and counties, as well as the states of Vermont, Alaska and Hawaii, have adopted resolutions criticizing the law. And Attorney General John Ashcroft recently went on a nationwide speaking tour to defend the law after the House voted overwhelmingly, with the support of 113 Republicans, to bar the application of a provision that allows police to conduct searches and seize evidence without notifying the subjects in advance. (*2003 CQ Weekly, p. 1905*)

"The whole Patriot Act is one big se-

The celebration at the signing of the homeland defense spending bill Oct. 1 belied tensions between Congress and Bush, shown shaking hands with Sen. Patrick J. Leahy, D-Vt.

cret," said Rep. C. L. "Butch" Otter, the Idaho Republican who sponsored the amendment, noting that the Justice Department has refused to release records of how it has been used in most cases.

Any legislative backlash, however, will be piecemeal. Otter is preparing a second amendment that would strip the attorney general's power to investigate religious institutions. And Sen. Larry E. Craig of Idaho, a former member of the GOP leadership, is planning to introduce a bill with Democrat Richard J. Durbin of Illinois that would rein in the FBI's subpoena powers and the power of law enforcement agencies to use "roving wiretaps," which follow suspects to any telephone lines they use.

But Otter says he has no intention of challenging the entire law. He believes some of it was necessary.

The Medicare Challenge

Overhauling Medicare, a potentially defining issue for Bush, may prove to be the exception to the rule of the Bush-Congress relationship.

Thirteen conservative Republicans who voted for the House version of the bill (HR 1) signed a letter to Speaker J. Dennis Hastert, R-Ill., saying they will not do so again if the final agreement does not include private competition and cost controls. These Republicans say the letter is not an idle threat, because the idea of creating a new, open-ended entitlement truly contradicts their basic view of the proper size and cost of the federal government. (2003 CQ Weekly, p. 2446)

"The letter should be taken quite literally," said its lead author, Rep. Patrick J. Toomey of Pennsylvania. "It's much more important to get a good bill than to get just any bill, and we're very serious about that."

Rep. Marsha Blackburn of Tennessee, a co-author of the letter, said she could no longer keep silent. "One of the things I learned while I was in the statehouse is that it's very easy to just keep your mouth shut and vote no," she said. "But that's not fair to everyone who's involved. It's much more honest to get involved in how the legislation is shaped."

These Republicans insist their letter was meant more to help the House negotiators' bargaining position than to challenge the president, and they say their goal is to improve the bill rather than to kill it. Some conservative leaders outside Congress, however, are open about their desire to stop the Medicare bill entirely.

"I think the question is whether or not we can change the political dynamics enough so that the bill becomes stymied," said Moore of the Club for Growth. The administration, he said, may "see it as a political winner in 2004, and our job as conservatives is to convince them that the politics actually work the other way."

Although Bush insists he wants a bill, and held a highly publicized meeting with House and Senate negotiators Sept. 25 to urge them to keep working, he has not been personally involved in the negotiations and therefore has plenty of room to distance himself if the negotiations fail.

Furthermore, there is some question whether Bush is using all of the tools at his disposal to make sure the bill passes. Three of the Republicans who signed the letter said they have gotten no feedback from the White House at all since they released it Sept. 17.

The fact that Republicans are venting their concerns at all is remarkable for a party that historically has frowned upon airing its differences in public.

That level of party discipline has helped Bush, for the most part, win greater compliance from a Republican Congress than the most recent Democratic presidents, Bill Clinton and Jimmy Carter, did from Congresses that were even more solidly Democratic.

"The prevailing wisdom is, 'If we fight in public, that's what Democrats do,' " said Lewis L. Gould, a professor emeritus in American history at the University of Texas at Austin and author of the forthcoming "Grand Old Party: A History of the Republicans." "When it's a president they agree with, and they endorse the policies in their general concept, it wouldn't make sense to get into fratricidal conflicts like the Democrats do."

Republicans are also aware that despite his declining overall approval ratings, Bush is still tremendously popular with their core supporters. "Most Republican voters still love him, and certainly the activists do," Sinclair said.

In addition, they are conscious of the presidential election politics that are already well under way, and the mileage Democratic presidential candidates are getting from criticizing Bush's policies on Iraq and the economy and his efforts to safeguard, if not expand, the Patriot Act.

Not all Republicans buy the argument that they should keep their differences private, however. "Our role now, as stewards of the funds, is to make sure the money is being spent wisely, with benchmarks to make sure it's being spent wisely," Kolbe said of the Iraq supplemental.

"It's never easy to criticize a president who you love and respect, and who is, of course, of your own party," said Feeney, who has advocated loans rather than grants for Iraq and was also one of the 13 House Republicans who signed the Medicare letter. "You have an obligation, when you think your friends are making mistakes, to speak up."

And the fact that other Republicans have been relatively restrained in questioning the administration in public on Iraq does not mean the tough questions have not been raised in private, some are quick to point out.

"They have been. It's just that they haven't been public," said Sen. George V. Voinovich, R-Ohio, a member of the Foreign Relations Committee.

By using the hearings and the floor debate to vent their frustrations over the cost of the Iraq request — even while making it clear they will ultimately vote for it — congressional Republicans say they are still having an impact by putting pressure on the administration to be more careful with its cost estimates and funding requests in the future.

Loyalty vs. Self-Preservation

"The administration is going to be put on notice that it can't just waltz in here and say, 'We're in charge of the foreign policy, you just give us the money,' " said Hagel.

Analysts agree. "The message is, 'This ticket is good for this trip only, and don't come back and ask us for another one,' " said Gould. "The peril for the administration is . . . what if they have to come back in June or July and say, 'Uh, we need another supplemental'?"

If that happens, the Republican tradition of discipline and loyalty will be pitted against the oldest tradition in politics: self-preservation. "The first rule of politics is to protect yourself," said former Democratic Rep. Dan Glickman of Kansas (1977-95), who now directs the Institute of Politics at Harvard's John F. Kennedy School of Government. "Yeah, party loyalty is important, but a smart senator or representative isn't going to do anything willingly that jeopardizes his or her career." ◆

GOP Draws on Image Of American Icon for 2004

Analysts say history is of little help in predicting election that could go either way

Ask Republican loyalists which recent election the 2004 presidential campaign will most resemble, and they are likely to say President Ronald Reagan's 1984 landslide victory.

They say George W. Bush will be a two-term president because he favors the muscular projection of the United States' power in global affairs, as did Reagan. They note that Bush mirrors Reagan in his frequent calls to patriotism and in his image as a rugged, ranch-living man of the West.

Moreover, Bush, as did Reagan, is running against a Democratic Party that is taking one of the greatest of all political risks: criticizing tax cuts that the incumbent pushed to enactment.

And even as they idolize Reagan and his legacy, some Republicans argue that Bush may be able to go one better: They say he might win big enough to establish his Republican Party — which already controls both houses of Congress — as the nation's majority party for many years to come.

But Democrats point to their own parallel bid for the White House, one that is more recent and closer to home for Bush. They predict that 2004 will be a sequel of the 1992 election — the one that handed Democrat Bill Clinton the presidency and made the first George Bush a one-termer.

The current incumbent, just like his father/predecessor, saw his public approval ratings soar following a quick victory by U.S.-led forces over the army of Iraqi dictator Saddam Hussein that occurred early in the year before his re-election campaign.

But like his father, Bush has presided during a period of national economic stagnation. Democrats say that will be his political undoing.

For political forecasters, either party's metaphor can appear plausible, which may leave the success or failure of Bush's re-election campaign in his own hands.

Bush "appears to have learned from his father's mistakes,"

Republicans are counting on Bush's re-election campaign to resemble Ronald Reagan's of 20 years ago, not Bill Clinton's.

BLOOMBERG NEWS PHOTO / ERIC DRAPER: KRT PHOTO

Election 2004

2004 OVERVIEW	**p. 2010**
Is Bush another Reagan... or another Bush?	
DEMOCRATS FOR PRESIDENT	**p. 2011**
Columnist Craig Crawford parses the field.	
ELECTION CALENDAR	**p. 2012**
Primaries, caucuses and filing deadlines.	
SENATE OUTLOOK	**p. 2015**
So near — yet so far — for the Democrats.	
SENATE RACE RANKINGS	**p. 2018**
CQ's "morning line" on the 2004 contests.	
HOUSE OUTLOOK	**p. 2021**
GOP majority enjoys structural advantages.	

said Paul Herrnson, the director of the Center for American Politics and Citizenship at the University of Maryland. "He is shrewd about dealing with the media, and he knows how to run a campaign while in office."

The 2004 campaign has begun during a particularly turbulent period of American history. It will be the first since the devastating al Qaeda attacks of Sept. 11, 2001; the first since Bush launched an international war on terrorism and ended the rule of al Qaeda sympathizers in Afghanistan; the first since he obligated U.S. troops and money in Iraq by toppling Saddam's dictatorial regime; and the first since the country's longest run of prosperity dissolved into the first recession in a decade.

Much more will happen over the next 15 months that will affect what voters decide Nov. 2, 2004 — from the staged fanfare of the 2004 conventions, which will be held by the Democrats in Boston on July 26-29 and the Republicans in New York City on Aug. 30 through Sept. 2, to events on the national and world stages that are impossible to predict.

Incumbent Favored to Win

To borrow the standard formulation used by pollsters, if the election were held today, Bush would have to be favored to win.

As the incumbent, he sets the national agenda and dominates media coverage of public affairs. His assertively conservative program has helped him maintain astounding loyalty among his voting base: A recent poll by the Pew Center for the People and the Press showed that 89 percent of self-described Republicans said they were inclined to vote for Bush, while 3 percent said they would favor a Democrat.

Bush also will have an unprecedented opportunity to broadcast his message unfiltered by others. After spending a record $100 million on his 2000 campaign, Bush raised more than $35 million in just six weeks after establishing his 2004 campaign committee May 16. He may spend as much as $150 million touting his record before next year's Republican convention — even though he is expected to

2004 Election Calendar Appears

Here are the dates for each state's key events in the 2004 campaign. The filing deadlines listed are for congressional and gubernatorial contests where applicable. Primary dates are designated based on which offices are on the ballot.

KEY

Text:
Blue — Primary election
Red — Caucus
Black — Filing deadline
Red dot 1 — National events

(P) — Event dealing with the presidential election
(C) — Congressional election
(G) — Gubernatorial and/or statewide election.

Shaded areas:
Critical early presidential primary and caucus dates

DECEMBER 2003

Dec. 5 — California filing deadline
Dec. 15 — Illinois filing deadline
Dec. 22 — Maryland filing deadline

JANUARY 2004

Jan. 2 — Ohio filing deadline
Texas filing deadline
Jan. 9 — Mississippi filing deadline
Jan. 13 — District of Columbia primary (P)[1]
Jan. 19 — Iowa caucuses (P)
Jan. 27 — New Hampshire primary (P)
Kentucky filing deadline
Jan. 31 — West Virginia filing deadline

FEBRUARY 2004

Feb. 3 — Arizona primary (P)
Delaware primary (P)
Missouri primary (P)
New Mexico caucuses (P)
North Dakota caucuses (P)
Oklahoma primary (P)
South Carolina primary (P)
Feb. 7 — Michigan caucuses (P)
Washington caucuses (P)
Feb. 8 — Maine caucuses (P)
Feb. 10 — Tennessee primary (P)
Virginia primary (P)
New Mexico filing deadline
Feb. 14 — District of Columbia caucuses (P)
Nevada caucuses (P)
Feb. 15 — Nebraska filing deadline (C — incumbents only)
Feb. 17 — Wisconsin primary (P)
Pennsylvania filing deadline
Feb. 20 — Indiana filing deadline
Feb. 24 — Hawaii caucuses (P)
Idaho caucuses (P)
Feb. 27 — Utah primary (P)
North Carolina filing deadline

MARCH 2004

March 1 — Nebraska filing deadline (C — non-incumbents)
March 2 — California primary (PC)
Connecticut primary (P)
Georgia primary (P)
Maryland primary (PC)
Massachusetts primary (P)
Minnesota caucuses (P)
New York primary (P)
Ohio primary (PC)
Rhode Island primary (P)
Texas primary (PC)
Vermont primary (P)
Washington primary (P)[2]
March 9 — Florida primary (P)
Louisiana primary (P)
Mississippi primary (PC)
Oregon filing deadline
March 13 — Kansas caucuses (P)
March 15 — Maine filing deadline
March 16 — Illinois primary (PC)
March 17 — Utah filing deadline
March 19 — Idaho filing deadline
Iowa filing deadline
March 20 — Alaska caucuses (P)
Wyoming caucuses (P)
March 25 — Montana filing deadline
March 30 — Arkansas filing deadline
Missouri filing deadline
South Carolina filing deadline

APRIL 2004

April 1 — Tennessee filing deadline
April 2 — Alabama filing deadline
April 6 — South Dakota filing deadline
April 9 — North Dakota filing deadline
Virginia filing deadline
April 12 — New Jersey filing deadline
April 13 — Colorado caucuses (P)
April 27 — Pennsylvania primary (PC)
April 30 — Georgia filing deadline

New Hampshire voters, shown casting primary ballots four years ago, will go to the polls next Jan. 27.

face no competition for the party's nomination.

Meanwhile, the voting public — paying scant attention to presidential campaign developments, as is typical in a pre-election year — is expressing few strong opinions about the nine candidates who are seeking the Democratic nomination to oppose Bush. After more than half a year of full-fledged campaigning, no front-runner has emerged from a field that includes Sens. John Edwards of North Carolina, Bob Graham of Florida, John Kerry of Massachusetts and Joseph I. Lieberman of Connecticut; Reps. Richard A. Gephardt of Missouri and Dennis J. Kucinich of Ohio; former Vermont Gov. Howard Dean; former Illinois Sen. Carol Moseley Braun; and civil rights activist Al Sharpton.

Congressional Hegemony

The outlook also appears positive for Republicans who are working to maintain their party's control of the House and the Senate in the 109th Congress that begins in January 2005.

As has been the case for many years, the national Republican Party campaign organizations will have much more money to spend on congressional races than their Democratic counter-

Packed With Critical Dates

The presidential primary dates listed are specifically for the Democrats, as President Bush is not expected to face competition for the Republican nomination. Under Louisiana's unique law, all candidates will run in an open primary Nov. 2.

MAY 2004	JUNE 2004	JULY 2004	AUGUST 2004	SEPTEMBER 2004
May 4 — Indiana primary (PCG)¹ North Carolina primary (PCG) **May 7** — Florida filing deadline **May 11** — Nebraska primary (PC) West Virginia primary (PCG) Michigan filing deadline **May 17** — Nevada filing deadline **May 18** — Arkansas primary (PC) Kentucky primary (PC) Oregon primary (PC) **May 25** — Idaho primary (C) ² **May 28** — Wyoming filing deadline	**June 1** — Alabama primary (PC) New Mexico primary (C) South Dakota primary (PC) Alaska filing deadline Colorado filing deadline Massachusetts filing deadline **June 8** — Iowa primary (C) Maine primary (C) Montana primary (PCG) New Jersey primary (PC) North Dakota primary (CG) South Carolina primary (C) Virginia primary (C) **June 9** — Arizona filing deadline **June 10** — Kansas filing deadline **June 11** — New Hampshire filing deadline **June 22** — Utah primary (CG) **June 23** — Oklahoma filing deadline **June 30** — Rhode Island filing deadline	**July 7** — District of Columbia filing deadline **July 13** — Wisconsin filing deadline **July 15** — New York filing deadline **July 19** — Vermont filing deadline **July 20** — Georgia primary (C) Hawaii filing deadline Minnesota filing deadline ● **July 26-29** — Democratic National Convention, Boston **July 27** — Oklahoma primary (C) **July 30** — Delaware filing deadline Washington filing deadline	**Aug. 3** — Kansas primary (C) Michigan primary (C) Missouri primary (CG) **Aug. 5** — Tennessee primary (C) **Aug. 6** — Louisiana filing deadline **Aug. 10** — Colorado primary (C) Connecticut primary (C) **Aug. 17** — Wyoming primary (C) **Aug. 24** — Alaska primary (C) ● **Aug. 30-Sept. 2** — Republican National Convention, New York **Aug. 31** — Florida primary (C)	**Sept. 7** — Arizona primary (C) Nevada primary (C) **Sept. 11** — Delaware primary (CG) **Sept. 14** — District of Columbia primary (C) Massachusetts primary (C) Minnesota primary (C) New Hampshire primary (CG) New York primary (C) Rhode Island primary (C) Vermont primary (CG) Wisconsin primary (C) **Sept. 18** — Hawaii primary (C) **Sept. 21** — Washington primary (CG) ● **Nov. 2** — National Election Day Louisiana primary (C) ³

BLOOMBERG PHOTO / TANNEN MAURY

BLOOMBERG PHOTO / KEVIN P. COUGHLIN

¹ — Will be a non-binding "beauty contest" primary, since an official delegate-selection event this early would violate Democratic Party rules.

² — Also will hold non-binding presidential "beauty contest" vote on this date.

³ — Candidates will run on this date in all-party, single-ballot primaries. Candidates who win a majority of votes are deemed elected. In contests in which there is no majority winner, the top two vote-getters regardless of party compete in runoffs to be held Dec. 4.

parts. In fact, the Republican advantage may loom larger because of the newly implemented campaign finance law that was enacted mainly with the support of Democrats in Congress.

Democrats hoped that voters would honor their commitment to reducing the influence of money in politics when they pushed the bill sponsored by Sens. John McCain, R-Ariz., and Russell D. Feingold, D-Wis., to passage in 2002. They did so over complaints by many Republicans that the measure would infringe upon Americans' freedom of political expression.

But the practical effect of the law has been to eliminate the large, mainly unregulated "soft money" donations to federal campaigns from individuals, unions, businesses and other entities — a form of fundraising at which Democrats had grown to be almost as adept as Republicans — while amplifying the importance of smaller, regulated "hard money" donations, which the GOP is the master at collecting.

The political landscape may accrue to the Republicans' benefit as they work to hold on to Congress.

Numerically, the Democrats do not appear to face an insuperable challenge in their effort to take control of the Senate. There now are 51 Republican senators, 48 Democrats and an independent, Vermont's James M. Jeffords, who quit the Republican Party in 2001 and declared his independence while aligning himself with the Democrats.

As a result, the Democrats need a net gain of just two seats to guarantee a majority — and just one if their party succeeds in evicting Bush from the White House, since that victory would allow a Democratic vice president, in the constitutional role as president of the Senate, to break a 50-50 tie.

But a close look at the 34 seats that will be up for election in 2004 suggests the Democrats may have their hands full holding their ground, much less making the gains they need to reclaim the Senate gavel.

Democrats will be defending 19 seats that they currently hold, compared with 15 now held by Republicans. Many of next year's Senate contests will take place in parts of the South and West that are Republican-friendly — 10 of the Democratic seats are in states that favored Bush for president in 2000, while only three of the Republican seats are in states that supported 2000 Democratic presidential nominee Al Gore.

Majority Wins?

The Republicans also appear to have a built-in advantage in the elections for the House, which they now control with a 229-205-1 majority.

The congressional reapportionment that followed the 2000 census continued a longstanding trend of shifting seats from the North and East, where Democrats are most competitive, to the South and West, where Republicans thrive best.

Republicans also got the better of the redistricting process that preceded the 2002 elections. In states where the GOP controlled the process, Republicans drew maps that gave their party gains. And they reached compromises protecting GOP incumbents in states where they shared control with Democrats.

The result was a net six-seat Republican gain in 2002 that added a cushion to what had been a perilously narrow majority.

Democrats would need to add at least 12 seats to their total to reclaim the majority they surrendered in the 1994 elections — and even top party officials concede that that is unlikely unless national and world events provoke a backlash against Bush and his Republican allies in Congress.

Still, the political environment in these first years of the 21st century creates enough uncertainty to mitigate Republican overconfidence.

It has been many years since a presidential election has been so affected by a confluence of concerns about the economy, national security and America's role in the world.

A vibrant rebound from the 1981-82 recession and the neutralization of America's main international adversary, the Soviet Union, undergirded Reagan's 1984 rout and the easy 1988 presidential victory for the elder Bush, Reagan's vice president. By 1992, the economy had soured, but it was virtually the only issue in the Bush-Clinton matchup: The end of the Cold War and collapse of the Soviet Union essentially removed foreign policy as a major campaign issue.

With the economy thriving and Americans enjoying what turned out to be a false sense of security, the last two presidential campaigns were dominated by narrowly focused themes.

Clinton's emphasis on political esoterica in 1996 was symbolized by his proposal to improve educational discipline by encouraging school systems to require students to wear uniforms. While Bush in 2000 broadly promised to address long-term problems in such areas as Social Security, health care and education, much of his rhetoric focused on restoring moral rectitude to the White House following the scandals of the Clinton years.

Parallels With 1980

The contrast with the current campaign is striking: Not since the presidential election of 1980 has the nation faced so much volatility and uncertainty on both the domestic and international fronts.

The parallel with 1980 is not especially attractive for the party in control of the White House. That year, a combination of raging inflation, high interest rates, energy shortages and public outrage over the taking of American hostages by Iran's Islamic revolutionaries resulted in Reagan's defeat of Democratic incumbent Jimmy Carter.

There is little similarity to Carter, though, in the manner in which Bush has conducted America's affairs. Carter was widely viewed, even by many in his own party, as timid in addressing the nation's well-being. Bush has governed boldly, as he has attempted to stamp his conservative political philosophy indelibly on government policy-making.

The political rewards for boldness can be great — if the voters view those policies as making them better off and more secure than they were four years earlier. The penalties can be just as great if the public sees those policies as failing.

The degree to which preservation of Republican congressional majorities may be tied to Bush's success is uncertain: Presidential "coattails," positive or negative, have not been a major factor in most recent elections. The Republicans endured net losses of one House seat and four Senate seats even as Bush was narrowly elected president in 2000. Clinton failed to restore his party to power in Congress even as he won easily in 1996.

Sharing the Wealth

But with their party in complete control of the federal government, and with their membership providing near-lockstep support for Bush's major policy initiatives, the fate of congressional Republicans may be linked more closely than usual to that of the president.

"In the case of unified government, there is accountability," Herrnson said.

If the economy improves, congressional Republicans will share credit with Bush for the big tax cut packages they supported this year and in 2001. If the economy fails to generate jobs and the ballooning federal deficit becomes a matter of voter dissent, Republicans in Congress could find themselves vulnerable.

If Iraq is pacified and appears on its way to democratic stability, the Republicans who gave near-unanimous support to the resolution authorizing the use of military force may benefit politically. If the public decides Iraq is becoming a military quagmire, there may be a price paid at the polls.

The degree to which voters believe that progress is being made on critical domestic issues such as health care and education will also affect Bush and congressional Republicans alike.

It was Bush himself who set a high standard for his party in his speech accepting the presidential nomination at the 2000 convention in Philadelphia. He ticked off a list of national problems that he said were unsolved after eight years of Clinton-Gore administration, following each with the mantra, "They have not led. We will."

Voters in the past two elections have given the Republicans the opportunity to lead. Their views of how well the party has kept Bush's promise will influence the outcome in 2004. ◆

A Full Reservoir of Trust

President Bush's Timetable

President Bush enjoys solid public backing for the way he is handling the situation in Iraq, but as American casualties have mounted, that support has begun to erode slightly.

Bush Has Confidence Of the Majority

How Americans responded to the question, "Do you think the Bush administration deliberately misled the American public about whether Iraq had weapons of mass destruction or not?"

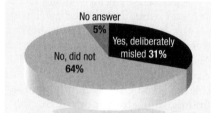

No answer **5%**

No, did not **64%**

Yes, deliberately misled **31%**

SOURCE: June 9-10 USA TODAY/CNN/Gallup telephone poll of 1,029 adults nationwide. Margin of sampling error, plus or minus 3 percentage points.

The phrase "as long as it takes" is President Bush's ready answer to questions about how long American troops and civilian officials will remain in Iraq: to rebuild that nation's war-ravaged economy, to set up democratic institutions — and especially to locate the alleged arsenal of weapons of mass destruction that Bush used as the leading justification to crush the regime of Saddam Hussein.

The president's stay-the-course rhetoric conveys his determination to combat threats to national security while countering critics who contend that he is seeking to turn the United States into an imperial power.

But his assertion also relies on a political calculation — that Congress and the American public are willing to grant him all the time and money he needs to find hidden biological, chemical and/or nuclear weapons, pacify an increasingly restive Iraqi population, and create enough order there to allow some of the roughly 146,000 American occupation forces to start coming home.

Bush thus far is bolstered by the fact that his fellow Republicans control Congress, and most continue to rally around him. Allies such as California Republican Duncan Hunter, chairman of the House Armed Services Committee, speak rousingly of the need to "persevere" in Iraq. Bush may have bought more time in the weapons search last week, when American forces uncovered a long-buried centrifuge — a device that could be used in nuclear weapons production — in the garden of a former Iraqi scientist.

Most Americans continue to give the president the benefit of the doubt. Bush maintains soaring support for his handling of national security issues since the terrorist attacks of Sept. 11, 2001. A Washington Post-ABC News poll published June 24 showed that 67 percent of the respondents approved of the way Bush was handling the situation in Iraq.

But the president and his supporters on Capitol Hill also know the public can lose its patience with America's incomplete victory.

Another poll — by the Democracy Corps, made up of veteran Democratic strategists James Carville, Stan Greenberg and Bob Shrum — showed a declining majority in favor of the war. The poll taken June 23 showed a 14 percentage-point margin between the 55 percent who said the war was worth the cost of U.S. lives and dollars and the 41 percent who said it was not. That was exactly half the 28 percentage-point margin in favor of the "worth it" side (61 percent to 33 percent) in a Democracy Corps poll taken May 15.

Greenberg described the decline in support as significant. "It is a very dramatic drop," he said. "That's a very big shift in one month." He noted that there was no similar backtrack in the immediate aftermath of the 1991 Persian Gulf War, in which a U.S.-led coalition built by President George Bush ended an Iraqi occupation of neighboring Kuwait.

A continued slippage in public support for the Iraq engagement could spur some sort of congressional action, such as potentially embarrassing open hearings into the possible manipulation before the war of intelligence reports concerning Iraq's weapons by Bush administration officials.

The flames are being fanned by contenders for the 2004 Democratic nomination to challenge Bush. Most of these Democrats were cautious about criticizing any aspect of Bush's policy in the weeks after the Iraqi regime fell, but have grown increasingly bold in recent weeks.

But the situation in Iraq is not strictly a partisan issue. Among those questioning Bush's approach are a number of Republicans, some of whom criticize the president for lacking an exit strategy.

Other Republicans insist that realistically it will be at least five years before all American troops can be withdrawn from Iraq and that Bush must tell that to the nation now. They also say Bush needs to be forthright with Congress about how much such a lengthy occupation will cost.

As prominent a Republican as Indiana's Richard G. Lugar, chairman of the Senate Foreign Relations Committee, told a news conference June 25 that the time had come for the administration to drop the "as long as it takes" line and tell the American public that the occupation will probably last at least five years.

"This idea that we will be in just as long as we need to and not a day more, we've got to get over that rhetoric. It is rubbish!" said Lugar, who was among a group of senators who had just returned to Washington after checking out the scene in Iraq.

Further afield, Bush faces a different challenge from the international community. Officials from countries such as France, Russia and China, which worry about America's pre-emptive policies and its awesome global reach, are in no hurry to see Bush extricate himself from his problems in Iraq.

The longer he flounders, this thinking goes, the weaker the position of the United States in the world — and the better their chances of restoring a measure of equilibrium to the U.S.-dominated world order.

Reading the Polls

For now, at least, most polling about Iraq brings solace to Bush. Perhaps the best news for the president is that most Americans do not seem overly concerned about whether those weapons of mass destruction — said by Bush to have posed an imminent threat to the welfare of the American people — are ever found.

Ending the 34-year rule of Iraqi tyrant Saddam is enough justification for most poll respondents. The recent Washington Post-ABC News poll showed that 63 percent of the respondents said the war was justified even if no such weapons are ever found.

Yet even the positive numbers in this poll show some signs of slippage. A Washington Post-ABC News poll taken April 3, before the outcome of the war had been decided, showed that 69 percent thought the war was justified even if no weapons of mass destruction were found.

There is little question, however, that national security and foreign policy issues are Bush's strongest suit as he prepares for his 2004 re-election campaign.

The reservoir of trust in Bush as commander in chief in the wake of military victories in Afghanistan and Iraq is underscored by an unusual dichotomy in the Democracy Corps poll. When asked if they trusted what the government in general is saying about weapons of mass destruction in Iraq, 49 percent of the respondents said no, while 46 percent said yes. But when asked if they trusted Bush himself on this issue, 56 percent said yes and 40 percent said no.

The poll also showed that on key domestic issues such as health care, federal deficits, the economy and Social Security, respondents said they favored a "significantly different direction" from Bush's approach — a reason why Carville, Greenberg and Shrum contend that Bush is potentially vulnerable to defeat next year.

But Bush held the edge on the four foreign policy-related questions. His most lopsided advantage concerned the war on terrorism: 67 percent of those polled said they favored Bush's direction, compared with 30 percent for a significantly different direction.

"There has been a widespread perception that he has been a strong leader since 9/11," said James M. Lindsay, senior fellow in foreign policy studies at the Brookings Institution, a liberal Washington think tank.

But, Lindsay said, "That is not inexhaustible. The public has the right to change its direction."

Lindsay added that if serious problems developed in the postwar effort in Iraq, "issues that aren't sticking now would stick like glue."

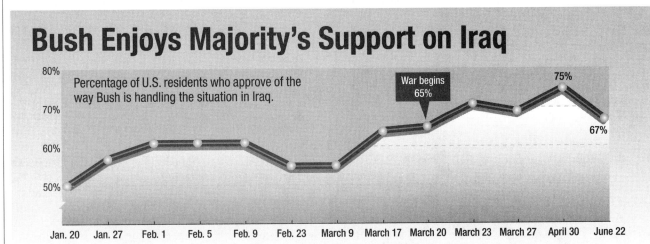

Bush Enjoys Majority's Support on Iraq

Percentage of U.S. residents who approve of the way Bush is handling the situation in Iraq.

War begins 65% 75% 67%

Jan. 20 Jan. 27 Feb. 1 Feb. 5 Feb. 9 Feb. 23 March 9 March 17 March 20 March 23 March 27 April 30 June 22

SOURCE: Washington Post-ABC News telephone polls of more than 1,000 adults nationwide. Margin of sampling error, plus or minus 3 percentage points.

How Patient?

"A lot of people basically said we went in, we did this and that it was a good thing. That we did a human and beneficial act, at some sacrifice, for the good of the Iraqi people," said George Rabinowitz, a political science professor at the University of North Carolina.

The degree of patience also may be affected by how much this effort, probably years long, to pacify and rebuild Iraq in America's image will cost American taxpayers.

"The occupation will be a much bigger issue than weapons of mass destruction," Carville said.

"Winning the peace," as it is often called, is proving more difficult than Bush administration planners appeared to allow for.

War damage, sabotage, looting and the collapse of the existing administrative structure have caused frustrating delays in restoration of basic public services in much of Iraq. And while Bush's strategists hoped the United States would be viewed as a liberator, many Iraqis have remained wary of, if not downright hostile to, the American presence.

"If there is a point in time when it seems the Iraqi people are really collectively dissatisfied with American presence, and it becomes obvious that it is [financially] costly, then [American] people might start to say, 'How did we get into this in the first place?' " Rabinowitz said.

The most sensitive issue of all may be the slowly mounting toll of U.S. troop casualties. "There are a lot of people in Iraq and around Iraq who don't want us to succeed," Lindsay said.

After enduring deaths of 138 service personnel during the war, U.S. forces have lost an additional 60 people since Bush declared an end to major combat operations on May 1, as of June 27. While many died in accidents, 20 have been killed in attacks by individuals or guerrilla groups opposed to the U.S. occupation.

Yet some conservative analysts expect the public to maintain its tolerance of some losses as long as there are no devastating setbacks.

"As long as we have a military victory and no additional big attack, [the public] is happy to see our military forces prevail and someone whom they acknowledge as evil defeated,"

said Michael Franc, vice president of government relations at The Heritage Foundation, a conservative think tank.

Even some Democrats are sanguine about the leeway that the public is giving Bush as the difficult postwar scenario unfolds.

"It is really not a big surprise. The public is not as fickle as some presume. They think it's going to be tough, but they are patient," said Will Marshall, president of the Progressive Policy Institute, which is associated with the centrist Democratic Leadership Council.

Democrats Probe

That, however, has not prevented several of the Democratic presidential hopefuls from testing whether Iraq-related issues could be harmful to Bush's political standing.

At the core of most Democratic criticisms is the question of whether the administration, and the president himself, manipulated or exaggerated evidence of Iraqi weapons capability to hype the imminence of the threat to national security.

Among those taking this tack are two candidates — former Vermont Gov. Howard Dean and Ohio Rep. Dennis J. Kucinich — who are appealing to the liberal anti-war constituency that is part of the Democratic political base.

Appearing on CNN's "American Morning" on June 23, Dean said, "This president has really not been terribly truthful to the American people. On Iraq, he told us a whole lot of things about Iraq that weren't so. We knew where the chemical weapons were, that Saddam was going to use chemical weapons on us. That didn't happen."

Kucinich went even further, implying that Bush was a liar. "America faces a crisis of legitimacy of the administration itself, which lied to the American people to get approval for a war," Kucinich said in a House floor speech June 24.

Also hitting hard at Bush has been Florida Sen. Bob Graham.

In a June 26 news release, Graham cited a New York Times article concerning a dispute between the State Department and the CIA over whether a pair of trailers impounded in Iraq were mobile biological laboratories. Bush had publicly cited the

CIA's conclusion that the trucks were germ warfare laboratories.

"The steady dripping sound of conflicting information coming from the administration is confirming the worst fears of the American people: Their government is not being honest and forthright about the intelligence surrounding weapons of mass destruction in Iraq," said Graham.

Like the dovish Kucinich, Graham voted against the resolution authorizing Bush to use military force against Iraq last October.

But Graham — a political moderate who chaired the Senate Intelligence Committee during much of the 107th Congress — said he opposed the measure because he believed it would sap military and financial resources from what he viewed as the more crucial war against terrorism.

Voting for the war resolution were the other four members of Congress who are running for president: Rep. Richard A. Gephardt of Missouri and Sens. John Edwards of North Carolina, Joseph I. Lieberman of Connecticut and John Kerry of Massachusetts.

Kerry skewered Bush on Iraq during an appearance June 18 in the crucial early primary state of New Hampshire. "I will not let him off the hook throughout this campaign with respect to America's credibility and credibility to me, because if he lied, he lied to me personally," Kerry said.

But Brookings' Lindsay said Kerry could face credibility questions of his own on the issue because he supported the war resolution.

"To the extent that there will be politicians who say they were fooled, I think that is far too charitable about their gullibility," Lindsay said. "Why weren't you asking those tough questions? Where were your critical analytical faculties back then?"

Franc, of the Heritage Foundation, said the Democrats' criticisms of Bush are not aimed so much at changing voters' minds at this early stage of the campaign as they are "setting the table" in case the Iraq mission ultimately goes sour.

"The kind of attacks the Democrats are mounting are prophylactic," Franc said. "The remarks they are making today might have more loft if, God forbid, there's some major disaster."

But, he added, "if forces do find weapons of mass destruction, there will be a lot of crow to eat." ◆

Can Deal-Making Survive Bush's Falling Numbers?

As the president's polls go down, the congressional landscape is changing

As he left his ranch house in Crawford, Texas, before dawn Aug. 19 for a golf outing, President Bush could not have known how fully the next few hours would demonstrate the uncertainty of the nation's affairs at home and abroad — a volatility that could now affect his ability to get his way this fall on Capitol Hill.

His first stop before he arrived at the Ridgewood Country Club was at a FINA gasoline station, where he relayed assurances from congressional leaders that work on energy legislation would resume within 20 days. Five days earlier, the worst-ever power outage in North America had exposed the vulnerability of the nation's aged electricity delivery system and had created a new imperative to act in coming weeks.

Lost in Bush's optimism was the reality that the energy policy package (HR 6) had been dragged down the last two years by partisan, regional and environmental policy divides.

Less than three hours later, Bush's working vacation was rocked by another crisis. National security adviser Condoleezza Rice telephoned the president with news of a terrorist bombing of the United Nations headquarters in Baghdad. Bush left the golf course after the 11th hole and asserted his command before a television audience over an issue that has increasingly placed him in a defensive position.

The bombing underscored his administration's miscalculations about what it will take to stabilize Iraq after this year's U.S.-led war. Costs have risen, more soldiers have died since May than during the six weeks of combat, and congressional oversight is intensifying.

Indeed, the power blackout, turmoil in Iraq and the Middle East, and other events during August as the president and the 108th Congress vacationed shook Bush's political standing

CQ Weekly Aug. 30, 2003

slightly, but enough to change the political environment for the critical fall legislative season. The result was that the enactment of bills considered "must do" before the 2004 election year arrives — adding a prescription drug benefit to Medicare (HR 1) and energy legislation — now seems less certain.

The only mandatory items on the agenda now are the fiscal 2004 appropriations bills, which may keep Congress in session to Veterans' Day or beyond. (*2003 CQ Weekly, p. 2086*)

Swinging Numbers

Growing public unease over Iraq and the general direction of the country has placed Bush's once-solid footing in public opinion polls on softer ground.

Fully 49 percent of 1,009 adults polled by Gallup on Aug. 25-26 described the war as going "badly," up from 29 percent in May. A Princeton Survey Research Associates poll of 1,011 adults Aug. 21-22 found 44 percent want to see Bush re-elected, down from 51 percent in May. And while the economy is showing signs of a turnaround, critics note that so far during Bush's presidency there has been a net loss of jobs — the first time that has happened since Herbert Hoover was president during the Depression.

More bad news for Republicans came Aug. 26, when the Congressional Budget Office reported that the federal budget deficits for the foreseeable future will be deeper than previously forecast — even without a new Medicare drug benefit or an extension of current tax cuts. (*2003 CQ Weekly, p. 2088*)

Though Bush remains popular, the perception that he is weakening politically only intensifies partisan competition and diminishes the likelihood of legislative deal-making.

"I'm actually quite pessimistic," said Thomas E. Mann, a senior fellow at the Brookings Institution, a liberal Washington think tank. "I actually think the fate of the election has now moved from the legislative battlefield to the real econo-

President Losing Ground to Democrats

When asked whether President Bush or the Democrats have a better approach in the following issues, recent polling notes that Bush is losing ground almost across the board:

■ President Bush　　　▨ Democrats

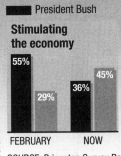
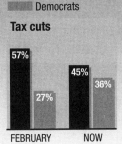
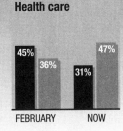
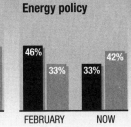

Stimulating the economy — FEBRUARY: 55% / 29% — NOW: 36% / 45%

Tax cuts — FEBRUARY: 57% / 27% — NOW: 45% / 36%

Health care — FEBRUARY: 45% / 36% — NOW: 31% / 47%

Energy policy — FEBRUARY: 46% / 33% — NOW: 33% / 42%

SOURCE: Princeton Survey Research Associates telephone poll of 1,011 adults nationwide taken Aug. 21-22 for Newsweek. Margin of sampling error, plus or minus 3 percentage points.

CQ PHOTO

CQ GRAPHIC / MARILYN GATES-DAVIS

my and to the situation on the ground in the Middle East. That's why I think you are going to see a lot of fighting and a lot of irresolution" in Congress.

The shift in momentum was signaled by a senior House Republican aide, who labeled Medicare and energy "top legislative priorities, but not necessarily 'must-do' bills." In other words, he said, Republicans expect there will be great pressure on both parties to get the bills finished, but his party is not ready to compromise its free-market principles for the sake of getting just any bill.

Political Calculations

If Bush wants Medicare and energy legislation to show voters that a Republican-controlled government produces solutions, he must decide how he will gamble. Does he bet on hard-line GOP leaders who will try to force Democrats to fold by accusing them of blocking progress if they do not go along? Or does he deal with Democrats and count on loyal Republicans to back him, no matter how dissatisfied the conservative base is with the final bills?

"The public demands for action [on Medicare] are so great, you may find in the end that the Democrats cannot sustain a filibuster," said Norman J. Ornstein, a resident scholar at the American Enterprise Institute, a conservative think tank. "Or, the president decides, and enough Republicans decide, to give up a share of their base. But the weaker he is politically, the more sensitive he is to that base."

There was a time when Bush forced his will on Republican loyalists and brought along reluctant Democrats. In the wake of the 2001 terrorist attacks, Democrats calculated that it was better to cut a deal on an education overhaul (PL 107-110) and go along with Bush on an anti-terrorism law (PL 107-56) than to take on an unusually popular president.

But the mood to compromise is long gone. Tensions between the parties increased during August in the home states of 50 House Democrats: in California, where Republicans forced a recall election of Democratic Gov. Gray Davis; and in Texas, where House Majority Leader Tom DeLay is trying to orchestrate a redrawing of congressional district boundaries. (*2003 CQ Weekly, p. 1728*)

"There's hardly any trust, let alone flexibility," Democratic consultant Donna Brazile said of the prevailing mood in Washington.

At best, completion of a Medicare bill that, as currently drafted, would not take effect until 2006 would only give politicians bragging rights in the 2004 election. Meanwhile, grousing over the plan's shortcomings would probably intensify.

"With this plan, he has bought a bag of trouble," said Democratic pollster Mark Mellman. "But if he does not have it, he's open to attack on that front."

But Democrats also learned in the 2002 election, when they lost control of the Senate, the cost of not producing a bill when given a chance. They will be under pressure to avoid looking like obstructionists of a GOP-backed Medicare bill, warned Republican pollster David Winston.

"If it is perceived that the Democrats are stopping it in an unfair way, the Democrats have a problem" because of the public's demand for a solution, he said. "However, if it is perceived as the Republicans not getting it through, that's a different problem for Republicans."

There is a bit more optimism for the energy bill, though again, it will require breaking stalemates on several points. Chiefly, Bush will have to decide whether he would veto a bill that did not include drilling in the Arctic National Wildlife Refuge. But an energy bill would help the GOP on another weak front: the economy. Republicans estimate the House version would create 300,000 jobs. Similarly, the Medicare bill will be cast in terms of how it will help the economy, as will a bill to curb medical malpractice awards.

The House passed its malpractice bill (HR 5) in March, but the Senate version (S 11) was blocked in July. In an effort to get a bill to conference this year, Senate Republicans now plan to vote on narrow legislation that would only limit lawsuits against obstetrician-gynecologists.

At fundraisers this summer, Bush has argued for reducing litigation, which he says drives up health care costs and hurts the federal budget. "It is time for the United States Senate to realize that no one has ever been healed by a frivolous lawsuit," Bush said Aug. 26 at a campaign stop in Minnesota.

Heavy Load in the Senate

The Senate bears the greatest legislative burden this fall as it plays catch-up to House action.

The House already has passed 11 of the 13 appropriations bills, Bush's medical malpractice measure, a permanent repeal of the estate tax (HR 8), and health care savings accounts (HR 2596), among other things. Much of its focus will be on negotiating final bills with the Senate on other priority issues, including legislation to expand the tax benefits of charitable giving (HR 7) and to ban a procedure that opponents call "partial birth" abortion (S 3).

Majority Leader Bill Frist, R-Tenn., has said the Senate will spend September on appropriations. But he has also pledged to continue the fight to confirm more of Bush's judicial nominees — an effort meant to paint Democrats as obstructionists — and he intends to bring several social policy bills to the floor before the end of the year.

"The challenge for Republicans here is to continue to offer solutions," Winston said. "Democrats, on the other hand, need to focus on where they are going to go, as opposed to saying, 'Bush has done it all wrong.'"

But Democrats plan to continue their criticism on all fronts, including a stalled bill that would extend to low-income parents the benefits of the recently increased child tax credit (HR 1308).

Said Mellman: "Republicans control Congress, the White House, and God knows, they control the Supreme Court. If things go well, they will get credit, and they may even deserve it. And if things go poorly, they will get blamed, and they will certainly deserve that." ◆

INDEX OF ISSUES				
'Partial birth' abortion	2084	Freddie Mac, Fannie Mae	2080
Amtrak reauthorization	2073	Head Start	2082
Bankruptcy overhaul	2079	Human cloning ban	2083
Business tax	2079	Intelligence authorization	2078
Child tax credit	2079	Media ownership	2075
Civil justice overhaul	2082	Medicare overhaul	2083
Clear skies	2074	Pension and retirement	2081
Defense authorization	2077	Philanthropy	2081
Energy	2074	Spam limits	2076
FAA reauthorization	2075	Special education	2084
Filibuster rule change	2073	Surface transportation	2076
Financial privacy	2080	Tobacco regulation	2077
Foreign relations	2078	Unborn victims	2085
Forests restoration act	2075	Welfare reauthorization	2085

Senate Traditions a Casualty In Judicial Nominees Spat

Blue slips and proposed changes in voting procedures put comity on ice

When Democrats decided to filibuster nominees to the U.S. Court of Appeals this year, they did away with a longstanding gentlemen's agreement in the Senate. Never before had a filibuster been successful in blocking a lower court nominee.

Now, Senate Republicans are weighing a strategy that could trample on another time-honored Senate tradition: the blue slip policy that gives senators great control over judicial nominees from their states.

Under the blue slip tradition, home-state senators can approve or disapprove judicial nominees, and traditionally, Senate leaders have abided by their recommendations out of collegial courtesy. Michigan Democrats Carl Levin and Debbie Stabenow, who remain angry at the Republican-controlled Senate's treatment of President Bill Clinton's nominees to the U.S. Court of Appeals for the 6th Circuit, have used their blue slip power to object to President Bush's four nominees for that court, effectively blocking the nominations from advancing. Three of the nominations have been on hold since late 2001.

During the week of July 7, though, Judiciary Committee Chairman Orrin G. Hatch, R-Utah, said GOP leaders are urging him to begin the confirmation process on the four with

CQ Weekly July 12, 2003

hearings in his panel — despite the blue slip objections of Levin and Stabenow.

In the heated judicial confirmation battles that have plagued recent Congresses, Democrats and Republicans alike have grabbed any available tool to advance their side of the issue. In so doing, they are dispensing with more and more of the Senate's norms and customs.

"It seems like these traditions are beginning to be eroded gradually," said Brannon P. Denning, a professor at Samford University's Cumberland School of Law who has studied the blue slip process extensively.

Deep-Seated Argument

The first unwritten rule to go might have been the notion that divisive fights over federal court candidates should take place mostly behind closed doors. In the 107th and 108th Congresses, more and more of those messy battles have taken place in full view, either in the Judiciary Committee or on the Senate floor. (*2003 CQ Weekly, p. 1078*)

But the blue slip policy now at issue is a Senate norm that has long guided the way the chamber handles judicial nominations. If Republicans proceed with their plan of holding hearings, and possibly having committee votes on the four stalled judicial nominees from Michigan, they will be diffusing the power of a tradition that dates back to at

Quick Contents

Senators are on the verge of entering a new front in the ongoing war over judicial nominations. Now the right of senators to block nominees from their home states faces a major challenge as Republicans try to loosen Democrats' grip on four of President Bush's appellate candidates.

Nominations Stalled by Senators

President Bush has nominated these four judges, all from Michigan, to the U.S. Court of Appeals for the 6th Circuit. But the state's two Democratic senators have effectively stalled the nominations using the blue slip process.

● **David W. McKeague**
U.S. District Judge, Western District of Michigan, 1992-present
Born: Nov. 5, 1946, Pittsburgh
Education: U. of Michigan, B.A. 1968, J.D. 1971
Originally nominated: Nov. 8, 2001

● **Susan Bieke Neilson**
Judge, 3rd Judicial Circuit Court of Michigan, 1991-present
Born: Aug. 27, 1956, Ann Arbor, Mich.
Education: U. of Michigan, A.B. 1977; Wayne State U., J.D. 1980.
Originally nominated: Nov. 8, 2001

McKeague   **Neilson**   **Saad**   **Griffin**

● **Henry W. Saad**
Judge, Michigan Court of Appeals, 1994-present
Born: July 15, 1948, Detroit
Education: Wayne State U., BSBA 1971, J.D. 1974
Originally nominated: Nov. 8, 2001

● **Richard A. Griffin**
Judge, Michigan Court of Appeals, 1989-present
Born: April 15, 1952, Traverse City, Mich.
Education: Western Michigan U. B.A. 1973; U. of Michigan J.D. 1977
Originally nominated: June 26, 2002

Source: U.S. Department of Justice

least 1917. (*Blue slips, p. 80*)

Bush originally nominated three of the four — David W. McKeague, Susan Bieke Neilson and Henry W. Saad — on Nov. 8, 2001. Richard Griffin was nominated June 26, 2002.

Levin and Stabenow's fight against the four has its roots in the late 1990s — before Stabenow had been elected. It centers on two of Clinton's nominees: Helene N. White and Kathleen McCree Lewis, whose nominations languished for years in the Judiciary Committee, themselves the subject of blue slip objections. (*1999 Almanac, p. 18-49; Background, 2002 CQ Weekly, p. 531*)

Clinton originally nominated White to the 6th Circuit at the beginning of his second term, in January 1997, and again at the beginning of the 106th Congress. Clinton first nominated Lewis, Levin's cousin-in-law, in September 1999.

Neither nominee ever had a hearing in the Judiciary Committee. White's four-year wait for a confirmation hearing remains a Senate record.

Levin attributes White's blocked nomination to "Republican delaying tactics" and to opposition from former Republican Sen. Spencer Abraham of Michigan (1995-2001). It is widely believed by both Democrats and Republicans that an unreturned or negative blue slip from Abraham sealed White's fate, but Abraham never publicly took credit for White's delays. Blue slips were not made public until 2001.

No Compromise

Since Bush took office in 2001, Levin and Stabenow have traded letters with administration officials seeking some kind of resolution. Generally, the pair would like to see at least one of Clinton's failed 6th Circuit nominees get another shot at the federal appellate bench. But the administration has flatly rejected their proposals — including one for a bipartisan nominating commission that would help vet potential nominees and submit them to Bush for his consideration.

Levin and Stabenow now are pitching a bipartisan commission modeled after one in Wisconsin that was revived — over administration objections — late last month to help fill a vacancy on the 7th Circuit.

That 12-member panel, which is expected to offer the White House the names of roughly five potential nominees later this month, includes two members named by the Wisconsin bar,

Blue Slips Seen in New Light

As with so many matters in the Senate, it often is long-held tradition rather than specified rule that guides the handling of presidents' nominations, especially those to the federal judiciary.

And few senatorial traditions have so tangible a manifestation to identify them as the blue slip, the method by which senators signal their approval or disapproval of nominees from their home states. (*2002 CQ Weekly, p. 531*)

The blue slip process is unique to the Senate Judiciary Committee. When any judicial nominee — as well as any U.S. marshal or U.S. attorney nominee — is sent to the panel, aides send a form to the nominee's home-state senators.

On the form, printed on blue paper, members can circle "approve" or "disapprove" to indicate their feelings about the nominee. Home-state senators also may opt not to return the blue slip at all, which is seen as the equivalent of a note of disapproval. Judiciary Committee chairmen decide how much weight to give blue slips, but traditionally, negative or unreturned blue slips halt a nomination's progress.

The blue slip process is a way for senators to retain some authority over presidential appointments to positions in their states. Or at the very least, a way for senators to express their views about a nominee or the extent to which the senator was consulted by the administration.

"The blue slip is a longstanding tradition of the Senate," said Judiciary member Mike DeWine, R-Ohio. "And, like most longstanding traditions of the Senate, it is one members will be reluctant to change."

The blue slip policy has been in use since at least 1917, according to the Congressional Research Service.

During the Clinton administration, more than a dozen nominees — including two to the U.S. Court of Appeals for the 6th Circuit — were blocked by negative or unreturned blue slips. In some instances, one senator endorsed a nominee while the other disapproved.

Judiciary Chairman Orrin G. Hatch, R-Utah, said earlier this year such blue slip conflicts were the reason at least 17 of President Bill Clinton's nominees stalled in committee. "There was no way to confirm those nominations without completely ignoring the senatorial courtesy we afford to home-state senators in the nominations process."

As a result, Hatch has said he will not consider a single blue slip rejection to be sufficient for stopping a nomination. He and other Republicans say blue slips are important, but should not determine a nominee's future, especially for appeals courts that handle cases from several states.

"The so-called blue slip has never been dispositive when it comes to circuit nominees," said Majority Leader Bill Frist, R-Tenn. "Negative blue slips can always be overcome by a record that the home-state senators were consulted."

In the late 1970s, when Edward M. Kennedy, D-Mass., headed the Judiciary Committee, the panel had a similar policy on blue slips.

Kennedy knew "you can't just blow off senatorial courtesy," said Brannon P. Denning, a law professor at Samford University in Alabama. "But Kennedy said at the time that he wasn't going to unilaterally table a nomination simply because of a blue slip."

four members named by Wisconsin Democrats Herb Kohl and Russell D. Feingold, and four members named by Rep. F. James Sensenbrenner Jr., R-Wis.

"We're continually trying to work out a bipartisan compromise with the president, and I think Wisconsin has a great model," Stabenow said. "We're looking at their language."

But Republicans and White House officials say that giving commissions and individual senators too much control in the judicial selection process runs roughshod over the Constitution, which awards the president the power to make nominations with the "advice and consent" of the Senate.

"The president is the one under the Constitution who gets to nominate judges," said Republican Whip Mitch McConnell of Kentucky. "It seems to me inappropriate for the other party to assume that they can dictate choices to the president for the circuit court, and failing to do that, be in a position to prevent action on them."

GOP leaders also say blue slips are not dispositive when it comes to appeals court nominees. Although home-state senators should be given deference when it comes to filling district court vacancies, Republicans say, that should not be the case when it comes to the appeals courts, which handle cases from a number of states. The 6th Circuit for instance, includes Kentucky, Ohio and Tennessee as well as Michigan.

"We do have a good deal more to say about who gets to be a district judge," McConnell said. "But circuit judges have not historically been senatorial prerogative."

"Tell that to Helene White and Kathleen McCree Lewis," Stabenow said, in response to the GOP argument. "It was a blue slip [that stalled them]. And it was not even from both senators. It was from one."

Democrats say current Republican attitudes are a reversal from their treatment of blue slips when the GOP controlled the Senate and Clinton was in the White House.

"When Clinton would send up somebody, and a home-state senator didn't return a blue slip, they just would stop them altogether," Denning said.

Hatch himself has acknowledged that blue slip problems halted more than a dozen of Clinton's nominees.

In the case of White and Lewis, "it had to do with Sen. Spencer Abraham believing that he had been wronged by the Clinton administration, which had failed to consult him after a commitment to do so," said Judiciary Republican Jon Kyl of Arizona. "So there's a perfectly legitimate case to be made for what Spencer Abraham did at that time."

That argument mimics the one Levin is now espousing.

"You see the same arguments being recycled, side to side, just because there's been a change in the party holding the reins of power," Denning said. "Both sides tend to come off looking quite hypocritical.

"Neither the Democrats nor the Re-publicans have suffered any penalties for being rank hypocrites on this issue, so they can just sort of trade these arguments, and the public will just sort of tune in — 'Oh, the Democrats are being obstructionists' — and then, if the worm turns — 'Oh, it's terrible the Republicans are being obstructionists.' "

Chipping Away at Tradition

But there is a price to the arguments and actions each party uses to bolster its side in the struggle over who controls the shape of the federal judiciary.

When both Republicans and Democrats are willing "to take advantage of all their tools — formal and informal — and traditions and customs" to advance their views, Denning said, they end up bending rules and dispensing with Senate customs.

In addition to considering hearings on the stalled 6th Circuit nominees despite their blue slip problems, GOP leaders are advancing a plan that would rewrite the Senate's filibuster rule, so that its power to block all nominations would be gradually weakened. (2003 CQ Weekly, p. 1375)

"Republicans are showing shockingly little regard for the very things that have made this Senate a successful institution," Feingold said.

Perhaps the one unwritten law that remains in place, much to the aggravation of whatever party is in the majority, is what goes around comes around.

"There's an old saying — two wrongs don't make a right," Kyl said. "Certainly, retribution for [Abraham's opposition to White and Lewis] is inappropriate. Does that make it right what's being done here? Is that fair to these nominees? Is it fair to the people in that circuit? No."

With the apparent tit-for-tat approach of the administration and the Senate to the 6th Circuit, resolution appears a long way off. As long as Michigan Democrats and Senate Republicans hold firm in their demands, the standoff is sure to continue.

"It seems like to me there has to be some unilateral disarmament somewhere," Denning said. "Somebody in power is going to have to say, 'We're going to change this, and even though it will hurt us in the short run, in the long run it's going to help us.' As awful as the confirmation process has gotten with judges, it'd be nice to think some statesmen will emerge and try to see if they can bring order out of chaos." ◆

GOP Trying Again on Child Credit

A new effort to advance child tax credit legislation is expected during the week of July 14, as Republican leaders seek to pre-empt Democratic plans to turn up the pressure with parliamentary maneuvers.

Senate Majority Leader Bill Frist, R-Tenn., said he hopes to resolve differences between the House and Senate versions of the legislation (HR 1308).

Leaders also need to settle a dispute over whether a conference on the bill will be chaired by Senate Finance Committee Chairman Charles E. Grassley, R-Iowa, or by House Ways and Means Committee Chairman Bill Thomas, R-Calif. Frist said Grassley will probably preside.

The largest obstacle to a compromise remains House GOP resistance to the demand by Senate moderates that any child tax credit expansion be offset by revenue increases. While the cost of the Senate version would be covered by extending Customs user fees, the House bill includes no revenue increases and carries an $82 billion 11-year price tag.

Both versions of the bill would expand the child credit's refundability to low-income working families and allow more upper-income taxpayers to claim the credit, which was temporarily increased to $1,000 per child by this year's budget reconciliation tax package (PL 108-27). The House measure includes tax breaks for military personnel and would extend the increased credit through 2010.

House Majority Leader Tom DeLay, R-Texas, and Speaker J. Dennis Hastert, R-Ill., declined to say whether they will join Frist's effort to clear the child credit bill before the August recess.

The Senate voted 51-45 along party lines July 9 to block consideration of another child credit bill (S 1162). Minority Leader Tom Daschle, D-S.D., said he will try to move that bill alone or as an amendment to other legislation during the week of July 14. House Democrats may offer a new motion to instruct conferees to accept the Senate version of HR 1308. (2003 CQ Weekly, p. 1782) ◆

Religion Takes Center Stage In Fight Over Judicial Nominee

Pryor becomes third nominee under filibuster, with fourth expected after recess

Quick Contents

Allegations of anti-Catholic bias added to pre-recess tensions as Senate Republican leaders called for three cloture votes on judicial nominees during the last week of legislative work before September.

For weeks, the Senate Judiciary Committee has been embroiled in a nasty fight after Republicans accused Democrats of anti-Catholic bias in their opposition to appeals court nominee William H. Pryor Jr.

On July 30, the furor exploded on the Senate floor and slowed action on energy legislation as senators of both parties engaged in heated debate over the role of religion in shaping the federal bench.

The discourse served as a preview of the next day's 53-44 vote to invoke cloture, or cut off debate, on the nomination of Pryor, Alabama's attorney general, to the U.S. Court of Appeals for the 11th Circuit.

With the vote July 31, Republicans fell seven votes shy of the 60 necessary to break a Democratic filibuster against Pryor. Leaders held similar votes all week to highlight what they called "obstructionism" by Democrats.

A July 29 cloture motion on the nomination of Priscilla Owen to the 5th Circuit failed, 53-43, and on July 30 the Senate voted 55-43 to limit debate on Miguel A. Estrada's nomination to the District of Columbia Circuit. Another cloture test had been expected Aug. 1 on 9th Circuit nominee Carolyn Kuhl, but that was postponed late in the week until after the August recess. (*2003 CQ Weekly, p. 1991; votes 312 and 316, p. 1992*)

The weeklong series of votes on President

CQ Weekly Aug. 2, 2003

Bush's most contentious judicial nominees, coupled with the allegations of religious bias, thrust a new bitterness into the already intensely partisan judicial confirmation process. "Something very ugly has been injected" into the system, said Sen. Dianne Feinstein, D-Calif.

Moreover, the fight spilled into other Senate business as debate over nominees and the anti-Catholic accusations stymied the chamber in the final week before recess.

Tying Up the Floor

Democrats and a handful of Republicans complained about the GOP leadership's decision to schedule votes on four of Bush's nominees, including two who already had been unable to survive cloture tests a total of eight times before. The hours devoted to debate on the nominees and on the resulting votes frustrated attempts to push an omnibus energy bill (S 14) through the Senate before members left for a monthlong break. (*2003 CQ Weekly, p. 1967*)

"It is absolutely impossible to do the people's business if, in fact, during the next 12 hours we have six or eight hours taken up by speeches with reference to a judge," Energy and Natural Resources Committee Chairman Pete V. Domenici, R-N.M., said during floor debate July 30.

The atmosphere was especially tense that night. For more than 15 minutes, members

GOP 0-for-11 in Effort to Get Votes on Some Nominees

Senate Republicans have tried, or plan to try, to force confirmation votes on these nominees by moving to invoke cloture, thus ending debate. Such a motion must get 60 votes to succeed, a goal not achieved in any of the 11 efforts so far.

MIGUEL A. ESTRADA

March 13	May 5
Senate vote 53	Senate vote 140
Denied, 55-42	Denied, 52-39

March 18	May 8
Senate vote 56	Senate vote 143
Denied, 55-45	Denied, 54-43

March 6	April 2	July 30
Senate vote 40	Senate vote 114	Senate vote 312
Denied, 55-44	Denied, 55-44	Denied, 55-43

PRISCILLA OWEN

May 1
Senate vote 137
Denied, 52-44

May 8
Senate vote 144
Denied, 52-45

July 29
Senate vote 308
Denied, 53-43

WILLIAM H. PRYOR JR.

July 31
Senate vote 316
Denied, 53-44

CAROLYN KUHL

Expected Aug. 1
Postponed until after August recess. Motion for cloture not expected to succeed.

squabbled over who had the right to control time on the floor — and whether the pending business was the energy measure or judicial nominees.

Even after the procedural questions were answered, members spent hours discussing the nominations and the role of religion in the confirmation process — a subject that had dominated debate throughout the week.

At issue were the anti-Catholic accusations, made most visibly in newspaper ads run by the conservative Committee for Justice, that depict courthouse doors and a sign saying "Catholics need not apply." (*2003 CQ Weekly, p. 1894*)

Some Republicans and the Committee for Justice, which lobbies for Bush's judicial nominees, have said that by asking Pryor questions about his views on abortion, Democrats were crossing the line and vetting his religious beliefs.

"They are referring to it [religion] all the time," said Judiciary Chairman Orrin G. Hatch, R-Utah. "And it's almost always in the context of abortion — almost every question they ask about abortion with what they consider to be controversial nominees."

Rick Santorum, R-Pa., said if the Senate disqualifies people with "deeply held beliefs," the logical result could be that only dispassionate, non-religious nominees make it through the confirmation process.

"What appears to be going on in the Judiciary Committee by members of the other side of the aisle is not a separation of church and state, but a separation of anybody who believes in church and faith from any public role," Santorum said.

Is Religion Relevant?

Democrats insisted that a nominee's religion is not relevant but that his or her personal views can be, even if they coincide with the judicial candidate's faith. Furthermore, Democrats argued, there is no way to draw a bright line separating a nominee's religious, personal and political views.

"Whether you are Jewish, Catholic, Protestant or Muslim, it is appropriate to ask any nominee for a judicial position," said Richard J. Durbin, D-Ill. For instance, Durbin said, "Where do you stand on the death penalty? That is a political issue. It is a social issue. And yes, it is also a religious issue."

Democrats argued that the opposi-

> **"** *Nominees who have religious beliefs are being asked to renounce their religious beliefs.* **"**
>
> — Sen. Jeff Sessions, R-Ala.

> **"** *The arguments you are using are the last refuge of scoundrels. . . . You ought to be ashamed.* **"**
>
> — Sen. Charles E. Schumer, D-N.Y.

tion to Pryor was about his fitness for a lifetime seat on the federal bench — not his Catholic faith. And Democrats repeatedly called on Republicans to disavow any notion that they were acting out of a bias against Catholic nominees.

Jeff Sessions, R-Ala., defended the newspaper ads that launched the religious debate. "It reflected and reflects a deep concern among many that nominees who have religious beliefs are being asked to renounce their religious beliefs," Sessions said.

But Democrats said the ad and its accusation were beneath the dignity of the Senate. Patrick J. Leahy, D-Vt., called the ads tantamount to "religious McCarthyism."

"The arguments you are using are the last refuge of scoundrels," said Charles E. Schumer, D-N.Y., to Senate Republicans. "They're debasing of our society and this chamber. They are hits below the belt. You ought to be ashamed."

Feinstein complained that the charges were the latest in a series against those who opposed Bush's judicial nominees.

"Each time we have opposed a nominee, there has been bias used as a rationale," Feinstein said. "It happened with an anti-Hispanic charge with Miguel Estrada, an anti-woman charge with Priscilla Owen, an anti-Baptist charge with [5th Circuit nominee] Charles Pickering, and now with William Pryor, an anti-Catholic charge."

Even Catholic leaders and social groups began weighing in on the situation throughout the week.

Denver Archbishop Charles J. Chaput wrote a column in a church newspaper saying the opposition to Pryor was reminiscent of the anti-Catholic sentiment in many cities just two generations ago. He specifically took aim at Durbin, a supporter of abortion rights, who opposes Pryor.

Before a Judiciary Committee vote on Pryor's nomination July 23, Durbin said many anti-abortion Catholics do not believe federal laws should outlaw the procedure in all instances.

"This kind of propaganda makes the abortion lobby proud," the archbishop wrote, "but it should humiliate any serious Catholic."

Chaput suggested that Durbin and other Catholic senators should "read and pray over" the catechism of the Catholic Church "before they explain the Catholic faith to anyone."

In response, Durbin noted that there is a great diversity among the beliefs of Catholics. "On certain issues, they are allowed to turn to their conscience rather than church elders," he said.

Republicans found themselves on the defensive, too, after liberal religious groups and Democratic senators criticized Hatch for directly asking Pryor about his religion during the nominee's confirmation hearing in June.

Proposed Rules Change

Democrats proposed a change in the Senate rules that would bar members from asking nominees about their "religious status" during any committee meeting or hearing. Hatch objected to the proposal, but he promised never to ask about a nominee's religion again.

Still other Republicans said the question should be an option.

"If you've got a concern about their religion and whether it might affect their decision-making process, you have a right to ask them about it," Sessions said. But, he added, the next and most fundamental question is, "If you're going to be a judge, [will] you follow the government's law?"

The week's cloture votes were the first on Pryor's nomination, the third on Owen's and the seventh on Estrada's. Democrats are expected to add Kuhl to the list of nominees under filibuster when Republicans file for cloture after the recess. ◆

Court Challenge a Sure Thing For 'Partial Birth' Abortion Ban

House passes its version of ban on controversial procedure, which may be ready for Bush to sign this summer — but how much weight will high court give Hill 'findings'?

With House passage of a ban on the procedure critics call "partial birth" abortion, social conservatives are closer than ever to seeing enactment of the first federal law restricting abortion since the Supreme Court ruled in favor of abortion rights in *Roe v. Wade*.

The 282-139 House vote June 4 to pass the legislation (HR 760) represented a huge win for foes of abortion, who have pushed a broad array of bills in Congress and elsewhere seeking to limit abortions ever since the high court ruled they were legal in 1973. (*2003 CQ Weekly, p. 1410*)

But even after the bill clears Congress and President Bush signs it into law — both considered inevitable — the fight will continue. Abortion rights advocates are ready to challenge the law in federal courts, drawing heavily on a 2000 Supreme Court ruling that a similar Nebraska state law was unconstitutional. (*2003 CQ Weekly, p. 765*)

On a basic level, the new court fight will test the assertion of bill supporters that Congress has made a persuasive argument in 17 pages of congressional "findings" that such a procedure is never medically necessary. But at a time when the Supreme Court has been increasingly willing to limit Congress' power to legislate under the Constitution's Commerce Cause and 14th Amendment, the answer to that question will be an important arbiter of Congress' authority.

The findings are an attempt to respond to one of the high court's main objections to the Nebraska law: that it did not include an exception for cases where the banned procedure was needed to protect a woman's health.

The House bill would ban the procedure in all instances except when the woman's life was endangered "by a physical disorder, physical illness, or physical injury." The measure does not have an exception for cases in which a

Since Roe v. Wade, *abortion foes in Congress have tried to curtail the procedure legislatively, with limited success.*

woman's health alone — not her life — is in jeopardy.

"We believe those findings are sufficient to deal with the Supreme Court's concern about a health exception," said bill sponsor Steve Chabot, R-Ohio. "The legislative branch has the authority to find the findings we did based on the evidence . . . from extensive hearings."

Legislative History

Since *Roe v. Wade*, abortion foes in Congress have tried to curtail the procedure legislatively, with limited success. Social conservatives' main victories have come in attaching abortion funding restrictions to appropriations bills.

The partial-birth ban — the Senate passed its version (S 3) in March — is expected to become law this year after a nine-year effort by abortion opponents. Previous versions of the bill cleared Congress twice but were vetoed by President Bill Clinton. But Bush has promised to sign the measure into law.

Now, only a few small hurdles — including a House-Senate conference on the Senate bill — are all that is standing in the way of enactment. The main difference between the two is that the

Senate version contains language affirming support for the *Roe v. Wade* ruling. The non-binding language was added as an amendment by Sen. Tom Harkin, D-Iowa, and has more political value than legislative substance. Chabot said the language would not survive in conference.

Bill supporters said they expect a conference to wrap up quickly. Congress could clear a conference report and send the measure to Bush before the August recess.

But they also expect a case challenging the law to be heard by the Supreme Court at some point, and to prepare for that probability they devoted several pages in the House Judiciary Committee's report on the bill to bolstering their argument that the court should accede to Congress.

But all but two of the Supreme Court cases cited by bill supporters come before 1982. They are cases decided by a court far more willing to give ground to Congress, said A. E. Dick Howard, a constitutional law professor at the University of Virginia. The change in the court's composition, and its view of Congress, gives opponents of the ban cause to hope their side will prevail.

From the late 1930s — when President Franklin D. Roosevelt tried to add members to the Supreme Court to gain support for his New Deal — until the late 1980s, the high court upheld every law passed under the authority of the Commerce Clause, which gives Congress the authority to regulate interstate business. For more than four decades, the court maintained a broad reading of the clause, allowing Congress to legislate in areas even if they were only tangentially related to interstate or foreign commerce.

But a decade ago, the court started taking a significantly different — and far more aggressive — approach to vetting acts of Congress. In recent years it has swatted down a number of federal laws — or portions of them. (*Important cases, p. 85*)

"Until the 1990s, the dominant assumption was the courts might be suspicious of the states and the cities, but by and large where there was a national problem the court would respect Congress' judgment," Howard said. "That was a way of thinking for 40 years, probably, and it seemed to be a crosscutting assumption."

But it is jurisprudence the Supreme Court appears to have taken pains to dispel in recent years, much to lawmakers' chagrin.

Democrats and Republicans alike have bristled at court-imposed limitations on the reach of laws such as the Americans With Disabilities Act (PL 101-336) and the Violence Against Women Act (PL 103-322). Laws that attempt to block "virtual" child pornography — images that only appear to be of children — and aim to prevent age discrimination have also been turned back by the Supreme Court.

"These cases stem from the proposition that the Supreme Court can narrow the authority of Congress," said Jerrold Nadler of New York, the top Democrat on the House Judiciary Subcommittee on the Constitution.

The court has increasingly required Congress to demonstrate that its laws are addressing a real evil and that lawmakers' remedy is proportionate to the problem at hand, Nadler said.

"That's a limitation on the power of Congress — and in my view an improper limitation," he said.

'Findings' Questioned

The Supreme Court's recent willingness to whittle away at Congress' legislative authority might show that the court will pay little attention to the findings in the abortion measure.

"The post-New Deal consensus has clearly broken down, and it has broken down not only in respect for the court's respect for Congress' primacy in dealing with issues," Howard said, "[but also] the court's willingness to allow Congress to produce much more by way of findings."

Bill opponents point to the words of Justice Clarence Thomas in an unrelated 1992 case. "We know of no support . . . for the proposition that if the constitutionality of a statute depends in part on the existence of certain facts, a court may not review [Congress'] judgment that the facts exist," Thomas said. "If [Congress] could make a

Rulings on Congressional Power

While the Supreme Court was extremely deferential to Congress from the late 1930s until the late 1980s, it has taken a far more critical stance in recent years.

ISSUE	DESCRIPTION
1966 *Katzenbach v. Morgan* 7-2	In *Katzenbach*, the court upheld a provision of the 1965 Voting Rights Act (PL 89-110) barring literacy tests that prohibited some who were schooled in Puerto Rico from voting. "It was for Congress, as the branch that made this judgment, to assess and weigh the various conflicting considerations. . . . It is not for us to review the congressional resolution of these factors. It is enough that we be able to perceive a basis upon which the Congress might resolve the conflict as it did."
1980 *Fullilove v. Klutznick* 6-3	In *Fullilove v. Klutznick*, the court upheld a provision of the Public Works Employment Act of 1977 (PL 94-369), which required that at least 10 percent of all federal funds disbursed for local construction projects be set aside for minority business owners. "Here we pass, not on a choice made by a single judge or a school board, but on a considered decision of the Congress and the president. ... We are bound to approach our task with appropriate deference to the Congress, a co-equal branch."
1981 *Rostker v. Goldberg* 6-3	In *Rostker v. Goldberg*, the court said it was constitutional for Congress to require only men to register for selective service. "The fact that th[e] court is not exercising a primary judgment but sitting in judgment upon those who also have taken the oath to observe the Constitution and who have the responsibility for carrying on government [compels the court to be] particularly careful not to substitute our judgment of what is desirable for that of Congress, or our own evaluation of evidence for a reasonable evaluation by the legislative branch."
1995 *U.S. v. Lopez* 5-4	*Lopez* launched the beginning of a string of Supreme Court cases restricting Congress' power to legislate under the Commerce Clause. In the case, the high court struck down a federal law (PL 103-382) banning the possession of guns near schools. "Although as part of our independent evaluation of constitutionality under the Commerce Clause, we of course consider legislative findings, and indeed even congressional committee findings, regarding effect on interstate commerce . . . the government concedes that '(n)either the statute nor its legislative history contains express congressional findings regarding the effects upon interstate commerce of gun possession in a school.'"
1997 *City of Boerne v. Flores* 6-3	In *Boerne v. Flores*, the Supreme Court struck down the Religious Freedom Restoration Act (PL 103-141), which was designed to protect virtually all religious expression from state and local interference. "There must be a congruence and proportionality between the injury to be prevented or remedied and the means adopted to that end."
2000 *United States v. Morrison* 5-4	In *Morrison*, the Supreme Court struck down part of the 1994 Violence Against Women Act (PL 103-322) that allowed victims of gender-motivated violence to sue their attackers for monetary damages in federal civil court. Lawmakers had justified the federal court remedy through extensive hearings and legislative language detailing the effects of violence against women on interstate commerce and the purportedly inadequate protections for women in state courts. "Even under our modern, expansive interpretation of the Commerce Clause, Congress' regulatory authority is not without effective bounds."
2001 *Board of Trustees of the University of Alabama v. Garrett* 5-4	In *Garrett*, the Supreme Court ruled that state employees cannot use federal courts to sue for discrimination under the 1990 Americans With Disabilities Act (PL 101-336). The court ruled that the 11th Amendment to the Constitution, which the court said prohibits individuals from suing states, trumps the discrimination protections of the ADA. "It is the responsibility of this court, not Congress, to define the substance of constitutional guarantees."

statute constitutional simply by 'finding' that black is white, or freedom slavery, judicial review would be an elaborate farce."

Opponents of the partial-birth ban said it was ludicrous to think that the Supreme Court would blindly accept Congress' findings that the procedure is never medically necessary.

Abortion rights supporters say the procedure is medically necessary in some cases, such as when a fetus has an abnormal fluid accumulation in the brain. Because of the swelling in the fetus' head, the procedure — technically known as dilation and extraction or intact dilation and evacuation — might be safer for the pregnant woman, they say.

"The authors of this bill hope that the federal courts — most especially the United States Supreme Court — will defer to these congressional findings and waive this constitutional requirement, but the court has unequivocally said that the power to interpret the Constitution in a case or controversy remains in the judiciary," Rep. Louise M. Slaughter, D-N.Y., said during floor debate June 4.

The amount of attention the Supreme Court gives to congressional findings is unclear, Howard said. In recent cases, the court has signaled its desire for Congress to document the need for federal laws.

But at the same time, "the massive congressional activity is not enough," Howard said. "The court is less willing to take Congress' conclusions; they are much more willing to go" and investigate on their own.

Even supporters of the partial-birth abortion bill said their odds in court are less than certain.

"We can't know for sure," said Rep. Mike Pence, R-Ind. "The reason we're optimistic is because we are working with some of the best legal minds in the country. We analyzed what was missing in the Nebraska law. We just tightened the whole thing up."

Pence and other anti-abortion lawmakers said they are counting on the bill's definition of the banned abortion procedure — which they say is more narrow than the definition in the unconstitutional Nebraska law — to satisfy the Supreme Court.

The bill would ban any procedure in which "the person performing the abortion deliberately and intentionally vaginally delivers a living fetus until, in the case of a head-first presentation, the en-

Roe Provision Likely to Go

To supporters of legislation that would ban a procedure they call "partial birth" abortion, the only difference between the House- and Senate-passed bills is minor — language that can be easily stripped out in conference.

But to opponents of the ban, the one provision contained in the Senate bill (S 3) but not the House version (HR 760) is significant. That provision, added as an amendment by Sen. Tom Harkin, D-Iowa, affirms the Supreme Court's landmark 1973 ruling in *Roe v. Wade* that made abortion legal.

Abortion rights advocates value the vote on the non-binding language as a barometer measuring *Roe*'s support in the Senate.

"I want to make sure with all of this going on that we send a strong signal to the women of this country that *Roe v. Wade* is appropriate, it was a good decision, and it is not going to be overturned," Harkin said at the time.

When adopted by the Senate on a 52-46 vote on March 12, the amendment helped to define some of the smaller, subtle demarcations in the divisive, often black-and-white debate over abortion.

The language first appeared in the Senate the last time the cham-

ber took up a partial-birth abortion bill in 1999.

Then, Harkin and Barbara Boxer, D-Calif., offered similar sense-of-Congress language to smoke out those Republicans who said the bill had nothing to do with the broader issue of abortion rights.

The 1999 vote firmly identified those Democrats — such as Harry Reid of Nevada — who take anti-abortion stances. It also showed clearly which Republicans — such as Arlen Specter of Pennsylvania and Ted Stevens of Alaska — supported abortion rights.

It was the first time the Senate had held an up-or-down vote on whether *Roe* should stand, and abortion rights supporters promised to use the tally in future political campaigns. (*1999 Almanac, p. 3-5*)

The language was removed from the 1999 bill in conference, just as is expected this year.

Republican sponsors Sen. Rick Santorum of Pennsylvania and Rep. Steve Chabot of Ohio say they plan to ensure that the provision is quickly killed in conference.

"I expect to go through the conference to strip out the *Roe* language," Chabot said. "It would be totally unacceptable in the House."

tire fetal head is outside the body of the mother, or, in the case of breech presentation, any part of the fetal trunk past the navel is outside the body of the mother, for the purpose of performing an overt act that the person knows will kill the partially delivered living fetus."

Doctors who performed the banned procedure would be subject to fines and up to two years in prison

Civil cases also could be brought against doctors performing the procedure. The bill specifically would allow the woman's husband — or her parents if she was under 18 — to file civil lawsuits seeking monetary damages for psychological or physical injuries.

When the measure was considered on the House floor, Republican leaders allowed one amendment — a proposal

from Democratic Whip Steny H. Hoyer of Maryland and Republican James C. Greenwood of Pennsylvania. Their amendment would have outlawed abortions conducted after a fetus would be viable outside the womb. It also would have provided exceptions for both the health and the life of a pregnant woman.

But abortion foes said the Hoyer-Greenwood alternative amounted to a "phony ban" on late-term abortions, because it would leave the determination of viability up to doctors performing the procedure and could allow post-viability abortions even in instances when a woman's mental health was threatened. Their amendment was rejected, 133-287. (*2003 CQ Weekly, p. 1410*) ◆

High Court Ruling on Internet Filters Acknowledges Power of the Purse

Upholding of requirement for libraries and schools to safeguard against pornography affirms legislative branch's ability to make policy via appropriations process

One of the most significant legacies of the Supreme Court under Chief Justice William H. Rehnquist has been a reining in of Congress' power to write laws that impose new requirements on the states.

Despite this federalist trend of the past decade, however, the Rehnquist court generally has maintained the judicial branch's respect for the use of the power of the purse by Congress as a means of rewarding behavior it endorses and punishing those who do not do what it wants.

"There's no doubt about Congress' authority to legislate this way," Steven S. Smith, a political science professor at Washington University in St. Louis, said of the court's view of the congressional power under Article I of the Constitution to set conditions on the receipt of federal funds.

That was affirmed yet again as the court's 2002-03 term came to an end. A June 23 opinion, written by Rehnquist himself, reaffirmed the constitutionality of making policy through the appropriations process. The court held, 6-3, that Congress acted within its authority in writing a law three years ago (PL 106-554) that required libraries and schools that accept federal grants for computer equipment and discounted Internet access to install filtering software on their computer terminals in order to shield children from pornography on the Web. (*2000 Almanac, pp. 2-3, 2-97*)

The ruling reversed a lower court decision that held that the law was an unconstitutional infringement on free speech and blocked it from taking effect.

The organizations that had challenged the law, including the American Library Association and the American Civil Liberties Union (ACLU), argued that Congress was requiring libraries to perform an unconstitutional act in order to receive federal funds. But the court concluded that because libraries can disable the filters whenever they are asked to by adult patrons, there was no First Amendment violation. More important for the conduct of routine legislative business, the justices affirmed the permissibility of Congress to use the threat of withheld money for advancing its agenda.

"Congress has wide latitude to attach conditions to the receipt of federal assistance in order to further its policy objectives," Rehnquist wrote.

Justices John Paul Stevens, David H. Souter and Ruth Bader Ginsburg dissented. The law "impermissibly conditions the receipt of government funding on the restriction of significant First Amendment rights," Stevens said. The other two, in a separate dissent, also said

the law should be struck down because it effectively "mandates action" that would be unconstitutional if the libraries took it on their own.

A 'Carrot Approach'

The law that was challenged in *United States v. American Library Association* applies to libraries and schools that receive tens of millions of dollars annually in grant money under two federal programs: E-Rate, created as part of the 1996 telecommunications policy overhaul (PL 104-104), which allows schools and libraries to buy Internet service at a discount; and a program established under the fiscal 1997 omnibus appropriations law (PL 104-208) that provides funds for computers and other equipment. (*1996 Almanac, p. 3-43; 1996 Almanac, p. 10-20*)

Congress enacted the filtering law in an effort to curb minors' access to adult content on the Internet via computer terminals at schools and libraries.

"It's a carrot approach to the exercise of legislative power rather than a stick approach," said David Garrow, a law professor at Emory University.

At the behest of Rep. Ernest Istook, R-Okla., and Sen. John McCain, R-Ariz., the provision was included in an omnibus appropriations and policy package enacted in December 2000 to conclude a politically charged lame-

CQ Weekly June 28, 2003

"Congress has wide latitude to attach conditions to the receipt of federal assistance in order to further its policy objectives."
— Chief Justice William H. Rehnquist, for the majority in *U.S. v. American Library Association*

"[The law] impermissibly conditions the receipt of government funding on the restriction of significant First Amendment rights."
— Justice John Paul Stevens, in dissent

duck session convened during the uncertainty about the outcome of the disputed 2000 presidential election.

Opponents contended that software filters are not sufficiently sophisticated to weed out adult content without also blocking innocuous Web sites. They argued that requiring libraries to use them as a condition of federal funding was a violation of freedom of speech.

Writing for a plurality, Rehnquist said libraries have the right to choose what Web content to make available to their patrons, just as they have the right to choose what books to put on their shelves.

Citing an assurance during oral arguments by Solicitor General Theodore B. Olson that libraries can turn off filters at an adult's request, Rehnquist said, "The Constitution does not guarantee the right to acquire information at a public library without any risk of embarrassment."

Scholars say imposing such a restriction as a condition of appropriations is a much safer route for Congress than simply passing a law that mandates the use of filters.

"A law written that way would be significantly more open to challenge because it would not allow libraries to avoid the statutory requirement simply by declining to accept the funds," Garrow said.

Giving Congress Latitude

It was not the first time the Rehnquist court has been giving Congress wide latitude in deciding how to condition the receipt of federal funds. In 1991 it held on a 5-4 vote in *Rust v. Sullivan* that it was permissible for Congress to stipulate in a 1970 law (PL 91-572) that federal assistance to family planning clinics could not be used to subsidize clinics where abortions were performed. Abortion rights advocates had argued that the stipulation amounted to a gag rule that violated the First Amendment. (*1970 Almanac, p. 570*)

Since 1996, Congress has passed several laws to regulate content transmission on the Internet. The high court in two instances ruled that lawmakers had overreached and infringed on First Amendment rights guaranteeing free speech. One provision, part of the 1996 telecommunications law, barred the online transmission of "patently offensive" communications. By 7-2 the next year, the court held in *Reno v. ACLU* that the statute was so broad that it would

not only protect children but could unconstitutionally limit adult conversation. (*1997 Almanac, p. 5-25*)

Last year, the court ruled that another 1996 law (PL 104-208) outlawing virtual child pornography was an overbroad violation of the First Amendment. (*1996 Almanac, p. 5-38*)

Because this year's decision found that the anti-pornography filtering incentives were narrowly drawn, libraries are left to decide whether they want to install filters on their computers or forgo federal grant money that helps them make the equipment available to their patrons.

Claudette Tennant, an Internet policy specialist at the American Library Association, said some libraries have already decided not to install filters. Tennant said that contrary to the government's assertion, it is not easy for libraries to turn off filters at individual terminals.

"The management issue of responding to these requests is just going to be mind-boggling for libraries to address," Tennant said.

Curbing Congress

In the decades since the New Deal, Congress has steadily expanded federal powers through legislation. Lawmakers had wide latitude to make laws under the clause of Article 1 that gave the legislative branch power to "regulate commerce . . . among the several states."

When Rehnquist joined the Supreme Court in 1972, he was a lonely voice advocating a federalist approach that aimed to devolve power back to the states. But since he became chief justice in 1986, the court — often on a 5-4 vote — has invalidated several statutes.

In 1995, the court ruled 5-4 in *United States v. Lopez* that a 1990 law (PL 101-647) that made it a federal crime to possess a firearm in or near a school relied on an unconstitutionally broad interpretation of the Commerce Clause. Rehnquist wrote that in passing the law, Congress had failed to make a convincing case that such regulation was linked to interstate commerce. The court held that the authority to govern firearms possession in that manner was reserved for the states. (*1995 Almanac, p. 6-40*)

In 1997, the court ruled 5-4 in *Printz v. United States* that the 1993 gun control law popularly known as the Brady bill (PL 103-159) unconsti-

tutionally violated states' rights by requiring local law enforcement to conduct background checks on gun buyers. Writing for the majority, Justice Antonin Scalia said Congress could not compel states to help run a federal program. (*1997 Almanac, p. 5-21*)

Two days before that decision was handed down, the court ruled 6-3 that a 1993 law (PL 103-141) that sought to define the First Amendment clause dealing with the exercise of religion was unconstitutional. (*1997 Almanac, p. 5-23*)

Congress said the law was within its authority to enforce under the Equal Protection Clause of the 14th Amendment. But Justice Anthony M. Kennedy, writing for the majority in *City of Boerne v. Flores*, rejected the idea that Congress could claim authority under one part of the Constitution to define another part. Congress "has been given the power 'to enforce,' not the power to determine what constitutes a constitutional violation," he wrote.

'Activist' Legal Theories?

Two years ago, the court ruled 5-4 that state employees may not sue their employers for relief under the Americans With Disabilities Act (ADA), the 1990 law (PL 101-336) that sought to bar discrimination on the basis of disability. The court held in *Alabama v. Garrett* that such lawsuits were prohibited by the 11th Amendment, which the court said bars suits against states in federal court. (*1990 Almanac, p. 447*)

"That case is part of a recent trend in which a narrow majority of the Supreme Court creates new restrictions on federal rights and protections," said Patrick J. Leahy of Vermont, the ranking Democrat on the Senate Judiciary Committee, in a June 25 speech at the National Press Club.

He said the court was acting "in accord with new legal theories that are being promoted by a cadre of dedicated conservative activists, often in alliance with powerful special interests," comments suggesting that he and other Senate Democrats would closely question any nominee for a Supreme Court vacancy on his or her views on federalism.

But no justice had announced plans for retirement by the end of the week of June 23. (*2003 CQ Weekly, p. 1329*)

The court announced June 23 that in its next term it will hear a case in which the state of Tennessee is challenging the ADA on similar grounds. ◆

Politics and Public Policy

The term *public policymaking* refers to action that the government takes to address issues on the public agenda; it also refers to the process of reaching a decision about what action to take. The work of the president, Congress, the judiciary and the bureaucracy is to make, implement and rule on policy decisions. Articles in this section discuss the most important policy issues that came before the federal government in summer and fall 2003.

The first article describes the struggles of congested metropolitan areas to strike a balance between building more highways while adhering to federal air quality rules. A dramatic increase in traffic has created levels of auto and truck emissions that have kept government officials frantically trying to meet federal clean air standards—and sometimes failing. The Bush administration and some key Republicans in Congress want to shorten the time it takes to review the environmental impact of major transportation projects and allow metropolitan areas some leeway in meeting federal air quality standards. Environmental organizations worry that such changes, along with administration regulatory policies that favor business and industry, will erode air quality protection in metropolitan areas. Congress will have to reconcile these often opposing interests in the new surface transportation bill.

The second and third articles address the deepening Medicare debate. In expanding Medicare to pay for beneficiaries' prescription drugs, Congress must choose between covering everybody—including the affluent—at an astronomical cost or limiting the benefit and thus changing the character of Medicare. Democrats fear that a drug benefit for lower-income seniors only will make Medicare a social welfare program that will lose its universal mission and constituency. That, they fear, would endanger its long-term survival. It is a dilemma that challenges fundamental notions about parity and the limits of government.

Just as Congress must perform a balancing act when debating the environment or Medicare, it also walks a tightrope when it comes to balancing homeland security and trade. As the fourth article notes, businesses across the country knew that commerce would be more difficult and more expensive because of stepped-up security after the September 11 attacks. But two years later, the issue is far from resolved. Industries large and small are still coming to grips with ever-increasing levels of inspection, caution, restriction and paperwork.

As Congress pushes ahead with its review of prewar U.S. intelligence on Iraq's weapons of mass destruction, some on Capitol Hill worry that such weapons were secretly hustled out of the country. The fifth article in this section examines how this theory, if substantiated, could ease the pressure on search teams to make a big discovery soon. Yet the same theory may also confirm critics' prewar warnings that the world may not be safer as a result of Saddam Hussein's removal if his weapons are dispersed into other dangerous hands.

The last article in this section returns to environmental policy. Environmental groups lined up early to oppose President Bush's "Clear Skies" proposal, but energy companies opposed it as well. That opposition is stalling the plan in Congress, as environmentalists argue that its pollution standards are too lax and coal-burning energy companies contend they are too strict.

Searching For Clean Air On the Road More Traveled

Cities desperate to keep traffic moving struggle to reach a difficult balance

The challenge in rapidly growing cities is how to improve the air quality of residents without impeding their economic well-being.

Atlanta was born at the junction of two railroads, but in the half-century since World War II the city has grown and thrived on the strength of its airport and its roads. In fact, Atlanta is belted and quartered by Interstate highways as broad and fast as runways and packed with thundering traffic that can frighten visiting motorists.

With that explosive growth and traffic comes pollution — a level of auto and truck emissions that has kept the region's planners frantically trying to meet federal clean air standards and sometimes losing the challenge. *(Clean air, p. 93)*

"It's the growth," said Jane Hayse, chief of transportation planning for the Atlanta Regional Commission. "We have unprecedented growth in Atlanta, and it's forecast to continue."

During the 1990s, the 13 counties of metro Atlanta added 1 million residents. Business recessions have hardly slowed the flood of new residents, and by 2030, the area is projected to grow by another 2.3 million, to a total of 6 million people.

The challenge faced by Hayse and government officials in other rapidly growing metropolitan areas across the country is how to preserve or improve air quality and the health of their residents while not impeding their economic well-being.

That is a balance that most business interests and environmental activists agree they want to achieve, a balance that Congress sought to promote in both the 1991 and 1998 surface transportation bills when it required the government to take the environment into consideration in planning transportation projects.

But this year, with a new highway and transit authorization bill on the drawing boards, federal and state transportation officials warn that the country faces a crisis if it does not immediately act to ease highway congestion and repair aging roads and bridges. Indeed, cities across the country, and particularly in the rapidly growing Sunbelt, are strangling on their own traffic.

Under pressure from the transportation industry and metropolitan areas struggling to comply with federal air quality rules while relieving crowded highways, the pendulum may be swinging back toward building roads.

Jonathan D. Weiss, executive director of the George Washington University Center on Sustainable Growth, acknowledges that the Bush administration's proposed highway and transit legislation "does preserve the general framework of the current law." However, he says, "it undercuts some of the environmental protections that currently exist."

The administration's proposal, he said, "appears to be more weighted toward building roads without as strongly incorporating the concerns of public transportation and the environment."

Striking a Balance

This year, both the administration and key members of Congress have said they remain committed to environmental protection. But they also talk about achieving a balance between programs to relieve the nation's worsening highway congestion by improving its roads and programs to protect metropolitan environmental quality.

Though there is no indication of a broad effort to rewrite environmental sections of transportation policy, the Bush administration and some key Republicans in Congress want to shorten the time it takes to review the environmental impact of major transportation projects — an effort called environmental "stream-lining" — and allow metropolitan areas some leeway in meeting federal air quality standards — an issue called transportation "conformity."

Environmental organizations worry that these changes, along with administration regulatory policies that generally favor business and industry, will erode environmental policies on transportation in metropolitan areas. They also say a renewed emphasis on highway building, which was bolstered by big authorization increases in 1998, will simply lead to more uncontrolled urban sprawl.

"There is big pressure from the road lobby," said Michael Replogle, transportation director of Environmental Defense, a national environmental group. The road construction industry and state highway departments, he said, "see an opportunity . . . to take us back to the days when the road lobby didn't have to pay attention to environmental consequences."

But highways in metropolitan areas across the country have grown more crowded. Since 1970, annual vehicle miles have increased 123 percent, while road capacity has grown by only 5 percent, according to the U.S. Chamber of Commerce.

The administration says its promise to streamline the environmental review of transportation projects is based on a desire to get more roads, bridges and transit systems built more quickly in order to alleviate congestion.

"There's an attitude, 'not in my back yard.' Nobody wants a road next to their house," said Ed Mortimer, senior manager of transportation infrastructure at the Chamber of Commerce. "At the same time, these roads bring economic development; they bring jobs and growth. There needs to be a balance on that. It appears from our perspective that right now there isn't a balance."

Background

In the spring of 1991, Democratic Sen. Daniel Patrick Moynihan of New York (1977-2001) and members of his Environment and Public Works Committee touched off a revolution in U.S. transportation policy with their decision to emphasize environmental protection in what had been called "the highway bill." The year before, the committee had helped overhaul the Clean Air Act with strict new standards on smog, auto exhaust and toxic air pollution that caused acid rain. Now the committee and environmental lobbyists turned to highways and transit with much the same frame of mind. (*Clean air, 1990 Almanac, p. 229*)

The 44,328-mile National System of Interstate and Defense Highways, which had shaped federal highway policy since 1956, was nearing completion, and the Senate committee and its staff sensed an opportunity to fashion a new, broader vision for the nation's transportation system. (*1991 Almanac, p. 137*)

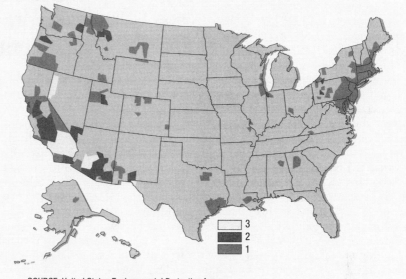

The Air Out There

Traffic and air pollution are worst on the coasts, where population is densest. Counties shown violate air standards for one or more pollutants.

3
2
1

SOURCE: United States Environmental Protection Agency

The legislation that emerged from the committee and was passed by Congress later in the year elevated urban planning and environmental considerations to central roles in transportation policy for the first time. It directed federal agencies to take environmental issues into account in all transportation projects. It also put a new emphasis on the connection between different modes of travel and allowed states the flexibility to spend road money on transit systems if they chose.

"This is not a highway bill, it's a surface transportation bill," Sen. John H. Chafee, R-R.I. (1976-99), said at the time. And the law indeed became the Intermodal Surface Transportation Efficiency Act of 1991 (PL 102-240), called ISTEA.

Democrats controlled both houses of Congress at the time, but highways have never been a partisan issue on Capitol Hill. When Congress wrote its next surface transportation bill in 1998, Bud Shuster, R-Pa. (1973-2001), then chairman of the House Transportation and Infrastructure Committee, defied some party leaders by passing a 40 percent increase in authorized spending. He had plenty of backing from Republicans and Democrats for the Transportation Equity Act for the 21st Century (PL 105-178) called TEA-21 for short. (*1998 Almanac, p. 24-3*)

The divisions that do exist are between urban and rural states, between the East and West, and between those who think the government should focus primarily on building more highways and those who think it has a broader obligation.

The 1998 law continued and strengthened the emphasis on environmental protection and planning. The Senate Environment and Public Works Committee wrote in its report on the bill that it "retains a strong commitment of the transportation sector to finance and contribute to the protection of our environment."

Following the Money

As Congress gathers itself to write the surface transportation bill this year, attention has focused on how much money should be spent on the nation's highways — the bidding is anywhere from $247 billion to $375 billion — where the money should be raised, and which states and projects should get the most.

Shuster wrote his 1998 bill in a boom economy, and the measure passed on a wave of cash for highways, transit and environmental protection.

This year, the transportation authorizing committees in the House and Senate are trying to find the resources for a similar, if less ambitious, commitment to highway and transit projects. The debate has divided Republicans in Congress between those led by House Transportation and Infrastructure Committee Chairman Don Young of Alaska, who want to increase the gas tax to pay for more highways, and those for whom any new taxes are anathema.

According to Bill Fulton, president of the Solimar Research Group in Ventura, Calif., and co-author of a book on regional planning and sprawl, "The road-building crowd loves Republicans, but they also love taxes. The Republicans love roads, but they hate taxes."

Environmental and transit groups worry that their programs might be cut in order to finance the building of more roads. Senate Finance Committee Chairman Charles E. Grassley, R-Iowa, and ranking Democrat Max Baucus of Montana stirred up a hornet's nest this spring when they suggested that the portion of the federal gasoline tax now allocated to transit — 2.9 cents of an 18.4 cents-per-gallon tax — be shifted instead to highway projects, and that transit work be financed through revenue bonds. Their suggestions have not been put into legislation.

Richard C. Shelby, R-Ala., chairman of the Senate Banking, Housing and Urban Affairs Committee, which has jurisdiction over transit programs, along with three of his committee members fired off a letter to Grassley about his "scheme" and warned that "any effort to divert the historic share of gas tax revenues that transit currently benefits from will be met with strong resistance from the [Banking] committee."

The administration's own proposal for transit contained in its surface transportation bill — the Safe, Accountable, Flexible, and Efficient Transportation Equity Act, or SAFETEA — would increase the local share of transit construction from 20 percent to 50 percent and consolidate funding for new transit projects in an account outside budgetary "firewalls" that now ensure that the money can be used only for transit.

The advantage that highway interests have in this year's debate, besides strong support from the White House and congressional Republicans, is a clear, concise message that resonates with millions of motorists stuck in traffic: More and better highways will ease congestion.

"Building roads is a simple, compelling vision," Fulton said. "The problem for the anti-pavement crowd is that the solution is complicated and hard to measure, while for the pavement crowd the solution is easy to articulate: Give us more money and we'll build more roads."

Atlanta has no heavy industry to speak of. It is a distribution center, a warehouse town and a regional headquarters. Set in a wooded landscape of gentle, parallel ridges and val-

QUESTION #1

Should Congress continue to require metropolitan areas to take drastic measures to reduce pollution in their transportation systems?

leys, it has sprawled across parts of 13 counties. Its commerce is decentralized in suburban office parks. Though its subway system was designed to carry commuters from their homes to downtown, most commuting is now suburb-to-suburb.

As a consequence, Atlanta's air pollution is caused primarily by the tens of thousands of automobiles, trucks and sport utility vehicles (SUVs) on its streets and highways.

The city's air quality grew so bad in 1998 that it exceeded levels in the plan that regional authorities had devised to gradually bring Atlanta into compliance with national clean air standards. The result was that for two years, until a new plan was written and approved, the city was prohibited from using federal money for transportation projects that might make the air worse, such as building new roads or adding lanes.

Dealing with the level of traffic growth that plagues Atlanta and other cities "is a huge question," said Jane Hayse, chief of transportation planning for the Atlanta Regional Commission.

The commission's remedy has been to use a variety of strategies to try to control vehicle emissions, including high-occupancy vehicle [HOV] lanes with express buses, and it is investigating new types of transit. But there is, Hayse said, "no silver bullet."

As Congress casts a new surface transportation bill, the White House and some lawmakers want to take some of the pressure off cities such as Atlanta by lengthening the time between their regular assessments of air quality and shortening the time frame they must now plan for.

The subject is complex, and the arguments are as heated as Atlanta's summer air.

Staying in Conformity

The environmental requirements of transportation programs are based on the 1963 Clean Air Act (PL 88-206), which was designed to bring the nation's deteriorating air quality under control. That was an era before fuel efficiency standards for cars and trucks, catalytic converters or smokestack scrubbers. The law was substantially rewritten in 1970 (PL 91-604), and major amendments were added in 1990 (PL 101-549). (*1963 Almanac, p. 236; 1970 Almanac, p. 472*)

Under the law, the Environmental Protection Agency (EPA) has set National Ambient Air Quality Standards for seven pollutants considered serious health risks — carbon monoxide, sulfur dioxide, nitrogen dioxide, ozone, large- and small-diameter particulate matter (soot), and lead. The standards are framed in terms of the concentration of a particular pollutant that is permitted in a region's air. For instance, the standards allow nine parts of carbon monoxide per million parts of ambient air.

Metropolitan areas must keep their emissions below the standards for each pollutant or be classified as a "non-

attainment" area. There are just over 100 such areas that do not meet federal air quality standards. The worst are Southern California and the urban Northeast stretching from Washington, D.C., to the coast of Maine.

Areas that exceed the standards must come up with a plan to meet them eventually — a State Implementation Plan, or SIP. Such acronyms will be common in this year's congressional debate.

These plans usually include emissions limits on factories and other stationary sources of pollution and requirements for mobile pollution sources, including cars and trucks, airplanes, trains, and even neighborhood devices such as leaf blowers, lawn mowers and barbecue grills.

"States do a lot of SIPs," said Deron Lovaas, deputy director of the smart growth and transportation program of the Natural Resources Defense Council. He used to help draft such plans for the state of Maryland.

These plans are crucial because federal agencies are prohibited from giving money to any project that might make an area's air quality worse. So projects with federal aid, including road and transit programs, must conform to the State Implementation Plan.

As one federal highway official describes it, "Any federal action has to conform and demonstrate that it is consistent with the air quality goals of the area."

An area's plans for future transportation projects — both its short-range Transportation Improvement Program (TIP) and its 20-year transportation plan — must not conflict with the emissions reduction goals of the SIP. In other words, if a region wants to build a highway that will add 5,000 cars a day to the traffic flow, it must have a way to cut emissions to accommodate the attendant boost in pollution.

This requirement that transportation plans conform to clean air plans is at the heart of the clean air debate on the surface transportation bill.

Most metropolitan areas have plans, some of them innovative, for offsetting auto emissions by such measures as express bus lanes, congestion improvements, land use planning and time-of-day pricing for toll roads. But cities are being squeezed between stricter air quality standards and a growing volume of larger cars and trucks that produce more pollution.

The Heat Is On

In 2004, the EPA plans to start enforcing new standards for soot and ozone, standards that could force a number of other metropolitan areas into non-attainment and thus the task of drawing up SIPs.

And ozone, for which the standard is becoming stricter, is

Issues on the Web

Spend some time with the arguments for and against environmental provisions in the next surface transportation bill and learn highway issues at the same time. All sides in the debate have extensive Web sites:

• **Department of Transportation**
www.fhwa.dot.gov/reauthorization

• **U.S. Chamber of Commerce**
www.uschamber.com/portal/atm

• **Surface Transportation Policy Project**
www.tea3.org

• **Environmental Defense**
www.environmentaldefense.org

• **Northwestern University**
www.library.northwestern.edu/transportation

Atlanta's big problem.

Ozone in the upper atmosphere helps protect the Earth from harmful solar radiation, and scientists worry when an ozone hole develops over Antarctica, for instance. But at ground level, ozone is a major ingredient of smog and a threat to people's lungs.

It is not produced directly by cars and trucks but is the result of a chemical reaction between volatile organic compounds — the type of chemicals found in paint and household cleaners that readily evaporate — and nitrogen oxides from auto exhausts. The reaction needs sunlight, so ozone creation is highest in summer months and during the day, the times when people are most likely to be on the road. For a Sunbelt city such as Atlanta, that is a particular challenge.

Metropolitan areas must show every three years that their transportation plans conform to their clean air goals, and that is done by looking down the road with computer models of population and economy growth and trends.

The EPA allows metropolitan areas little leeway before their conformity lapses, and it is a constant worry for metro officials, particularly in fast-growing cities such as Atlanta.

"We're all struggling to different degrees," Hayse said.

A recent study by the General Accounting Office, the investigative arm of Congress, found that in the past six years, 56 of 159 transportation planning areas with air quality problems had lost their conformity at least once. In 26 cases, transportation planners said they lacked the time and resources to finish their reviews by the federal deadlines. A number of the planners complained that the required assessments came too close together.

That is an issue that the Bush administration's surface transportation bill addresses and one that congressional committees are considering. The idea is to shorten the horizon that metropolitan planners take into account when they decide whether a transportation plan meets air quality goals, reducing it from 20 years to 10.

The other proposal is to lengthen the time between assessments of a transportation plan from three years to five.

With the new standards in the offing for ozone and fine soot, "some reasonableness needs to be applied," said Federal Highway Administrator Mary Peters, whose hometown of Phoenix suffers from bad air. "Maybe not relief" from the rules, she said, "maybe a bit more time to comply."

Many of those who study the issue contend that simply getting traffic moving will do wonders for air quality, even if the plans do not include express buses and other methods of cutting traffic volume.

"Relieving congestion is usually the best way to get to conformity," said Ed Mortimer, senior manager of transportation infrastructure for the U.S. Chamber of Commerce.

But allowing cities more time between evaluations of their transportation plans is much like the difference between balancing your checkbook weekly or once a month, said Replogle of Environmental Defense.

More frequent assessments, he said, ensure that "you can catch problems early when they're simple and easy to fix."

According to Paul Billings, an assistant vice president of the American Lung Association, "Clearly there is a danger that we, through the magic of a stroke of a pen, would ignore days when we have bad air pollution."

Shortening the planning horizon to 10 years, critics worry, would mean that some major road projects, those that would not be finished for 12 or 15 years, might not be accounted for in the computer modeling of traffic emissions until it was too late.

"Unless we address [transportation's] impact on air quality," Billings said, "we'll never solve our air pollution problem."

Helping Hand

To help states and metropolitan areas such as Atlanta achieve their pollution goals, Congress created the Congestion Mitigation and Air Quality Improvement Program (CMAQ), which provides money for projects such as bus lanes, ride share programs, traffic flow improvements and other ideas that the Transportation Departments thinks will lower vehicle emissions. "Everything we fund under CMAQ has to improve air quality," said a federal transportation official.

But environmentalists question the value of adding HOV lanes without express bus service, or the value to clean air of synchronized traffic signals or informational signs. HOV lanes, grumbles Replogle, are sometimes "a Trojan horse for simply widening roads."

The administration says it is committed to CMAQ, though its proposed transportation bill would reduce authorized funding for the program from $1.4 billion in fiscal 2003 to $1.1 billion in fiscal 2004 before gradually raising the level to $1.6 billion in fiscal 2007. Over the life of the authorization bill, the program would receive about $8.9 billion, slightly more than the $8.1 billion authorization in the last surface transportation bill.

Atlanta area officials have used every strategy they can think of to hold down air pollution, but still the traffic grows.

"People still want to come and live in Atlanta," Hayse said. "It's just a matter of creating options for folks to have a quality of life within an urban area."

It was in 1953, during the first Eisenhower administration, that state highway officials in Connecticut first suggested building a modern expressway that would provide a direct link between the southeast coast near New London and the interior of the state around Hartford, the capital. Construction began on this road in 1966, and the first section of 7.5 miles — roughly half the planned 16-mile route — was finished in 1972. That is as far as it got.

Over the next 30 years, as plans and reviews and arguments came and went, Connecticut Route 11 came to be known as the "Highway to Nowhere."

Around the Bush administration, the unfinished road that ends in a welter of gravel and dirt nine miles from the coast is a strong argument for "streamlining" the process by which transportation projects are reviewed and sometimes challenged for their environmental impacts.

Connecticut officials nominated Route 11 — along with a similar and even more controversial project to replace a section of U.S. Route 6 with an expressway — for a list of high-priority transportation projects the administration is affording special attention and rapid environmental reviews.

Route 11 did not make the cut for projects announced last fall, but it remains on the waiting list.

Federal Highway Administrator Peters used the road in a recent interview as an example of the havoc that project delays can cause, adding millions of dollars to the cost of stalled highways, if and when they are eventually built, and even putting a burden on the environment the government might be trying to protect. Route 11, she said, was to have green space around it to keep development at bay, but now the development is occurring anyway because the road has taken so long to build.

But the story of Route 11 is more complicated than it seems at first, and its disputed history illustrates the issues and conflicting viewpoints at stake in the coming congressional debate over streamlining.

There is little dispute over the fact that reviewing the environmental impact of transportation projects can take a long time and hold up the projects for years — in rare cases, for a decade or more. There is great disagreement, however, over the reasons for these delays and whether arbitrarily imposing deadlines, as the administration and some lawmakers have suggested, would be a good idea for the nation's environment.

Though environmental reviews can be complex, involving several different state and federal agencies, efforts have been made over the past five years to improve coordination and speed up the process. A few states such as Florida have been particularly successful.

But in many cases, reviews are late simply because the agencies charged with doing them are overworked.

When the General Accounting Office earlier this year contacted a number of state governments and transportation industry associations about their perceptions of what causes delays in environmental reviews, a major factor cited was the inability of state transportation departments and federal resource agencies, such as the Fish and Wildlife Service, to handle their workloads.

"The report showed an overwhelming consensus that getting more resources is the single most effective way of moving these projects along," said Replogle.

Bruce Katz, director of the Center on Urban and Metropolitan Policy at the Brookings Institution, a Washington think tank, said he knows from his days of working at the Department of Housing and Urban Development that government reviews of any type of project often take a long time.

QUESTION #2

Should Congress go along with President Bush's request to streamline environmental reviews as a way to speed construction of road and bridge projects?

But the solution, Katz said, is not in changing the underlying environmental laws. "There's an overreaction here of major proportions," he said. "The solution is to re-engineer the processes by which transportation projects get implemented."

Following NEPA

Environmental reviews of transportation projects are rooted in the 1969 National Environmental Policy Act, known as NEPA (PL 91-190), which, along with such laws as the Clean Air Act, is considered the foundation of U.S. environmental policy. (*1969 Almanac, p. 525*)

Under NEPA, all federal agencies are required to consider the environmental impact of any action they propose to take or pay for, such as road and transit projects. If such an action or project is thought to have a significant impact on the environment, an Environmental Impact Statement is required.

Other federal environmental laws that apply to transportation projects, such as the National Historic Preservation Act or the Endangered Species Act, are handled within the NEPA process.

The universe of projects that need review is small — 90 percent of highway projects, for instance, require no environmental assessment at all beyond a determination by state transportation officials that they do not qualify. Of the remainder, only 3 percent require the full treatment, most often because they are large and would affect wetlands or forests and other environmentally sensitive or historically significant areas.

Such a review, according to the recent GAO study, can involve upward of 11 federal agencies — everything from the Fish and Wildlife Service to the National Oceanic and Atmospheric Administration — along with state agencies. And it can be excruciating.

Here is how a federal transportation official describes the process: "Imagine the most complicated income taxes you've ever done, and now imagine that instead of doing them just for federal and state [governments] you had to do them for any number of different governments that had jurisdiction over your income," the official said. "And there wasn't a single unified system agreed to by all of those taxing authorities . . . and you could be taken into tax court by any citizen. That's what you're faced with."

According to the Federal Highway Administration, it typically takes from nine to 19 years to design, review and build a major highway project with a significant environmental impact. The entire process can involve as many as 200 or more steps. Planning takes four to six years, design and environmental review takes one to six years, final design and right-of-way acquisition takes two to three years, and construction about two to six years.

Environmental reviews are not the main holdup. Often, communities cannot agree on a highway project or cannot come up with the money necessary to match the federal contribution. Acquiring right-of-way and clear titles to land can be time-consuming. Roads run into design and engineering problems. In some cases, states change their minds about a project.

Delivering a Product

For those who must answer to restless commuters, or for those with a background in business where delay is death,

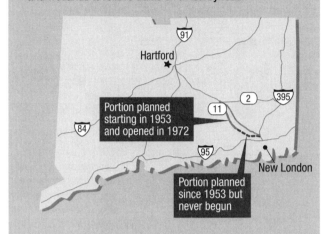

Highway to Nowhere

Connecticut built less than half of four-lane Route 11 before the money ran out and environmental concerns closed in. Finishing the highway would mean plowing through forest and wetlands to relieve traffic on a nearby road.

the years that go by waiting for a road or a bridge or a transit line to be built can be infuriating.

According to Mortimer of the U.S. Chamber of Commerce, 20 percent of the cost of an average transportation project is consumed by planning and approval.

"In this time of limited funds, trying to streamline the process and accelerating product delivery is going to be really key to delivering more projects to the public," he said.

And that, Mortimer added, "is obviously very key to the business community, which relies on a good transportation system."

Because of such complaints about delays in environmental reviews, Congress included a provision in the 1998 surface transportation law (PL 105-178) requiring the Transportation Department to develop a "coordinated environmental review process." The idea was that if all of the agencies with a say in a project knew about it early and participated promptly and jointly in the review, the environmental impact statements could be done much faster.

It turned out that even agreeing on the rules for such coordination was impossible.

According to a federal official involved in the rulemaking process, President Bill Clinton's Transportation secretary, Rodney E. Slater, wanted to take his time and listen to those with a stake in the process. That took some months. Agency staffs put together lists of options for the rules and gathered information on literally dozens of laws that pertained to the environmental aspects of transportation projects.

When draft regulations were finally finished, "there was something for everybody to dislike in our proposal," the official, who asked not to be named, said. "In a series of hearings in 2000 we got a strong message that we were on the wrong track."

As an analyst for the Congressional Research Service has wryly described it, "Some commentators indicated that the proposed rule failed to streamline the review process. Elements of the rule presented an increased burden of paper-

The Givers and Takers Of Environmental Funds

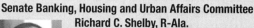

House Transportation and Infrastructure Committee

Don Young, R-Alaska
An ally of energy, mining and timber interests, Young dislikes environmental groups that have blocked some logging and oil drilling in his state. His main concern is raising substantially more money for highway programs through an increase in the gasoline tax.

James L. Oberstar, D-Minn.
Though he strongly supports highway programs, Oberstar generally fights Republican efforts to scale back environmental protections. A dedicated bicyclist, Oberstar included provisions in the 1998 law to encourage biking and convert abandoned railways into bike paths.

Senate Environment and Public Works Committee

James M. Inhofe, R-Okla.
A Western conservative, Inhofe has no patience with environmentalists; he once called the Environmental Protection Agency one of the government's "Gestapo bureaucracies." He is unlikely to go along with any expansion of environmental protections in the surface transportation bill.

Max Baucus, D-Mont.
In the 1998 bill, Baucus helped engineer an allocation formula for highway funds more friendly to Western states, such as Montana, and his focus is sure to remain on road funds. Baucus is ranking Democrat on the Finance Committee, where he and Chairman Charles E. Grassley, R-Iowa, have suggested taking away transit's portion of the federal gas tax and paying for transit projects with revenue bonds instead.

Senate Banking, Housing and Urban Affairs Committee

Richard C. Shelby, R-Ala.
Shelby's committee has jurisdiction over the transit portion of the transportation bill, and he has made it clear he will defend transit's portion of the gasoline tax.

Paul S. Sarbanes, D-Md.
Coming from a state with large urban areas dependent on public transit, Sarbanes is expected to strongly back transit funding.

work and procedural requirements, they said, and increased the potential for litigation."

In September 2002, the administration decided to pull the plug on the rules.

At the same time, President Bush issued his executive order for federal agencies to expedite environmental reviews for high-priority transportation projects picked by the Transportation Department from those, such as Connecticut's Route 11, that were nominated by the states.

Highway to Nowhere

The southern half of Route 11 had, indeed, been held up for three decades, but by more than environmental issues and by local as well as federal government concerns.

The road was designed as a connector between I-95, running along the coast, and four-lane Route 2, trending southeastward from Hartford. Route 11 was supposed to replace a two-lane highway that gets clogged and dangerous with holiday beach traffic.

But the route chosen for Route 11 ran through undeveloped land including acres of wetlands and forest.

Though state and local governments have long wanted to finish Route 11, many local residents were not so sure. Organizations sprang up to defeat the half-finished project, and the U.S. Environmental Protection Agency recommended against it partly because it would carve a path through open country.

"The questions are: Was it a good idea to build it at all,

and is it a good idea to complete it? The answer is no," said Dan Lorimier, outreach director for the Connecticut Fund for the Environment, who helps assemble coalitions of groups to oppose such projects.

"It's out in the middle of nowhere," Lorimier said. "If it's completed at this exorbitant dollar amount [approaching $500 million], everything that's been developed on the other road is going to shrivel up, and development is going to center around the exits of this road."

It would be better, Lorimier contends, to make safety improvements on the parallel two-lane highway. Besides, he said, the road is "only overloaded on holiday weekends."

What Route 11 has faced, in fact, is not so much a delay as a roadblock, which critics say is warranted because of its environmental destruction.

"There are some projects that have such severe impacts that they should not go forward unless they're fundamentally changed," said Replogle. The reason they are not, he said, is "obstinacy on the part of some transportation agency."

The administration, however, contends that environmental reviews are holding up roads that would relieve traffic congestion and help the economy.

In its proposed surface transportation bill, SAFETEA, the administration would impose time frames for environmental reviews and a six-month time limit for court reviews of project approvals.

The White House bill also would modify environmental reviews for projects that would affect parklands, wildlife refuges and historic properties, what transportation officials call "fine tuning" a 1966 law to eliminate duplication. Critics say it would eliminate a requirement that road builders should consider "prudent or feasible alternatives" for encroaching on such lands.

The general concept of streamlining is popular with the Bush administration and many lawmakers, and transportation officials are optimistic that it will encounter less opposition in Congress than other proposals on clean air requirements.

The administration's forestry plan, for instance, would streamline environmental review of forest thinning projects and limit the time for court review. And a House bill (HR 2115) to reauthorize federal aviation programs includes a provision that environmental reviews for proposed airport capacity projects, such as runway construction, would be shortened by requiring different agency reviews to be conducted simultaneously, rather than one after another. HR 2115 is now in a House-Senate conference committee. (*2003 CQ Weekly, p. 1626*)

"Nobody wants to change environmental law," said Mortimer. "Nobody wants to take away the public's right to express their views and participate in the plan approval of transportation projects. But there needs to be some reasonable time lines."

QUESTION #3

Should highway programs be designed so they do not aggravate metropolitan sprawl?

Federal Highway Administrator Peters grew up in a middle-class suburb of Phoenix in the late 1950s and early 1960s, just as the city was starting to grow. The population of Phoenix and surrounding Maricopa County was about 663,000 then; it is an estimated 3.3 million today. In fact, the Phoenix area is adding about 100,000 new residents a year, most of them in the outer suburbs. Only Atlanta has been able to keep up such a torrid pace.

Phoenix lies on the griddle-flat floor of a broad desert valley — the "Valley of the Sun" — where there are no barriers to growth save an uncertain supply of water. As a result, the city has spread out in all directions, eating up the high Sonoran Desert with its cactus and creosote bushes at the rate of an acre a day. In a 2000 study of the city's growth, the Morrison Institute for Public Policy at Arizona State University found that between 1975 and 1995, an estimated 40 percent of the area's agricultural land and a third of its desert had been urbanized.

"The vivid Sonoran Desert is what makes metropolitan Phoenix unique and gives it a special character," the institute wrote. "Losing huge tracts of land threatens the region with the loss of its most famous lifestyle and environmental asset."

Environmentalists and some urban planners argue that building and widening highways ostensibly to relieve traffic congestion in metropolitan areas actually leads to more congestion because the roads make possible more development farther and farther from the city center.

"They're like can openers to development," said Lorimier,

of the Connecticut Fund for the Environment.

In writing a new surface transportation bill, environmentalists and urban planners say, Congress should put more emphasis and money behind the idea of "smart growth" — that metropolitan areas redevelop land they have, repair urban roads and streets rather than build new ones, promote communities people can walk in from homes to shopping and jobs, and better develop transportation alternatives such as light rail systems and buses.

However, highway officials such as Peters say that local decisions on land use and planning, not highways, are setting the pattern of metropolitan development. Peters said that when she became Arizona's highway director, she found that "transportation decisions were being made in the aftermath of these other decisions."

"We should suggest, as we have done, that land use planning and zoning decisions be incorporated as part of transportation planning," Peters said in a recent interview. "What we suggest is that you should not do transportation planning in a vacuum, because it really is affected by so many other things."

However, "at the end of the day," she said, "what happens with land use and how zoning considerations and decisions are made by local government much more affects sprawl than anything that transportation does."

This chicken-and-egg debate over whether highways or zoning decisions are the primary cause of sprawl has been going on for decades and seems no closer to a resolution, though both sides are calling for better coordination in their planning.

The idea of induced demand — that a new or wider highway quickly fills up with new traffic — "is really to some extent a red herring," said a federal highway official who asked not to be named.

"There is some travel that's created as you increase accessibility to an area that previously had poor accessibility," he said. "But it's not just the transportation system that's going to make that area more attractive — permissive land use controls, zoning, other infrastructure. If you don't put water and sewer out to an area and you provide highway access, you're still not going to get development."

In Atlanta, much of the growth in development has been on the city's north side, which is where most of the highway construction has been. Though widening routes such as Interstate 85 no doubt accelerated suburban development in the past 20 years, some planners say the city would have sprawled anyway. The quest for spacious yet affordable housing and a decent back yard helps push people farther out.

"It comes down to the growth. People still want to come and live in Atlanta," said Jane Hayse of the Atlanta Regional Commission. She pointed out that in the northern end of Fulton County there have been limited road improvements, yet "there still is tremendous development pressure" even without new highways.

Metropolitan Atlanta officials have used a variety of programs aside from new highways to try to ease congestion and control sprawl, including mass transit, bike and pedestrian paths, and redevelopment of suburban towns into "livable centers" with shopping and employment opportunities so that people will be drawn to the city rather than forced farther out.

But such programs require local and federal resources, and the pressure in Congress this year will be to cut back such spending, rather than increase it. Transit advocates worry that the search for more highway money will cost their program financial support. The administration wants to increase the required local share of new transit starts from 20 percent to 50 percent, for instance, and Senate Finance Chairman Grassley has suggested that transit's share of federal highway taxes should be rescinded and that a bond program be used to pay for transit projects.

"Investing in public transportation is a vital element of our economy," the American Public Transportation Association said in response to Bush's budget proposal in February. "Unfortunately, America's transit systems are struggling to keep up with the strain of increasing demands and aging infrastructure."

One possible solution, in keeping with the past two surface transportation laws, is to give metropolitan governments more flexibility in how they spend federal transportation funds, tailoring the programs to meet local needs.

Bruce Katz, director of the Center on Urban and Metropolitan Policy at the Brookings Institution and an expert on sprawl, said that "resources need to shift more to the metropolitan areas" that have to deal directly with the problems of traffic congestion and suburban development.

"The real geography of our economy is metropolitan now and regional, yet we tend to still administer transportation at a state level," Katz said. "State transportation departments for the most part are not incredibly sensitive to the complex kind of issues that are playing out in metropolitan areas, and to some extent are exacerbating them because they tend to take a fairly narrow focus on many of these issues and really treat it almost as a kind of traffic engineering issue, as opposed to a complex [set] of housing, land use, and economic development and transportation issues."

Some states, in fact, spend a disproportionate share of their federal highway funds on roads in rural areas even though metropolitan areas pay most of the federal gasoline taxes and have the worst congestion problems.

"The genie's out of the bottle," Katz said. "Population and employment decentralization is the dominant trend in American life today. Congestion is becoming an issue in small and large metropolitan areas alike. That should be the geography of decision-making."

Local governments also are where innovation is strongest, and analysts such as Katz say local officials should be encouraged and rewarded for trying new methods to remedy congestion, such as "value pricing" roads by charging different tolls depending on the time of day, and using new types of buses or jitneys to move people around in the suburbs.

Bill Fulton, president of the Solimar Research Group in Ventura, Calif., which studies land use issues, said "part of the solution is to adjust to congestion, which we're doing. People are absorbing higher housing costs to live close."

Businesses are responding, he said, "which is why so many businesses locate in the suburbs rather than downtown, because it's easier for some of their employees to get there. That's the reason why people in suburbs drive cars, so they can have access to lots and lots of jobs. There is a combination of solutions here, some of which are occurring naturally without the government's help."

Fulton calls it the "Starbucks' solution," which "is to make it unnecessary to drive to a Starbucks by putting them on every corner."

Outlook

The debate over highway revenue threatens to stall the surface transportation bill this year, which means Congress probably will pass a one-year or two-year extension of current programs. If Congress does pass a long-term authorization bill this year, environmental provisions are expected to change only marginally.

A requirement to accelerate the environmental review of transportation projects is the most likely change, though some environmental groups have dubbed it "steamrolling" rather than streamlining. Proposed changes in Clean Air Act requirements, such as reducing the frequency with which cities must assess the environmental effects of their transportation plans, could run into more opposition.

The central issue in the transportation debate remains the gasoline tax. Don Young, R-Alaska, chairman of the House Transportation and Infrastructure Committee, and the American Road and Transportation Builders Association say that an increase in the tax is the only way to raise the kind of money needed for roads and bridges. The White House is dead set against increasing any tax, and many Republicans in Congress agree.

However, Peters said, "If we don't get a transportation bill this year, and a six-year bill at that, it's really going to wreak havoc with our ability to promote good, long-range transportation planning and deal with important environmental issues." ◆

Plans for Targeted Benefits Deepen Medicare Debate

Any move affecting program's equal coverage is heavy with political risk

Senate Finance Chairman Grassley and ranking Democrat Baucus, above, intensified the debate over the future of Medicare by introducing an overhaul bill on June 5. But criticism from Daschle, left, and other Democrats could scuttle the effort when the bill reaches the Senate floor.

For a program designed to provide health insurance to some of the most vulnerable Americans, Medicare is curiously unconcerned with such details as what recipients earn, where they live or what kind of coverage they already may have. The Great Society initiative was created on the notion of equality as an essential covenant that would reduce elderly and disabled citizens' medical expenses and ensure that future retirees would not see their savings eaten away.

But for almost as long as the 38-year-old program has existed, policymakers have grappled with how to tailor a prescription drug benefit to those who need it the most — the approximately 10 million seniors who do not have any drug coverage — without altering the wider program's universal heritage. It is a dilemma that challenges fundamental notions of parity and the limits of government. And it is a question that once again is hanging over Congress as the House and Senate begin efforts to create a Medicare prescription drug benefit and debate other changes to the program.

The problem is that extending the benefit to all Medicare recipients would cost more than the $400 billion lawmakers allocated in the fiscal 2004 budget resolution (H Con Res 95) to overhaul the program. Further complicating matters is the fact that the Bush administration and its allies have designs on doing much more than adding a drug benefit, most notably establishing new benefit packages managed by private health plans. (*2003 CQ Weekly, p. 1332*)

But to attempt to limit the benefit to a specific group — by, for example, tying the benefit to income — politicians open up a debate fraught with political risk. Targeting benefits to the poorest seniors could alienate middle-class and well-heeled voters, who finance the system through payroll taxes. At the same time it would anger liberals, who view Medicare's balanced approach as one of the most cherished legacies of the Great Society.

"We're taking a Medicare system we've had where everyone is treated the same, but now we'll have a two-tiered system," said Sen. Tom Harkin, D-Iowa, echoing the sentiments of Democrats who view the overhaul efforts as a threat to Medicare's egalitarian roots. "What they're trying to do here is destroy the underpinnings of the entire system."

Senators began exchanging Medicare drug proposals the week of June 2 in anticipation of a potentially lengthy debate that could consume most of the summer.

Senate Finance Chairman Charles E. Grassley, R-Iowa, and ranking Democrat Max Baucus of Montana, who will have to shepherd any Medicare bill through that chamber, unveiled draft legislation June 5 that resembles a "tripartisan" bill the Senate debated but did not pass last year. (2002 *CQ Weekly*, p. 3196)

Grassley and Baucus say the Senate Finance proposal would offer an equivalent level of drug coverage to all seniors beginning in 2006 and provide a discount drug card in the interim that supporters say would help save 10 percent to 25 percent of drug costs.

But the bill, and other measures that are expected to materialize in the coming weeks, will serve only as opening salvos in a broader philosophical battle about whether Medicare should remain a program for all classes or be converted into a social welfare initiative.

Lawmakers will have to make a series of critical trade offs regardless of the path they choose. Spending more to cover everyone could be a budget-wrecker, forcing Congress to justify hundreds of billions of dollars of additional costs at a time of deepening budget deficits. Adding benefits to maintain the "universal" nature of Medicare also could prompt messy questions, such as why multimillionaire seniors qualify for the same drug benefit as those who have no coverage. There also is concern that private employers may stop offering health care coverage for retirees if the government provides such a benefit. (2003 *CQ Weekly*, p. 1360)

Undaunted, at least a dozen well-placed Republicans on committees with jurisdiction over Medicare are openly discussing targeting a proposed drug benefit to the approximately 24 percent of Medicare beneficiaries — some 10 million people — who have no drug coverage.

Advocates say the strategy would allow lawmakers to use the government's limited resources to develop a more generous benefit for a defined population instead of giving a skimpy package to all of the more than 40 million Medicare beneficiaries. Past unsuccessful GOP efforts to create a universal drug benefit for all seniors were criticized for creating gaps in coverage and uncovered expenses for certain groups.

Limiting the number of people who qualify for the benefit also would appeal to fiscal conservatives, who want to insulate the Treasury from the brunt of future drug price increases. So would linking the level of benefits provided to beneficiaries' income — a concept that has been embraced by some House Republicans.

The lawmakers have suggested that the federal government's share of drug coverage for those beneficiaries who incur the highest costs, otherwise known as catastrophic coverage, be gradually phased out for seniors with incomes of $60,000 or higher.

"It's a cost container. It's the right thing to do. It's making sure that Medicare doesn't crumble under the weight of that one aspect of the program," said Rep. Mark Foley, R-Fla., who sits on the Ways and Means Committee, one of two House panels that will mark up a Medicare drug bill.

Tying the level of benefits to recipients' incomes "directs most of the help to people who need help," said Ways and Means member Jim McCrery, R-La., adding that the concept

Prescription Drug Coverage An Uneven Landscape

Prescription drug coverage currently is obtained by a majority of over-65 Medicare recipients. With new Medicare benefits looming, however, the picture could change quickly. Below are figures showing who has prescription coverage and how it is used.

Who has prescription coverage:

By age
- 65-69: 80%
- 70-74: 78%
- 75-79: 79%
- 80-84: 74%
- 85+: 72%

By race
- White: 77%
- Black: 80%
- Others: 84%

By gender
- Men: 78%
- Women: 77%

By residence
- Metro: 81%
- Rural: 67%

Those with coverage fill more prescriptions per year...

	65-69	70-74	75-79	80-84	85+
Covered	23.1	25.8	27.6	27.8	27.6
Not covered	14	17.9	21.9	24.2	22.2

...and pay more for them...

	65-69	70-74	75-79	80-84	85+
Covered	$1,141	$1,284	$1,281	$1,275	$1,101
Not covered	$534	$689	$826	$907	$791

...but pay less out of pocket.

	65-69	70-74	75-79	80-84	85+
Not covered	$534	$689	$826	$907	$791
Covered	$345	$402	$412	$421	$405

SOURCE: Medicare Current Benefit Survey (2000, latest data available)

CQ GRAPHIC / MARILYN GATES-DAVIS

"has a lot of support in the [House GOP] conference."

Undercutting Congressional Support?

Restricting benefits could stoke some Democrats' charges that the GOP's real goal is to dismantle Medicare over time. The Democrats fear that a targeted Medicare drug benefit will change the nature of the program and make it resemble welfare. That could reduce congressional support and affect future decisions about how the program is financed.

Democrats appear reluctant to "give up or cede what they regard as the high political ground" that Medicare is a universal benefit for all and that it should not be changed, said Robert D. Reischauer, the former director of the Congressional Budget Office (CBO) who is now president of the Urban Institute, a nonpartisan think tank.

Sen. Edward M. Kennedy of Massachusetts and other Democrats contend that there would be sufficient funding for a more generous drug benefit if President Bush and his congressional allies had not pressed for the $350 billion tax cut package that was signed into law (PL 108-27) on May 28. (*2003 CQ Weekly, p. 1404*)

Voters "understand that extravagant tax breaks for the rich mean that the resources will not be available to address America's real needs," Kennedy said. "They would prefer to use limited public dollars to help pay for health care than to finance a tax cut."

The push to limit Medicare benefits is more popular in the House than in the Senate, where Republicans are focused on developing a bipartisan bill that can attract a 60-vote majority to stave off the possibility of a filibuster. Still, some conservatives, such as Finance Committee member Don Nickles, R-Okla., are trying to design a bill that would target benefits to certain groups as part of broader overhaul plans. Some ideas include raising Medicare's eligibility age or phasing in any drug benefit slowly, with coverage extended only to lower income beneficiaries in the early years.

"It's very easy to add benefits and not reform the system," said Nickles, who is also chairman of the Senate Budget Committee. "I'd like to have a little more reform than some of my colleagues want."

Sen. Rick Santorum, R-Pa., has indicated that he will not block a bill from advancing out of the Senate, but will seek to modify the measure in conference.

Majority Leader Bill Frist, R-Tenn., wants the Finance Committee to mark up the draft the week of June 9 and bring the measure to a floor vote before the July Fourth recess.

Down a Familiar Road

Since the late 1980s, Congress has considered linking Medicare benefits to incomes on several occasions by charging well-heeled beneficiaries more for supplementary Part B coverage. The Senate in 1997 added a provision to its version of a tax cut bill. While the language won an endorsement from President Bill Clinton, it was dropped during conference negotiations at the insistence of House lawmakers. (*1997 Almanac, p. 6-3*)

The idea also sparked a tempest after Congress passed the 1988 Medicare Catastrophic Coverage Act, which raised Part B premiums for wealthy beneficiaries. The outcry from seniors was so great that Congress took the unusual step of repealing the measure in a separate bill (PL 101-234) the following year. (*2003 CQ Weekly, p. 1362*)

The idea endures, however, because Medicare beneficiaries make up nearly 15 percent of the population but account for about 40 percent of prescription drug spending, according to CBO. Medicare now covers drugs only when they are administered to patients in a hospital setting or in a physician's office.

The CBO estimates that the amount spent by Medicare beneficiaries on drugs will rise 12 percent per year over the next decade, regardless of whether lawmakers create a new prescription drug benefit. Some Republicans worry that creating a new drug benefit now will effectively leave the government with the bill if drug expenditures explode.

Five Republicans on the House Energy and Commerce Committee, which shares jurisdiction over Medicare with the Ways and Means panel, are drafting a bill that addresses the concern by proposing to create a prescription drug card that would link drug coverage to income. Low-income seniors would receive more aid from the federal government. Employers could contribute to the cards' coverage level, and states could do the same for poorer seniors.

Rep. Charlie Norwood, R-Ga., one of the plan's proponents, said it would control the government's costs of providing drug coverage by specifying the total amount the government contributes. That, in Norwood's view, is preferable to relying on private insurers to provide a drug benefit and risking their withdrawal from the program if costs run higher than expected. Other Energy and Commerce Republicans allied with Norwood include the panel's vice chairman, Richard M. Burr of North Carolina, and John Shadegg of Arizona.

A similar group that favors linking coverage to incomes exists on the Ways and Means Committee and includes Foley, McCrery and Dave Camp, R-Mich. The chairmen of the two committees of jurisdiction — Ways and Means' Bill Thomas, R-Calif., and Energy and Commerce's Billy Tauzin, R-La., have not yet committed to a specific Medicare drug plan.

Some House Democrats also are backing legislation that would contain the federal government's share of a Medicare drug benefit and that could form the basis of a possible bipartisan compromise.

Centrist Democrat Cal Dooley of California has introduced a bill (HR 1568) that would subsidize low-income seniors' drug costs and require Medicare to cover 80 percent of other beneficiaries' annual out-of-pocket expenses above $4,000.

Though House Republican leaders have publicly said they, too, want to bring Medicare drug legislation to the floor by the July Fourth recess, the disagreements about targeting benefits are contributing to a delay in bill markups until the week of June 16. House leaders also are waiting to gauge the Senate's reaction to any Senate Finance Committee bill, before moving any legislation.

Dealing With Doughnuts

If Congress does not link benefits to income, it will probably mean the final product would have coverage gaps, as Congress has just $400 billion to spend on drugs for all beneficiaries.

The Senate Finance bill, for example, would cover half of a beneficiary's drug costs up to $3,450. Coverage would not begin again until the senior's out-of-pocket spending hit $3,700, at which point the government would pick up 90 percent of the tab. A House Republican drug bill that passed the chamber last year similarly would have had a gap in coverage from $2,000 to $3,700. (*2002 CQ Weekly, p. 1667*)

On top of those gaps, seniors also would have to pay monthly premiums and an annual deductible before drug coverage would start. In the Finance bill, those premiums would be about $35, and the annual deductible would be $275, although the bill's specifics could change once CBO completes its cost analysis, which Grassley and Baucus hope is done before the scheduled June 12 markup.

When lawmakers and their constituents do the math, they may determine that proposals such as the Finance bill cost too much for the coverage they provide. Seniors' groups will not be happy, either. An AARP advertising campaign unveiled June 5 — the day the Senate Finance Committee bill was unveiled — urged Congress to make "every effort . . . to reduce caps in coverage."

A factor working in favor of the Finance Committee bill is the qualified and surprising endorsement of Kennedy, one of the chamber's staunchest liberals, but a lawmaker also known for cutting deals with Republicans.

Kennedy on June 5 called the Grassley-Baucus package "a major breakthrough in our effort to give senior citizens the prescription drug coverage under Medicare they need and deserve." One reason the bill appeals to Kennedy is because the measure does not offer enhanced drug benefits to seniors who leave traditional Medicare for private plans.

However, Senate Minority Leader Tom Daschle, D-S.D., sounded an entirely different note, saying the bill falls "significantly short" of Democratic ideas for drug coverage. "We have strongly opposed plans that would privatize Medicare; that would include large gaps in coverage that require seniors to pay premiums when they don't receive benefits, that allow insurance companies rather than Medicare to set premiums and determine coverage," he said.

Floor Fight Expected

While Daschle has said repeatedly that he has no intention of filibustering Medicare prescription drug legislation, he said Democrats would offer amendments in committee and on the floor "to improve this bill."

Such a scenario could lead to fierce partisan floor fights and derail the measure, even if the Finance panel approves it largely intact.

If senators cannot unite behind the Finance bill, they may return to a fallback position: the politically safe alternative of passing a bill that provides drug coverage to the poorest seniors and those with the highest drug bills.

In the 107th Congress, Democrats and Republicans supported plans that would have targeted the majority of a Medicare drug benefit to those two groups. None of the plans, however, received the 60 votes needed to overcome procedural hurdles that were raised against them.

Sens. Chuck Hagel, R-Neb., and John Ensign, R-Nev., are considering reviving language they introduced last

---

Congress Has a Difficult Time Discriminating by Income

Lawmakers have frequently debated charging well-off individuals more for their coverage under entitlement programs such as Medicare and Social Security since the late 1980s. The issue is again in the spotlight as House Ways and Means Committee Republicans consider phasing out proposed catastrophic Medicare drug coverage for seniors with incomes of $60,000 or higher. Following are some examples where lawmakers considered imposing, or lifting, restrictions tied to beneficiaries' incomes.

1997: The Senate Finance Committee in 1997 included an amendment in its version of budget-reconciliation legislation linking Medicare beneficiaries' insurance deductibles under Medicare Part B to their incomes. The theory was that the change would influence beneficiaries' behavior and make them think twice about spending their own money on health services. The language by John H. Chafee, R-R.I., and Bob Kerrey, D-Neb., was adopted by the committee, 18-2, and included in the Senate version of the bill. President Bill Clinton endorsed the idea. However, it was dropped in conference in the face of strong opposition from House lawmakers.

1996: Congress reversed a means test, of sorts, in 1996 by increasing the Social Security earnings limit as part of legislation raising the federal statutory debt limit (PL 104-121). The legislation allowed the working elderly to earn up to $30,000 and continue to receive full Social Security benefits. Under existing law, recipients age 65 to 69 could earn up to $11,520 and continue to receive full benefits. For every $3 earned over the limit, a recipient lost $1 in benefits. The language raised the maximum earnings threshold over seven years.

1995: Congress in 1995 attempted to charge wealthy Medicare beneficiaries more for their Part B coverage, including language to that effect in a budget-reconciliation bill that Clinton vetoed. The bill would have required the wealthiest beneficiaries to pay the entire cost of their Part B coverage. The existing Part B subsidy would begin to phase out for individuals making $60,000 annually and couples making $90,000, with costs gradually increasing until the subsidy ended at $110,000 for singles and $150,000 for couples.

1988-93: Congress voted to charge well-heeled Medicare recipients an extra sum for stop-loss coverage of hospital, doctor and prescription drug costs and expanded coverage of nursing home, home health and hospice care when it passed the 1988 Medicare Catastrophic Coverage Act (PL 100-360), a landmark expansion of the Medicare program. But lawmakers did a stunning about-face the next year and repealed the law (PL 101-234) after senior citizens angrily protested being forced to pay the entire costs of new benefits. Particularly outraged were the 40 percent of Medicare's then-33 million beneficiaries who would have had to pay an income surtax of up to $800 per person in 1989, climbing to $1,050 in 1993. The outcry led to a particularly memorable scene in which then-House Ways and Means Committee Chairman Dan Rostenkowski, D-Ill., was assailed by angry seniors in his district.

SOURCE: CQ Almanac

---

year that would have given all Medicare beneficiaries access to discount drug cards and provided catastrophic coverage based on recipients' incomes.

Ensign said he and Hagel are trying to gauge Democratic support for their bill. Ensign sees the plan as an alternative if the chamber becomes deadlocked over other plans. "The people who need the benefit the most get the most benefit under our plan," he said.

For now, Republican leaders are hoping the Finance Committee bill will remain relatively untouched, and

that they can pick up the votes of such lawmakers as independent James M. Jeffords of Vermont, one of the authors of last year's "tripartisan" plan. Another Republican target is Democrat Blanche Lincoln of Arkansas, who is up for re-election next year.

Frist, a Finance Committee member who advocated a bipartisan bill from the start, has urged skeptical lawmakers to hold their fire until they read the final legislation. "If the pieces come together as envisioned, it will have significant reform," he said. ◆

Medicare Rewrite: Prescription For Disappointing Everyone?

Hill leaders vow to 'get it right,' but list of potentially crushing problems is daunting

After more than five years of stalemate, members of Congress seem stunned by the passage of Medicare overhaul bills in the House and Senate — a feat many regarded as unthinkable even a few months ago.

Soon, they will begin writing a final version designed to win enough votes to get through the chambers one last time. But winning votes is not the only test this conference report will have to pass. It will also have to produce a Medicare prescription drug benefit that works.

"This will be the last real shot to get this perfect," acknowledged Senate Majority Leader Bill Frist, R-Tenn., hours after the Senate passed its version June 27. "So we will spend whatever time it takes, working together . . . to get it right." *(2003 CQ Weekly, p. 1611)*

The measure of success is whether the revamped Medicare program will truly address seniors' needs. With all of the things that can go wrong in the health care marketplace — and considering all of the tradeoffs that have already been made in the legislation — analysts and policymakers from across the political spectrum are warning that this overhaul has a good chance of disappointing nearly everybody. That could create a political backlash that would make members of Congress wish they had never heard of Medicare and prescription drugs.

"It bothers me a lot that we are setting up a system to take care of my mother that we know in advance is not bound to work," said Sen. Jon Kyl, R-Ariz. The conservative lawmaker voted for the Senate bill despite misgivings that it would fall short of GOP goals of giving private health plans a bigger role in Medicare.

"There is no way to legislate on a program of such great importance to the citizens of the country," Democrat Robert C. Byrd of West Virginia, who voted against the Senate bill, warned colleagues in a floor speech. "They may revolt, and members of Congress could be back here scratching their heads and scrambling to find a solution and save their seats."

Analysts say the list of potential problems is long and will give negotiators plenty to worry about.

The proposed prescription drug coverage would contain so many gaps due to budget constraints in both bills (HR 1, S 1) that seniors may feel cheated and unwilling to pay for the new coverage. There also is no guarantee that private health plans will be any more eager to administer Medicare benefits than they have been since 1997, when Congress created a Medicare managed care program called Medicare+Choice (PL 105-33). *(1997 Almanac, p. 6-3)*

Employers struggling in the economic downturn could stop offering prescription drug coverage to their retirees, transferring the burden to the new government plan and leaving retirees with potentially skimpier benefits. Lawmakers aware of the threat of so-called "employer crowd-out" already have loaded up the bills with subsidies to employers to continue retiree coverage — which itself could become a political issue.

The costs to the federal government could explode for any number of reasons, deepening the federal deficit. It could be difficult creating a new federal bureaucracy to run the revamped program, as both bills propose. And the program as envisioned already is so complex that some critics believe it will simply confuse and overwhelm seniors.

All of this assumes the conference committee can write a final bill capable of passing Congress, and that is not necessarily a safe

Hastert and other congressional leaders face thorny questions about how to address seniors' needs as they head into conference on Medicare drug legislation.

assumption. Negotiators will somehow have to straddle the issue of whether to allow competitive bidding between private plans and traditional, fee-for-service Medicare, a central feature of the House bill. That is not an easy issue to finesse because 42 House Republicans have warned their leaders that they will not support a conference report that does not include it, and key Senate Democrats say they will not support a conference report that does. (*Premium support, p. 105*)

Even if the political divide can be bridged, the long-term policy challenges are so difficult that many of the 76 senators who voted for the bill did so with a deep sense of unease.

"Those of our friends on the other side of the aisle and in the administration who believe the government does everything badly have designed legislation to prove themselves right," said Sen. Mark Dayton, D-Minn., one of those who could barely bring himself to vote for the bill.

No Shortage of Critics

The effort is also being criticized by an unusually wide variety of experts off the Hill.

"It could be a political disaster as well as an epitome of confusion," said Bruce C. Vladeck, who headed the agency now known as the Centers for Medicare and Medicaid Services (CMS) under President Bill Clinton from 1993 to 1997.

"The whole concept of creating a universal health benefit is wrong from the beginning," said Robert E. Moffitt, director of the Center for Health Policy Studies at the conservative Heritage Foundation, because most seniors already have some kind of drug coverage. "So what's wrong with it? Just about everything."

Aware of the deep discontent with the legislation, as well as the potential for all kinds of policy problems, Republican leaders insist they will pay attention to the details and let the conference committee take the time it needs to get the final product right.

President Bush, however, is already leaning on Congress to finish the Medicare bill sooner rather than later. In a

Bush stands to win credit for breaking the Medicare logjam while avoiding complaints about specifics in the drug bill.

BLOOMBERG NEWS PHOTO / CHRIS KLEPONIS

June 30 speech in Miami, he urged lawmakers to "get to work, iron out the differences in a constructive way and get a good bill to my desk, so that I can then say, and all of us can say, we've done our jobs on behalf of America's seniors."

Bush has good reason to keep the pressure on GOP lawmakers. Passage of a Medicare bill would achieve a long-sought Republican goal of overhauling an entitlement program that is financially unprepared for the looming eligibility of the baby boom generation.

Bush also will have more to gain politically if the years-long deadlock on Medicare prescription drugs is finally broken. And he will have less on the line than Congress if the benefit does not live up to seniors' expectations.

"There's no question that it will help the president. . . . They'll give the president credit for breaking the logjam," said Robert J. Blendon, director of Harvard University's Program on Public Opinion and Health and Social Policy. However, when seniors start to find out about the limits of the benefit, it is more likely to be members of Congress who will bear the brunt of the complaints, he said.

That might not happen for a while. Under both the House and the Senate bills, the benefit would not actually start until 2006, long after the presidential election was over. Instead, during the 2004 election, seniors would have access to Medicare-endorsed dis-

count cards to help them buy prescription drugs — an interim step that would bear little resemblance to the benefit that would kick in two years later. Low-income seniors would get additional subsidies.

Political strategists disagree on how much information seniors will hear about the real benefit, and its many limits, during 2004. But all agree that in 2006, seniors will know about it from first-hand experience. And in the focus groups that have been conducted so far, seniors have not liked what they have heard.

GOP strategists are aware of this, and are advising Republicans not to try to oversell the prescription drug benefit. "We can't frame this as a replacement for the coverage they have now," said Republican pollster Bill McInturff, who has conducted focus groups on the Medicare prescription drug benefit. "If they compare this to private coverage, it doesn't stack up."

Instead, the new Medicare benefit should be described to seniors only as a new option, a backup for those who do not have private drug coverage or lose it in the future, McInturff said. The message, he said, should be that "if you like your current coverage, you can keep it."

To some, the legislation has already become so convoluted, thanks to the tradeoffs between two parties with completely different visions of the future of Medicare, that it would be better to simply stop the entire effort and let the bill die in conference committee rather than create a flawed program that could be impossible to fix later.

"A transformation of Medicare which involves major concessions to both sides . . . would be worth avoiding and blocking rather than conceding to it," said Theodore R. Marmor, a Department of Health, Education and Welfare aide at the time when the original Medicare system was launched, in the mid-1960s.

Unlike 1965 — when Democrats had a 2-to-1 majority in Congress and could prevail in efforts to create national health insurance — the political conditions now are not right to create a coherent program, Marmor said. Republicans enjoy only a narrow majority over Democrats, leading to awkward compromises between public and private coverage that will only ensure that neither side's goals will be realized, he said. *(1965 Almanac, p. 236)*

Blendon, however, thinks the reaction will not all be negative. Seniors will simply put pressure on members of Congress from both parties to make the existing benefits more generous — just as lawmakers have faced pressure to raise the minimum wage over the years when the public believes it has not kept pace with the cost of living.

"They're going to find out that they're not off the hook on this at all," Blendon said.

Sticker Shock

By 2006, the year the new Medicare prescription drug coverage would take effect, the average Medicare beneficiary is expected to spend $3,160 a year on prescription drugs, according to the Henry J. Kaiser Family Foundation.

One of the main goals of the legislation is to cut those bills down to a more manageable figure. But seniors might be surprised to learn that their new Medicare prescription drug coverage would still leave them paying more than half of the costs themselves.

Under the Senate legislation, the average Medicare beneficiary would still have to pay about $1,718 in drug costs, according to Kaiser estimates. The House measure would leave them paying $1,760 in out-of-pocket costs.

That includes the annual deductible — $275 under the Senate bill, $250 under the House bill — and the cost-sharing requirements that would kick in after the deductibles were paid. Neither figure counts the estimated $35-a-month premium, or $420 a year. Since the $35 a month figure is only an estimate, not written into the legislation, the actual premium any senior might pay could be considerably different.

How will seniors react, after six years of promises from Congress and two more years of preparation before the coverage starts, when they find that Medicare still cannot even cover half of their drug costs? To some lawmakers and health care experts, the greatest danger of the legislation is that seniors will resist the changes and vent their frustrations at elected officials.

"There will be anger," said Rep. Benjamin L. Cardin, D-Md., a member of the House Ways and Means Committee. "When you compare what was promised in the 30-second ads that were run by our colleagues across the

aisle in the last election and what they [seniors] are actually going to get, there's a real disconnect."

The structure would be far different than most private prescription drug benefits, which have no deductible and nominal copayments for each drug purchase. For example, the standard option under the BlueCross BlueShield Federal Employees Program requires federal workers to pay 25 percent of the cost of a drug if they buy it at a pharmacy within their preferred provider organization (PPO) network. For mail orders, the cost is $10 for a generic drug and $35 for a brand-name drug.

The biggest danger in designing the Medicare coverage plan is that "seniors see what the benefits are, and they say, 'Yuck!' " said Paul B. Ginsburg, president of the nonpartisan Center for Studying Health System Change.

The gaps in coverage became inevitable, however, once Congress decided that it would not spend more than $400 billion over 10 years — the maximum amount that Republicans were willing to spend — while agreeing to Democrats' insistence that all seniors be eligible for the coverage. *(2003 CQ Weekly, p. 1358)*

The most-discussed effect of the budget limit is the large gap in cover-

Understanding 'Premium Support'

Among the difficult political tradeoffs House and Senate conferees will confront while developing compromise Medicare drug legislation is what role they should give private health insurers in a revamped Medicare system. The House bill revives the controversial concept of "premium support," which was endorsed in 1999 by a bipartisan commission studying proposals to overhaul the system. Premium support assumes the federal government will subsidize a portion of the out-of-pocket costs that beneficiaries would pay to belong to private plans. The Senate bill does not call for premium support.

any plan, including Medicare, exceeded the established rate, beneficiaries would have to make up the extra amount through out-of-pocket costs. This system would, in theory, reward efficiency because a plan that can keep its costs below the weighted average would still be guaranteed to receive the average payment. Seniors theoretically could benefit if they choose programs that bid below the benchmark rate.

HOUSE BILL

• The bill would require private plans to bid against each other to offer Medicare services in geographic regions established by the government. The three lowest bidders would offer PPO-type service, and Medicare beneficiaries would be able to choose traditional fee-for-service Medicare or one of the three private options.

• Starting in 2010, in areas where competition exists, the bill would require the traditional Medicare fee-for-service plan to compete directly on price against the private plans. The government would consider all bids and establish a weighted average that would be used to establish payment rates. Traditional Medicare would have to be able to provide services according to those rates. If the cost of

SENATE BILL

• Private plans could bid against each other on price to provide Medicare benefits, but could not bid directly against the traditional Medicare fee-for-service program.

• Includes an additional $12 billion in funds, to be spent after 2009, half of which would go toward bolstering Medicare's fee-for-service system to help it compete against private plans. The other $6 billion would fund payments to private plans to encourage participation in the overhauled program.

• Has a "fallback" provision that would offer a government-run Medicare drug benefit in geographic areas where not enough private plans bid for a government contract to offer a drug-only benefits for seniors who stay in fee-for-service plans.

age, known as the "doughnut hole," between the end of the bills' initial coverage and the start of their catastrophic coverage.

One of the biggest issues the conference committee will have to decide is how large that gap will be. In the Senate version, seniors would have to pay all of their costs between $4,500 and $5,813. Under the House bill, the gap is much larger, leaving seniors on the hook for all of their coverage between $2,000 and $4,900.

The size of the coverage gap drew so much notice during the Senate and House debates that Republican leaders have been trying to stress how few seniors would ever spend enough to experience it. Frist, for example, noted that "the vast majority" of seniors would never have prescription drug costs high enough to put them in the doughnut hole.

While it is true that most seniors would not experience it, more beneficiaries than Frist suggests could have expenses that fall into that gap. In 2006, according to the nonprofit Kaiser Family Foundation, 19.6 percent of seniors — or one in five — will probably have drug expenses over $5,000, putting them well within the gap in the Senate bill. Moreover, 33 percent — one in three — will probably have drug costs between $2,000 and $5,000, the size of the House gap.

Will Private Plans Play?

In addition to dealing with the issue of whether seniors will pay for the new coverage, conferees will be haunted by a second fundamental question: Will private insurers, on whom the entire program rests, participate?

Both bills would allow seniors to get drug coverage in two main ways. Beneficiaries could join a new managed care network similar to a preferred provider organization (PPO), a structure that many workers use now but most current seniors do not. Or seniors could stay in the traditional fee-for-service Medicare program and buy a separate, drug-only insurance plan — an option that does not now exist.

The insurance industry is offering no assurances that health plans will sign up to offer coverage. Many health plan executives hope that they will benefit from the increased volume that the Medicare market might provide, but they still are seeking a number of concessions.

Lawmakers are calling on health plans to offer PPO coverage in one of 10 regions, which could be as large as a state. But if those regions were too large, insurers might find it onerous to offer coverage in such a wide geographical area. They also would like the government to allow more than three plans to participate per region, as both bills currently stipulate. (*2003 CQ Weekly*, p. 1692)

Insurers additionally would like to change provisions, particularly in the Senate bill, that would require them to disclose the rebates that they win from drug companies.

And insurers offering Medigap policies, which provide supplemental coverage to Medicare beneficiaries, are concerned about the way that those plans could change. Under both bills, the few Medigap plans that provide drug benefits, among other coverage, would change when the new program goes into effect on Jan. 1, 2006.

In the House bill, those plans would continue in a new form without the drug benefits. Seniors who are already in those Medigap plans could keep them, but the plans would be discounted to reflect the elimination of the drug benefits. But the Senate bill would just eliminate the three plans, which insurers oppose.

Even if insurers win all of the changes that they are seeking, no company is willing to guarantee that it will stay in the Medicare business. All expect to constantly re-evaluate the business climate to gauge whether it makes sense to participate.

"They may well come in at the beginning if they perceive it to be profitable, but there's nothing to hold them in the market over the long term, so there's no way to ensure that seniors will get stable, predictable coverage over time," said Tricia Neuman, director of the Medicare Policy Project of the Kaiser Family Foundation. "It's just really uncertain."

Questions About Complexity

When Hillary Rodham Clinton, D-N.Y., stood up on the Senate floor June 20 to warn that the Medicare bill was needlessly complicated, the irony all but drowned out her message. Many remembered Clinton's role as spokeswoman for her husband's unsuccessful health care plan, which was similarly derided as convoluted and unworkable. (*1994 Almanac*, p. 319)

But Clinton was not the only critic to make that point. Many of her Democratic colleagues, and numerous outside analysts, raised the same concern about the Senate bill. At a time when seniors will be looking for a simple, understandable drug benefit, one of the biggest jobs of the House-Senate conference committee will be to produce a benefit structure that accomplishes that goal.

"I foresee a great deal of confusion and dismay occurring around kitchen tables and in corporate boardrooms across America," said Byrd. "I am confused just trying to describe it."

The Senate bill was the product of political tradeoffs between Republicans and Democrats on the Finance Committee, where it originated.

It would let seniors obtain their drug coverage through a private health plan, such as a PPO or a health maintenance organization, or a private stand-alone drug policy. If two private plans did not stay in an area, there would be a government-run "fallback" plan. Bush does not like that arrangement, but it is crucial to Democrats, who cite the history of Medicare+Choice plans pulling out of the program. (*Medicare+Choice*, 2002 *CQ Weekly*, p. 3071)

Still, some Democrats worry that the arrangement will leave seniors shifting back and forth between plans from year to year if insurers pull out of an area and then re-enter.

In addition, Clinton described the problems a Medicare beneficiary could have if he or she signed up for a private plan, found out it did not cover a needed drug, appealed the decision, and went through a drawn-out appeals process — only to have the plan pull out of the market and be replaced by a fallback plan, and possibly replaced again by another private plan a year later.

The House bill, meanwhile, could create bureaucratic hassles for wealthier beneficiaries. It would set higher out-of-pocket spending limits for seniors with incomes over $60,000, or $120,000 for couples. To make that work, the Treasury Department would have to send tax return information to the Department of Health and Human Services (HHS). The beneficiary could send a more recent tax return to HHS, if it would work to his or her advantage, but the newer return would have to be verified by the Treasury Department.

Such complexities would make it vital for Congress to invest in beneficiary education, according to Vladeck, the former CMS administrator. Both bills call for a Medicare ombudsman, the establishment of a toll-free phone number to answer beneficiaries' questions (1-800-MEDICARE), and a demonstration program in six locations in which Medicare specialists would work with beneficiaries at local Social Security offices. Neither bill would set a specific funding level for those efforts.

McInturff, the Republican pollster, believes much of the talk of complexity is overblown. While seniors in the focus groups did have a hard time understanding the plan, he said, any new benefit would be confusing at first, and seniors would learn their way around the new system over time.

Fearing 'Crowd-Out'

Liberals and conservatives alike are concerned about the threat that employers could see the new Medicare program as an opportunity to shift the costs of providing health benefits for their retirees to the government.

"You don't want to replace private dollars with public dollars," said House Ways and Means Committee Chairman Bill Thomas, R-Calif.

Most employers are hoping to retain current benefits for those seniors already receiving them, according to surveys by the Kaiser Family Foundation and others. But some companies stung by rising health care costs already are planning to scale back coverage for future retirees. Lawmakers fear that the promise of government coverage could entice some employers to drop coverage sooner.

The Congressional Budget Office has estimated that under the Senate bill, 37 percent of retirees would lose their current coverage. Under the House bill, that number is about 32 percent.

Some lobbyists for employers' groups dispute that number and say that the bills have essentially removed the concern about reduced coverage as much as possible. Both bills would allow employers who now offer drug coverage to continue offering those benefits — but receive new government subsidies for doing so.

"I can't tell you that each and every one of our members that provides drug coverage to retirees will continue to, but at least there's a better environment for them under these bills than in the current climate," said Neil Trautwein, a lobbyist for the National Association of Manufacturers.

Because each company offers a different set of health and prescription drug benefits, business lobbyists say they cannot predict precisely how companies will react. "Some may be in a position to do business directly with the government right away, others may evolve in, and then others may evolve out," said Kate Sullivan, a top health care lobbyist for the U.S. Chamber of Commerce.

Labor unions have made it a priority to ensure the continuation of benefits for retirees. Business lobbyists also have signaled an interest in expanding subsidies for employers who keep offering the same benefits that they do now —but only if the costs remain under the $400 billion price tag for Medicare overhaul that lawmakers approved in the fiscal 2004 budget resolution (H Con Res 95). Employers, who pay half of the 5.8 percent Medicare payroll tax, are more concerned about keeping those taxes low than providing additional subsidies for the declining number of companies that offer retiree coverage.

The Price Tag

For liberal Democrats such as Sen. Edward M. Kennedy of Massachusetts, the best argument for supporting the bill is that Congress will be forced to come back and make the benefits more generous once seniors start complaining about them.

That is exactly what makes conservative Republicans nervous.

Still, public pressure is not the only reason to expect that a drug benefit would escalate well beyond $400 billion over 10 years once it was in place.

If employers dropped their retiree coverage, those retirees could be added to the Medicare benefit. The same thing could happen if states scaled back or dropped their pharmaceutical programs.

There is also the issue of keeping private plans from dropping out. If the final version resembles the House bill, which would offer higher payments to private plans to keep them in an area rather than relying on a government fallback plan, some analysts say the price of keeping private plans in business could be far higher than Congress expects.

And then, of course, there is a history of incorrect assumptions about the growth in Medicare spending.

"One potential bombshell out there is what it actually costs as opposed to what it's projected to cost," said Gail Wilensky, who headed Medicare under President George Bush from 1990 to 1992. "History is terrible" on predicting Medicare and Medicaid costs in advance, she said.

At a news conference hours after the House barely passed its bill June 27, Speaker J. Dennis Hastert, R-Ill., acknowledged that he faces resistance from conservative Republicans who are "concerned that this is a government entitlement that will get out of hand." However, he said the role of the private sector in the House bill is "a way that you can really hold and tie down a future benefit without added government cost."

"The fact is that it's a mix of government entitlement, because certainly Medicare is an entitlement, but it's also a commitment to the private sector that they will have a role, and cost containment will be part of that role," Hastert said.

The New Agency

With all eyes focused on the new prescription drug benefit and the fight over the role of the private sector, most members of Congress have been curiously silent on another detail of both bills: the creation of a new agency to oversee the prescription drug program.

The agency would run the program as well as the effort to draw more private health plans into Medicare. It would exist side by side with CMS, which would continue to run the rest of Medicare.

That raises a host of potential implementation problems. For one thing, analysts say, most of the officials with the strongest expertise on Medicare are already at CMS, leading to the prospect of a "brain drain" away from the old agency if too many experts move to the new one.

In addition, they say, Congress needs to think more about the bureaucratic problems that could arise if a program as big as Medicare is split between two agencies, particularly if the best experts leave CMS.

"Do you move them all out of CMS?" asked Vladeck. "If you move them all over from CMS . . . who's responsible for [the Medicare beneficiaries]? Who keeps track of their enrollment records?" ◆

Lawmakers Walk a Tightrope On Economic, Security Issues

Security delays threaten 'just in time' delivery system that serves U.S. so well

In Union City, Calif., just south of San Francisco, food importer Albert Lin has had shipments from Asia delayed for two weeks awaiting inspectors from the Food and Drug Administration to make sure snacks such as his company's "Sultana" raisin biscuits are not tainted.

"Because of the bioterrorism law, there's lots more inspections, and more delays," said Lin, who is executive vice president of Singapore-based food company Khong Guan Corp. "We'll have to raise our prices easily another 10 percent."

To the south in Long Beach, port director Richard D. Steinke says he hears daily complaints about containers sitting idle on docks waiting for customs inspectors, who are now part of the Department of Homeland Security. And in Charleston, S.C., on the East Coast, the port authority has $10 million in security needs. It may not be able to build a new security fence because the port is not expected to receive enough in federal grants in fiscal 2004, according to Byron Miller, spokesman for the South Carolina State Ports Authority.

Businesses across the country knew commerce would be more difficult, and more expensive, because of stepped-up security after the Sept. 11 terrorist attacks. But nearly two years later the issue is far from resolved. From the air cargo hub of Anchorage to the docks of Los Angeles, to the Ambassador Bridge connecting Detroit and Windsor, Ontario, industries large and small are still coming to grips with ever-increasing levels of inspection, caution, restriction and paperwork.

For Congress and the executive branch, protecting the nation from terrorism has meant trying to find a balance between an adequate level of vigilance and a comfortable level of trade. Tighten security, and commerce can suffer with long lines of idling trucks, spoiled goods and empty warehouses. Loosen trade, and terrorists might sneak through weapons of mass destruction.

Much of the burden of making things work falls on the new Department of Homeland Security, an agglomeration of 22 agencies that are supposed to protect the nation's borders, transportation and critical infrastructure. But Congress is still trying to find the right balance on a range of national security issues. Though it swiftly passed aviation security legislation (PL 107-71) and financial aid for the airline industry in the closing months of 2001 (PL 107-42), because of the clear threat and damage done by airborne attacks, writing laws to protect other modes of travel and a far-flung infrastructure has been more difficult. (*2001 Almanac, p. 20-4*)

Industries and individual companies recognize the need

"*We have to balance freedom with restrictions. It's the fundamental challenge in American society.*"

— Sen. Thad Cochran, R-Miss., chairman of the Homeland Security Appropriations Subcommittee

for homeland security, but they bridle at what they consider unreasonable requirements, restrictions or inspections, particularly when those requirements and scrutiny might help competitors or increase the cost of doing business.

Many have lobbied Congress to avoid or adjust security legislation. As a result, lawmakers have not been able to finish bills to increase security in the chemical industry, railroads and air cargo. A port security law passed in 2002 calls for grants and harbor surveys but authorizes almost no funding; lawmakers could not agree on how to pay for it, and shippers balked at new fees.

Security legislation Congress has passed sometimes imposes conflicting requirements on business.

The Trade Act of 2002 (PL 107-210), for instance, led to regulations still under debate that would require trucks headed for the United States from Canada or Mexico to notify customs inspectors an hour before reaching the border. Meanwhile, working from the 2002 bioterrorism prevention law (PL 107-188), the Food and Drug Administration (FDA) came up with a proposed regulation requiring that details of a shipment be provided at least by noon of the day before the truck crosses the border. (*Trade, 2002 Almanac, p. 18-3; bioterrorism, p. 10-10*)

Shippers say such rules, though intended to help homeland security, will cause problems with the "just in time" delivery that American retailers and manufacturers have come to rely on.

"We're afraid there's going to be a congestion problem" with some security rules, said Sandra Scott, an international trade and government affairs official for Roadway Express Inc., one of the country's largest trucking companies. "You add gas cost, shipment delays. You've got Homeland Security with one rule and the FDA with other rules."

Critics of relaxing security, including some congressional Democrats, say some industries are trying to water down proposed regulations to save money or annoyance. Industry heads and Republican congressional leaders counter that the security legislation they are writing strikes a good balance

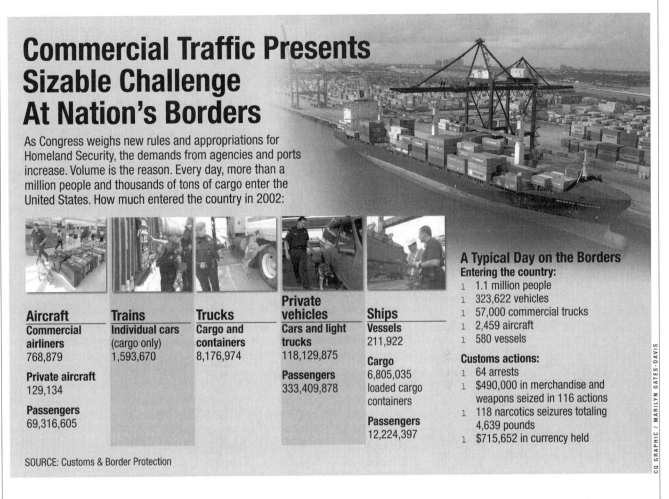

Commercial Traffic Presents Sizable Challenge At Nation's Borders

As Congress weighs new rules and appropriations for Homeland Security, the demands from agencies and ports increase. Volume is the reason. Every day, more than a million people and thousands of tons of cargo enter the United States. How much entered the country in 2002:

Aircraft
Commercial airliners
768,879

Private aircraft
129,134

Passengers
69,316,605

Trains
Individual cars (cargo only)
1,593,670

Trucks
Cargo and containers
8,176,974

Private vehicles
Cars and light trucks
118,129,875

Passengers
333,409,878

Ships
Vessels
211,922

Cargo
6,805,035
loaded cargo containers

Passengers
12,224,397

A Typical Day on the Borders
Entering the country:
1 1.1 million people
1 323,622 vehicles
1 57,000 commercial trucks
1 2,459 aircraft
1 580 vessels

Customs actions:
1 64 arrests
1 $490,000 in merchandise and weapons seized in 116 actions
1 118 narcotics seizures totaling 4,639 pounds
1 $715,652 in currency held

SOURCE: Customs & Border Protection

CQ GRAPHIC / MARILYN GATES-DAVIS

between security and free commerce.

"We have to balance freedom with restrictions," said Sen. Thad Cochran, R-Miss., chairman of the Homeland Security Appropriations Subcommittee. "It's the fundamental challenge in American society."

Difficult Climb

As Congress and the Bush administration picked up the pieces of the nation's shattered confidence after the Sept. 11 attacks, both knew that reassurance — in the form of homeland security — would be vital. Members of Congress, in fact, were the first to call for a new federal department devoted to domestic protection. The administration, dedicated as it is to reducing the size of government, was at first wary of creating such a super-agency and later argued for broad new personnel power in order to control it.

But as the two branches set about creating legislation and regulations to guard at least the borders and transportation, they knew it would be a major challenge to secure the country without shutting down the economy. The United States is a vast, porous country with 12,000 miles of coastline, a tradition of free-market capitalism, and a suspicion of government and restriction. As former House Speaker Newt Gingrich, R-Ga. (1979-99), once observed, Americans want highway speed limits posted so they know by how much to exceed them.

The changeover from private security companies to a federalized workforce at the nation's airports was marked by long lines, confusion over aviation security rules and frustration on the part of American travelers. Though the changes were meant to calm travelers who had deserted the airlines

in droves, the added security made travel, and commerce, more difficult.

And passenger airliners are just one mode of travel. Some lawmakers worried about freight carriers, as well as the cargo carried aboard airliners that was not checked in the same way as passenger baggage. Trains, subways, private aircraft and ships were virtually not inspected at all. And most of the nation's critical infrastructure — telecommunications networks, pipelines, nuclear power plants, chemical factories, water reservoirs and oil refineries — was in the hands of private business or local government.

The shipping industry is just one example.

Worry on the Wharves

Each year, an estimated 6 million loaded cargo containers arrive at the United States' 361 commercial seaports. Each of these standardized 20- or 40-foot-long containers has room for the entire contents of a house; the larger ones can hold up to 34 tons of cargo. Containers arrive sealed, and because the sizes are standard, in minutes they can be lifted from a ship, loaded onto a flatcar or truck chassis and be on their way anywhere in the country. Only 2 percent are inspected.

Concern over the vulnerability of the nation's sprawling ports led some lawmakers, such as Democratic Sen. Ernest F. Hollings from coastal Charleston, S.C., to push for legislation to tighten security. Hollings' 2002 Maritime Transportation Security Act (PL 107-295), in fact, was supposed to be the major port security law, except that almost no money was authorized to carry it out.

Lobbying by shipping companies helped scotch Hollings' plan to impose a shipping fee to pay for security surveys and enhancements at the ports, some of which spread for miles along tidal rivers and bays. Labor unions complained about plans to require security checks and identification for dockworkers.

The fiscal 2004 Homeland Security appropriations bill (HR 2555) would provide $150 million for port security grants, but the Coast Guard has said at least $1 billion is needed in fiscal 2004 alone to carry out mandates for security assessments and upgrades at all the major U.S. ports.

Steinke, the Port of Long Beach director, calls the port security law an unfunded mandate. He has identified $60 million in security needs; his port has received $18 million in federal grants. "Where are we going to get the revenue to pay for these programs?" Steinke said. "We have to balance the flow of commerce with the need for security. But we could use more resources."

Lobbyists who represent port authorities, meanwhile, oppose a bill (HR 1010) introduced by Rep. Jerrold Nadler, D-N.Y., that would require inspection of every shipping container that comes into U.S. ports every year. Though few are inspected now, Homeland Security officials have said that almost all high-risk or questionable shipments are inspected. Most containers are moved by large corporations with their own security procedures.

"It's a tricky proposition" trying to have good security while keeping shipments moving, said Maureen Ellis, a spokeswoman for the American Association of Port Authorities. "Screening every single piece of commerce just can't happen. Industry would come to a screeching halt. What you need is risk assessments" to figure out which shipments to inspect.

Chemical Headache

In New Jersey, the issue is not just the mammoth Port of New York but the chemical industry that hugs the state's major highways with factories, plastics plants and storage tanks.

Sen. Jon Corzine, D-N.J., has been trying since autumn of 2001 to pass legislation — the current version is S 157 — that would require vulnerability assessments and make chemical companies consider using safer technologies, in hopes that facilities would move away from chemicals that could cause a

The Port of Long Beach has $60 million in security needs but received $18 million in federal aid. "Where are we going to get the revenue to pay for these programs?" Steinke asks.

deadly plume if an attack occurred.

The industry has opposed Corzine's measure, embracing instead legislation (S 994) by Sen. James M. Inhofe, R-Okla., under which chemical plants would conduct vulnerability studies but would be allowed to keep those documents on file and not have to give them to the Department of Homeland Security unless requested. Inhofe's bill has no provision on safer chemicals.

"The administration is supporting a weak alternative by Sen. Inhofe," said Jon Devine, an attorney with the Natural Resources Defense Council. "It's hard to understand opposition to doing something that is affordable and available and will improve facilities' vulnerability. There is currently no federal mandate for chemical plant security."

Industry lobbyists say requiring "inherently safer technologies" as advocated by Corzine's bill is just a meddlesome way of telling industry what types of chemicals it can and cannot use.

"We're an industry that wants national standards for chemical plant security," said Martin Durbin, director of federal relations for the American Chemistry Council. "A rigorous, voluntary program backed up by government oversight is the right thing to do."

Durbin contends that Corzine's proposals go beyond security and try to micromanage what types of chemicals are used. Corzine warns that industry opposition could come back to bite it if a chemical facility is attacked.

"It's a major, major problem that we

don't have vulnerability assessments. We are just stalling, stalling, stalling, for the benefit of some in the industry to the detriment of the public," Corzine said. "There is no serious risk-reward measurement going on right now."

A study by the Brookings Institution suggested that public-private partnerships, along with federal funding, are needed to protect terrorist targets that are owned by the private sector.

"Private markets will often not provide adequate protection against terrorist attacks on their own, since individual citizens and businessmen tend to worry more about the immediate challenge of making a profit than about the extremely unlikely possibility that their properties and facilities will be attacked," Brookings scholars wrote in a January report.

The nuclear power industry is considered one of the most secure in the country through its own efforts. Most plants have close surveillance and private security forces that carry semiautomatic weapons. According to the Nuclear Energy Institute, the country's 103 nuclear plants have invested $400 million in security upgrades since the Sept. 11 attacks.

The industry generally supports a bill (S 1043) that would require more security reports and more public inspections of nuclear power plants, but has lobbied for changes in the legislation.

The measure, sponsored by Inhofe, has been approved by the Senate Environment and Public Works Commit-

Laws Passed And Pending Bills

As the second anniversary of the Sept. 11 attacks approaches, Congress still has unfinished business in security legislation. Here's a look at laws passed and those pending:

Laws Enacted

● **Aviation Security Act (PL 107-71).** Created the Transportation Security Administration and federalized the airport security workforce.

● **Homeland Security Act (PL 107-296).** Created the Department of Homeland Security.

● **Bioterrorism prevention law (PL 107-188).** Authorized funds to increase the stockpiles of medicines and vaccines. Provided aid to state and local governments to help them prepare for possible attacks.

● **Maritime Transportation Security Act (PL 107-295).** Mandated security assessments for ports nationwide.

Pending security bills

● **S 994.** A chemical plant security bill, sponsored by Sen. James M. Inhofe, R-Okla., would mandate security assessments for chemical facilities. Sen. Jon Corzine, D-N.J., has written a stricter bill (S 157), but it has been sidelined.

● **S 165.** An air cargo security bill, sponsored by Sens. Dianne Feinstein, D-Calif., and Kay Bailey Hutchison, R-Texas, would require the Transportation Security Administration to come up with a program for screening air cargo.

● **HR 2555.** The Homeland Security appropriations bill now headed for a House-Senate conference. Both versions would provide about $30 billion for security agencies and programs.

● **S 930.** It would change the formula for how homeland security grants are distributed so money goes to cities and states based on the threat of terrorism, rather than by traditional per capita formulas.

tee. It would require nuclear power plants to update their security plans and have them reviewed by the Nuclear Regulatory Commission. It would also require criminal background checks for employees who had unescorted access to the nuclear facilities.

"We are trying to make sure the provisions are going to improve security and are not being done for the sake of public perception," said Stephen Floyd, vice president of regulatory affairs for the Nuclear Energy Institute. "We will fight regulations that go beyond what is reasonable."

Securing Cargo Bays

But as other industries get used to the idea of more federally mandated security regulations, aviation remains the center of government attention.

The U.S. airline industry as a whole has lost 127,000 jobs since Sept. 11 and is facing projected losses of $7 billion in 2003, according to the Air Transport Association, comprised of major carriers. The next debate on Capitol Hill may be on cargo security, and Sen. Ted Stevens, R-Alaska, promises to play a major role.

The Ted Stevens International Airport in Anchorage has the second-largest cargo hub in the country, and the cargo industry is resisting an amendment added to the House version of the fiscal 2004 Homeland Security spending bill that would require inspection of all air cargo that travels on commercial passenger jets.

The provision would cover packages sent through cargo companies but carried in the holds of passenger airliners. The amendment was sponsored by Rep. Edward J. Markey, D-Mass., who said he fears that the current lack of inspection could allow a package bomb to end up in a cargo hold. Stevens says something needs to be done for air cargo security, but in a way that does not slow down the flow of freight through Anchorage and other hubs. One option would be a "trusted shipper" program similar to the "trusted traveler" system airlines want for their steady customers.

"We want inspections done, but it's a question of where they're inspected and how they're inspected," Stevens said.

The power of the transportation and shipping industries was on display with a recent rulemaking process under Homeland Security.

As part of its effort to have better intelligence on what is being shipped by

rail, highway, waterway and airplane, the department came up with rules that would require up to 24-hour notification for shipment of some goods. With such notice, Homeland Security agents could flag shipments that have suspicious origins or incomplete information on bills of lading. The idea is to stop something such as a dirty bomb before it arrives at a U.S. port or airport, rather than catching it once it has arrived.

The U.S. Chamber of Commerce opposed the initial rule, saying it would completely upend the time-sensitive delivery of everything from perishable flowers to important documents that are shipped on short notice.

In the end, it looked as if the Chamber would win. The new rule, which will soon be finalized, would require trucking shipments to give only 30 minutes' to an hour's notice on their shipping manifests, and railroads would have to give only two hours' notice.

"We understand the need to improve security of our transportation systems, our cargo and our shipping," said Ed Mortimer, director of transportation infrastructure for the U.S. Chamber of Commerce. "But there has to be a balance between improving security and maintaining the just-in-time movement of goods that makes our economy the envy of the world."

But Mortimer acknowledges that "without a specific threat, it's very hard to convince businesses to make the investment."

Debate Expected to Last

The debate over aviation, port security and other critical industries is not likely to end any time soon. The specter of another hijacking loomed yet again with fresh warnings July 30 that terrorists may try to commandeer airplanes for an attack.

Democrats promise to use homeland security as a political issue in the 2004 election, and have accused Republicans of not spending enough on safety. Republicans, on the other hand, realize they face a complex challenge, trying to remain the party that promotes free markets and less government regulation, while trying to maintain a strong, sturdy image on national security.

"The challenge is to improve security without encroaching on individual liberties," said Cochran, who will be part of the conference committee that determines final funding allocations for Homeland Security programs. ◆

'Privatization' of Iraq's Weapons A Growing Postwar Concern

Have Saddam's weapons changed hands and become a greater threat than before?

Quick Contents

The theory that Iraq's elusive weapons may have been spirited out of the country is buying some lawmakers more time as the arms search continues. But others see it as a damning confirmation of their worst prewar fears.

As Congress pushes ahead with its review of prewar U.S. intelligence on Iraq's weapons of mass destruction, the question of the weapons' whereabouts has taken on new urgency among some lawmakers.

According to several congressional leaders on intelligence and homeland security issues, the failure to find the weapons could be explained by a terrifying scenario: Either before the war or during the anarchy and looting that followed, Saddam Hussein may have spirited the banned materials out of Iraq or sold them to third parties, including terrorist groups.

Politically, this theory is a double-edged sword. On one hand, it could provide lawmakers — both Republicans and Democrats who voted for the war — with more time by deflecting the argument that the weapons threat was overblown before the fighting began. But if this theory gains credence, it would seriously undermine the prewar contention of the Bush administration and its supporters in Congress that conquering Iraq would make the United States safer.

Indeed, it would reinforce the argument made before the war by some terrorism experts, including those who worked in the Clinton administration, that invading Iraq could result in dangers even greater than the one posed by Saddam, including the dispersal of his weapons.

Already, some Democrats are using this latest theory on the whereabouts of Iraq's weapons to intensify their demands for a full investigation into prewar intelligence and to criticize the military's postwar failure to safeguard known Iraqi nuclear weapons research sites.

New Warnings

Some Republicans have responded by scaling back expectations for the teams that are still scouring Iraq for evidence of the weapons. Pat Roberts of Kansas, chairman of the Senate Intelligence Committee, says that now those teams are focusing on finding evidence of weapons programs rather than existing weapons, mostly in documents and interviews with Iraqi scientists.

"That will lead to the final puzzle to prove without a doubt [Saddam] had the weapons of mass destruction," Roberts said July 3, after returning from a visit to Iraq.

But he added: "The most important thing is, where is it now?"

Jane Harman of California, the top Democrat on the House Intelligence Committee and a supporter of the war, tried to answer that question on the House floor June 25.

Saddam, Harman said, had most likely "buried or dispersed the [weapons of mass destruction]. . . . Some may now be in the hands of terrorist groups outside of Iraq or counterinsurgents in Iraq who continue to harm and kill U.S. and British troops."

On the same day that Harman made her remarks, Christopher Cox — the California Republican who chairs the House Homeland Security Committee — also underscored that fear.

"We know that Saddam had 8,500 liters of anthrax, but there's no evidence inside Iraq that he destroyed it," Cox warned. "My most ominous concern is that there's no evidence of [its] destruction in the country."

The possibility of the "privatization" of Iraq's weapons of mass destruction by rogue elements willing to sell to terrorist groups has started to affect legislation as well.

On June 26, the House Homeland Securi-

CQ Weekly July 5, 2003

U.S. Navy Special Warfare forces search an Iraqi vessel for weapons. Concerns are growing in Congress that the weapons were spirited out of the country.

ty Committee met to approve a bill (HR 2122) that would authorize, among other things, $5.6 billion for President Bush's Project Bioshield, a 10-year initiative to develop and stockpile vaccines and medications against biological, chemical and radiological attacks.

Framing Project Bioshield as a reaction to proliferation concerns, the committee's ranking Democrat, Jim Turner of Texas, cautioned that "despite our belief that Iraq possessed significant stockpiles of such weapons, we have to date found none, leading to the very real possibility that those weapons may be in the hands of our terrorist enemies."

The CIA is also expected to take a look at the missing weapons mystery. The House intelligence authorization bill (HR 2417), which the House passed 410-9 on June 27, includes a provision requiring that the CIA conduct its own review of the intelligence lessons learned from the war with Iraq.

Although the bill's report called the CIA review "consistent with previous after-action studies undertaken following past conflicts," it adds that the current task for the intelligence community "is to try to figure out who has the [weapons of mass destruction] and how they got there."

Even among those lawmakers who believe that the ouster of Saddam made the United States more secure, some are starting to express concerns more openly about the ramifications of the weapons' disappearance.

"There is now less of a chance that the United States will be attacked with Saddam Hussein gone, but it is disconcerting that we can't pinpoint his weapons," said John E. Sweeney, a New York Republican on the House Homeland Security Committee.

Added Jennifer Dunn, a Washington state Republican who also sits on the Homeland Security panel: "I definitely think that there is a genuine risk. . . . The feeling in Congress now is that there is more of a concern now."

Privatized Weapons

Those in Congress who opposed the Iraq war resolution (PL 107-243) deployed a variety of arguments against invading Iraq. But the fear that the proscribed weapons would fall into the wrong hands as a consequence of the war was not frequently cited last fall. (2002 CQ Weekly, p. 2671)

Levin Starts His Own Inquiry

Levin

While Republican lawmakers wait for the House and Senate Intelligence committees to complete their review of the intelligence reports that led to the Iraq war, Sen. Carl Levin of Michigan is striking out on his own.

Levin, the ranking Democrat on the Armed Services Committee, announced June 27 that his staff would begin an inquiry into the "objectivity and credibility" of prewar intelligence reports about Iraq's weapons of mass destruction, Baghdad's alleged ties to al Qaeda, and the effect of those reports on Pentagon war plans and operations. Levin, who returned from a fact-finding trip to Iraq on July 3, would like the inquiry to begin soon.

"I believe that the Armed Services Committee has a heavy responsibility to review . . . the intelligence produced by, made available to and used by the Department of Defense before and during the Iraq war," Levin said in a statement.

Levin was disappointed when committee Chairman John W. Warner, R-Va., who previously had called for a joint inquiry by the Armed Services and Intelligence committees, later bowed to the intelligence panels. But it is not clear what more Levin could accomplish, given that the two intelligence panels are conducting bipartisan reviews of the same information. (2003 CQ Weekly pp. 1564, 1397)

A Whiff of Politics

Also unclear is how much cooperation Levin will get from the Bush administration. Its Democratic cast could leave the proposal vulnerable to charges of partisan politics. Levin was one of 23 senators who voted against giving President Bush the authority to attack Iraq unilaterally, preferring that U.N. inspectors be given all the information and time they needed to find those weapons before multilateral military action was brought to bear. Levin also has strongly questioned whether the CIA provided inspectors with all the data it possessed.

As an Intelligence Committee member, Levin has access to the CIA and other intelligence documents gathered there. Levin says he also plans to seek documents from the departments of Defense, State and Energy, the National Intelligence Council and the Joint Atomic Energy Intelligence Committee and have his staff interview defense, military and intelligence personnel. Then he would like to hold "hearings — both open and closed, as appropriate, and [issue] a public report, with classified annex if necessary, at the end of the inquiry."

Given the political and security sensitivities surrounding the issue, Levin could face real obstacles in conducting a meaningful inquiry.

But the Harvard-trained lawyer is a skillful investigator. He made his mark on that score last year when, as chairman of the Governmental Affairs' Permanent Subcommittee on Investigations, he looked into the cause of the Enron Corp. collapse. (2002 CQ Weekly, p. 129)

His reading glasses perched at the end of his nose, Levin meticulously unraveled the complex financial transactions Enron used to hide its losses and enable it to report better financial results than it had earned.

Levin also appears to have the sympathy of Warner. While declining Levin's invitation to join a bipartisan probe, Warner appears to be keeping his options open.

In giving Levin the go-ahead to conduct the inquiry, Warner wrote in a letter: "This is clearly your prerogative, and as you keep me informed, there may be instances where my staff would join."

Instead, anti-war lawmakers mostly criticized the notion of pre-emption as a national security doctrine, the risk of American diplomatic isolation at the United Nations, and the question of whether Iraq posed a truly imminent danger to the United States.

Among some terrorism and intelligence experts, however, the "privatization" scenario posed a very real threat last fall — and still does today.

One was Daniel Benjamin, who served on the National Security Council under President Bill Clinton as a counterterrorism official. He warned in The Washington Post last October that a U.S. occupation of Iraq could backfire in two serious ways.

Benjamin wrote that a U.S. occupation of Iraq could provide a magnet for fundamentalist Islamic militants intent on exacting revenge on the United States. But even more worrisome was the prospect that the weapons material would be "liberated by colonels, security service operatives and soon-to-be unemployed scientists" eager to sell, during and after the war's chaos.

Today, Benjamin says, the privatization of Iraq's weapons remains "a real possibility," especially in the case of biological weapons and nuclear waste material that could produce a "dirty bomb" — a crude device that uses conventional explosives to disperse radioactive waste across a wide area.

"If you assume that Saddam Hussein was not in production mode but wanted to reconstitute his stockpile when he was out from under the inspections, he probably kept small amounts of biological weapons and the things needed to produce them," said Benjamin, now a senior fellow at the Center for Strategic and International Studies.

"It's possible that he hid them somewhere and they've now made their way into untrustworthy hands," he warned.

Touching on the "dirty bomb" threat, Benjamin pointed to the postwar looting of the al Tuwaitha nuclear research facility outside Baghdad as another area of grave concern.

"The looting at Tuwaitha leaves ample room for terrorists to get their hands on radioactive material," Benjamin explained. "It would be tempting for former Iraqi Secret Service types, who know their future isn't appealing, to make as much money as they can by selling that material."

In a June 16 letter to Bush, 16 House Democrats also broached the "dirty bomb" scenario.

Citing the deliberate steps that U.S. forces took to secure Iraqi oil fields, the letter asked why "similar precautions were not taken with respect to nuclear facilities."

Separately, 23 House Democrats introduced a bill (HR 2625) June 26 that would establish an independent commission to investigate how U.S. intelligence was used before the war. Among the group's concerns, according to Rep. Edward J. Markey, D-Mass., is that weapons of mass destruction "are now in the hands of al Qaeda, Baathist separatist groups, other terrorist groups, or in Syria."

The House Intelligence Committee is conducting its own review into the matter, but some Democrats have said they want more committees to be involved and more open hearings held.

Mission Impossible

Whether some stockpiles may have indeed been looted during and after the war, most terrorism analysts discount the possibility that Saddam could have shipped his proscribed weapons or their precursor materials out of Iraq undetected.

"It seems implausible that large quantities could have been spirited away without leaving some trace," said Gregory F. Treverton, senior analyst at the RAND Corporation and former vice chairman of the National Intelligence Council in the first Clinton administration.

"There wasn't enough coherence in the regime to do such a thing ahead of the war. Even if it was done in a chaotic way, it would have left some traces," he explained, adding that the privatization scenario remains "a legitimate fear," especially regarding biological agents.

Richard A. Clarke, a former White House adviser on counterterrorism and intelligence who served under Ronald Reagan, George Bush, Clinton and George W. Bush, also discounts the possibility of a massive illegal weapons transfer before the war, even if some material did fall into the hands of rogue parties.

"It would have been hard to secretly move the large amounts of anthrax and sarin that the United Nations described. Besides, some of that material has a limited shelf life," he explained. "The toxicity falls over time.

"But small amounts, or small amounts of precursor materials, may

well have been smuggled out," he said.

Clarke thinks that "the notion that it all went to Syria or to terrorists doesn't answer the question." The Syria option was first raised by Israel, which has an interest in getting the United States to focus on Damascus' unconventional weapons programs.

"The bulk of the missing weapons were either hidden or destroyed, or a combination of the two," he concluded.

The Search for Intelligence

For many in Congress, the debate over the accuracy of prewar intelligence on the Iraqi threat is now part of a larger discussion over how good the intelligence is on developing threats, such as those that could grow out of Iraq's missing weapons.

"We're concerned about the lack of good intelligence on this issue. Where are these weapons? Where do we stand on bioterrorism?" asked Rep. Karen McCarthy of Missouri, ranking Democrat on the House Homeland Security Subcommittee on Counterterrorism.

"We do not have the intelligence we need, and not having it heightens our concern about rogue actors in Iraq," she said.

Meanwhile, both the House and Senate Intelligence committees continue to conduct their reviews on the performance of U.S. intelligence before the Iraq war behind closed doors. (2003 CQ Weekly, p. 1564)

Some members, such as Harman, already have brought up troubling scenarios on the whereabouts of Iraq's weapons. And if the House Intelligence Committee conducts its first open hearing on the missing weapons issue later in July, as Harman has said it will, it could provide a forum for more members to openly express their concerns on the topic.

Referring to the possibility of Iraq's weapons falling into the wrong hands, Olympia J. Snowe, R-Maine, a member of the Senate Intelligence Committee, said "there is a higher probability of thinking on the issue" on the panel.

"But I don't know if it is seen as more probable than other scenarios," she cautioned.

"The main idea is that we now have a greater commitment to find the truth. If [privatization] did occur, it opens the door to all kinds of potentially threatening scenarios," she added. "We certainly don't want the materials to fall into the wrong hands, in different countries." ◆

Prospects Dim for 'Clear Skies' As Industry Joins List of Foes

Democrats say Bush clean air proposal was never more than legislative theater

When the Senate Environment and Public Works Committee approved legislation in June 2002 aimed at reducing industrial air pollution, Max Baucus of Montana was the only Democrat to vote against it.

His state mines about 38,000 tons of coal a year, and much of it is sold to power plants whose owners would be forced to spend money to curb emissions under the bill. While his Democratic colleagues cheered the legislation — sponsored by James M. Jeffords, I-Vt., who was then chairman of the committee — Baucus was critical. (*2002 CQ Weekly, p. 1742*)

"We're here primarily for political reasons," he said. "We're not trying to craft legislation that is achievable."

In the year since that committee markup, Congress has made little headway on clean air legislation. Jeffords' bill, which the electric power industry and most Republicans said would hurt the economy even though it was intended to control pollution, never made it to the Senate floor last year.

President Bush's plan — dubbed "Clear Skies" by the White House and vehemently opposed by environmental groups — has been introduced for the second time, but there has been little progress on it in either the House or the Senate.

Environmental organizations are particularly critical of Bush's decision not to regulate carbon dioxide, which most scientists say is the principal cause of global warming because it traps the sun's heat in the atmosphere. Bush instead proposed a voluntary program to reduce CO_2.

The utility industry does not like Bush's plan because it would regulate emissions of mercury, which is found in the coal burned in power plants. These plants now emit an estimated 48 tons of mercury a year in vapor form, and, according to industry officials testifying before the Clean Air, Climate Change and Nuclear Safety Subcommittee on June 5, there is no proven technology to cut that significantly.

Industry opposition, in fact, is the main reason the Bush bill has not moved this year. "Basically, no one likes it," said Myron Ebell, director of global warming and international environmental policy for the Competitive Enterprise Institute, a pro-business Washington think tank.

Ebell said the Bush initiative could have been better if the White House had asked for more congressional input. "I think this was dropped on the Hill with no consultation," he said.

Privately, some Republicans say they expect that the legislation will not really have a chance until 2005. The topic is too politically touchy for an election year, they say, and few are pleased with it now.

"The odds are heavily against it passing the Senate at this point," said one Republican aide. "I don't see it on the priority list."

The current chairman of the Environment and Public Works Committee, James M. Inhofe, R-Okla., insists that some "amended form" of the legislation will pass the Senate this session. He said the Bush plan deals too stringently with mercury emissions and that it would fail in the Senate if the current language were brought to the floor. But he says the committee will work on the bill this year in an attempt to find a compromise.

"We've got to make some changes and that's what we intend to do," he said.

Quick Contents

Environmentalists do not like President Bush's plan for reducing industrial pollution, but they are not the main reason the legislation has stalled this year. Electric power companies that burn coal think the Bush plan's proposed limits on mercury emissions are too strict, and they have lobbied against the measure.

CQ PHOTO / SCOTT J. FERRELL

Kroszner told the Senate Environment and Public Works Committee on June 5 it would be more difficult to cut mercury emissions than the administration earlier thought.

In what could be a boost to the bill's support — at least with industry — an administration official indicated at the June 5 hearing that the White House might go along with less restrictive standards for mercury emissions than Bush proposed.

The administration said its estimates for how much mercury could be removed from power plant emissions with current technology may have been overly optimistic.

High on the Wish List

Bush plugged his clean air plan in his State of the Union address, and it has been an administration priority ever since. Though Republicans contend that voters are not overly concerned about the environment — compared with security and the economy — the White House recognizes that Bush could be vulnerable on the issue and has taken remedial steps.

But passing any environmental legislation is difficult, particularly in the closely divided Senate.

When asked how he thought Bush might handle the political fallout if his clean air legislation failed with an election approaching, Inhofe said:

"I think what he would say is that this was the most far-reaching [clean air] proposal in the history of America, and we were rejected. And I would be standing right beside him, saying we did all we could."

Democrats contend that this has been the plan from the start — for the Bush administration to introduce broad anti-pollutant legislation that would never pass and then to campaign on the fact that they tried.

"There has been zero negotiation," said one Democratic Senate aide, who asked not to be identified. "What they are trying to do is set this up to blame the Democrats for not moving it, and label us as obstructionists."

John Stanton, who works on clean air issues at the environmental group National Environmental Trust, said lawmakers are not doing and saying the same thing.

"Everyone says what the White House wants to hear, but they aren't doing what you need to do to pass a bill," he said. "They don't want to cross the White House publicly."

Aides at the White House's Council on Environmental Quality contend that is not the case. They say the legislation is on the right track and has in-

The Four-Pollutant Conundrum

The debate over revising the Clean Air Act centers on four pollutants from coal-burning power plants. President Bush has proposed further controls on three of the pollutants — nitrogen oxides, sulfur dioxide and mercury. Some lawmakers want to add carbon dioxide. Here is a look at the pollutants:

Nitrogen oxides (NOx)
Produced mainly by motor vehicles and power plants, nitrogen oxides such as nitrogen dioxide (NO_2) and nitric oxide (NO) are a major cause of smog and contribute to acid rain. They also can cause respiratory problems. Nitrogen oxide emissions already are regulated by the Clean Air Act.

Sulfur dioxide (SO_2)
Produced by motor vehicles, coal-fired power plants and smelters, this gas is an ingredient of acid rain and can cause respiratory problems. SO_2 emissions currently are regulated by the Clean Air Act. Atmospheric concentrations of sulfur dioxide and nitrogen oxides have declined over the past decade, though emissions of nitrogen oxides have increased.

Mercury (Hg)
Produced primarily as mercury vapor by coal-fired power plants and incinerators, this volatile element can contaminate water supplies as methylmercury, which accumulates in fish and in mammals that eat fish. It is a neurotoxin that, because it is readily absorbed in the bloodstream, is a particular threat to developing fetuses. Mercury emissions are in the process of being regulated by the EPA and many states have warned consumers about consumption of certain fish.

Carbon dioxide (CO_2)
Produced by the burning of fossil fuels, such as in power plants, factories and motor vehicles, this oxidized form of carbon is considered the principal cause of global warming. It is also produced by wildfires and, like sulfur dioxide, is generated by volcanoes. CO_2 is a "greenhouse" gas that traps solar radiation and therefore raises the atmospheric temperature. The present concentration of CO_2 in the atmosphere is the highest in at least 420,000 years. CO_2 emissions are not regulated.

Source: Environmental Protection Agency

creasing enthusiasm on and off the Hill. "People are actually talking about moving it, where last year they just introduced it," said one aide.

Phasing In Changes

Bush's air pollution legislation (S 485, HR 999) — introduced by Inhofe and Rep. Joe L. Barton, R-Texas — would phase in new emissions limits for three power-plant emissions: sulfur dioxide (SO_2) and nitrogen oxides (NOx), which both contribute to acid rain, and mercury, which is toxic to humans in concentrated amounts and can impair children's development.

The White House says the plan would cut emissions of those three pollutants by 70 percent by 2018 under national limits. The legislation is based on a "cap and trade" program that would allow power plants that produce more than their allotted share of pollution to buy credits from companies that reduce their emissions levels below the federal standards.

Instead of a limit on carbon dioxide

emissions, the administration has proposed a voluntary reduction program to reduce "greenhouse gas intensity" — a measurement linked to the rate of economic output — by 18 percent by 2012.

The administration says its overall plan would curb pollution but not cause electricity prices to rise and affect economic growth.

But environmentalists say Bush's claims for what his plan would accomplish in cutting emissions would actually be less than what is forecast under current policies.

Bush's timetable would set limits for sulfur dioxide and mercury in two phases targeted for 2010 and 2018. The limits for nitrogen oxides would be in two phases targeted for 2008 and 2018. The administration says that would give industry time to plan for the reductions.

Opponents say this would allow companies to pollute for too long. Under the current Clean Air Act (PL 101-549), according to Jeffords, utilities would have to cut emissions by as much as 90 percent by 2008.

The opponents also say Bush has included other benefits for industry in the bill. The legislation would help highway builders, for instance, by delaying "transitional" highway construction areas from some of the requirements.

Opponents also say the legislation would eliminate a provision of the Clean Air Act that requires the cleanup of pollution sources that threaten national parks.

Inhofe indicated in February that he thought the makeup of the Environment and Public Works committee meant that it would more likely approve a bill that would regulate carbon dioxide in addition to sulfur dioxide, nitrogen oxides and mercury.

The panel has 10 Republicans and nine Democrats, and Republican Sen. Lincoln Chafee of Rhode Island, who is often a swing vote on the committee, supports adding carbon dioxide to whatever legislation the committee produces. The committee approved Jeffords' four-pollutant legislation on a 10-9 vote in 2002, and Chafee was the only Republican to vote for the bill.

In the House, Energy and Commerce Chairman Billy Tauzin, R-La., has been largely silent on the legislation. And Barton, chairman of the Energy and Air Quality Subcommittee, has not worked to move it. Tauzin, Barton and Inhofe all introduced the legislation Feb. 27 after Bush mentioned it in his speech.

"He has not ruled it out, but we don't have a timetable," said Barton spokeswoman Samantha Jordan.

Tauzin spokesman Ken Johnson said the committee plans hearings on the legislation in July. "We are going to hold hearings on it, and if nothing else we will be better informed," Johnson said.

Bush administration proposals usually have an easier time in the House, but in this case the House could be more troublesome. About 40 House Republicans support adding carbon dioxide controls to the bill, and if some conservatives remain opposed because of the mercury restrictions, the measure could be doomed.

Mercury Standards

Industry is divided on the bill. Some companies would like to see the legislation pass because it is less stringent than standards in the current Clean

Going the Regulatory Route

President Bush may not get his air pollution plan through Congress this year, but some analysts say he doesn't need to. The administration has implemented a series of regulations that have advanced Bush's agenda on clean air issues:

New Source Review

The Environmental Protection Agency finalized rules in March that would ease New Source Review restrictions on companies rebuilding or updating coal-fired power plants and similar factories in ways that significantly increase pollution. Under current law, such modified power plants and factory units must undergo an EPA review as if they were a new source of pollution, and companies often are required to add expensive emissions reduction equipment.

The new rules change the way emissions levels are determined, allow some projects to proceed without permits, and allow those with state-of-the-art pollution equipment an exemption from review for 10 years.

The new rules are being challenged in court by nine Northeastern states. Bush's "Clear Skies" legislation (S 485, HR 999) would eliminate the New Source Review program entirely.

Diesel Standards

The EPA announced a proposed rule in April designed to reduce air pollution from off-road diesel equipment, such as tractors and construction machinery. The proposed rules, which were praised by environmental organizations, would require diesel engine manufacturers to reduce the content of nitrogen oxides and other pollutants in engine exhaust. EPA officials said the plan could prevent as many as 9,600 deaths a year.

Ozone Standards

The EPA announced May 14 that it would delay implementing new smog standards for more than 30 urban areas. All of them would be in violation of rules that have been tied up in court since they were proposed in 1997, but which are expected to be implemented later this year.

The EPA now plans to give the cities an extra year to adopt more effective smog-control measures for automobiles, power plants and other polluting sources.

Mercury

The EPA is required by a court order to propose a rule by Dec. 15 of this year that would reduce industrial emissions of mercury. The power and coal industries oppose such requirements and may try to block or delay any such rule. Bush's legislation would impose different mercury restrictions.

Air Act, and it would give them more certainty than the patchwork of rules that has developed to regulate emissions. Many of the standards are due for implementation since the Supreme Court ruled in 2001 to dismiss industry lawsuits aimed at delaying them.

Other executives are worried that the standards in the bill are too strict. Mercury has been a sticking point.

There are only minute quantities of mercury in coal, and it costs a lot of money to get it out.

"Mercury is the trickiest of the three emissions," said Scott Segal, a lobbyist for power companies and spokesman for the Electric Reliability Coordinating Council. "The dynamics of mercury are less understood, many mercury control strategies are unproven or expensive, and an inflexible mercury standard causes too much fuel switching from coal to natural gas."

Segal says there is a consensus in the industry that some form of multipollutant legislation would be a good thing, "but there are still some important issues to be resolved, mostly mercury."

At the June 5 hearing, however, the White House released new data on mercury controls that could alter the debate. Randall S. Kroszner, a member of the Council of Economic Advisers, testified that the method of reducing mercury called for in the first phase of Bush's proposal — co-benefit reduction — would not be as effective as the administration originally thought.

The idea behind co-benefit reduction is that in removing sulfur dioxide and nitrogen oxides from power plant emissions, a certain amount of mercury will also be removed without additional effort or equipment.

Power and coal companies prefer this method because it would not require them to purchase new technologies for mercury extraction, few of which are fully developed.

The first phase would end in 2010; it is generally assumed that technology to extract mercury from coal will be available by the start of the second phase, which is scheduled to end in 2018.

The Bush legislation would require that mercury emissions be reduced from the current level of approximately 48 tons a year to 26 tons in 2010. Studies within the administration said co-benefit reduction would be able to achieve that.

Several coal and power companies have objected to that goal, however, saying co-benefit reduction would probably not be able to reduce mercury emissions that much. In order to reach 26 tons, they said, they would probably have to purchase new technologies that are not fully developed.

Kroszner said that two new studies by the EPA and the Energy Department's Energy Information Administration found that the earlier estimates were too optimistic. The EPA said co-benefit reduction would lower mercury emissions to 34 tons a year; the Energy Department agency estimated 46 tons a year.

That could be good news for the power industry because its congressional allies would gain an argument for more modest mercury emission restrictions or no restrictions at all — the technology may not be available to do what the administration has proposed by 2010.

In the hearing, Sen. Craig Thomas, R-Wyo., asked Kroszner if his testimony was an indication that the White House wanted Congress to change the targets.

Kroszner said that could be "a possibility."

"We just wanted to provide you with the updated information," he said.

Advocates and opponents of Clear Skies said the new information could improve the bill's chances.

"It raises the stakes, certainly," said Frank O'Donnell, executive director of the Clean Air Trust. "The administration sent Congress an invitation to change the number. I think this is a bombshell development, and it is definitely going to give impetus to industry to weaken an already bad bill."

A Republican Senate aide said the implied go-ahead to eliminate the mercury cap could change the minds of some companies that have opposed the bill. "It could consolidate things on our side."

Carbon Cycle

The carbon dioxide debate remains a major obstacle, however.

Senate Democrats have threatened to boycott a markup of Bush's bill in the Environment and Public Works Committee, and Northeastern lawmakers from both parties in the Senate and House say they will work to stop the bill in its tracks if it does not regulate carbon emissions.

However, Ohio Republican Sen. George V. Voinovich, chairman of the Clean Air Subcommittee, said limits on carbon dioxide are not an option. "The political realities of Congress are that a cap will not be placed on carbon for quite some time," he said.

There are other bills that could contribute to a compromise on clean air.

Jeffords has reintroduced a version of his legislation that was approved by the Environment and Public Works Committee in 2002. The bill (S 366) would limit carbon dioxide emissions, in addition to sulfur dioxide, nitrogen oxides and mercury, and it would speed up the compliance process. It has 19 cosponsors, including two Republicans — Olympia J. Snowe and Susan Collins of Maine.

Another alternative is a measure (S 843) by Sen. Thomas R. Carper, D-Del., that would limit carbon dioxide emissions but give companies more time to comply with the standards.

Though that bill has only two cosponsors, one of them is Chafee and the other is Republican Judd Gregg of New Hampshire.

Bush's "Clear Skies" bill is part of what he has described as a realistic approach to environmental protection that takes economics into account and is designed to encourage rather than

force industries to reduce pollution and to preserve open spaces.

In the 107th Congress, lawmakers say the most significant environmental legislation was a relatively modest law (PL 107-118) to help state and local governments continue cleaning up former industrial sites known as brownfields. The law also protects some small businesses and landowners from superfund liability. (*2001 Almanac, p. 9-11*)

Even that legislation, which was scaled back from earlier efforts to overhaul the superfund program, came close to being killed several times and took most of the year to complete. It was not cleared until Dec. 20, 2001.

This year, Bush's "Healthy Forests" legislation (HR 1904), aimed at reducing the risk of disastrous wildfires by thinning public forests, was passed by the House and is now headed to the Senate, where it is likely to encounter more opposition. Environmental groups contend that the bill is mainly designed to help the timber industry. (*2003 CQ Weekly, p. 1259*)

If both bills stall, it could be a problem for Bush next year, or at least that is what Democrats hope.

They will focus on global warming and other environmental issues they think will resonate with suburban voters.

Bush pledged in the 2000 election to regulate carbon dioxide emissions, but later changed his mind. He also briefly delayed implementation of tighter standards for arsenic in drinking water.

"It's a big issue to soccer moms," said Erik Smulson, spokesman for Jeffords. "It may not appeal to the Republican base, but elections are not won and lost on appealing to the base."

President Bill Clinton was not much more successful in persuading Congress to pass environmental legislation.

During the Clinton years, only two significant environmental laws were enacted: the 1996 Safe Drinking Water Act Amendments (PL 104-182), which Republicans accepted as a way to shore up their environmental credentials, and a 1996 rewrite of pesticide laws (PL 104-170). (*1996 Almanac, pp. 4-4, 3-27*)

"Maybe the reason people think Clear Skies will be so difficult to get through is because nothing like this has been done in 10 years," said a White House aide. ◆

Appendix

The Legislative Process in Brief

Note: Parliamentary terms used below are defined in the glossary.

Introduction of Bills

A House member (including the resident commissioner of Puerto Rico and nonvoting delegates of the District of Columbia, Guam, the Virgin Islands and American Samoa) may introduce any one of several types of bills and resolutions by handing it to the clerk of the House or placing it in a box called the hopper. A senator first gains recognition of the presiding officer to announce the introduction of a bill.

As the usual next step in either the House or Senate, the bill is numbered, referred to the appropriate committee, labeled with the sponsor's name and sent to the Government Printing Office so that copies can be made for subsequent study and action. House and Senate bills may be jointly sponsored and carry several senators' names. A bill written in the executive branch and proposed as an administration measure usually is introduced by the chairman of the congressional committee that has jurisdiction, as a courtesy to the White House.

Bills—Prefixed with HR in the House, S in the Senate, followed by a number. Used as the form for most legislation, whether general or special, public or private.

Joint Resolutions—Designated H J Res or S J Res. Subject to the same procedure as bills, with the exception of a joint resolution proposing an amendment to the Constitution. The latter must be approved by two-thirds of both houses and is then sent directly to the administrator of general services for submission to the states for ratification instead of being presented to the president for his approval.

Concurrent Resolutions—Designated H Con Res or S Con Res. Used for matters affecting the operations of both houses. These resolutions do not become law.

Resolutions—Designated H Res or S Res. Used for a matter concerning the operation of either house alone and adopted only by the chamber in which it originates.

Committee Action

With few exceptions, bills are referred to the appropriate standing committees. The job of referral formally is the responsibility of the Speaker of the House and the presiding officer of the Senate, but this task usually is carried out on their behalf by the parliamentarians of the House and Senate. Precedent, statute and the jurisdictional mandates of the committees as set forth in the rules of the House and Senate determine which committees receive what kinds of bills. Bills are technically considered "read for the first time" when referred to House committees.

When a bill reaches a committee it is placed on the committee's calendar. Failure of a committee to act on a bill is equivalent to killing it and most fall by the legislative roadside. The measure can be withdrawn from the committee's purview only by a discharge petition signed by a majority of the House membership on House bills, or by adoption of a special resolution in the Senate. Discharge attempts rarely succeed and the Senate procedure has not been used for decades.

The first committee action taken on a bill usually is a request for comment on it by interested agencies of the government. The committee chairman may assign the bill to a subcommittee for study and hearings, or it may be considered by the full committee. Hearings may be public, closed (executive session) or both. A subcommittee, after considering a bill, reports to the full committee its recommendations for action and any proposed amendments.

The full committee then votes on its recommendation to the House or Senate. This procedure is called "ordering a bill reported." Occasionally a committee may order a bill reported unfavorably; most of the time a report, submitted by the chairman of the committee to the House or Senate, calls for favorable action on the measure since the committee can effectively "kill" a bill by simply failing to take any action.

After the bill is reported, the committee chairman instructs the staff to prepare a written report. The report describes the purposes and scope of the bill, explains the committee revisions, notes proposed changes in existing law and, usually, includes the views of the executive branch agencies consulted. Often committee members opposing a measure issue dissenting minority statements that are included in the report.

Usually, the committee "marks up" or proposes amendments to the bill. If the amendments are substantial and the measure is complicated, the committee may order a "clean bill" introduced, which will embody the proposed amendments. The original bill then is put aside and the clean bill, with a new number, is reported to the floor.

The chamber must approve, alter or reject the committee amendments before the bill itself can be put to a vote.

Floor Action

After a bill is reported back to the house where it originated, it is placed on the calendar.

There are five legislative calendars in the House, issued in one cumulative calendar titled *Calendars of the United States House of Representatives and History of Legislation*. The House calendars are:

The Union Calendar to which are referred bills raising revenues, general appropriations bills and any measures directly or indirectly appropriating money or property. It is the Calendar of the Committee of the Whole House on the State of the Union.

This graphic shows the most typical way in which proposed legislation is enacted into law. There are more complicated, as well as simpler, routes, and most bills never become law. The process is illustrated with two hypothetical bills, House bill No. 1 (HR 1) and Senate bill No. 2 (S 2). Bills must be passed by both houses in identical form before they can be sent to the president. The path of HR 1 is traced by a gray line, that of S 2 by a black line. In practice, most bills begin as similar proposals in both houses.

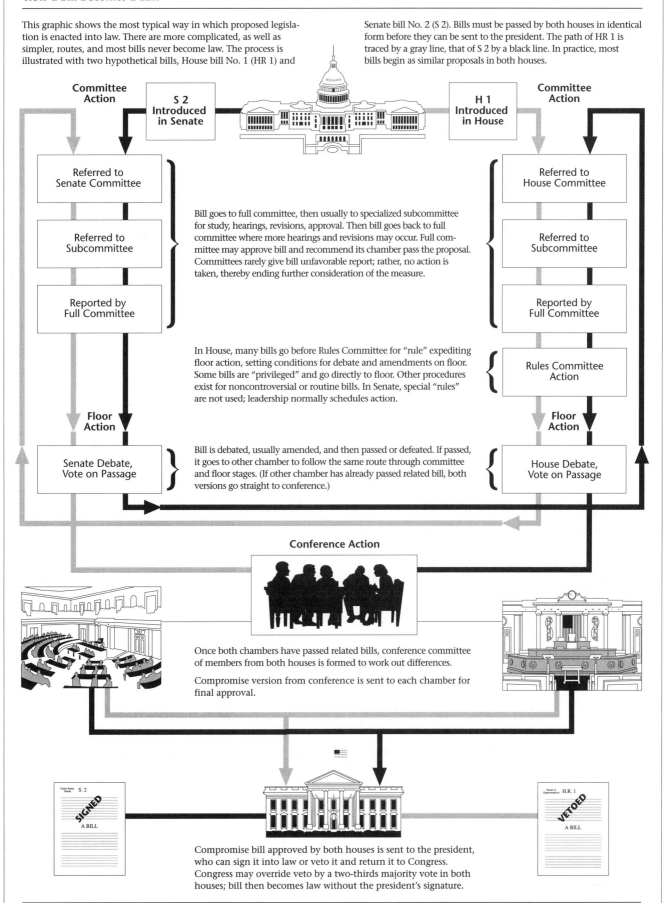

Committee Action

S 2 Introduced in Senate

H 1 Introduced in House

Committee Action

Referred to Senate Committee

Referred to Subcommittee

Reported by Full Committee

Referred to House Committee

Referred to Subcommittee

Reported by Full Committee

Bill goes to full committee, then usually to specialized subcommittee for study, hearings, revisions, approval. Then bill goes back to full committee where more hearings and revisions may occur. Full committee may approve bill and recommend its chamber pass the proposal. Committees rarely give bill unfavorable report; rather, no action is taken, thereby ending further consideration of the measure.

In House, many bills go before Rules Committee for "rule" expediting floor action, setting conditions for debate and amendments on floor. Some bills are "privileged" and go directly to floor. Other procedures exist for noncontroversial or routine bills. In Senate, special "rules" are not used; leadership normally schedules action.

Rules Committee Action

Floor Action

Floor Action

Senate Debate, Vote on Passage

House Debate, Vote on Passage

Bill is debated, usually amended, and then passed or defeated. If passed, it goes to other chamber to follow the same route through committee and floor stages. (If other chamber has already passed related bill, both versions go straight to conference.)

Conference Action

Once both chambers have passed related bills, conference committee of members from both houses is formed to work out differences.

Compromise version from conference is sent to each chamber for final approval.

United States Senate S. 2

SIGNED

A BILL

House of Representatives H.R. 1

VETOED

A BILL

Compromise bill approved by both houses is sent to the president, who can sign it into law or veto it and return it to Congress. Congress may override veto by a two-thirds majority vote in both houses; bill then becomes law without the president's signature.

The House Calendar to which are referred bills of public character not raising revenue or appropriating money.

The Corrections Calendar to which are referred bills to repeal rules and regulations deemed excessive or unnecessary when the Corrections Calendar is called the second and fourth Tuesday of each month. (Instituted in the 104th Congress to replace the seldom-used Consent Calendar.) A three-fifths majority is required for passage.

The Private Calendar to which are referred bills for relief in the nature of claims against the United States or private immigration bills that are passed without debate when the Private Calendar is called the first and third Tuesdays of each month.

The Discharge Calendar to which are referred motions to discharge committees when the necessary signatures are signed to a discharge petition.

There is only one legislative calendar in the Senate and one "executive calendar" for treaties and nominations submitted to the Senate.

Debate. A bill is brought to debate by varying procedures. In the Senate the majority leader, in consultation with the minority leader and others, schedules the bills that will be taken up for debate. If it is urgent or important it can be taken up in the Senate either by unanimous consent or by a majority vote.

In the House, precedence is granted if a special rule is obtained from the Rules Committee. A request for a special rule usually is made by the chairman of the committee that favorably reported the bill. The request is considered by the Rules Committee in the same fashion that other committees consider legislative measures. The committee proposes a resolution providing for immediate consideration of the bill. The Rules Committee reports the resolution to the House where it is debated and voted on in the same fashion as regular bills.

The resolutions providing special rules are important because they specify how long the bill may be debated and whether it may be amended from the floor. If floor amendments are banned, the bill is considered under a "closed rule."

When a bill is debated under an "open rule," amendments may be offered from the floor. Committee amendments always are taken up first but may be changed, as may all amendments up to the second degree; that is, an amendment to an amendment to an amendment is not in order.

Duration of debate in the House depends on whether the bill is under discussion by the House proper or before the House when it is sitting as the Committee of the Whole House on the State of the Union. In the former, the amount of time for debate is allocated with an hour for each member if the measure is under consideration without a rule. In the Committee of the Whole the amount of time agreed on for general debate is equally divided between proponents and opponents. At the end of general discussion, the bill is often read section by section for amendment. Debate on an amendment is limited to five minutes for each side; this is called the "five-minute rule." In practice, amendments regularly are debated more than ten minutes, with members gaining the floor by offering pro forma amendments or obtaining unanimous consent to speak longer than five minutes.

Senate debate usually is unlimited. It can be halted only by unanimous consent or by "cloture," which requires a three-fifths majority of the entire Senate except for proposed changes in the Senate rules. The latter requires a two-thirds vote.

The House considers almost all important bills within a parliamentary framework known as the Committee of the Whole. It is not a committee as the word usually is understood; it is the full House meeting under another name for the purpose of

speeding action on legislation. Technically, the House sits as the Committee of the Whole when it considers any tax measure or bill dealing with public appropriations. Upon adoption of a special rule, the Speaker declares the House resolved into the Committee of the Whole and appoints a member of the majority party to serve as the chairman. The rules of the House permit the Committee of the Whole to meet when a quorum of 100 members is present on the floor and to amend and act on bills. When the Committee of the Whole has acted, it "rises," the Speaker returns as the presiding officer of the House and the member appointed chairman of the Committee of the Whole reports the action of the committee and its recommendations. The Committee of the Whole cannot pass a bill; instead it reports the measure to the full House with whatever changes it has approved. The full House then may pass or reject the bill — or, on occasion, recommit the bill to committee. Amendments adopted in the Committee of the Whole may be put to a second vote in the full House.

Votes. Voting on bills may occur repeatedly before they are finally approved or rejected. The House votes on the rule for the bill and on various amendments to the bill. Voting on amendments often is a more illuminating test of a bill's support than is the final tally. Sometimes members approve final passage of bills after vigorously supporting amendments that, if adopted, would have scuttled the legislation.

The Senate has three different methods of voting: an untabulated voice vote, a standing vote (called a division) and a recorded roll call to which members answer "yea" or "nay" when their names are called. The House also employs voice and standing votes, but since January 1973 yeas and nays have been recorded by an electronic voting device, eliminating the need for time-consuming roll calls.

After amendments to a bill have been voted upon, a vote may be taken on a motion to recommit the bill to committee. If carried, this vote is usually a death blow to the bill. If the motion is unsuccessful, the bill then is "read for the third time." After the third reading a vote on passage is taken. The final vote may be followed by a motion to reconsider, and this motion may be followed by a move to lay the motion on the table. Usually, those voting for the bill's passage vote for the tabling motion, thus safeguarding the final passage action. With that, the bill has been formally passed by the chamber.

Action in Second Chamber

After a bill is passed it is sent to the other chamber. This body may then take one of several steps. It may pass the bill as is — accepting the other chamber's language. It may send the bill to committee for scrutiny or alteration, or reject the entire bill, advising the other chamber of its actions. Or it simply may ignore the bill submitted while it continues work on its own version of the proposed legislation. Frequently, one chamber may approve a version of a bill that is greatly at variance with the version already passed by the other chamber, and then substitute its contents for the language of the other, retaining only the latter's bill number.

Often the second chamber makes only minor changes. If these are readily agreed to by the other chamber, the bill then is routed to the president. However, if the opposite chamber significantly alters the bill submitted to it, the measure usually is "sent to conference." The chamber that has possession of the "papers" (engrossed bill, engrossed amendments, messages of transmittal) requests a conference and the other chamber may agree to it. If the second chamber does not agree, the bill dies.

Conference Action

A conference works out conflicting House and Senate versions of a legislative bill. The conferees usually are senior members from the committees that managed the legislation who are appointed by the presiding officers of the two houses. Under this arrangement the conferees of one house have the duty of trying to maintain their chamber's position in the face of amending actions by the conferees (also referred to as "managers") of the other house.

The number of conferees from each chamber may vary, the range usually being from seven to nine members in each group, depending on the length or complexity of the bill involved. But a majority vote controls the action of each group so that a large representation does not give one chamber a voting advantage over the other chamber's conferees.

Theoretically, conferees are not allowed to write new legislation in reconciling the two versions before them, but this curb sometimes is bypassed. Many bills have been put into acceptable compromise form only after new language was provided by the conferees. Frequently the ironing out of difficulties takes days or even weeks. Conferences on involved, complex and controversial bills sometimes are particularly drawn out.

As a conference proceeds, conferees reconcile differences between the versions, but generally they grant concessions only insofar as they remain sure that the chamber they represent will accept the compromises. Occasionally, uncertainty over how either house will react, or the positive refusal of a chamber to back down on a disputed amendment, results in an impasse, and the bills die in conference even though each was approved by its sponsoring chamber.

When the conferees have reached agreement, they prepare a conference report embodying their recommendations (compromises) and a joint explanatory statement. The report, in document form, must be submitted to each house. The conference report must be approved by each house. Consequently, approval of the report is approval of the compromise bill. In the order of voting on conference reports, the chamber that asked for a conference yields to the other chamber the opportunity to vote first.

Final Action

After a bill has been passed by both the House and Senate in identical form, all of the original papers are sent to the enrolling clerk of the chamber in which the bill originated. The clerk then prepares an enrolled bill, which is printed on parchment paper.

When this bill has been certified as correct by the secretary of the Senate or the clerk of the House, depending on which chamber originated the bill, it is signed first (no matter whether it originated in the Senate or House) by the Speaker of the House and then by the president of the Senate. It is next sent to the White House to await action.

If the president approves the bill, he signs it, dates it and usually writes the word "approved" on the document. If the president does not sign it within 10 days (Sundays excepted) and Congress is in session, the bill becomes law without his signature.

If Congress adjourns *sine die* at the end of the second session the president can pocket veto a bill and it dies without Congress having the opportunity to override.

A president vetoes a bill by refusing to sign it and, before the ten-day period expires, returning it to Congress with a message stating his reasons. The message is sent to the chamber that originated the bill. If no action is taken on the message, the bill dies. Congress, however, can attempt to override the president's veto and enact the bill, "the objections of the president to the contrary notwithstanding." Overriding a veto requires a two-thirds vote of those present in each chamber, who must number a quorum and vote by roll call.

If the president's veto is overridden by a two-thirds vote in both houses, the bill becomes law. Otherwise it is dead.

When bills are passed finally and signed, or passed over a veto, they are given law numbers in numerical order as they become law. There are two series of numbers, one for public and one for private laws, starting at the number "1" for each two-year term of Congress. They are then identified by law number and by Congress — for example, Private Law 10, 105th Congress; Public Law 33, 106th Congress (or PL 106-33).

The Budget Process in Brief

Through the budget process, the president and Congress decide how much to spend and tax during the upcoming fiscal year. More specifically, they decide how much to spend on each activity, ensure that the government spends no more than that and spends it only for that activity and report on that spending at the end of each budget cycle.

The President's Budget

The law requires that, by the first Monday in February, the president submit to Congress his proposed federal budget for the next fiscal year, which begins on October 1. To accomplish this the president establishes general budget and fiscal policy guidelines. Based on these guidelines, executive branch agencies make requests for funds and submit them to the White House's Office of Management and Budget (OMB) nearly a year before the start of a new fiscal year. The OMB, receiving direction from the president and administration officials, reviews the agencies' requests and develops a detailed budget by December. From December to January the OMB prepares the budget documents, so that the president can deliver it to Congress in February.

The president's budget is the executive branch's plan for the next year — but it is just a proposal. After receiving it, Congress has its own budget process to follow from February to October. Only after Congress passes the required spending bills — and the president signs them — has the government created its actual budget.

Action in Congress

Congress first must pass a "budget resolution" — a framework within which the members of Congress will make their decisions about spending and taxes. It includes targets for total spending, total revenues and the deficit, and allocations within the spending target for the two types of spending — discretionary and mandatory.

Discretionary spending, which currently accounts for about 33 percent of all federal spending, is what the president and Congress must decide to spend for the next year through the thirteen annual appropriations bills. It includes money for such activities as the FBI and the Coast Guard, for housing and education, for NASA and highway and bridge construction and for defense and foreign aid.

Mandatory spending, which currently accounts for 67 percent of all spending, is authorized by laws that have already been passed. It includes entitlement spending — such as for Social Security, Medicare, veterans' benefits and food stamps — through which individuals receive benefits because they are eligible based on their age, income or other criteria. It also includes interest on the national debt, which the government pays to individuals and institutions that hold Treasury bonds and other government securities. The only way the president and Congress can change the spending on entitlement and other mandatory programs is if they change the laws that authorized the programs.

Currently, the law requires that legislation that would raise mandatory spending or lower revenues — compared to existing law — be offset by spending cuts or revenue increases. This requirement, called "pay-as-you-go" is designed to prevent new legislation from increasing the deficit.

Once Congress passes the budget resolution, legislators turn their attention to passing the 13 annual appropriations bills and, if they choose, "authorizing" bills to change the laws governing mandatory spending and revenues.

Congress begins by examining the president's budget in detail. Scores of committees and subcommittees hold hearings on proposals under their jurisdiction. The House and Senate Armed Services Authorizing Committees, and the Defense and Military Construction Subcommittees of the Appropriations Committees, for instance, hold hearings on the president's defense budget. The White House budget director, cabinet officers and other administration officials work with Congress as it accepts some of the president's proposals, rejects others and changes still others. Congress can change funding levels, eliminate programs or add programs not requested by the president. It can add or eliminate taxes and other sources of revenue, or make other changes that affect the amount of revenue collected. Congressional rules require that these committees and subcommittees take actions that reflect the congressional budget resolution.

The president's budget, the budget resolution and the appropriations or authorizing bills measure spending in two ways — "budget authority" and "outlays." Budget authority is what the law authorizes the federal government to spend for certain programs, projects or activities. What the government actually spends in a particular year, however, is an outlay. For example, when the government decides to build a space exploration system, the president and Congress may agree to appropriate $1 billion in budget authority. But the space system may take ten years to build. Thus, the government may spend $100 million in outlays in the first year to begin construction and the remaining $900 million during the next nine years as the construction continues.

Congress must provide budget authority before the federal agencies can obligate the government to make outlays. When Congress fails to complete action on one or more of the regular annual appropriations bills before the fiscal year begins on October 1, budget authority may be made on a temporary basis through continuing resolutions. Continuing resolutions make budget authority available for limited periods of time, generally at rates related through some formula to the rate provided in the previous year's appropriation.

Monitoring the Budget

Once Congress passes and the president signs the federal appropriations bills or authorizing laws for the fiscal year, the government monitors the budget through (1) agency program managers and budget officials, including the Inspectors General, who report only to the agency head; (2) the Office of Management and Budget; (3) congressional committees; and (4) the General Accounting Office, an auditing arm of Congress.

This oversight is designed to (1) ensure that agencies comply with legal limits on spending and that agencies use budget authority only for the purposes intended; (2) see that programs are operating consistently with legal requirements and existing policy; and (3) ensure that programs are well managed and achieving the intended results.

The president may withhold appropriated amounts from obligation only under certain limited circumstances — to provide for contingencies, to achieve savings made possible through changes in requirements or greater efficiency of operations or as otherwise provided by law. The Impoundment Control Act of 1974 specifies the procedures that must be followed if funds are withheld. Congress can also cancel previous authorized budget authority by passing a rescissions bill — but it also must be signed by the president.

Glossary of Congressional Terms

AA—(See Administrative Assistant.)

Absence of a Quorum—Absence of the required number of members to conduct business in a house or a committee. When a quorum call or roll-call vote in a house establishes that a quorum is not present, no debate or other business is permitted except a motion to adjourn or motions to request or compel the attendance of absent members, if necessary by arresting them.

Absolute Majority—A vote requiring approval by a majority of all members of a house rather than a majority of members present and voting. Also referred to as constitutional majority.

Account—Organizational units used in the federal budget primarily for recording spending and revenue transactions.

Act—(1) A bill passed in identical form by both houses of Congress and signed into law by the president or enacted over the president's veto. A bill also becomes an act without the president's signature if he does not return it to Congress within ten days (Sundays excepted) and if Congress has not adjourned within that period. (2) Also, the technical term for a bill passed by at least one house and engrossed.

Ad Hoc Select Committee—A temporary committee formed for a special purpose or to deal with a specific subject. Conference committees are ad hoc joint committees. A House rule adopted in 1975 authorizes the Speaker to refer measures to special ad hoc committees, appointed by the Speaker with the approval of the House.

Adjourn—A motion to adjourn is a formal motion to end a day's session or meeting of a house or a committee. A motion to adjourn usually has no conditions attached to it, but it sometimes may specify the day or time for reconvening or make reconvening subject to the call of the chamber's presiding officer or the committee's chairman. In both houses, a motion to adjourn is of the highest privilege, takes precedence over all other motions, is not debatable and must be put to an immediate vote. Adjournment of a house ends its legislative day. For this reason, the House or Senate sometimes adjourns for only one minute, or some other very brief period of time, during the course of a day's session. The House does not permit a motion to adjourn after it has resolved into Committee of the Whole or when the previous question has been ordered on a measure to final passage without an intervening motion.

Adjourn for More Than Three Days—Under Article I, Section 5 of the Constitution, neither house may adjourn for more than three days without the approval of the other. The necessary approval is given in a concurrent resolution to which both houses have agreed.

Adjournment *Sine Die*—Final adjournment of an annual or two-year session of Congress; literally, adjournment without a day. The two houses must agree to a privileged concurrent resolution for such an adjournment. A sine die adjournment precludes Congress from meeting again until the next constitutionally fixed date of a session (Jan. 3 of the following year) unless Congress determines otherwise by law or the president calls it into special session. Article II, Section 3 of the Constitution authorizes the president to adjourn both houses until such time as the president thinks proper when the two houses cannot agree to a time of adjournment. No president, however, has ever exercised this authority.

Adjournment to a Day (and Time) Certain—An adjournment that fixes the next date and time of meeting for one or both houses. It does not end an annual session of Congress.

Administration Bill—A bill drafted in the executive office of the president or in an executive department or agency to implement part of the president's program. An administration bill is introduced in Congress by a member who supports it or as a courtesy to the administration.

Administrative Assistant (AA)—The title usually given to a member's chief aide, political advisor and head of office staff. The administrative assistant often represents the member at meetings with visitors or officials when the member is unable (or unwilling) to attend.

Adoption—The usual parliamentary term for approval of a conference report. It is also commonly applied to amendments.

Advance Appropriation—In an appropriation act for a particular fiscal year, an appropriation that does not become available for spending or obligation until a subsequent fiscal year. The amount of the advance appropriation is counted as part of the budget for the fiscal year in which it becomes available for obligation.

Advance Funding—A mechanism whereby statutory language may allow budget authority for a fiscal year to be increased, and obligations to be incurred, with an offsetting decrease in the budget authority available in the succeeding fiscal year. If not used, the budget authority remains available for obligation in the succeeding fiscal year. Advance funding is sometimes used to provide contingency funding of a few benefit programs.

Adverse Report—A committee report recommending against approval of a measure or some other matter. Committees usually pigeonhole measures they oppose instead of reporting them adversely, but they may be required to report them by a statutory rule or an instruction from their parent body.

Advice and Consent—The Senate's constitutional role in consenting to or rejecting the president's nominations to executive branch and judicial offices and treaties with other nations. Confirmation of nominees requires a simple majority vote of senators present and voting. Treaties must be approved by a two-thirds majority of those present and voting.

Aisle—The center aisle of each chamber. When facing the presiding officer, Republicans usually sit to the right of the aisle, Democrats to the left. When members speak of "my side of the aisle" or "this side," they are referring to their party.

Amendment—A formal proposal to alter the text of a bill, resolution, amendment, motion, treaty or some other text. Technically, it is a motion. An amendment may strike out (eliminate) part of a text, insert new text or strike out and insert — that is, replace all or part of the text with new text. The texts of amendments considered on the floor are printed in full in the Congressional Record.

Amendment in the Nature of a Substitute—Usually, an amendment to replace the entire text of a measure. It strikes out everything after the enacting clause and inserts a version that may be somewhat, substantially or entirely different. When a committee adopts extensive amendments to a measure, it often incorporates them into such an amendment. Occasionally, the term is applied to an amendment that replaces a major portion of a measure's text.

Amendment Tree—A diagram showing the number and types of amendments that the rules and practices of a house permit to be offered to a measure before any of the amendments is voted on. It shows the relationship of one amendment to the others, and it may also indicate the degree of each amendment, whether it is a perfecting or substitute amendment, the order in which amendments may be offered and the order in which they are put to a vote. The same type of diagram can be used to display an actual amendment situation.

Annual Authorization—Legislation that authorizes appropriations for a single fiscal year and usually for a specific amount. Under the rules of the authorization-appropriation process, an annually authorized agency or program must be reauthorized each year if it is to receive appropriations for that year. Sometimes Congress fails to enact the reauthorization but nevertheless provides appropriations to continue the program, circumventing the rules by one means or another.

Appeal—A member's formal challenge of a ruling or decision by the presiding officer. On appeal, a house or a committee may overturn the ruling by majority vote. The right of appeal ensures the body against arbitrary control by the chair. Appeals are rarely made in the House and are even more rarely successful. Rulings are more frequently appealed in the Senate and occasionally overturned, in part because its presiding officer is not the majority party's leader, as in the House.

Apportionment—The action, after each decennial census, of allocating the number of members in the House of Representatives to each state. By law, the total number of House members (not counting delegates and a resident commissioner) is fixed at 435. The number allotted to each state is based approximately on its proportion of the nation's total population. Because the Constitution guarantees each state one representative no matter how small its population, exact proportional distribution is virtually impossible. The mathematical formula currently used to determine the apportionment is called the Method of Equal Proportions. (See Method of Equal Proportions.)

Appropriated Entitlement—An entitlement program, such as veterans' pensions, that is funded through annual appropriations rather than by a permanent appropriation. Because such an entitlement law requires the government to provide eligible recipients the benefits to which they are entitled, whatever the cost, Congress must appropriate the necessary funds.

Appropriation—(1) Legislative language that permits a federal agency to incur obligations and make payments from the Treasury for specified purposes, usually during a specified period of time. (2) The specific amount of money made available by such language. The Constitution prohibits payments from the Treasury except "in Consequence of Appropriations made by Law." With some exceptions, the rules of both houses forbid consideration of appropriations for purposes that are unauthorized in law or of appropriation amounts larger than those authorized in law. The House of Representatives claims the exclusive right to originate appropriation bills — a claim the Senate denies in theory but accepts in practice.

At-Large—Elected by and representing an entire state instead of a district within a state. The term usually refers to a representative rather than to a senator. (See Apportionment; Congressional District; Redistricting.)

August Adjournment—A congressional adjournment during the month of August in odd-numbered years, required by the Legislative Reorganization Act of 1970. The law instructs the two houses to adjourn for a period of at least thirty days before the second day after Labor Day, unless Congress provides otherwise or if, on July 31, a state of war exists by congressional declaration.

Authorization—(1) A statutory provision that establishes or continues a federal agency, activity or program for a fixed or indef-

inite period of time. It may also establish policies and restrictions and deal with organizational and administrative matters. (2) A statutory provision, as described in (1), may also, explicitly or implicitly, authorize congressional action to provide appropriations for an agency, activity or program. The appropriations may be authorized for one year, several years or an indefinite period of time, and the authorization may be for a specific amount of money or an indefinite amount ("such sums as may be necessary"). Authorizations of specific amounts are construed as ceilings on the amounts that subsequently may be appropriated in an appropriation bill, but not as minimums; either house may appropriate lesser amounts or nothing at all.

Authorization-Appropriation Process—The two-stage procedural system that the rules of each house require for establishing and funding federal agencies and programs: first, enactment of authorizing legislation that creates or continues an agency or program; second, enactment of appropriations legislation that provides funds for the authorized agency or program.

Automatic Roll Call—Under a House rule, the automatic ordering of the yeas and nays when a quorum is not present on a voice or division vote and a member objects to the vote on that ground. It is not permitted in the Committee of the Whole.

Backdoor Spending Authority—Authority to incur obligations that evades the normal congressional appropriations process because it is provided in legislation other than appropriation acts. The most common forms are borrowing authority, contract authority and entitlement authority.

Baseline—A projection of the levels of federal spending, revenues and the resulting budgetary surpluses or deficits for the upcoming and subsequent fiscal years, taking into account laws enacted to date and assuming no new policy decisions. It provides a benchmark for measuring the budgetary effects of proposed changes in federal revenues or spending, assuming certain economic conditions.

Bells—A system of electric signals and lights that informs members of activities in each chamber. The type of activity taking place is indicated by the number of signals and the interval between them. When the signals are sounded, a corresponding number of lights are lit around the perimeter of many clocks in House or Senate offices.

Bicameral—Consisting of two houses or chambers. Congress is a bicameral legislature whose two houses have an equal role in enacting legislation. In most other national bicameral legislatures, one house is significantly more powerful than the other.

Bigger Bite Amendment—An amendment that substantively changes a portion of a text including language that had previously been amended. Normally, language that has been amended may not be amended again. However, a part of a sentence that has been changed by amendment, for example, may be changed again by an amendment that amends a "bigger bite" of the text — that is, by an amendment that also substantively changes the unamended parts of the sentence or the entire section or title in which the previously amended language appears. The biggest possible bite is an amendment in the nature of a substitute that amends the entire text of a measure. Once adopted, therefore, such an amendment ends the amending process.

Bill—The term for the chief vehicle Congress uses for enacting laws. Bills that originate in the House of Representatives are designated as HR, those in the Senate as S, followed by a number assigned in the order in which they are introduced during a two-year Congress. A bill becomes a law if passed in identical language by both houses and signed by the president, or passed over the president's veto, or if the president fails to sign it within ten days after receiving it while Congress is in session.

Bill of Attainder—An act of a legislature finding a person guilty of treason or a felony. The Constitution prohibits the passage of such a bill by the U.S. Congress or any state legislature.

Bills and Resolutions Introduced—Members formally present measures to their respective houses by delivering them to a clerk in the chamber when their house is in session. Both houses permit any number of members to join in introducing a bill or resolution. The first member listed on the measure is the sponsor; the other members listed are its cosponsors.

Bills and Resolutions Referred—After a bill or resolution is introduced, it is normally sent to one or more committees that have jurisdiction over its subject, as defined by House and Senate rules and precedents. A Senate measure is usually referred to the committee with jurisdiction over the predominant subject of its text, but it may be sent to two or more committees by unanimous consent or on a motion offered jointly by the majority and minority leaders. In the House, a rule requires the Speaker to refer a measure to the committee that has primary jurisdiction. The Speaker is also authorized to refer measures sequentially to additional committees and to impose time limits on such referrals.

Bipartisan Committee—A committee with an equal number of members from each political party. The House Committee on Standards of Official Conduct and the Senate Select Committee on Ethics are the only bipartisan, permanent full committees.

Borrowing Authority—Statutory authority permitting a federal agency, such as the Export-Import Bank, to borrow money from the public or the Treasury to finance its operations. It is a form of backdoor spending. To bring such spending under the control of the congressional appropriation process, the Congressional Budget Act requires that new borrowing authority shall be effective only to the extent and in such amounts as are provided in appropriations acts.

Budget—A detailed statement of actual or anticipated revenues and expenditures during an accounting period. For the national government, the period is the federal fiscal year (Oct. 1 to Sept. 30). The budget usually refers to the president's budget submission to Congress early each calendar year. The president's budget estimates federal government income and spending for the upcoming fiscal year and contains detailed recommendations for appropriation, revenue and other legislation. Congress is not required to accept or even vote directly on the president's proposals, and it often revises the president's budget extensively. (See Fiscal Year.)

Budget Act—Common name for the Congressional Budget and Impoundment Control Act of 1974, which established the basic procedures of the current congressional budget process; created the House and Senate Budget Committees; and enacted procedures for reconciliation, deferrals and rescissions. (See Budget Process; Deferral; Impoundment; Reconciliation; Rescission. See also Gramm-Rudman-Hollings Act of 1985.)

Budget and Accounting Act of 1921—The law that, for the first time, authorized the president to submit to Congress an annual budget for the entire federal government. Before passage of the act, most federal agencies sent their budget requests to the appropriate congressional committees without review by the president.

Budget Authority—Generally, the amount of money that may be spent or obligated by a government agency or for a government program or activity. Technically, it is statutory authority to enter into obligations that normally result in outlays. The main forms of budget authority are appropriations, borrowing authority and contract authority. It also includes authority to obligate and expend the proceeds of offsetting receipts and collections. Congress may

make budget authority available for only one year, several years or an indefinite period, and it may specify definite or indefinite amounts.

Budget Enforcement Act of 1990—An act that revised the sequestration process established by the Gramm-Rudman-Hollings Act of 1985, replaced the earlier act's fixed deficit targets with adjustable ones, established discretionary spending limits for fiscal years 1991 through 1995, instituted pay-as-you-go rules to enforce deficit neutrality on revenue and mandatory spending legislation and reformed the budget and accounting rules for federal credit activities. Unlike the Gramm-Rudman-Hollings Act, the 1990 act emphasized restraints on legislated changes in taxes and spending instead of fixed deficit limits.

Budget Enforcement Act of 1997—An act that revised and updated the provisions of the Budget Enforcement Act of 1990, including by extending the discretionary spending caps and pay-as-you-go rules through 2002.

Budget Process—(1) In Congress, the procedural system it uses (a) to approve an annual concurrent resolution on the budget that sets goals for aggregate and functional categories of federal expenditures, revenues and the surplus or deficit for an upcoming fiscal year; and (b) to implement those goals in spending, revenue and, if necessary, reconciliation and debt-limit legislation. (2) In the executive branch, the process of formulating the president's annual budget, submitting it to Congress, defending it before congressional committees, implementing subsequent budget-related legislation, impounding or sequestering expenditures as permitted by law, auditing and evaluating programs and compiling final budget data. The Budget and Accounting Act of 1921 and the Congressional Budget and Impoundment Control Act of 1974 established the basic elements of the current budget process. Major revisions were enacted in the Gramm-Rudman-Hollings Act of 1985 and the Budget Enforcement Act of 1990.

Budget Resolution—A concurrent resolution in which Congress establishes or revises its version of the federal budget's broad financial features for the upcoming fiscal year and several additional fiscal years. Like other concurrent resolutions, it does not have the force of law, but it provides the framework within which Congress subsequently considers revenue, spending and other budget-implementing legislation. The framework consists of two basic elements: (1) aggregate budget amounts (total revenues, new budget authority, outlays, loan obligations and loan guarantee commitments, deficit or surplus and debt limit); and (2) subdivisions of the relevant aggregate amounts among the functional categories of the budget. Although it does not allocate funds to specific programs or accounts, the budget committees' reports accompanying the resolution often discuss the major program assumptions underlying its functional amounts. Unlike those amounts, however, the assumptions are not binding on Congress.

By Request—A designation indicating that a member has introduced a measure on behalf of the president, an executive agency or a private individual or organization. Members often introduce such measures as a courtesy because neither the president nor any person other than a member of Congress can do so. The term, which appears next to the sponsor's name, implies that the member who introduced the measure does not necessarily endorse it. A House rule dealing with by-request introductions dates from 1888, but the practice goes back to the earliest history of Congress.

Byrd Rule—The popular name of an amendment to the Congressional Budget Act that bars the inclusion of extraneous matter in any reconciliation legislation considered in the Senate. The ban is enforced by points of order that the presiding officer sustains. The provision defines different categories of extraneous matter, but it also permits certain exceptions. Its chief sponsor was Sen. Robert C. Byrd, D-W.Va.

Calendar—A list of measures or other matters (most of them favorably reported by committees) that are eligible for floor consideration. The House has five calendars; the Senate has two. A place on a calendar does not guarantee consideration. Each house decides which measures and matters it will take up, when and in what order, in accordance with its rules and practices.

Calendar Wednesday—A House procedure that on Wednesdays permits its committees to bring up for floor consideration nonprivileged measures they have reported. The procedure is so cumbersome and susceptible to dilatory tactics, however, that it is rarely used.

Call Up—To bring a measure or report to the floor for immediate consideration.

Casework—Assistance to constituents who seek assistance in dealing with federal and local government agencies. Constituent service is a high priority in most members' offices.

Caucus—(1) A common term for the official organization of each party in each house. (2) The official title of the organization of House Democrats. House and Senate Republicans and Senate Democrats call their organizations "conferences." (3) A term for an informal group of members who share legislative interests, such as the Black Caucus, Hispanic Caucus and Children's Caucus.

Censure—The strongest formal condemnation of a member for misconduct short of expulsion. A house usually adopts a resolution of censure to express its condemnation, after which the presiding officer reads its rebuke aloud to the member in the presence of his or her colleagues.

Chairman—The presiding officer of a committee, a subcommittee or a task force. At meetings, the chairman preserves order, enforces the rules, recognizes members to speak or offer motions and puts questions to a vote. The chairman of a committee or subcommittee usually appoints its staff and sets its agenda, subject to the panel's veto.

Chamber—The Capitol room in which a house of Congress normally holds its sessions. The chamber of the House of Representatives, officially called the Hall of the House, is considerably larger than that of the Senate because it must accommodate 435 representatives, four delegates and one resident commissioner. Unlike the Senate chamber, members have no desks or assigned seats. In both chambers, the floor slopes downward to the well in front of the presiding officer's raised desk. A chamber is often referred to as "the floor," as when members are said to be on or going to the floor. Those expressions usually imply that the member's house is in session.

Christmas Tree Bill—Jargon for a bill adorned with amendments, many of them unrelated to the bill's subject, that provide benefits for interest groups, specific states, congressional districts, companies and individuals.

Classes of Senators—A class consists of the thirty-three or thirty-four senators elected to a six-year term in the same general election. Because the terms of approximately one-third of the senators expire every two years, there are three classes.

Clean Bill—After a House committee extensively amends a bill, it often assembles its amendments and what is left of the bill into a new measure that one or more of its members introduces as a "clean bill." The revised measure is assigned a new number.

Clerk of the House—An officer of the House of Representatives responsible principally for administrative support of the legislative process in the House. The clerk is invariably the candidate of the majority party.

Cloakrooms—Two rooms with access to the rear of each chamber's floor, one for each party's members, where members may confer privately, sit quietly or have a snack. The presiding officer sometimes urges members who are conversing too loudly on the floor to retire to their cloakrooms.

Closed Hearing—A hearing closed to the public and the media. A House committee may close a hearing only if it determines that disclosure of the testimony to be taken would endanger national security, violate any law or tend to defame, degrade or incriminate any person. The Senate has a similar rule. Both houses require roll-call votes in open session to close a hearing.

Closed Rule—A special rule reported from the House Rules Committee that prohibits amendments to a measure or that only permits amendments offered by the reporting committee.

Cloture—A Senate procedure that limits further consideration of a pending proposal to thirty hours in order to end a filibuster. Sixteen senators must first sign and submit a cloture motion to the presiding officer. One hour after the Senate meets on the second calendar day thereafter, the chair puts the motion to a yea-and-nay vote following a live quorum call. If three-fifths of all senators (sixty if there are no vacancies) vote for the motion, the Senate must take final action on the cloture proposal by the end of the thirty hours of consideration and may consider no other business until it takes that action. Cloture on a proposal to amend the Senate's standing rules requires approval by two-thirds of the senators present and voting.

Code of Official Conduct—A House rule that bans certain actions by House members, officers and employees; requires them to conduct themselves in ways that "reflect creditably" on the House; and orders them to adhere to the spirit and the letter of House rules and those of its committees. The code's provisions govern the receipt of outside compensation, gifts and honoraria and the use of campaign funds; prohibit members from using their clerk-hire allowance to pay anyone who does not perform duties commensurate with that pay; forbids discrimination in members' hiring or treatment of employees on the grounds of race, color, religion, sex, handicap, age or national origin; orders members convicted of a crime who might be punished by imprisonment of two or more years not to participate in committee business or vote on the floor until exonerated or reelected; and restricts employees' contact with federal agencies on matters in which they have a significant financial interest. The Senate's rules contain some similar prohibitions.

College of Cardinals—A popular term for the subcommittee chairmen of the appropriations committees, reflecting their influence over appropriation measures. The chairmen of the full appropriations committees are sometimes referred to as popes.

Comity—The practice of maintaining mutual courtesy and civility between the two houses in their dealings with each other and in members' speeches on the floor. Although the practice is largely governed by long-established customs, a House rule explicitly cautions its members not to characterize any Senate action or inaction, refer to individual senators except under certain circumstances, or quote from Senate proceedings except to make legislative history on a measure. The Senate has no rule on the subject but references to the House have been held out of order on several occasions. Generally the houses do not interfere with each other's appropriations although minor conflicts sometimes occur. A refusal to receive a message from the other house has also been held to violate the practice of comity.

Committee—A panel of members elected or appointed to perform some service or function for its parent body. Congress has four types of committees: standing, special or select, joint, and, in the House, a Committee of the Whole. Committees conduct investigations, make studies, issue reports and recommendations and, in the case of standing committees, review and prepare measures on their assigned subjects for action by their respective houses. Most committees divide their work among several subcommittees. With rare exceptions, the majority party in a house holds a majority of the seats on its committees, and their chairmen are also from that party.

Committee Jurisdiction—The legislative subjects and other functions assigned to a committee by rule, precedent, resolution or statute. A committee's title usually indicates the general scope of its jurisdiction but often fails to mention other significant subjects assigned to it.

Committee of the Whole—Common name of the Committee of the Whole House on the State of the Union, a committee consisting of all members of the House of Representatives. Measures from the union calendar must be considered in the Committee of the Whole before the House officially completes action on them; the committee often considers other major bills as well. A quorum of the committee is 100, and it meets in the House chamber under a chairman appointed by the Speaker. Procedures in the Committee of the Whole expedite consideration of legislation because of its smaller quorum requirement, its ban on certain motions and its five-minute rule for debate on amendments. Those procedures usually permit more members to offer amendments and participate in the debate on a measure than is normally possible. The Senate no longer uses a Committee of the Whole.

Committee Ratios—The ratios of majority to minority party members on committees. By custom, the ratios of most committees reflect party strength in their respective houses as closely as possible.

Committee Report on a Measure—A document submitted by a committee to report a measure to its parent chamber. Customarily, the report explains the measure's purpose, describes provisions and any amendments recommended by the committee and presents arguments for its approval.

Committee Veto—A procedure that requires an executive department or agency to submit certain proposed policies, programs or action to designated committees for review before implementing them. Before 1983, when the Supreme Court declared that a legislative veto was unconstitutional, these provisions permitted committees to veto the proposals. Committees no longer conduct this type of policy review, and the term is now something of a misnomer. Nevertheless, agencies usually take the pragmatic approach of trying to reach a consensus with the committees before carrying out their proposals, especially when an appropriations committee is involved.

Concur—To agree to an amendment of the other house, either by adopting a motion to concur in that amendment or a motion to concur with an amendment to that amendment. After both houses have agreed to the same version of an amendment, neither house may amend it further, nor may any subsequent conference change it or delete it from the measure. Concurrence by one house in all amendments of the other house completes action on the measure; no vote is then necessary on the measure as a whole because both houses previously passed it.

Concurrent Resolution—A resolution that requires approval by both houses but does not need the president's signature and therefore cannot have the force of law. Concurrent resolutions deal with the prerogatives or internal affairs of Congress as a whole. Designated H. Con. Res. in the House and S. Con. Res. in the Senate, they are numbered consecutively in each house in their order of introduction during a two-year Congress.

Conferees—A common title for managers, the members from each house appointed to a conference committee. The Senate usually authorizes its presiding officer to appoint its conferees. The Speaker appoints House conferees, and under a rule adopted in 1993, can remove conferees "at any time after an original appointment" and also appoint additional conferees at any time. Conferees are expected to support the positions of their houses despite their personal views, but in practice this is not always the case. The party ratios of conferees generally reflect the ratios in their houses. Each house may appoint as many conferees as it pleases. House conferees often outnumber their Senate colleagues; however, each house has only one vote in a conference, so the size of its delegation is immaterial.

Conference—(1) A formal meeting or series of meetings between members representing each house to reconcile House and Senate differences on a measure (occasionally several measures). Because one house cannot require the other to agree to its proposals, the conference usually reaches agreement by compromise. When a conference completes action on a measure, or as much action as appears possible, it sends its recommendations to both houses in the form of a conference report, accompanied by an explanatory statement. (2) The official title of the organization of all Democrats or Republicans in the Senate and of all Republicans in the House of Representatives. (See Party Caucus.)

Conference Committee—A temporary joint committee formed for the purpose of resolving differences between the houses on a measure. Major and controversial legislation usually requires conference committee action. Voting in a conference committee is not by individuals but within the House and Senate delegations. Consequently, a conference committee report requires the support of a majority of the conferees from each house. Both houses require that conference committees open their meetings to the public. The Senate's rule permits the committee to close its meetings if a majority of conferees in each delegation agree by a roll-call vote. The House rule permits closed meetings only if the House authorizes them to do so on a roll-call vote. Otherwise, there are no congressional rules governing the organization of, or procedure in, a conference committee. The committee chooses its chairman, but on measures that go to conference annually, such as general appropriation bills, the chairmanship traditionally rotates between the houses.

Conference Report—A document submitted to both houses that contains a conference committee's agreements for resolving their differences on a measure. It must be signed by a majority of the conferees from each house separately and must be accompanied by an explanatory statement. Both houses prohibit amendments to a conference report and require it to be accepted or rejected in its entirety.

Congress—(1) The national legislature of the United States, consisting of the House of Representatives and the Senate. (2) The national legislature in office during a two-year period. Congresses are numbered sequentially; thus, the 1st Congress of 1789–1791 and the 106th Congress of 1999–2001. Before 1935, the two-year period began on the first Monday in December of odd-numbered years. Since then it has extended from January of an odd-numbered year through noon on Jan. 3 of the next odd-numbered year. A Congress usually holds two annual sessions, but some have had three sessions and the 67th Congress had four. When a Congress expires, measures die if they have not yet been enacted.

Congressional Accountability Act of 1995 (CAA)—An act applying eleven labor, workplace and civil rights laws to the legislative branch and establishing procedures and remedies for legislative branch employees with grievances in violation of these laws. The following laws are covered by the CAA: the Fair Labor

Standards Act of 1938; Title VII of the Civil Rights Act of 1964; Americans with Disabilities Act of 1990; Age Discrimination in Employment Act of 1967; Family and Medical Leave Act of 1993; Occupational Safety and Health Act of 1970; Chapter 71 of Title 5, U.S. Code (relating to federal service labor-management relations); Employee Polygraph Protection Act of 1988; Worker Adjustment and Retraining Notification Act; Rehabilitation Act of 1973; and Chapter 43 of Title 38, U.S. Code (relating to veterans' employment and reemployment).

Congressional Budget and Impoundment Control Act of 1974—The law that established the basic elements of the congressional budget process, the House and Senate Budget Committees, the Congressional Budget Office and the procedures for congressional review of impoundments in the form of rescissions and deferrals proposed by the president. The budget process consists of procedures for coordinating congressional revenue and spending decisions made in separate tax, appropriations and legislative measures. The impoundment provisions were intended to give Congress greater control over executive branch actions that delay or prevent the spending of funds provided by Congress.

Congressional Budget Office (CBO)—A congressional support agency created by the Congressional Budget and Impoundment Control Act of 1974 to provide nonpartisan budgetary information and analysis to Congress and its committees. CBO acts as a scorekeeper when Congress is voting on the federal budget, tracking bills to ensure they comply with overall budget goals. The agency also estimates what proposed legislation would cost over a five-year period. CBO works most closely with the House and Senate Budget Committees.

Congressional Directory—The official who's who of Congress, usually published during the first session of a two-year Congress.

Congressional District—The geographical area represented by a single member of the House of Representatives. For states with only one representative, the entire state is a congressional district. As of 2001 seven states had only one representative each: Alaska, Delaware, Montana, North Dakota, South Dakota, Vermont and Wyoming.

Congressional Record—The daily, printed and substantially verbatim account of proceedings in both the House and Senate chambers. Extraneous materials submitted by members appear in a section titled "Extensions of Remarks." A "Daily Digest" appendix contains highlights of the day's floor and committee action plus a list of committee meetings and floor agendas for the next day's session.

Although the official reporters of each house take down every word spoken during the proceedings, members are permitted to edit and "revise and extend" their remarks before they are printed. In the Senate section, all speeches, articles and other material submitted by senators but not actually spoken or read on the floor are set off by large black dots, called bullets. However, bullets do not appear when a senator reads part of a speech and inserts the rest. In the House section, undelivered speeches and materials are printed in a distinctive typeface. The term "permanent Record" refers to the bound volumes of the daily Records of an entire session of Congress.

Congressional Research Service (CRS)—Established in 1917, a department of the Library of Congress whose staff provide nonpartisan, objective analysis and information on virtually any subject to committees, members and staff of Congress. Originally the Legislative Reference Service, it is the oldest congressional support agency.

Congressional Support Agencies—A term often applied to three agencies in the legislative branch that provide nonpartisan information and analysis to committees and members of Congress: the Congressional Budget Office, the Congressional Research Service of the Library of Congress and the General Accounting Office. A fourth support agency, the Office of Technology Assessment, formerly provided such support but was abolished in the 104th Congress.

Congressional Terms of Office—A term normally begins on Jan. 3 of the year following a general election and runs two years for representatives and six years for senators. A representative chosen in a special election to fill a vacancy is sworn in for the remainder of the predecessor's term. An individual appointed to fill a Senate vacancy usually serves until the next general election or until the end of the predecessor's term, whichever comes first. Some states, however, require their governors to call a special election to fill a Senate vacancy shortly after an appointment has been made.

Constitutional Rules—Constitutional provisions that prescribe procedures for Congress. In addition to certain types of votes required in particular situations, these provisions include the following: (1) the House chooses its Speaker, the Senate its president pro tempore and both houses their officers; (2) each house requires a majority quorum to conduct business; (3) less than a majority may adjourn from day to day and compel the attendance of absent members; (4) neither house may adjourn for more than three days without the consent of the other; (5) each house must keep a journal; (6) the yeas and nays are ordered when supported by one-fifth of the members present; (7) all revenue-raising bills must originate in the House, but the Senate may propose amendments to them. The Constitution also sets out the procedure in the House for electing a president, the procedure in the Senate for electing a vice president, the procedure for filling a vacancy in the office of vice president and the procedure for overriding a presidential veto.

Constitutional Votes—Constitutional provisions that require certain votes or voting methods in specific situations. They include (1) the yeas and nays at the desire of one-fifth of the members present; (2) a two-thirds vote by the yeas and nays to override a veto; (3) a two-thirds vote by one house to expel one of its members and by both houses to propose a constitutional amendment; (4) a two-thirds vote of senators present to convict someone whom the House has impeached and to consent to ratification of treaties; (5) a two-thirds vote in each house to remove political disabilities from persons who have engaged in insurrection or rebellion or given aid or comfort to the enemies of the United States; (6) a majority vote in each house to fill a vacancy in the office of vice president; (7) a majority vote of all states to elect a president in the House of Representatives when no candidate receives a majority of the electoral votes; (8) a majority vote of all senators when the Senate elects a vice president under the same circumstances; and (9) the casting vote of the vice president in case of tie votes in the Senate.

Contempt of Congress—Willful obstruction of the proper functions of Congress. Most frequently, it is a refusal to obey a subpoena to appear and testify before a committee or to produce documents demanded by it. Such obstruction is a misdemeanor and persons cited for contempt are subject to prosecution in federal courts. A house cites an individual for contempt by agreeing to a privileged resolution to that effect reported by a committee. The presiding officer then refers the matter to a U.S. attorney for prosecution.

Continuing Body—A characterization of the Senate on the theory that it continues from Congress to Congress and has existed continuously since it first convened in 1789. The rationale for the theory is that under the system of staggered six-year terms for senators, the terms of only about one-third of them expire after each Congress and, therefore, a quorum of the Senate is always in office. Consequently, under this theory, the Senate, unlike the House, does not have to adopt its rules at the beginning of each Congress because those rules continue from one Congress to the next. This makes it extremely difficult for the Senate to change its rules against the opposition of a determined minority because those rules require a two-thirds vote of the senators present and voting to invoke cloture on a proposed rules change.

Continuing Resolution (CR)—A joint resolution that provides funds to continue the operation of federal agencies and programs at the beginning of a new fiscal year if their annual appropriation bills have not yet been enacted; also called continuing appropriations. Continuing resolutions are enacted shortly before or after the new fiscal year begins and usually make funds available for a specified period. Additional resolutions are often needed after the first expires. Some continuing resolutions have provided appropriations for an entire fiscal year. Continuing resolutions for specific periods customarily fix a rate at which agencies may incur obligations based either on the previous year's appropriations, the president's budget request, or the amount as specified in the agency's regular annual appropriation bill if that bill has already been passed by one or both houses. In the House, continuing resolutions are privileged after Sept. 15.

Contract Authority—Statutory authority permitting an agency to enter into contracts or incur other obligations even though it has not received an appropriation to pay for them. Congress must eventually fund them because the government is legally liable for such payments. The Congressional Budget Act of 1974 requires that new contract authority may not be used unless provided for in advance by an appropriation act, but it permits a few exceptions.

Correcting Recorded Votes—The rules of both houses prohibit members from changing their votes after a vote result has been announced. Nevertheless, the Senate permits its members to withdraw or change their votes, by unanimous consent, immediately after the announcement. In rare instances, senators have been granted unanimous consent to change their votes several days or weeks after the announcement. Votes tallied by the electronic voting system in the House may not be changed. But when a vote actually given is not recorded during an oral call of the roll, a member may demand a correction as a matter of right. On all other alleged errors in a recorded vote, the Speaker determines whether the circumstances justify a change. Occasionally, members merely announce that they were incorrectly recorded; announcements can occur hours, days or even months after the vote and appear in the Congressional Record.

Cosponsor—A member who has joined one or more other members to sponsor a measure.

Credit Authority—Authority granted to an agency to incur direct loan obligations or to make loan guarantee commitments. The Congressional Budget Act of 1974 bans congressional consideration of credit authority legislation unless the extent of that authority is made subject to provisions in appropriation acts.

C-SPAN—Cable-Satellite Public Affairs Network, which provides live, gavel-to-gavel coverage of Senate floor proceedings on one cable television channel and coverage of House floor proceedings on another channel. C-SPAN also televises important committee hearings in both houses. Each house also transmits its televised proceedings directly to congressional offices.

Current Services Estimates—Executive branch estimates of the anticipated costs of federal programs and operations for the next and future fiscal years at existing levels of service and assuming no new initiatives or changes in existing law. The president submits these estimates to Congress with the annual budget and includes an explanation of the underlying economic and policy assumptions on which they are based, such as anticipated rates of inflation, real economic growth and unemployment, plus program caseloads and pay increases.

Custody of the Papers—Possession of an engrossed measure and certain related basic documents that the two houses produce as they try to resolve their differences over the measure.

Dance of the Swans and the Ducks—A whimsical description of the gestures some members use in connection with a request for a recorded vote, especially in the House. When members want their colleagues to stand in support of the request, they move their hands and arms in a gentle upward motion resembling the beginning flight of a graceful swan. When they want their colleagues to remain seated to avoid such a vote, they move their hands and arms in a vigorous downward motion resembling a diving duck.

Dean—Within a state's delegation in the House of Representatives, the member with the longest continuous service.

Debate—In congressional parlance, speeches delivered during consideration of a measure, motion or other matter, as distinguished from speeches in other parliamentary situations, such as one-minute and special order speeches when no business is pending. Virtually all debate in the House of Representatives is under some kind of time limitation. Most debate in the Senate is unlimited; that is, a senator, once recognized, may speak for as long as he or she chooses, unless the Senate invokes cloture.

Debt Limit—The maximum amount of outstanding federal public debt permitted by law. The limit (or ceiling) covers virtually all debt incurred by the government except agency debt. Each congressional budget resolution sets forth the new debt limit that may be required under its provisions.

Deferral—An impoundment of funds for a specific period of time that may not extend beyond the fiscal year in which it is proposed. Under the Impoundment Control Act of 1974, the president must notify Congress that he is deferring the spending or obligation of funds provided by law for a project or activity. Congress can disapprove the deferral by legislation.

Deficit—The amount by which the government's outlays exceed its budget receipts for a given fiscal year. Both the president's budget and the annual congressional budget resolution provide estimates of the deficit or surplus for the upcoming and several future fiscal years.

Degrees of Amendment—Designations that indicate the relationships of amendments to the text of a measure and to each other. In general, an amendment offered directly to the text of a measure is an amendment in the first degree, and an amendment to that amendment is an amendment in the second degree. Both houses normally prohibit amendments in the third degree — that is, an amendment to an amendment to an amendment.

Delegate—A nonvoting member of the House of Representatives elected to a two-year term from the District of Columbia, the territory of Guam, the territory of the Virgin Islands or the territory of American Samoa. By law, delegates may not vote in the full House but they may participate in debate, offer motions (except to reconsider) and serve and vote on standing and select committees. On their committees, delegates possess the same powers and privileges as other members and the Speaker may appoint them to appropriate conference committees and select committees.

Denounce—A formal action that condemns a member for misbehavior; considered by some experts to be equivalent to censure. (See Censure.)

Dilatory Tactics—Procedural actions intended to delay or prevent action by a house or a committee. They include, among others, offering numerous motions, demanding quorum calls and recorded votes at every opportunity, making numerous points of order and parliamentary inquiries and speaking as long as the applicable rules permit. The Senate rules permit a battery of dilatory tactics, especially lengthy speeches, except under cloture. In the House, possible dilatory tactics are more limited. Speeches are always subject to time limits and debate-ending motions. Moreover, a House rule instructs the Speaker not to entertain dilatory motions and lets the Speaker decide whether a motion is dilatory. However, the Speaker may not override the constitutional right of a member to demand the yeas and nays, and in practice usually waits for a point of order before exercising that authority. (See Cloture.)

Discharge a Committee—Remove a measure from a committee to which it has been referred in order to make it available for floor consideration. Noncontroversial measures are often discharged by unanimous consent. However, because congressional committees have no obligation to report measures referred to them, each house has procedures to extract controversial measures from recalcitrant committees. Six discharge procedures are available in the House of Representatives. The Senate uses a motion to discharge, which is usually converted into a discharge resolution.

District Office—Representatives maintain one or more offices in their districts for the purpose of assisting and communicating with constituents. The costs of maintaining these offices are paid from members' official allowances. Senators can use the official expense allowance to rent offices in their home state, subject to a funding formula based on their state's population and other factors.

District Work Period—The House term for a scheduled congressional recess during which members may visit their districts and conduct constituency business.

Division Vote—A vote in which the chair first counts those in favor of a proposition and then those opposed to it, with no record made of how each member votes. In the Senate, the chair may count raised hands or ask senators to stand, whereas the House requires members to stand; hence, often called a standing vote. Committees in both houses ordinarily use a show of hands. A division usually occurs after a voice vote and may be demanded by any member or ordered by the chair if there is any doubt about the outcome of the voice vote. The demand for a division can also come before a voice vote. In the Senate, the demand must come before the result of a voice vote is announced. It may be made after a voice vote announcement in the House, but only if no intervening business has transpired and only if the member was standing and seeking recognition at the time of the announcement. A demand for the yeas and nays or, in the House, for a recorded vote, takes precedence over a division vote.

Doorkeeper of the House—A former officer of the House of Representatives who was responsible for enforcing the rules prohibiting unauthorized persons from entering the chamber when the House is in session. The doorkeeper was usually the candidate of the majority party. In 1995 the office was abolished and its functions transferred to the sergeant at arms.

Effective Dates—Provisions of an act that specify when the entire act or individual provisions in it become effective as law. Most acts become effective on the date of enactment, but it is sometimes necessary or prudent to delay the effective dates of some provisions.

Electronic Voting—Since 1973 the House has used an electronic voting system to record the yeas and nays and to conduct recorded votes. Members vote by inserting their voting cards in one of the boxes at several locations in the chamber. They are given at least fifteen minutes to vote. When several votes occur immediately after each other, the Speaker may reduce the voting time to five minutes on the second and subsequent votes. The Speaker may allow additional time on each vote but may also close a vote at any time after the minimum time has expired. Members can change their votes at any time before the Speaker announces the result. The House also uses the electronic system for quorum calls. While a vote is in progress, a large panel above the Speaker's desk displays how each member has voted. Smaller panels on either side of the chamber display running totals of the votes and the time remaining. The Senate does not have electronic voting.

Enacting Clause—The opening language of each bill, beginning "Be it enacted by the Senate and House of Representatives of the United States of America in Congress assembled..." This language gives legal force to measures approved by Congress and signed by the president or enacted over the president's veto. A successful motion to strike it from a bill kills the entire measure.

Engrossed Bill—The official copy of a bill or joint resolution as passed by one chamber, including the text as amended by floor action and certified by the clerk of the House or the secretary of the Senate (as appropriate). Amendments by one house to a measure or amendments of the other also are engrossed. House engrossed documents are printed on blue paper; the Senate's are printed on white paper.

Enrolled Bill—The final official copy of a bill or joint resolution passed in identical form by both houses. An enrolled bill is printed on parchment. After it is certified by the chief officer of the house in which it originated and signed by the House Speaker and the Senate president pro tempore, the measure is sent to the White House for the president's signature.

Entitlement Program—A federal program under which individuals, businesses or units of government that meet the requirements or qualifications established by law are entitled to receive certain payments if they seek such payments. Major examples include Social Security, Medicare, Medicaid, unemployment insurance and military and federal civilian pensions. Congress cannot control their expenditures by refusing to appropriate the sums necessary to fund them because the government is legally obligated to pay eligible recipients the amounts to which the law entitles them.

Equality of the Houses—A component of the Constitution's emphasis on checks and balances under which each house is given essentially equal status in the enactment of legislation and in the relations and negotiations between the two houses. Although the House of Representatives initiates revenue and appropriation measures, the Senate has the right to amend them. Either house may initiate any other type of legislation, and neither can force the other to agree to, or even act on, its measures. Moreover, each house has a potential veto over the other because legislation requires agreement by both. Similarly, in a conference to resolve their differences on a measure, each house casts one vote, as determined by a majority of its conferees. In most other national bicameral legislatures, the powers of one house are markedly greater than those of the other.

Ethics Rules—Several rules or standing orders in each house that mandate certain standards of conduct for members and congressional employees in finance, employment, franking and other areas. The Senate Permanent Select Committee on Ethics and the House Committee on Standards of Official Conduct investigate alleged violations of conduct and recommend appropriate actions to their respective houses.

Exclusive Committee—(1) Under the rules of the Republican Conference and House Democratic Caucus, a standing committee whose members usually cannot serve on any other standing committee. As of 2000 the Appropriations, Energy and Commerce (beginning in the 105th Congress), Ways and Means and Rules Committees were designated as exclusive committees. (2) Under the rules of the two party conferences in the Senate, a standing committee whose members may not simultaneously serve on any other exclusive committee.

Executive Calendar—The Senate's calendar for committee reports on its executive business, namely treaties and nominations. The calendar numbers indicate the order in which items were referred to the calendar but have no bearing on when or if the Senate will consider them. The Senate, by motion or unanimous consent, resolves itself into executive session to consider them.

Executive Document—A document, usually a treaty, sent by the president to the Senate for approval. It is referred to a committee in the same manner as other measures. Resolutions to ratify treaties have their own "treaty document" numbers. For example, the first treaty submitted in the 106th Congress would be "Treaty Doc 106-1."

Executive Order—A unilateral proclamation by the president that has a policy-making or legislative impact. Members of Congress have challenged some executive orders on the grounds that they usurped the authority of the legislative branch. Although the Supreme Court has ruled that a particular order exceeded the president's authority, it has upheld others as falling within the president's general constitutional powers.

Executive Privilege—The assertion that presidents have the right to withhold certain information from Congress. Presidents have based their claim on (1) the constitutional separation of powers; (2) the need for secrecy in military and diplomatic affairs; (3) the need to protect individuals from unfavorable publicity; (4) the need to safeguard the confidential exchange of ideas in the executive branch; and (5) the need to protect individuals who provide confidential advice to the president.

Executive Session—(1) A Senate meeting devoted to the consideration of treaties or nominations. Normally, the Senate meets in legislative session; it resolves itself into executive session, by motion or by unanimous consent, to deal with its executive business. It also keeps a separate Journal for executive sessions. Executive sessions are usually open to the public, but the Senate may choose to close them.

Expulsion—A member's removal from office by a two-thirds vote of his or her house; the supermajority is required by the Constitution. It is the most severe and most rarely used sanction a house can invoke against a member. Although the Constitution provides no explicit grounds for expulsion, the courts have ruled that it may be applied only for misconduct during a member's term of office, not for conduct before the member's election. Generally, neither house will consider expulsion of a member convicted of a crime until the judicial processes have been exhausted. At that stage, members sometimes resign rather than face expulsion. In 1977 the House adopted a rule urging members convicted of certain crimes to voluntarily abstain from voting or participating in other legislative business.

Extensions of Remarks—An appendix to the daily Congressional Record that consists primarily of miscellaneous extraneous material submitted by members. It often includes members' statements not delivered on the floor, newspaper articles and editorials, praise for a member's constituents and noteworthy letters received by a member, among other material. Representatives supply the bulk of this material; senators submit very little. "Extensions of Remarks" pages are separately numbered, and each number is preceded by the letter "E." Materials may be placed in the Extensions of Remarks section only by unanimous consent. Usually, one member of each party makes the request each day on behalf of his or her party colleagues after the House has completed its legislative business of the day.

Federal Debt—The total amount of monies borrowed and not yet repaid by the federal government. Federal debt consists of public debt and agency debt. Public debt is the portion of the federal debt borrowed by the Treasury or the Federal Financing Bank directly from the public or from another federal fund or account. For example, the Treasury regularly borrows money from the Social Security trust fund. Public debt accounts for about 99 percent of the federal debt. Agency debt refers to the debt incurred by federal agencies such as the Export-Import Bank but excluding the Treasury and the Federal Financing Bank, which are authorized by law to borrow funds from the public or from another government fund or account.

Filibuster—The use of obstructive and time-consuming parliamentary tactics by one member or a minority of members to delay, modify or defeat proposed legislation or rules changes. Filibusters are also sometimes used to delay urgently needed measures to force the body to accept other legislation. The Senate's rules permitting unlimited debate and the extraordinary majority it requires to impose cloture make filibustering particularly effective in that chamber. Under the stricter rules of the House, filibusters in that body are short-lived and therefore ineffective and rarely attempted.

Fiscal Year—The federal government's annual accounting period. It begins Oct. 1 and ends on the following Sept. 30. A fiscal year is designated by the calendar year in which it ends and is often referred to as FY. Thus, fiscal year 1998 began Oct. 1, 1997, ended Sept. 30, 1998, and is called FY98. In theory, Congress is supposed to complete action on all budgetary measures applying to a fiscal year before that year begins. It rarely does so.

Five-Minute Rule—A House rule that limits debate on an amendment offered in Committee of the Whole to five minutes for its sponsor and five minutes for an opponent. In practice, the committee routinely permits longer debate by two devices: the offering of pro forma amendments, each debatable for five minutes, and unanimous consent for a member to speak longer than five minutes. Consequently, debate on an amendment sometimes continues for hours. At any time after the first ten minutes, however, the committee may shut off debate immediately or by a specified time, either by unanimous consent or by majority vote on a nondebatable motion. The motion, which dates from 1847, is also used in the House as in Committee of the Whole, where debate also may be shut off by a motion for the previous question.

Floor—The ground level of the House or Senate chamber where members sit and the houses conduct their business. When members are attending a meeting of their house they are said to be on the floor. Floor action refers to the procedural actions taken during floor consideration such as deciding on motions, taking up measures, amending them and voting.

Floor Manager—A majority party member responsible for guiding a measure through its floor consideration in a house and for devising the political and procedural strategies that might be required to get it passed. The presiding officer gives the floor manager priority recognition to debate, offer amendments, oppose amendments and make crucial procedural motions.

Frank—Informally, members' legal right to send official mail postage free under their signatures; often called the franking privilege. Technically, it is the autographic or facsimile signature used on envelopes instead of stamps that permits members and certain congressional officers to send their official mail free of charge. The franking privilege has been authorized by law since the first Congress, except for a few months in 1873. Congress reimburses the U.S. Postal Service for the franked mail it handles.

Function or Functional Category—A broad category of national need and spending of budgetary significance. A category provides an accounting method for allocating and keeping track of budgetary resources and expenditures for that function because it includes all budget accounts related to the function's subject or purpose such as agriculture, administration of justice, commerce and housing and energy. Functions do not necessarily correspond with appropriations acts or with the budgets of individual agencies. As of 2000 there were twenty functional categories, each divided into a number of subfunctions.

Gag Rule—A pejorative term for any type of special rule reported by the House Rules Committee that proposes to prohibit amendments to a measure or only permits amendments offered by the reporting committee.

Galleries—The balconies overlooking each chamber from which the public, news media, staff and others may observe floor proceedings.

General Accounting Office (GAO)—A congressional support agency, often referred to as the investigative arm of Congress. It evaluates and audits federal agencies and programs in the United States and abroad on its initiative or at the request of congressional committees or members.

General Appropriation Bill—A term applied to each of the thirteen annual bills that provide funds for most federal agencies and programs and also to the supplemental appropriation bills that contain appropriations for more than one agency or program.

Germaneness—The requirement that an amendment be closely related — in terms of subject or purpose, for example — to the text it proposes to amend. A House rule requires that all amendments be germane. In the Senate, only amendments offered to general appropriation bills and budget measures or proposed under cloture must be germane. Germaneness rules can be waived by suspension of the rules in both houses, by unanimous consent agreements in the Senate and by special rules from the Rules Committee in the House. Moreover, presiding officers usually do not enforce germaneness rules on their own initiative; therefore, a nongermane amendment can be adopted if no member raises a point of order against it. Under cloture in the Senate, however, the chair may take the initiative to rule amendments out of order as not being germane, without a point of order being made. All House debate must be germane except during general debate in the Committee of the Whole, but special rules invariably require that such debate be "confined to the bill." The Senate requires germane debate only during the first three hours of each daily session. Under the precedents of both houses, an amendment can be relevant but not necessarily germane. A crucial factor in determining germaneness in the House is how the subject of a measure or matter is defined. For example, the subject of a measure authorizing construction of a naval vessel is defined as being the construction of a single vessel; therefore, an amendment to authorize an additional vessel is not germane.

Gerrymandering—The manipulation of legislative district boundaries to benefit a particular party, politician or minority group. The term originated in 1812 when the Massachusetts legislature redrew the lines of state legislative districts to favor the party of Gov. Elbridge Gerry, and some critics said one district looked like a salamander. (See also Congressional District; Redistricting.)

Gramm-Rudman-Hollings Act of 1985—Common name for the Balanced Budget and Emergency Deficit Control Act of 1985, which established new budget procedures intended to balance the federal budget by fiscal year 1991. (The timetable subsequently was extended and then deleted.) The act's chief sponsors were senators Phil Gramm (R-Texas), Warren Rudman (R-N.H.)

Ernest Hollings (D-S.C.).

Grandfather Clause—A provision in a measure, law or rule that exempts an individual, entity or a defined category of individuals or entities from complying with a new policy or restriction. For example, a bill that would raise taxes on persons who reach the age of sixty-five after a certain date inherently grandfathers out those who are sixty-five before that date. Similarly, a Senate rule limiting senators to two major committee assignments also grandfathers some senators who were sitting on a third major committee before a specified date.

Grants-in-Aid—Payments by the federal government to state and local governments to help provide for assistance programs or public services.

Hearing—Committee or subcommittee meetings to receive testimony on proposed legislation during investigations or for oversight purposes. Relatively few bills are important enough to justify formal hearings. Witnesses often include experts, government officials, spokespersons for interested groups, officials of the General Accounting Office and members of Congress.

Hold—A senator's request that his or her party leaders delay floor consideration of certain legislation or presidential nominations. The majority leader usually honors a hold for a reasonable period of time, especially if its purpose is to assure the senator that the matter will not be called up during his or her absence or to give the senator time to gather necessary information.

Hold (or Have) the Floor—A member's right to speak without interruption, unless he or she violates a rule, after recognition by the presiding officer. At the member's discretion, he or she may yield to another member for a question in the Senate or for a question or statement in the House, but may reclaim the floor at any time.

Hold-Harmless Clause—In legislation providing a new formula for allocating federal funds, a clause to ensure that recipients of those funds do not receive less in a future year than they did in the current year if the new formula would result in a reduction for them. Similar to a grandfather clause, it has been used most frequently to soften the impact of sudden reductions in federal grants. (See Grandfather Clause.)

Hopper—A box on the clerk's desk in the House chamber into which members deposit bills and resolutions to introduce them. In House jargon, to drop a bill in the hopper is to introduce it.

Hour Rule—A House rule that permits members, when recognized, to hold the floor in debate for no more than one hour each. The majority party member customarily yields one-half the time to a minority member. Although the hour rule applies to general debate in Committee of the Whole as well as in the House, special rules routinely vary the length of time for such debate and its control to fit the circumstances of particular measures.

House As In Committee of the Whole—A hybrid combination of procedures from the general rules of the House and from the rules of the Committee of the Whole, sometimes used to expedite consideration of a measure on the floor.

House Calendar—The calendar reserved for all public bills and resolutions that do not raise revenue or directly or indirectly appropriate money or property when they are favorably reported by House committees.

House Manual—A commonly used title for the handbook of the rules of the House of Representatives, published in each Congress. Its official title is Constitution, Jefferson's Manual and Rules of the House of Representatives.

House of Representatives—The house of Congress in which states are represented roughly in proportion to their populations, but every state is guaranteed at least one representative. By law, the number of voting representatives is fixed at 435. Four delegates and one resident commissioner also serve in the House; they may vote in their committees but not on the House floor. Although the House and Senate have equal legislative power, the Constitution gives the House sole authority to originate revenue measures. The House also claims the right to originate appropriation measures, a claim the Senate disputes in theory but concedes in practice. The House has the sole power to impeach, and it elects the president when no candidate has received a majority of the electoral votes. It is sometimes referred to as the lower body.

Immunity—(1) Members' constitutional protection from lawsuits and arrest in connection with their legislative duties. They may not be tried for libel or slander for anything they say on the floor of a house or in committee. Nor may they be arrested while attending sessions of their houses or when traveling to or from sessions of Congress, except when charged with treason, a felony or a breach of the peace. (2) In the case of a witness before a committee, a grant of protection from prosecution based on that person's testimony to the committee. It is used to compel witnesses to testify who would otherwise refuse to do so on the constitutional ground of possible selfincrimination. Under such a grant, none of a witness's testimony may be used against him or her in a court proceeding except in a prosecution for perjury or for giving a false statement to Congress. (See also Contempt of Congress.)

Impeachment—The first step to remove the president, vice president or other federal civil officers from office and to disqualify them from any future federal office "of honor, Trust or Profit." An impeachment is a formal charge of treason, bribery or "other high Crimes and Misdemeanors." The House has the sole power of impeachment and the Senate the sole power of trying the charges and convicting. The House impeaches by a simple majority vote; conviction requires a two-thirds vote of all senators present.

Impeachment Trial, Removal and Disqualification—The Senate conducts an impeachment trial under a separate set of twenty-six rules that appears in the Senate Manual. Under the Constitution, the chief justice of the United States presides over trials of the president, but the vice president, the president pro tempore or any other senator may preside over the impeachment trial of another official.

The Constitution requires senators to take an oath for an impeachment trial. During the trial, senators may not engage in colloquies or participate in arguments, but they may submit questions in writing to House managers or defense counsel. After the trial concludes, the Senate votes separately on each article of impeachment without debate unless the Senate orders the doors closed for private discussions. During deliberations senators may speak no more than once on a question, not for more than ten minutes on an interlocutory question and not more than fifteen minutes on the final question. These rules may be set aside by unanimous consent or suspended on motion by a two-thirds vote.

The Senate's impeachment trial of President Clinton in 1999 was only the second such trial involving a president. It continued for five weeks, with the Senate voting not to convict on the two impeachment articles.

Senate impeachment rules allow the Senate, at its own discretion, to name a committee to hear evidence and conduct the trial, with all senators thereafter voting on the charges. The impeachment trials of three federal judges were conducted this way, and the Supreme Court upheld the validity of these rules in Nixon v. United States, 506 U.S. 224, 1993.

An official convicted on impeachment charges is removed from office immediately. However, the convicted official is not barred from holding a federal office in the future unless the Senate, after its conviction vote, also approves a resolution disqualifying the convicted official from future office. For example, federal judge Alcee L. Hastings was impeached and convicted in 1989, but the Senate did not vote to bar him from office in the future. In 1992 Hastings was elected to the House of Representatives, and no challenge was raised against seating him when he took the oath of office in 1993.

Impoundment—An executive branch action or inaction that delays or withholds the expenditure or obligation of budget authority provided by law. The Impoundment Control Act of 1974 classifies impoundments as either deferrals or rescissions, requires the president to notify Congress about all such actions and gives Congress authority to approve or reject them.

Inspector General (IG) In the House of Representatives—A position established with the passage of the House Administrative Reform Resolution of 1992. The duties of the office have been revised several times and are now contained in House Rule II. The inspector general (IG), who is subject to the policy direction and oversight of the Committee on House Administration, is appointed for a Congress jointly by the Speaker and the majority and minority leaders of the House. The IG communicates the results of audits to the House officers or officials who were the subjects of the audits and suggests appropriate corrective measures. The IG submits a report of each audit to the Speaker, the majority and minority leaders and the chairman and ranking minority member of the House Administration Committee; notifies these five members in the case of any financial irregularity discovered; and reports to the Committee on Standards of Official Conduct on possible violations of House rules or any applicable law by any House member, officer or employee. The IG's office also has certain duties to audit various financial operations of the House that had previously been performed by the General Accounting Office.

Instruct Conferees—A formal action by a house urging its conferees to uphold a particular position on a measure in conference. The instruction may be to insist on certain provisions in the measure as passed by that house or to accept a provision in the version passed by the other house. Instructions to conferees are not binding because the primary responsibility of conferees is to reach agreement on a measure and neither House can compel the other to accept particular provisions or positions.

Investigative Power—The authority of Congress and its committees to pursue investigations, upheld by the Supreme Court but limited to matters related to, and in furtherance of, a legitimate task of the Congress. Standing committees in both houses are permanently authorized to investigate matters within their jurisdictions. Major investigations are sometimes conducted by temporary select, special or joint committees established by resolutions for that purpose.

Some rules of the House provide certain safeguards for witnesses and others during investigative hearings. These permit counsel to accompany witnesses, require that each witness receive a copy of the committee's rules and order the committee to go into closed session if it believes the testimony to be heard might defame, degrade or incriminate any person. The committee may subsequently decide to hear such testimony in open session. The Senate has no rules of this kind.

Item Veto—Item veto authority, which is available to most state governors, allows governors to eliminate or reduce items in legislative measures presented for their signature without vetoing the entire measure and sign the rest into law. A similar authority was briefly granted to the U.S. president under the Line Item Veto Act of 1996. According to the majority opinion of the Supreme Court in its 1998 decision overturning that law, a constitutional amendment would be necessary to give the president such item veto authority.

Jefferson's Manual—Short title of Jefferson's Manual of Parliamentary Practice, prepared by Thomas Jefferson for his guidance when he was president of the Senate from 1797 to 1801. Although it reflects English parliamentary practice in his day, many procedures in both houses of Congress are still rooted in its basic precepts. Under a House rule adopted in 1837, the manual's provisions govern House procedures when applicable and when they are not inconsistent with its standing rules and orders. The Senate, however, has never officially acknowledged it as a direct authority for its legislative procedure.

Johnson Rule—A policy instituted in 1953 under which all Democratic senators are assigned to one major committee before any Democrat is assigned to two. The Johnson Rule is named after its author, Sen. Lyndon B. Johnson, D-Texas, then the Senate's Democratic leader. Senate Republicans adopted a similar policy soon thereafter.

Joint Committee—A committee composed of members selected from each house. The functions of most joint committees involve investigation, research or oversight of agencies closely related to Congress. Permanent joint committees, created by statute, are sometimes called standing joint committees. Once quite numerous, only four joint committees remained as of 2002: Joint Economic, Joint Taxation, Joint Library and Joint Printing. None has authority to report legislation.

Joint Resolution—A legislative measure that Congress uses for purposes other than general legislation. Similar to a bill, it has the force of law when passed by both houses and either approved by the president or passed over the president's veto. Unlike a bill, a joint resolution enacted into law is not called an act; it retains its original title. Most often, joint resolutions deal with such relatively limited matters as the correction of errors in existing law, continuing appropriations, a single appropriation or the establishment of permanent joint committees. Unlike bills, however, joint resolutions also are used to propose constitutional amendments; these do not require the president's signature and become effective only when ratified by three-fourths of the states. The House designates joint resolutions as H.J. Res., the Senate as S.J. Res. Each house numbers its joint resolutions consecutively in the order of introduction during a two-year Congress.

Joint Session—Informally, any combined meeting of the Senate and the House. Technically, a joint session is a combined meeting to count the electoral votes for president and vice president or to hear a presidential address, such as the State of the Union message; any other formal combined gathering of both houses is a joint meeting. Joint sessions are authorized by concurrent resolutions and are held in the House chamber, because of its larger seating capacity. Although the president of the Senate and the Speaker sit side by side at the Speaker's desk during combined meetings, the former presides over the electoral count and the latter presides on all other occasions and introduces the president or other guest speaker. The president and other guests may address a joint session or meeting only by invitation.

Joint Sponsorship—Two or more members sponsoring the same measure.

Journal—The official record of House or Senate actions, including every motion offered, every vote cast, amendments agreed to, quorum calls and so forth. Unlike the Congressional Record, it does not provide reports of speeches, debates, statements and the like. The Constitution requires each house to maintain a Journal and to publish it periodically.

Junket—A member's trip at government expense, especially abroad, ostensibly on official business but, it is often alleged, for pleasure.

Killer Amendment—An amendment that, if agreed to, might lead to the defeat of the measure it amends, either in the house in which the amendment is offered or at some later stage of the legislative process. Members sometimes deliberately offer or vote for such an amendment in the expectation that it will undermine support for the measure in Congress or increase the likelihood that the president will veto it.

King of the Mountain (or Hill) Rule—(See Queen of the Hill Rule.)

LA—(See Legislative Assistant.)

Lame Duck—Jargon for a member who has not been reelected, or did not seek reelection, and is serving the balance of his or her term.

Lame Duck Session—A session of a Congress held after the election for the succeeding Congress, so-called after the lame duck members still serving.

Last Train Out—Colloquial name for last must-pass bill of a session of Congress.

Law—An act of Congress that has been signed by the president, passed over the president's veto or allowed to become law without the president's signature.

Lay on the Table—A motion to dispose of a pending proposition immediately, finally and adversely; that is, to kill it without a direct vote on its substance. Often simply called a motion to table, it is not debatable and is adopted by majority vote or without objection. It is a highly privileged motion, taking precedence over all others except the motion to adjourn in the House and all but three additional motions in the Senate. It can kill a bill or resolution, an amendment, another motion, an appeal or virtually any other matter.

Tabling an amendment also tables the measure to which the amendment is pending in the House, but not in the Senate. The House does not allow the motion against the motion to recommit, in Committee of the Whole, and in some other situations. In the Senate it is the only permissible motion that immediately ends debate on a proposition, but only to kill it.

(The) Leadership—Usually, a reference to the majority and minority leaders of the Senate or to the Speaker and minority leader of the House. The term sometimes includes the majority leader in the House and the majority and minority whips in each house and, at other times, other party officials as well.

Legislation—(1) A synonym for legislative measures: bills and joint resolutions. (2) Provisions in such measures or in substantive amendments offered to them. (3) In some contexts, provisions that change existing substantive or authorizing law, rather than provisions that make appropriations.

Legislation on an Appropriation Bill—A common reference to provisions changing existing law that appear in, or are offered as amendments to, a general appropriation bill. A House rule prohibits the inclusion of such provisions in general appropriation bills unless they retrench expenditures. An analogous Senate rule permits points of order against amendments to a general appropriation bill that propose general legislation.

Legislative Assistant (LA)—A member's staff person responsible for monitoring and preparing legislation on particular subjects and for advising the member on them; commonly referred to as an LA.

Legislative Day—The day that begins when a house meets after an adjournment and ends when it next adjourns. Because the House of Representatives normally adjourns at the end of a daily session, its legislative and calendar days usually coincide. The Senate, however, frequently recesses at the end of a daily session, and its legislative day may extend over several calendar days, weeks or months. Among other uses, this technicality permits the Senate to save time by circumventing its morning hour, a procedure required at the beginning of every legislative day.

Legislative History—(1) A chronological list of actions taken on a measure during its progress through the legislative process. (2) The official documents relating to a measure, the entries in the Journals of the two houses on that measure and the Congressional Record text of its consideration in both houses. The documents include all committee reports and the conference report and joint explanatory statement, if any. Courts and affected federal agencies study a measure's legislative history for congressional intent about its purpose and interpretation.

Legislative Process—(1) Narrowly, the stages in the enactment of a law from introduction to final disposition. An introduced measure that becomes law typically travels through reference to committee; committee and subcommittee consideration; report to the chamber; floor consideration; amendment; passage; engrossment; messaging to the other house; similar steps in that house, including floor amendment of the measure; return of the measure to the first house; consideration of amendments between the houses or a conference to resolve their differences; approval of the conference report by both houses; enrollment; approval by the president or override of the president's veto; and deposit with the Archivist of the United States. (2) Broadly, the political, lobbying and other factors that affect or influence the process of enacting laws.

Legislative Veto—A procedure, declared unconstitutional in 1983, that allowed Congress or one of its houses to nullify certain actions of the president, executive branch agencies or independent agencies. Sometimes called congressional vetoes or congressional disapprovals. Following the Supreme Court's 1983 decision, Congress amended several legislative veto statutes to require enactment of joint resolutions, which are subject to presidential veto, for nullifying executive branch actions.

Limitation on a General Appropriation Bill—Language that prohibits expenditures for part of an authorized purpose from funds provided in a general appropriation bill. Precedents require that the language be phrased in the negative: that none of the funds provided in a pending appropriation bill shall be used for a specified authorized activity. Limitations in general appropriation bills are permitted on the grounds that Congress can refuse to fund authorized programs and, therefore, can refuse to fund any part of them as long as the prohibition does not change existing law. House precedents have established that a limitation does not change existing law if it does not impose additional duties or burdens on executive branch officials, interfere with their discretionary authority or require them to make judgments or determinations not required by existing law. The proliferation of limitation amendments in the 1970s and early 1980s prompted the House to adopt a rule in 1983 making it more difficult for members to offer them. The rule bans such amendments during the reading of an appropriation bill for amendments, unless they are specifically authorized in existing law. Other limitations may be offered after the reading, but the Committee of the Whole can foreclose them by adopting a motion to rise and report the bill back to the House. In 1995 the rule was amended to allow the motion to rise and report to be made only by the majority leader or his or her designee. The House Appropriations Committee, however, can include limitation provisions in the bills it reports.

Line Item—An amount in an appropriation measure. It can refer to a single appropriation account or to separate amounts within the account. In the congressional budget process, the term usually refers to assumptions about the funding of particular pro-

grams or accounts that underlie the broad functional amounts in a budget resolution. These assumptions are discussed in the reports accompanying each resolution and are not binding.

Line-Item Veto—(See Item Veto.)

Line Item Veto Act of 1996—A law, in effect only from January 1997 until June 1998, that granted the president authority intended to be functionally equivalent to an item veto, by amending the Impoundment Control Act of 1974 to incorporate an approach known as enhanced rescission. Key provisions established a new procedure that permitted the president to cancel amounts of new discretionary appropriations (budget authority), new items of direct spending (entitlements) or certain limited tax benefits. It also required the president to notify Congress of the cancellation in a special message within five calendar days after signing the measure. The cancellation would become permanent unless legislation disapproving it was enacted within thirty days. On June 25, 1998, in Clinton v. City of New York the Supreme Court held the Line Item Veto Act unconstitutional, on the grounds that its cancellation provisions violated the presentment clause in Article I, clause 7, of the Constitution.

Live Pair—A voluntary and informal agreement between two members on opposite sides of an issue, one of whom is absent for a recorded vote, under which the member who is present withholds or withdraws his or her vote to offset the failure to vote by the member who is absent. Usually the member in attendance announces that he or she has a live pair, states how each would have voted and votes "present." In the House, under a rules change enacted in the 106th Congress, a live pair is only permitted on the rare occasions when electronic voting is not used.

Live Quorum—In the Senate, a quorum call to which senators are expected to respond. Senators usually suggest the absence of a quorum, not to force a quorum to appear, but to provide a pause in the proceedings during which senators can engage in private discussions or wait for a senator to come to the floor. A senator desiring a live quorum usually announces his or her intention, giving fair warning that there will be an objection to any unanimous consent request that the quorum call be dispensed with before it is completed.

Loan Guarantee—A statutory commitment by the federal government to pay part or all of a loan's principal and interest to a lender or the holder of a security in case the borrower defaults.

Lobby—To try to persuade members of Congress to propose, pass, modify or defeat proposed legislation or to change or repeal existing laws. Lobbyists attempt to promote their preferences or those of a group, organization or industry. Originally the term referred to persons frequenting the lobbies or corridors of legislative chambers in order to speak to lawmakers. In a general sense, lobbying includes not only direct contact with members but also indirect attempts to influence them, such as writing to them or persuading others to write or visit them, attempting to mold public opinion toward a desired legislative goal by various means and contributing or arranging for contributions to members' election campaigns. The right to lobby stems from the First Amendment to the Constitution, which bans laws that abridge the right of the people to petition the government for a redress of grievances.

Lobbying Disclosure Act of 1995—The principal statute requiring disclosure of — and also, to a degree, circumscribing — the activities of lobbyists. In general, it requires lobbyists who spend more than 20 percent of their time on lobbying activities to register and make semiannual reports of their activities to the clerk of the House and the secretary of the Senate, although the law provides for a number of exemptions. Among the statute's prohibitions, lobbyists are not allowed to make contributions to the legal defense fund of a member or high government official or to reimburse for official travel. Civil penalties for failure to comply may include fines of up to $50,000. The act does not include grass-roots lobbying in its definition of lobbying activities.

The act amends several other lobby laws, notably the Foreign Agents Registration Act (FARA), so that lobbyists can submit a single filing. Since the measure was enacted, the number of lobby registrations has risen from about 12,000 to more than 20,000. In 1998 expenditures on federal lobbying, as disclosed under the Lobbying Disclosure Act, totaled $1.42 billion. The 1995 act supersedes the 1946 Federal Regulation of Lobbying Act, which was repealed in Section 11 of the 1995 Act.

Logrolling—Jargon for a legislative tactic or bargaining strategy in which members try to build support for their legislation by promising to support legislation desired by other members or by accepting amendments they hope will induce their colleagues to vote for their bill.

Lower Body—A way to refer to the House of Representatives, which is considered pejorative by House members.

Mace—The symbol of the office of the House sergeant at arms. Under the direction of the Speaker, the sergeant at arms is responsible for preserving order on the House floor by holding up the mace in front of an unruly member, or by carrying the mace up and down the aisles to quell boisterous behavior. When the House is in session, the mace sits on a pedestal at the Speaker's right; when the House is in Committee of the Whole, it is moved to a lower pedestal. The mace is forty-six inches high and consists of thirteen ebony rods bound in silver and topped by a silver globe with a silver eagle, wings outstretched, perched on it.

Majority Leader—The majority party's chief floor spokesperson, elected by that party's caucus — sometimes called floor leader. In the Senate, the majority leader also develops the party's political and procedural strategy, usually in collaboration with other party officials and committee chairmen. The majority leader negotiates the Senate's agenda and committee ratios with the minority leader and usually calls up measures for floor action. The chamber traditionally concedes to the majority leader the right to determine the days on which it will meet and the hours at which it will convene and adjourn. In the House, the majority leader is the Speaker's deputy and heir apparent and helps plan the floor agenda and the party's legislative strategy and often speaks for the party leadership in debate.

Managers—(1) The official title of members appointed to a conference committee, commonly called conferees. The ranking majority and minority managers for each house also manage floor consideration of the committee's conference report. (2) The members who manage the initial floor consideration of a measure. (3) The official title of House members appointed to present impeachment articles to the Senate and to act as prosecutors on behalf of the House during the Senate trial of the impeached person.

Mandatory Appropriations—Amounts that Congress must appropriate annually because it has no discretion over them unless it first amends existing substantive law. Certain entitlement programs, for example, require annual appropriations.

Markup—A meeting or series of meetings by a committee or subcommittee during which members mark up a measure by offering, debating and voting on amendments to it.

Means-Tested Programs—Programs that provide benefits or services to low-income individuals who meet a test of need. Most are entitlement programs, such as Medicaid, food stamps and Supplementary Security Income. A few—for example, subsidized housing and various social services—are funded through discretionary appropriations.

Members' Allowances—Official expenses that are paid for or for which members are reimbursed by their houses. Among these are the costs of office space in congressional buildings and in their home states or districts; office equipment and supplies; postage-free mailings (the franking privilege); a set number of trips to and from home states or districts, as well as travel elsewhere on official business; telephone and other telecommunications services; and staff salaries.

Member's Staff—The personal staff to which a member is entitled. The House sets a maximum number of staff and a monetary allowance for each member. The Senate does not set a maximum staff level, but it does set a monetary allowance for each member. In each house, the staff allowance is included with office expenses allowances and official mail allowances in a consolidated allowance. Representatives and senators can spend as much money in their consolidated allowances for staff, office expenses or official mail, as long as they do not exceed the monetary value of the three allowances combined. This provides members with flexibility in operating their offices.

Method of Equal Proportions—The mathematical formula used since 1950 to determine how the 435 seats in the House of Representatives should be distributed among the fifty states in the apportionment following each decennial census. It minimizes as much as possible the proportional difference between the average district population in any two states. Because the Constitution guarantees each state at least one representative, fifty seats are automatically apportioned. The formula calculates priority numbers for each state, assigns the first of the 385 remaining seats to the state with the highest priority number, the second to the state with the next highest number and so on until all seats are distributed. (See Apportionment.)

Midterm Election—The general election for members of Congress that occurs in November of the second year in a presidential term.

Minority Leader—The minority party's leader and chief floor spokesman, elected by the party caucus; sometimes called minority floor leader. With the assistance of other party officials and the ranking minority members of committees, the minority leader devises the party's political and procedural strategy.

Minority Staff—Employees who assist the minority party members of a committee. Most committees hire separate majority and minority party staffs but they also may hire nonpartisan staff. Senate rules state that a committee's staff must reflect the relative number of its majority and minority party committee members, and the rules guarantee the minority at least one-third of the funds available for hiring partisan staff. In the House, each committee is authorized thirty professional staff, and the minority members of most committees may select up to ten of these staff (subject to full committee approval). Under House rules, the minority party is to be "treated fairly" in the apportionment of additional staff resources. Each House committee determines the portion of its additional staff it allocates to the minority; some committees allocate one-third; and others allot less.

Modified Rule—A special rule from the House Rules Committee that permits only certain amendments to be offered to a measure during its floor consideration or that bans certain specified amendments or amendments on certain subjects.

Morning Business—In the Senate, routine business that is to be transacted at the beginning of the morning hour. The business consists, first, of laying before the Senate, and referring to committees, matters such as messages from the president and the House, federal agency reports and unreferred petitions, memorials, bills and joint resolutions. Next, senators may present additional petitions and memorials. Then committees may present their reports, after which senators may introduce bills and resolutions. Finally, resolutions coming over from a previous day are taken up for consideration. In practice, the Senate adopts standing orders that permit senators to introduce measures and file reports at any time, but only if there has been a morning business period on that day. Because the Senate often remains in the same legislative day for several days, weeks or months at a time, it orders a morning business period almost every calendar day for the convenience of senators who wish to introduce measures or make reports.

Morning Hour—A two-hour period at the beginning of a new legislative day during which the Senate is supposed to conduct routine business, call the calendar on Mondays and deal with other matters described in a Senate rule. In practice, the morning hour very rarely, if ever, occurs, in part because the Senate frequently recesses, rather than adjourns, at the end of a daily session. Therefore the rule does not apply when the senate next meets. The Senate's rules reserve the first hour of the morning for morning business. After the completion of morning business, or at the end of the first hour, the rules permit a motion to proceed to the consideration of a measure on the calendar out of its regular order (except on Mondays). Because that normally debatable motion is not debatable if offered during the morning hour, the majority leader may, but rarely does, use this procedure in anticipating a filibuster on the motion to proceed. If the Senate agrees to the motion, it can consider the measure until the end of the morning hour, and if there is no unfinished business from the previous day it can continue considering it after the morning hour. But if there is unfinished business, a motion to continue consideration is necessary, and that motion is debatable.

Motion—A formal proposal for a procedural action, such as to consider, to amend, to lay on the table, to reconsider, to recess or to adjourn. It has been estimated that at least eighty-five motions are possible under various circumstances in the House of Representatives, somewhat fewer in the Senate. Not all motions are created equal; some are privileged or preferential and enjoy priority over others. Some motions are debatable, amendable or divisible, while others are not.

Multiple and Sequential Referrals—The practice of referring a measure to two or more committees for concurrent consideration (multiple referral) or successively to several committees in sequence (sequential referral). A measure may also be divided into several parts, with each referred to a different committee or to several committees sequentially (split referral). In theory this gives all committees that have jurisdiction over parts of a measure the opportunity to consider and report on them.

Before 1975, House precedents banned such referrals. A 1975 rule required the Speaker to make concurrent and sequential referrals "to the maximum extent feasible." On sequential referrals, the Speaker could set deadlines for reporting the measure. The Speaker ruled that this provision authorized him to discharge a committee from further consideration of a measure and place it on the appropriate calendar of the House if the committee fails to meet the Speaker's deadline. The Speaker also used combinations of concurrent and sequential referrals. In 1995 joint referrals were prohibited. Now each measure is referred to a primary committee and also may be referred, either concurrently or sequentially, to one or more other committees, but usually only for consideration of portions of the measure that fall within the jurisdiction of each of those other committees.

In the Senate, before 1977 concurrent and sequential referrals were permitted only by unanimous consent. In that year, a rule authorized a privileged motion for such a referral if offered jointly by the majority and minority leaders. Debate on the motion and all amendments to it is limited to two hours. The motion may set deadlines for reporting and provide for discharging the committees involved if they fail to meet the deadlines. To date, this procedure has never been invoked; multiple referrals in the Senate continue to be made by unanimous consent.

Multiyear Appropriation—An appropriation that remains available for spending or obligation for more than one fiscal year; the exact period of time is specified in the act making the appropriation.

Multiyear Authorization—(1) Legislation that authorizes the existence or continuation of an agency, program or activity for more than one fiscal year. (2) Legislation that authorizes appropriations for an agency, program or activity for more than one fiscal year.

Nomination—A proposed presidential appointment to a federal office submitted to the Senate for confirmation. Approval is by majority vote. The Constitution explicitly requires confirmation for ambassadors, consuls, "public Ministers" (department heads) and Supreme Court justices. By law, other federal judges, all military promotions of officers and many high-level civilian officials must be confirmed.

Oath of Office—Upon taking office, members of Congress must swear or affirm that they will "support and defend the Constitution...against all enemies, foreign and domestic," that they will "bear true faith and allegiance" to the Constitution, that they take the obligation "freely, without any mental reservation or purpose of evasion," and that they will "well and faithfully discharge the duties" of their office. The oath is required by the Constitution, and the wording is prescribed by a statute. All House members must take the oath at the beginning of each new Congress. Usually, the member with the longest continuous service in the House swears in the Speaker, who then swears in the other members. The president of the Senate or a surrogate administers the oath to newly elected or reelected senators.

Obligation—A binding agreement by a government agency to pay for goods, products, services, studies and the like, either immediately or in the future. When an agency enters into such an agreement, it incurs an obligation. As the agency makes the required payments, it liquidates the obligation. Appropriation laws usually make funds available for obligation for one or more fiscal years but do not require agencies to spend their funds during those specific years. The actual outlays can occur years after the appropriation is obligated, as with a contract for construction of a submarine that may provide for payment to be made when it is delivered in the future. Such obligated funds are often said to be "in the pipeline." Under these circumstances, an agency's outlays in a particular year can come from appropriations obligated in previous years as well as from its current-year appropriation. Consequently, the money Congress appropriates for a fiscal year does not equal the total amount of appropriated money the government will actually spend in that year.

Off-Budget Entities—Specific federal entities whose budget authority, outlays and receipts are excluded by law from the calculation of budget totals, although they are part of government spending and income. As of early 2001, these included the Social Security trust funds (Federal Old-Age and Survivors Insurance Fund and the Federal Disability Insurance Trust Fund) and the Postal Service. Government-sponsored enterprises are also excluded from the budget because they are considered private rather than public organizations.

Office of Management and Budget (OMB)—A unit in the Executive Office of the President, reconstituted in 1970 from the former Bureau of the Budget. The Office of Management and Budget (OMB) assists the president in preparing the budget and in formulating the government's fiscal program. The OMB also plays a central role in supervising and controlling implementation of the budget, pursuant to provisions in appropriations laws, the Budget

Enforcement Act and other statutes. In addition to these budgetary functions, the OMB has various management duties, including those performed through its three statutory offices: Federal Financial Management, Federal Procurement Policy and Information and Regulatory Affairs.

Officers of Congress—The Constitution refers to the Speaker of the House and the president of the Senate as officers and declares that each house "shall chuse" its "other Officers," but it does not name them or indicate how they should be selected. A House rule refers to its clerk, sergeant at arms and chaplain as officers. Officers are not named in the Senate's rules, but Riddick's Senate Procedure lists the president pro tempore, secretary of the Senate, sergeant at arms, chaplain and the secretaries for the majority and minority parties as officers. A few appointed officials are sometimes referred to as officers, including the parliamentarians and the legislative counsels. The House elects its officers by resolution at the beginning of each Congress. The Senate also elects its officers, but once elected Senate officers serve from Congress to Congress until their successors are chosen.

Omnibus Bill—A measure that combines the provisions of several disparate subjects into a single and often lengthy bill.

One-Minute Speeches—Addresses by House members that can be on any subject but are limited to one minute. They are usually permitted at the beginning of a daily session after the chaplain's prayer, the pledge of allegiance and approval of the Journal. They are a customary practice, not a right granted by rule. Consequently, recognition for one-minute speeches requires unanimous consent and is entirely within the Speaker's discretion. The Speaker sometimes refuses to permit them when the House has a heavy legislative schedule or limits or postpones them until a later time of the day.

Open Rule—A special rule from the House Rules Committee that permits members to offer as many floor amendments as they wish as long as the amendments are germane and do not violate other House rules.

Order of Business (House)—The sequence of events prescribed by a House rule during the meeting of the House on a new legislative day that is supposed to take place, also called the general order of business. The sequence consists of (1) the chaplain's prayer; (2) reading and approval of the Journal; (3) the pledge of allegiance; (4) correction of the reference of public bills to committee; (5) disposal of business on the Speaker's table; (6) unfinished business; (7) the morning hour call of committees and consideration of their bills; (8) motions to go into Committee of the Whole; and (9) orders of the day. In practice, the House never fully complies with this rule. Instead, the items of business that follow the pledge of allegiance are supplanted by any special orders of business that are in order on that day (for example, conference reports; the corrections, discharge or private calendars; or motions to suspend the rules) and by other privileged business (for example, general appropriation bills and special rules) or measures made in order by special rules or unanimous consent. The regular order of business is also modified by unanimous consent practices and orders that govern recognition for one-minute speeches (which date from 1937) and for morning-hour debates, begun in 1994. By this combination of an order of business with privileged interruptions, the House gives precedence to certain categories of important legislation, brings to the floor other major legislation from its calendars in any order it chooses and provides expeditious processing for minor and noncontroversial measures.

Order of Business (Senate)—The sequence of events at the beginning of a new legislative day, as prescribed by Senate rules and standing orders. The sequence consists of (1) the chaplain's prayer; (2) the pledge of allegiance; (3) the designation of a temporary presiding officer if any; (4) Journal reading and approval; (5) recognition of the majority and minority leaders or their designees under the standing order; (6) morning business in the morning hour; (7) call of the calendar during the morning hour (largely obsolete); and (8) unfinished business from the previous session day.

Organization of Congress—The actions each house takes at the beginning of a Congress that are necessary to its operations. These include swearing in newly elected members, notifying the president that a quorum of each house is present, making committee assignments and fixing the hour for daily meetings. Because the House of Representatives is not a continuing body, it must also elect its Speaker and other officers and adopt its rules.

Original Bill—(1) A measure drafted by a committee and introduced by its chairman or another designated member when the committee reports the measure to its house. Unlike a clean bill, it is not referred back to the committee after introduction. The Senate permits all its legislative committees to report original bills. In the House, this authority is referred to in the rules as the "right to report at any time," and five committees (Appropriations, Budget, House Administration, Rules and Standards of Official Conduct) have such authority under circumstances specified in House Rule XIII, clause 5.

(2) In the House, special rules reported by the Rules Committee often propose that an amendment in the nature of a substitute be considered as an original bill for purposes of amendment, meaning that the substitute, as with a bill, may be amended in two degrees. Without that requirement, the substitute may only be amended in one further degree. In the Senate, an amendment in the nature of a substitute automatically is open to two degrees of amendment, as is the original text of the bill, if the substitute is offered when no other amendment is pending.

Original Jurisdiction—The authority of certain committees to originate a measure and report it to the chamber. For example, general appropriation bills reported by the House Appropriations Committee are original bills, and special rules reported by the House Rules Committee are original resolutions.

Other Body—A commonly used reference to a house by a member of the other house. Congressional comity discourages members from directly naming the other house during debate.

Outlays—Amounts of government spending. They consist of payments, usually by check or in cash, to liquidate obligations incurred in prior fiscal years as well as in the current year, including the net lending of funds under budget authority. In federal budget accounting, net outlays are calculated by subtracting the amounts of refunds and various kinds of reimbursements to the government from actual spending.

Override a Veto—Congressional enactment of a measure over the president's veto. A veto override requires a recorded two-thirds vote of those voting in each house, a quorum being present. Because the president must return the vetoed measure to its house of origin, that house votes first, but neither house is required to attempt an override, whether immediately or at all. If an override attempt fails in the house of origin, the veto stands and the measure dies.

Oversight—Congressional review of the way in which federal agencies implement laws to ensure that they are carrying out the intent of Congress and to inquire into the efficiency of the implementation and the effectiveness of the law. The Legislative Reorganization Act of 1946 defined oversight as the function of exercising continuous watchfulness over the execution of the laws by the executive branch.

Oxford-Style Debate—The House held three Oxford-style debates in 1994, modeled after the famous debating format favored by the Oxford Union in Great Britain. Neither chamber has held Oxford-style debates since then. The Oxford-style debates aired nationally over C-SPAN television and National Public Radio. The organized event featured eight participants divided evenly into two teams, one team representing the Democrats (then holding the majority in the chamber) and the other the Republicans. Both teams argued a single question chosen well ahead of the event. A moderator regulated the debate, and began it by stating the resolution at issue. The order of the speakers alternated by team, with a debater for the affirmative speaking first and a debater for the opposing team offering a rebuttal. The rest of the speakers alternated in kind until all gained the chance to speak.

Parliamentarian—The official advisor to the presiding officer in each house on questions of procedure. The parliamentarian and his or her assistants also answer procedural questions from members and congressional staff, refer measures to committees on behalf of the presiding officer and maintain compilations of the precedents. The House parliamentarian revises the House Manual at the beginning of every Congress and usually reviews special rules before the Rules Committee reports them to the House. Either a parliamentarian or an assistant is always present and near the podium during sessions of each house.

Party Caucus—Generic term for each party's official organization in each house. Only House Democrats officially call their organization a caucus. House and Senate Republicans and Senate Democrats call their organizations conferences. The party caucuses elect their leaders, approve committee assignments and chairmanships (or ranking minority members, if the party is in the minority), establish party committees and study groups and discuss party and legislative policies. On rare occasions, they have stripped members of committee seniority or expelled them from the caucus for party disloyalty.

Pay-as-You-Go (PAYGO)—A provision first instituted under the Budget Enforcement Act of 1990 that applies to legislation enacted before Oct. 1, 2002. It requires that the cumulative effect of legislation concerning either revenues or direct spending should not result in a net negative impact on the budget. If legislation does provide for an increase in spending or decrease in revenues, that effect is supposed to be offset by legislated spending reductions or revenue increases. If Congress fails to enact the appropriate offsets, the act requires presidential sequestration of sufficient offsetting amounts in specific direct spending accounts. Congress and the president can circumvent this requirement if both agree that an emergency requires a particular action or if a law is enacted declaring that deteriorated economic circumstances make it necessary to suspend the requirement.

Permanent Appropriation—An appropriation that remains continuously available, without current action or renewal by Congress, under the terms of a previously enacted authorization or appropriation law. One such appropriation provides for payment of interest on the public debt and another the salaries of members of Congress.

Permanent Authorization—An authorization without a time limit. It usually does not specify any limit on the funds that may be appropriated for the agency, program or activity that it authorizes, leaving such amounts to the discretion of the appropriations committees and the two houses.

Permanent Staff—Term used formerly for committee staff authorized by law, who were funded through a permanent authorization and also called statutory staff. Most committees were authorized thirty permanent staff members. Most committees also were permitted additional staff, often called investigative staff, who were authorized by annual or biennial funding resolutions. The Senate eliminated the primary distinction between statutory and investigative staff in 1981. The House eliminated the distinction in 1995 by requiring that funding resolutions authorize money to hire both types of staff.

Personally Obnoxious (or Objectionable)—A characterization a senator sometimes applies to a president's nominee for a federal office in that senator's state to justify his or her opposition to the nomination.

Pocket Veto—The indirect veto of a bill as a result of the president withholding approval of it until after Congress has adjourned sine die. A bill the president does not sign but does not formally veto while Congress is in session automatically becomes a law ten days (excluding Sundays) after it is received. But if Congress adjourns its annual session during that ten-day period the measure dies even if the president does not formally veto it.

Point of Order—A parliamentary term used in committee and on the floor to object to an alleged violation of a rule and to demand that the chair enforce the rule. The point of order immediately halts the proceedings until the chair decides whether the contention is valid.

Pork or Pork Barrel Legislation—Pejorative terms for federal appropriations, bills or policies that provide funds to benefit a legislator's district or state, with the implication that the legislator presses for enactment of such benefits to ingratiate himself or herself with constituents rather than on the basis of an impartial, objective assessment of need or merit. The terms are often applied to such benefits as new parks, post offices, dams, canals, bridges, roads, water projects, sewage treatment plants and public works of any kind, as well as demonstration projects, research grants and relocation of government facilities. Funds released by the president for various kinds of benefits or government contracts approved by him allegedly for political purposes are also sometimes referred to as pork.

Postcloture Filibuster—A filibuster conducted after the Senate invokes cloture. It employs an array of procedural tactics rather than lengthy speeches to delay final action. The Senate curtailed the postcloture filibuster's effectiveness by closing a variety of loopholes in the cloture rule in 1979 and 1986.

Power of the Purse—A reference to the constitutional power Congress has over legislation to raise revenue and appropriate monies from the Treasury. Article I, Section 8 states that Congress "shall have Power To lay and collect Taxes, Duties, Imposts and Excises, [and] to pay the Debts." Section 9 declares: "No Money shall be drawn from the Treasury, but in Consequence of Appropriations made by Law."

Preamble—Introductory language describing the reasons for and intent of a measure, sometimes called a whereas clause. It occasionally appears in joint, concurrent and simple resolutions but rarely in bills.

Precedent—A previous ruling on a parliamentary matter or a long-standing practice or custom of a house. Precedents serve to control arbitrary rulings and serve as the common law of a house.

President of the Senate—One constitutional role of the vice president is serving as the presiding officer of the Senate, or president of the Senate. The Constitution permits the vice president to cast a vote in the Senate only to break a tie, but the vice president is not required to do so.

President Pro Tempore—Under the Constitution, an officer elected by the Senate to preside over it during the absence of the vice president of the United States. Often referred to as the "pro tem," this senator is usually a member of the majority party with the longest continuous service in the chamber and also, by virtue of seniority, a committee chairman. When attending to committee and other duties the president pro tempore appoints other senators to preside.

Presiding Officer—In a formal meeting, the individual authorized to maintain order and decorum, recognize members to speak or offer motions and apply and interpret the chamber's rules, precedents and practices. The Speaker of the House and the president of the Senate are the chief presiding officers in their respective houses.

Previous Question—A nondebatable motion which, when agreed to by majority vote, usually cuts off further debate, prevents the offering of additional amendments and brings the pending matter to an immediate vote. It is a major debate-limiting device in the House; it is not permitted in Committee of the Whole in the House or in the Senate.

Private Bill—A bill that applies to one or more specified persons, corporations, institutions or other entities, usually to grant relief when no other legal remedy is available to them. Many private bills deal with claims against the federal government, immigration and naturalization cases and land titles.

Private Calendar—Commonly used title for a calendar in the House reserved for private bills and resolutions favorably reported by committees. The private calendar is officially called the Calendar of the Committee of the Whole House.

Private Law—A private bill enacted into law. Private laws are numbered in the same fashion as public laws.

Privilege—An attribute of a motion, measure, report, question or proposition that gives it priority status for consideration. Privileged motions and motions to bring up privileged questions are not debatable.

Privilege of the Floor—In addition to the members of a house, certain individuals are admitted to its floor while it is in session. The rules of the two houses differ somewhat but both extend the privilege to the president and vice president, Supreme Court justices, cabinet members, state governors, former members of that house, members of the other house, certain officers and officials of Congress, certain staff of that house in the discharge of official duties and the chamber's former parliamentarians. They also allow access to a limited number of committee and members' staff when their presence is necessary.

Pro Forma Amendment—In the House, an amendment that ostensibly proposes to change a measure or another amendment by moving "to strike the last word" or "to strike the requisite number of words." A member offers it not to make any actual change in the measure or amendment but only to obtain time for debate.

Pro Tem—A common reference to the president pro tempore of the Senate or, occasionally, to a Speaker pro tempore. (See President Pro Tempore; Speaker Pro Tempore.)

Procedures—The methods of conducting business in a deliberative body. The procedures of each house are governed first by applicable provisions of the Constitution, and then by its standing rules and orders, precedents, traditional practices and any statutory rules that apply to it. The authority of the houses to adopt rules in addition to those specified in the Constitution is derived from Article I, Section 5, clause 2, of the Constitution, which states: "Each House may determine the Rules of its Proceedings...." By rule, the House of Representatives also follows the procedures in Jefferson's Manual that are not inconsistent with its standing rules and orders. Many Senate procedures also conform with Jefferson's provisions, but by practice rather than by rule. At the beginning of each Congress, the House uses procedures in general parliamentary law until it adopts its standing rules.

Proxy Voting—The practice of permitting a member to cast the vote of an absent colleague in addition to his or her own vote. Proxy voting is prohibited on the floors of the House and Senate, but the Senate permits its committees to authorize proxy voting, and most do. In 1995, House rules were changed to prohibit proxy voting in committee.

Public Bill—A bill dealing with general legislative matters having national applicability or applying to the federal government or to a class of persons, groups or organizations.

Public Debt—Federal government debt incurred by the Treasury or the Federal Financing Bank by the sale of securities to the public or borrowings from a federal fund or account.

Public Law—A public bill or joint resolution enacted into law. It is cited by the letters "PL" followed by a hyphenated number. The digits before the hyphen indicate the number of the Congress in which it was enacted; the digits after the hyphen indicate its position in the numerical sequence of public measures that became law during that Congress. For example, the Budget Enforcement Act of 1990 became PL 101-508 because it was the 508th measure in that sequence for the 101st Congress. (See also Private Law.)

Qualification (of Members)—The Constitution requires members of the House of Representatives to be twenty-five years of age at the time their terms begin. They must have been citizens of the United States for seven years before that date and, when elected, must be "Inhabitant[s]" of the state from which they were elected. There is no constitutional requirement that they reside in the districts they represent. Senators are required to be thirty years of age at the time their terms begin. They must have been citizens of the United States for nine years before that date and, when elected, must be "Inhabitant[s]" of the states in which they were elected. The "Inhabitant" qualification is broadly interpreted, and in modern times a candidate's declaration of state residence has generally been accepted as meeting the constitutional requirement.

Queen of the Hill Rule—A special rule from the House Rules Committee that permits votes on a series of amendments, especially complete substitutes for a measure, in a specified order, but directs that the amendment receiving the greatest number of votes shall be the winning one. This kind of rule permits the House to vote directly on a variety of alternatives to a measure. In doing so, it sets aside the precedent that once an amendment has been adopted, no further amendments may be offered to the text it has amended. Under an earlier practice, the Rules Committee reported "king of the hill" rules under which there also could be votes on a series of amendments, again in a specified order. If more than one of the amendments was adopted under this kind of rule, it was the last amendment to receive a majority vote that was considered as having been finally adopted, whether or not it had received the greatest number of votes.

Quorum—The minimum number of members required to be present for the transaction of business. Under the Constitution, a quorum in each house is a majority of its members: 218 in the House and 51 in the Senate when there are no vacancies. By House rule, a quorum in Committee of the Whole is 100. In practice, both houses usually assume a quorum is present even if it is not, unless a member makes a point of no quorum in the House or suggests the absence of a quorum in the Senate. Consequently, each house transacts much of its business, and even passes bills, when only a few members are present. For House and Senate committees, chamber rules allow a minimum quorum of one-third of a committee's members to conduct most types of business.

Quorum Call—A procedure for determining whether a quorum is present in a chamber. In the Senate, a clerk calls the roll (roster) of senators. The House usually employs its electronic voting system.

Ramseyer Rule—A House rule that requires a committee's report on a bill or joint resolution to show the changes the measure, and any committee amendments to it, would make in existing law. The rule requires the report to present the text of any statutory provision that would be repealed and a comparative print showing, through typographical devices such as stricken-through type or italics, other changes that would be made in existing law. The rule, adopted in 1929, is named after its sponsor, Rep. Christian W. Ramseyer, R-Iowa. The Senate's analogous rule is called the Cordon Rule.

Rank or Ranking—A member's position on the list of his or her party's members on a committee or subcommittee. When first assigned to a committee, a member is usually placed at the bottom of the list, then moves up as those above leave the committee. On subcommittees, however, a member's rank may not have anything to do with the length of his or her service on it.

Ranking Member—(1) Most often a reference to the minority member with the highest ranking on a committee or subcommittee. (2) A reference to the majority member next in rank to the chairman or to the highest ranking majority member present at a committee or subcommittee meeting.

Ratification—(1) The president's formal act of promulgating a treaty after the Senate has approved it. The resolution of ratification agreed to by the Senate is the procedural vehicle by which the Senate gives its consent to ratification. (2) A state legislature's act in approving a proposed constitutional amendment. Such an amendment becomes effective when ratified by three-fourths of the states.

Reapportionment—(See Apportionment.)

Recess—(1) A temporary interruption or suspension of a meeting of a chamber or committee. Unlike an adjournment, a recess does not end a legislative day. Because the Senate often recesses from one calendar day to another, its legislative day may extend over several calendar days, weeks or even months. (2) A period of adjournment for more than three days to a day certain, especially over a holiday or in August during odd-numbered years.

Recess Appointment—A presidential appointment to a vacant federal position made after the Senate has adjourned sine die or has adjourned or recessed for more than thirty days. If the president submits the recess appointee's nomination during the next session of the Senate, that individual can continue to serve until the end of the session even though the Senate might have rejected the nomination. When appointed to a vacancy that existed thirty days before the end of the last Senate session, a recess appointee is not paid until confirmed.

Recommit—To send a measure back to the committee that reported it; sometimes called a straight motion to recommit to distinguish it from a motion to recommit with instructions. A successful motion to recommit kills the measure unless it is accompanied by instructions.

Recommit a Conference Report—To return a conference report to the conference committee for renegotiation of some or all of its agreements. A motion to recommit may be offered with or without instructions.

Recommit with Instructions—To send a measure back to a committee with instructions to take some action on it. Invariably in the House and often in the Senate, when the motion recommits to a standing committee, the instructions require the committee to report the measure "forthwith" with specified amendments.

Reconciliation—A procedure for changing existing revenue and spending laws to bring total federal revenues and spending within the limits established in a budget resolution. Congress has applied reconciliation chiefly to revenues and mandatory spending programs, especially entitlements. Discretionary spending is controlled through annual appropriation bills.

Recorded Vote—(1) Generally, any vote in which members are recorded by name for or against a measure; also called a record vote or roll-call vote. The only recorded vote in the Senate is a vote by the yeas and nays and is commonly called a roll-call vote. (2) Technically, a recorded vote is one demanded in the House of Representatives and supported by at least one-fifth of a quorum (forty-four members) in the House sitting as the House or at least twenty-five members in Committee of the Whole.

Recorded Vote by Clerks—A voting procedure in the House where members pass through the appropriate "aye" or "no" aisle in the chamber and cast their votes by depositing a signed green (yea) or red (no) card in a ballot box. These votes are tabulated by clerks and reported to the chair. The electronic voting system is much more convenient and has largely supplanted this procedure. (See Committee of the Whole; Recorded Vote; Teller Vote.)

Redistricting—The redrawing of congressional district boundaries within a state after a decennial census. Redistricting may be required to equalize district populations or to accommodate an increase or decrease in the number of a state's House seats that might have resulted from the decennial apportionment. The state governments determine the district lines. (See Apportionment; Congressional District; Gerrymandering.)

Referral—The assignment of a measure to committee for consideration. Under a House rule, the Speaker can refuse to refer a measure if the Speaker believes it is "of an obscene or insulting character."

Report—(1) As a verb, a committee is said to report when it submits a measure or other document to its parent chamber. (2) A clerk is said to report when he or she reads a measure's title, text or the text of an amendment to the body at the direction of the chair. (3) As a noun, a committee document that accompanies a reported measure. It describes the measure, the committee's views on it, its costs and the changes it proposes to make in existing law; it also includes certain impact statements. (4) A committee document submitted to its parent chamber that describes the results of an investigation or other study or provides information it is required to provide by rule or law.

Representative—An elected and duly sworn member of the House of Representatives who is entitled to vote in the chamber. The Constitution requires that a representative be at least twenty-five years old, a citizen of the United States for at least seven years and an inhabitant of the state from which he or she is elected. Customarily, the member resides in the district he or she represents. Representatives are elected in even-numbered years to two-year terms that begin the following January.

Reprimand—A formal condemnation of a member for misbehavior, considered a milder reproof than censure. The House of Representatives first used it in 1976. The Senate first used it in 1991. (See also Censure; Code of Official Conduct; Denounce; Ethics Rules; Expulsion; Seniority Loss.)

Rescission—A provision of law that repeals previously enacted budget authority in whole or in part. Under the Impoundment Control Act of 1974, the president can impound such funds by sending a message to Congress requesting one or more rescissions and the reasons for doing so. If Congress does not pass a rescission bill for the programs requested by the president within forty-five days of continuous session after receiving the message, the president must make the funds available for obligation and expenditure. If the president does not, the comptroller general of the

United States is authorized to bring suit to compel the release of those funds. A rescission bill may rescind all, part or none of an amount proposed by the president, and may rescind funds the president has not impounded.

Reserving the Right To Object—Members' declaration that at some indefinite future time they may object to a unanimous consent request. It is an attempt to circumvent the requirement that members may prevent such an action only by objecting immediately after it is proposed.

Resident Commissioner from Puerto Rico—A nonvoting member of the House of Representatives, elected to a four-year term. The resident commissioner has the same status and privileges as delegates. Like the delegates, the resident commissioner may not vote in the House or Committee of the Whole.

Resolution—(1) A simple resolution; that is, a nonlegislative measure effective only in the house in which it is proposed and not requiring concurrence by the other chamber or approval by the president. Simple resolutions are designated H. Res. in the House and S. Res. in the Senate. Simple resolutions express nonbinding opinions on policies or issues or deal with the internal affairs or prerogatives of a house. (2) Any type of resolution: simple, concurrent or joint. (See Concurrent Resolution; Joint Resolution.)

Resolution of Inquiry—A resolution usually simple rather than concurrent calling on the president or the head of an executive agency to provide specific information or papers to one or both houses.

Resolution of Ratification—The Senate vehicle for agreeing to a treaty. The constitutionally mandated vote of two-thirds of the senators present and voting applies to the adoption of this resolution. However, it may also contain amendments, reservations, declarations or understandings that the Senate had previously added to it by majority vote.

Revenue Legislation—Measures that levy new taxes or tariffs or change existing ones. Under Article I, Section 7, clause 1 of the Constitution, the House of Representatives originates federal revenue measures, but the Senate can propose amendments to them. The House Ways and Means Committee and the Senate Finance Committee have jurisdiction over such measures, with a few minor exceptions.

Revise and Extend One's Remarks—A unanimous consent request to publish in the Congressional Record a statement a member did not deliver on the floor, a longer statement than the one made on the floor or miscellaneous extraneous material.

Revolving Fund—A trust fund or account whose income remains available to finance its continuing operations without any fiscal year limitation.

Rider—Congressional slang for an amendment unrelated or extraneous to the subject matter of the measure to which it is attached. Riders often contain proposals that are less likely to become law on their own merits as separate bills, either because of opposition in the committee of jurisdiction, resistance in the other house or the probability of a presidential veto. Riders are more common in the Senate.

Roll Call—A call of the roll to determine whether a quorum is present, to establish a quorum or to vote on a question. Usually, the House uses its electronic voting system for a roll call. The Senate does not have an electronic voting system; its roll is always called by a clerk.

Rule—(1) A permanent regulation that a house adopts to govern its conduct of business, its procedures, its internal organization, behavior of its members, regulation of its facilities, duties of

an officer or some other subject it chooses to govern in that form. (2) In the House, a privileged simple resolution reported by the Rules Committee that provides methods and conditions for floor consideration of a measure or, rarely, several measures.

Rule Twenty-Two—A common reference to the Senate's cloture rule. (See Cloture)

Second-Degree Amendment—An amendment to an amendment in the first degree. It is usually a perfecting amendment.

Secretary of the Senate—The chief financial, administrative and legislative officer of the Senate. Elected by resolution or order of the Senate, the secretary is invariably the candidate of the majority party and usually chosen by the majority leader. In the absence of the vice president and pending the election of a president pro tempore, the secretary presides over the Senate. The secretary is subject to policy direction and oversight by the Senate Committee on Rules and Administration. The secretary manages a wide range of functions that support the administrative operations of the Senate as an organization as well as those functions necessary to its legislative process, including record keeping, document management, certifications, housekeeping services, administration of oaths and lobbyist registrations. The secretary is responsible for accounting for all funds appropriated to the Senate and conducts audits of Senate financial activities. On a semiannual basis the secretary issues the Report of the Secretary of the Senate, a compilation of Senate expenditures.

Section—A subdivision of a bill or statute. By law, a section must be numbered and, as nearly as possible, contain "a single proposition of enactment."

Select or Special Committee—A committee established by a resolution in either house for a special purpose and, usually, for a limited time. Most select and special committees are assigned specific investigations or studies but are not authorized to report measures to their chambers. However, both houses have created several permanent select and special committees and have given legislative reporting authority to a few of them: the Ethics Committee in the Senate and the Intelligence Committees in both houses. There is no substantive difference between a select and a special committee; they are so called depending simply on whether the resolution creating the committee calls it one or the other.

Senate—The house of Congress in which each state is represented by two senators; each senator has one vote. Article V of the Constitution declares that "No State, without its Consent, shall be deprived of its equal Suffrage in the Senate." The Constitution also gives the Senate equal legislative power with the House of Representatives. Although the Senate is prohibited from originating revenue measures, and as a matter of practice it does not originate appropriation measures, it can amend both. Only the Senate can give or withhold consent to treaties and nominations from the president. It also acts as a court to try impeachments by the House and elects the vice president when no candidate receives a majority of the electoral votes. It is often referred to as "the upper body," but not by members of the House.

Senate Manual—The handbook of the Senate's standing rules and orders and the laws and other regulations that apply to the Senate, usually published once each Congress.

Senator—A duly sworn elected or appointed member of the Senate. The Constitution requires that a senator be at least thirty years old, a citizen of the United States for at least nine years and an inhabitant of the state from which he or she is elected. Senators are usually elected in even-numbered years to six-year terms that begin the following January. When a vacancy occurs before the end of a term, the state governor can appoint a replacement to fill the position until a successor is chosen at the state's next general election or, if specified under state law, the next feasible date for such an election, to serve the remainder of the term. Until the Seventeenth Amendment was ratified in 1913, senators were chosen by their state legislatures.

Senatorial Courtesy—The Senate's practice of declining to confirm a presidential nominee for an office in the state of a senator of the president's party unless that senator approves.

Seniority—The priority, precedence or status accorded members according to the length of their continuous service in a house or on a committee.

Seniority Loss—A type of punishment that reduces a member's seniority on his or her committees, including the loss of chairmanships. Party caucuses in both houses have occasionally imposed such punishment on their members, for example, for publicly supporting candidates of the other party.

Seniority Rule—The customary practice, rather than a rule, of assigning the chairmanship of a committee to the majority party member who has served on the committee for the longest continuous period of time.

Seniority System—A collection of long-standing customary practices under which members with longer continuous service than their colleagues in their house or on their committees receive various kinds of preferential treatment. Although some of the practices are no longer as rigidly observed as in the past, they still pervade the organization and procedures of Congress.

Sequestration—A procedure for canceling budgetary resources — that is, money available for obligation or spending — to enforce budget limitations established in law. Sequestered funds are no longer available for obligation or expenditure.

Sergeant at Arms—The officer in each house responsible for maintaining order, security and decorum in its wing of the Capitol, including the chamber and its galleries. Although elected by their respective houses, both sergeants at arms are invariably the candidates of the majority party.

Session—(1) The annual series of meetings of a Congress. Under the Constitution, Congress must assemble at least once a year at noon on Jan. 3 unless it appoints a different day by law. (2) The special meetings of Congress or of one house convened by the president, called a special session. (3) A house is said to be in session during the period of a day when it is meeting.

Severability (or Separability) Clause—Language stating that if any particular provisions of a measure are declared invalid by the courts the remaining provisions shall remain in effect.

Sine Die—Without fixing a day for a future meeting. An adjournment sine die signifies the end of an annual or special session of Congress.

Slip Law—The first official publication of a measure that has become law. It is published separately in unbound, single-sheet form or pamphlet form. A slip law usually is available two or three days after the date of the law's enactment.

Speaker—The presiding officer of the House of Representatives and the leader of its majority party. The Speaker is selected by the majority party and formally elected by the House at the beginning of each Congress. Although the Constitution does not require the Speaker to be a member of the House, in fact, all Speakers have been members.

Speaker Pro Tempore—A member of the House who is designated as the temporary presiding officer by the Speaker or elected by the House to that position during the Speaker's absence.

Speaker's Vote—The Speaker is not required to vote, and the Speaker's name is not called on a roll-call vote unless so requested.

Usually, the Speaker votes either to create a tie vote, and thereby defeat a proposal or to break a tie in favor of a proposal. Occasionally, the Speaker also votes to emphasize the importance of a matter.

Special Session—A session of Congress convened by the president, under his constitutional authority, after Congress has adjourned sine die at the end of a regular session. (See Adjournment Sine Die; Session.)

Spending Authority—The technical term for backdoor spending. The Congressional Budget Act of 1974 defines it as borrowing authority, contract authority and entitlement authority for which appropriation acts do not provide budget authority in advance. Under the Budget Act, legislation that provides new spending authority may not be considered unless it provides that the authority shall be effective only to the extent or in such amounts as provided in an appropriation act.

Spending Cap—The statutory limit for a fiscal year on the amount of new budget authority and outlays allowed for discretionary spending. The Budget Enforcement Act of 1997 requires a sequester if the cap is exceeded.

Split Referral—A measure divided into two or more parts, with each part referred to a different committee.

Sponsor—The principal proponent and introducer of a measure or an amendment.

Staff Director—The most frequently used title for the head of staff of a committee or subcommittee. On some committees, that person is called chief of staff, clerk, chief clerk, chief counsel, general counsel or executive director. The head of a committee's minority staff is usually called minority staff director.

Standing Committee—A permanent committee established by a House or Senate standing rule or standing order. The rule also describes the subject areas on which the committee may report bills and resolutions and conduct oversight. Most introduced measures must be referred to one or more standing committees according to their jurisdictions.

Standing Order—A continuing regulation or directive that has the force and effect of a rule, but is not incorporated into the standing rules. The Senate's numerous standing orders, like its standing rules, continue from Congress to Congress unless changed or the order states otherwise. The House uses relatively few standing orders, and those it adopts expire at the end of a session of Congress.

Standing Rules—The rules of the Senate that continue from one Congress to the next and the rules of the House of Representatives that it adopts at the beginning of each new Congress.

Standing Vote—An alternative and informal term for a division vote, during which members in favor of a proposal and then members opposed stand and are counted by the chair.

Star Print—A reprint of a bill, resolution, amendment or committee report correcting technical or substantive errors in a previous printing; so called because of the small black star that appears on the front page or cover.

State of the Union Message—A presidential message to Congress under the constitutional directive that the president shall "from time to time give to the Congress Information of the State of the Union, and recommend to their Consideration such Measures as he shall judge necessary and expedient." Customarily, the president sends an annual State of the Union message to Congress, usually late in January.

Statutes at Large—A chronological arrangement of the laws enacted in each session of Congress. Though indexed, the laws are not arranged by subject matter nor is there an indication of how they affect or change previously enacted laws. The volumes are numbered by Congress, and the laws are cited by their volume and page number. The Gramm-Rudman-Hollings Act, for example, appears as 99 Stat. 1037.

Straw Vote Prohibition—Under a House precedent, a member who has the floor during debate may not conduct a straw vote or otherwise ask for a show of support for a proposition. Only the chair may put a question to a vote.

Strike From the *Record*—Expunge objectionable remarks from the Congressional Record, after a member's words have been taken down on a point of order.

Subcommittee—A panel of committee members assigned a portion of the committee's jurisdiction or other functions. On legislative committees, subcommittees hold hearings, mark up legislation and report measures to their full committee for further action; they cannot report directly to the chamber. A subcommittee's party composition usually reflects the ratio on its parent committee.

Subpoena Power—The authority granted to committees by the rules of their respective houses to issue legal orders requiring individuals to appear and testify, or to produce documents pertinent to the committee's functions, or both. Persons who do not comply with subpoenas can be cited for contempt of Congress and prosecuted.

Subsidy—Generally, a payment or benefit made by the federal government for which no current repayment is required. Subsidy payments may be designed to support the conduct of an economic enterprise or activity, such as ship operations, or to support certain market prices, as in the case of farm subsidies.

Sunset Legislation—A term sometimes applied to laws authorizing the existence of agencies or programs that expire annually or at the end of some other specified period of time. One of the purposes of setting specific expiration dates for agencies and programs is to encourage the committees with jurisdiction over them to determine whether they should be continued or terminated.

Sunshine Rules—Rules requiring open committee hearings and business meetings, including markup sessions, in both houses, and also open conference committee meetings. However, all may be closed under certain circumstances and using certain procedures required by the rules.

Supermajority—A term sometimes used for a vote on a matter that requires approval by more than a simple majority of those members present and voting; also referred to as extraordinary majority.

Supplemental Appropriation Bill—A measure providing appropriations for use in the current fiscal year, in addition to those already provided in annual general appropriation bills. Supplemental appropriations are often for unforeseen emergencies.

Suspension of the Rules (House)—An expeditious procedure for passing relatively noncontroversial or emergency measures by a two-thirds vote of those members voting, a quorum being present.

Suspension of the Rules (Senate)—A procedure to set aside one or more of the Senate's rules; it is used infrequently, and then most often to suspend the rule banning legislative amendments to appropriation bills.

Task Force—A title sometimes given to a panel of members assigned to a special project, study or investigation. Ordinarily, these groups do not have authority to report measures to their respective houses.

Tax Expenditure—Loosely, a tax exemption or advantage, sometimes called an incentive or loophole; technically, a loss of governmental tax revenue attributable to some provision of federal tax laws that allows a special exclusion, exemption or deduction from gross income or that provides a special credit, preferential tax rate or deferral of tax liability.

Televised Proceedings—Television and radio coverage of the floor proceedings of the House of Representatives has been available since 1979 and of the Senate since 1986. They are broadcast over a coaxial cable system to all congressional offices and to some congressional agencies on channels reserved for that purpose. Coverage is also available free of charge to commercial and public television and radio broadcasters. The Cable-Satellite Public Affairs Network (C-SPAN) carries gavel-to-gavel coverage of both houses.

Teller Vote—A voting procedure, formerly used in the House, in which members cast their votes by passing through the center aisle to be counted, but not recorded by name, by a member from each party appointed by the chair. The House deleted the procedure from its rules in 1993, but during floor discussion of the deletion a leading member stated that a teller vote would still be available in the event of a breakdown of the electronic voting system.

Third-Degree Amendment—An amendment to a second-degree amendment. Both houses prohibit such amendments.

Third Reading—A required reading to a chamber of a bill or joint resolution by title only before the vote on passage. In modern practice, it has merely become a pro forma step.

Three-Day Rule—(1) In the House, a measure cannot be considered until the third calendar day on which the committee report has been available. (2) In the House, a conference report cannot be considered until the third calendar day on which its text has been available in the Congressional Record. (3) In the House, a general appropriation bill cannot be considered until the third calendar day on which printed hearings on the bill have been available. (4) In the Senate, when a committee votes to report a measure, a committee member is entitled to three calendar days within which to submit separate views for inclusion in the committee report. (In House committees, a member is entitled to two calendar days for this purpose, after the day on which the committee votes to report.) (5) In both houses, a majority of a committee's members may call a special meeting of the committee if its chairman fails to do so within three calendar days after three or more of the members, acting jointly, formally request such a meeting.

In calculating such periods, the House omits holiday and weekend days on which it does not meet. The Senate makes no such exclusion.

Tie Vote—When the votes for and against a proposition are equal, it loses. The president of the Senate may cast a vote only to break a tie. Because the Speaker is invariably a member of the House, the Speaker is entitled to vote but usually does not. The Speaker may choose to do so to break, or create, a tie vote.

Title—(1) A major subdivision of a bill or act, designated by a roman numeral and usually containing legislative provisions on the same general subject. Titles are sometimes divided into subtitles as well as sections. (2) The official name of a bill or act, also called a caption or long title. (3) Some bills also have short titles that appear in the sentence immediately following the enacting clause. (4) Popular titles are the unofficial names given to some bills or acts by common usage. For example, the Balanced Budget and Emergency Deficit Control Act of 1985 (short title) is almost invariably referred to as Gramm-Rudman (popular title). In other cases, significant legislation is popularly referred to by its title number (see definition (1) above). For example, the federal legislation that requires equality of funding for women's and men's sports in educational institutions that receive federal funds is popularly called Title IX.

Track System—An occasional Senate practice that expedites legislation by dividing a day's session into two or more specific time periods, commonly called tracks, each reserved for consideration of a different measure.

Transfer Payment—A federal government payment to which individuals or organizations are entitled under law and for which no goods or services are required in return. Payments include welfare and Social Security benefits, unemployment insurance, government pensions and veterans benefits.

Treaty—A formal document containing an agreement between two or more sovereign nations. The Constitution authorizes the president to make treaties, but the president must submit them to the Senate for its approval by a two-thirds vote of the senators present. Under the Senate's rules, that vote actually occurs on a resolution of ratification. Although the Constitution does not give the House a direct role in approving treaties, that body has sometimes insisted that a revenue treaty is an invasion of its prerogatives. In any case, the House may significantly affect the application of a treaty by its equal role in enacting legislation to implement the treaty.

Trust Funds—Special accounts in the Treasury that receive earmarked taxes or other kinds of revenue collections, such as user fees, and from which payments are made for special purposes or to recipients who meet the requirements of the trust funds as established by law. Of the more than 150 federal government trust funds, several finance major entitlement programs, such as Social Security, Medicare and retired federal employees' pensions. Others fund infrastructure construction and improvements, such as highways and airports.

Unanimous Consent—Without an objection by any member. A unanimous consent request asks permission, explicitly or implicitly, to set aside one or more rules. Both houses and their committees frequently use such requests to expedite their proceedings.

Uncontrollable Expenditures—A frequently used term for federal expenditures that are mandatory under existing law and therefore cannot be controlled by the president or Congress without a change in the existing law. Uncontrollable expenditures include spending required under entitlement programs and also fixed costs, such as interest on the public debt and outlays to pay for prior-year obligations. In recent years, uncontrollables have accounted for approximately three-quarters of federal spending in each fiscal year.

Unfunded Mandate—Generally, any provision in federal law or regulation that imposes a duty or obligation on a state or local government or private sector entity without providing the necessary funds to comply. The Unfunded Mandates Reform Act of 1995 amended the Congressional Budget Act of 1974 to provide a mechanism for the control of new unfunded mandates.

Union Calendar—A calendar of the House of Representatives for bills and resolutions favorably reported by committees that raise revenue or directly or indirectly appropriate money or property. In addition to appropriation bills, measures that authorize expenditures are also placed on this calendar. The calendar's full title is the Calendar of the Committee of the Whole House on the State of the Union.

Upper Body—A common reference to the Senate, but not used by members of the House.

U.S. Code—Popular title for the United States Code: Containing the General and Permanent Laws of the United States in Force on.... It is a consolidation and partial codification of the general and permanent laws of the United States arranged by subject under 50 titles. The first six titles deal with general or political

subjects, the other forty-four with subjects ranging from agriculture to war, alphabetically arranged. A supplement is published after each session of Congress, and the entire Code is revised every six years.

User Fee—A fee charged to users of goods or services provided by the federal government. When Congress levies or authorizes such fees, it determines whether the revenues should go into the general collections of the Treasury or be available for expenditure by the agency that provides the goods or services.

Veto—The president's disapproval of a legislative measure passed by Congress. The president returns the measure to the house in which it originated without his signature but with a veto message stating his objections to it. When Congress is in session, the president must veto a bill within ten days, excluding Sundays, after the president has received it; otherwise it becomes law without his signature. The ten-day clock begins to run at midnight following his receipt of the bill. (See also Committee Veto; Item Veto; Line Item Veto Act of 1996; Override a Veto; Pocket Veto.)

Voice Vote—A method of voting in which members who favor a question answer aye in chorus, after which those opposed answer no in chorus, and the chair decides which position prevails.

Voting—Members vote in three ways on the floor: (1) by shouting "aye" or "no" on voice votes; (2) by standing for or against on division votes; and (3) on recorded votes (including the yeas and nays), by answering "aye" or "no" when their names are called or, in the House, by recording their votes through the electronic voting system.

War Powers Resolution of 1973—An act that requires the president "in every possible instance" to consult Congress before committing U.S. forces to ongoing or imminent hostilities. If the president commits them to a combat situation without congressional consultation, the president must notify Congress within forty-eight hours. Unless Congress declares war or otherwise authorizes the operation to continue, the forces must be withdrawn within sixty or ninety days, depending on certain conditions. No president has ever acknowledged the constitutionality of the resolution.

Well—The sunken, level, open space between members' seats and the podium at the front of each chamber. House members usually address their chamber from their party's lectern in the well on its side of the aisle. Senators usually speak at their assigned desks.

Whip—The majority or minority party member in each house who acts as assistant leader, helps plan and marshal support for party strategies, encourages party discipline and advises his or her leader on how colleagues intend to vote on the floor. In the Senate, the Republican whip's official title is assistant leader.

Yeas and Nays—A vote in which members usually respond "aye" or "no" (despite the official title of the vote) on a question when their names are called in alphabetical order. The Constitution requires the yeas and nays when a demand for it is supported by one-fifth of the members present, and it also requires an automatic yea-and-nay vote on overriding a veto. Senate precedents require the support of at least one-fifth of a quorum, a minimum of eleven members with the present membership of 100.

Congressional Information on the Internet

A huge array of congressional information is available for free at Internet sites operated by the federal government, colleges and universities and commercial firms. The sites offer the full text of bills introduced in the House and Senate, voting records, campaign finance information, transcripts of selected congressional hearings, investigative reports and much more.

THOMAS

The most important site for congressional information is THOMAS (*http://thomas.loc.gov*), which is named for Thomas Jefferson and operated by the Library of Congress. THOMAS' highlight is its databases containing the full text of all bills introduced in Congress since 1989, the full text of the *Congressional Record* since 1989 and the status and summary information for all bills introduced since 1973.

THOMAS also offers special links to bills that have received or are expected to receive floor action during the current week and newsworthy bills that are pending or that have recently been approved. Finally, THOMAS has selected committee reports, answers to frequently asked questions about accessing congressional information, publications titled *How Our Laws Are Made* and *Enactment of a Law* and links to lots of other congressional Web sites.

House of Representatives

The U.S. House of Representatives site (*http://www.house. gov*) offers the schedule of bills, resolutions and other legislative issues the House will consider in the current week. It also has updates about current proceedings on the House floor and a list of the next day's meeting of House committees. Other highlights include a database that helps users identify their representative, a directory of House members and committees, the House ethics manual, links to Web pages maintained by House members and committees, a calendar of congressional primary dates and candidate-filing deadlines for ballot access, the full text of all amendments to the Constitution that have been ratified and those that have been proposed but not ratified and lots of information about Washington, D.C., for visitors.

Another key House site is The Office of the Clerk On-line Information Center (*http://clerkweb.house.gov*), which has records of all roll-call votes taken since 1990. The votes are recorded by bill, so it is a lengthy process to compile a particular representative's voting record. The site also has lists of committee assignments, a telephone directory for members and committees, mailing label templates for members and committees, rules of the current Congress, election statistics from 1920 to the present, biographies of Speakers of the House, biographies of women who have served since 1917 and a virtual tour of the House Chamber.

One of the more interesting House sites is operated by the Subcommittee on Rules and Organization of the House Com-

mittee on Rules (*http://www.house.gov/rules/crs_reports. htm*). Its highlight is dozens of Congressional Research Service reports about the legislative process. Some of the available titles include *Legislative Research in Congressional Offices: A Primer, How to Follow Current Federal Legislation and Regulations; Investigative Oversight: An Introduction to the Law, Practice and Procedure of Congressional Inquiry;* and *Presidential Vetoes 1789 – Present: A Summary Overview.*

Senate

At least in the Internet world, the Senate is not as active as the House. Its main Web site (*http://www.senate.gov*) has records of all roll-call votes taken since 1989 (arranged by bill), brief descriptions of all bills and joint resolutions introduced in the Senate during the past week and a calendar of upcoming committee hearings. The site also provides the standing rules of the Senate, a directory of senators and their committee assignments, lists of nominations that the president has submitted to the Senate for approval, links to Web pages operated by senators and committees and a virtual tour of the Senate.

Information about the membership, jurisdiction and rules of each congressional committee is available at the U.S. Government Printing Office site (*http://www.access.gpo.gov/congress/ index.html*). It also has transcripts of selected congressional hearings, the full text of selected House and Senate reports and the House and Senate rules manuals.

General Reference

The U.S. General Accounting Office, the investigative arm of Congress, operates a site (*http://www.gao.gov*) that provides the full text of its reports from 1975 to the present. The reports cover a wide range of topics: aviation safety, combating terrorism, counternarcotics efforts in Mexico, defense contracting, electronic warfare, food assistance programs, Gulf War illness, health insurance, illegal aliens, information technology, long-term care, mass transit, Medicare, military readiness, money laundering, national parks, nuclear waste, organ donation and student loan defaults, among others.

The GAO Daybook is an excellent current awareness tool. This electronic mailing list distributes a daily list of reports and testimony released by the GAO. Subscriptions are available by sending an e-mail message to *majordomo@www.gao.gov*, and in the message area typing "subscribe daybook" (without the quotation marks).

Current budget and economic projections are provided at the Congressional Budget Office Web site (*http://www.cbo.gov*). The site also has reports about the economic and budget outlook for the next decade, the president's budget proposals, federal civilian employment, Social Security privatization, tax reform, water use conflicts in the West, marriage and the federal income tax and the role of foreign aid in development, among other topics. Other highlights include monthly budget updates, historical budget data, cost estimates for bills reported by congressional committees and transcripts of congressional testimony by CBO officials.

Campaign Finance

Several Internet sites provide detailed campaign finance data for congressional elections. The official site is operated by the Federal Election Commission *(http://www.fec.gov)*, which regulates political spending. The site's highlight is its database of campaign reports filed from May 1996 to the present by House and presidential candidates, political action committees and political party committees. Senate reports are not included because they are filed with the Secretary of the Senate. The reports in the FEC's database are scanned images of paper reports filed with the commission.

The FEC site also has summary financial data for House and Senate candidates in the current election cycle, abstracts of court decisions pertaining to federal election law from 1976 to 1997, a graph showing the number of political action committees in existence each year from 1974 to the present and a directory of national and state agencies that are responsible for releasing information about campaign financing, candidates on the ballot, election results, lobbying and other issues. Another useful feature is a collection of brochures about federal election law, public funding of presidential elections, the ban on contributions by foreign nationals, independent expenditures supporting or opposing a candidate for federal office, contribution limits, filing a complaint, researching public records at the FEC and other topics. Finally, the site provides the FEC's legislative recommendations, its annual report, a report about its first twenty years in existence, the FEC's monthly newsletter, several reports about voter registration, election results for the most re-

cent presidential and congressional elections and campaign guides for corporations and labor organizations, congressional candidates and committees, political party committees and nonconnected committees.

The best online source for campaign finance data is Political Money Line *(http://www.tray.com)*. The site's searchable databases provide extensive itemized information about receipts and expenditures by federal candidates and political action committees from 1980 to the present. The data, which are obtained from the FEC, are quite detailed. For example, for candidates contributions can be searched by Zip Code. The site also has lists of the top political action committees in various categories, lists of the top contributors from each state and much more.

Another interesting site is the American University Campaign Finance Website *(http://www1.soc.american.edu/campfin)*, which is operated by the American University School of Communication. It provides electronic files from the FEC that have been reformatted in .dbf format so they can be used in database programs such as Paradox, Access and FoxPro. The files contain data on PAC, committee and individual contributions to individual congressional candidates.

More campaign finance data is available from the Center for Responsive Politics *(http://www.opensecrets.org)*, a public interest organization. The center provides a list of all "soft money" donations to political parties of $100,000 or more in the current election cycle and data about "leadership" political action committees associated with individual politicians. Other databases at the site provide information about travel expenses that House members received from private sources for attending meetings and other events, activities of registered federal lobbyists and activities of foreign agents who are registered in the United States.

Index